BELT AND ROAD SME COOPERATION KEY PROJECT PROMOTION HANDBOOK
一带一路中小企业合作重点项目推介手册

主编：任兴磊　沈亚桂　孙士达
Chief Editor: Ren Xinglei　Shen Yagui　Sun Shida

世界知识出版社

图书在版编目（CIP）数据

一带一路中小企业合作·重点项目推介手册 / 任兴磊，沈亚桂，孙士达主编 . —北京：世界知识出版社，2017.11

ISBN 978-7-5012-5605-1

Ⅰ．①一⋯ Ⅱ．①任⋯ ②沈⋯ ③孙⋯ Ⅲ．①中小企业—国际合作—经济合作—中国—手册 Ⅳ．① F279.243-62

中国版本图书馆 CIP 数据核字（2017）第 259508 号

书　　名	一带一路中小企业合作·重点项目推介手册
主　　编	任兴磊　　沈亚桂　　孙士达
责任编辑	王瑞晴　　蔡金娣
责任出版	王勇刚
出版发行	世界知识出版社
地址邮编	北京市东城区干面胡同 51 号（100010）
电　　话	010-85112689（编辑部）
	010-65265923（发行部）　010-85119023（邮购电话）
网　　址	www.ishizhi.cn
印　　刷	北京京华虎彩印刷有限公司
经　　销	新华书店
开本印张	889×1194 毫米　1/16　　14½ 印张
版次印次	2018 年 1 月第一版　2018 年 1 月第一次印刷
标准书号	ISBN 978-7-5012-5605-1
定　　价	168.00 元

版权所有　侵权必究

《一带一路中小企业合作·重点项目推介手册》编委会
Editorial Board Members of *Belt and Road SME Cooperation · Key Project Promotion Handbook*

总　　编：王　民
Chief Editor：Wang Min

执行主编：任兴磊　沈亚桂　孙士达
Executive Editors：Ren Xinglei　Shen Yagui　Sun Shida

副 主 编：刘　珊　韩　旭　刘梦阳
Associate Editors：Liu Shan　Han Xu　Liu Mengyang

编　　委：马文锦　杨聪令　刘　丹　杨　猛
　　　　　陈　军　牛学文　王　浩　任红霞
　　　　　陈耀军　宋俊达　高　平　李双玲
　　　　　王俊娇　于　洋　许　湘　王　博
　　　　　汪健勇　武　征　刘志强　张桂华
　　　　　陈国强

Members：　Ma Wenjing　　Yang Congling　Liu Dan　　　Yang Meng
　　　　　Chen Jun　　　Niu Xuewen　　Wang Hao　　Ren Hongxia
　　　　　Chen Yaojun　　Song Junda　　Gao Ping　　Li Shuangling
　　　　　Wang Junjiao　 Yu Yang　　　 Xu Xiang　　 Wang Bo
　　　　　Wang Jianyong　Wu Zheng　　　Liu Zhiqiang　Zhang Guihua
　　　　　Chen Guoqiang

《一带一路中小企业合作·重点项目推介手册》顾问
Consultants of *Belt and Road SME Cooperation · Key Project Promotion Handbook*

机构	职务	姓名	Organization	Title	Name
埃及华人企业家协会	会长	李霞林	Chinese Entrepreneur Association in Egypt	President	Li Xialin
安徽福建总商会	秘书长	王军	Anhui Fujian General Chamber of Commerce	Secretary General	Wang Jun
澳中企业家总商会	中国区副会长	张强	Australia-China Chamber of CEO Inc.	Vice President, China region	Zhangqiang
包头市文化创意产业联合会	会长	刘俊伟	Baotou Culture and Creative Industry Federation	President	Liu Junwei
宝鸡市女企业家协会	秘书长	龚霖霞	Baoji Women Entrepreneurs Association	Secretary General	Gong Linxia
北京对外文化贸易协会	会长	张少龙	Beijing Foreign Cultural Trade Association	President	Zhang Shaolong
北京福州商会	秘书长	刘薇	Beijing Fuzhou Enterprise Chamber Commerce	Secretary General	Liu Wei
北京海归孵化器科学技术协会	主席	关帅	Beijing Returnees' Incubator Association for Science and Technology	Chairman	Guan Shuai
北京合益商会	会长	金普明	Beijing Heyi Chamber of Commerce	President	Jin Puming
北京河南中小企业商会	秘书长	贾振杰	Henan Small & Medium Enterprise Chamber of Commerce in Beijing	Secretary General	Jia Zhen
北京辽宁企业商会法律委员会	秘书长	邢宝军	Legal Council of Beijing Liaoning Enterprise Chamber of Commerce	Secretary General	Xing Baojun
北京能源协会国际分会	理事长	厉磊	Beijing Energy Association, International Branch	President	Li Lei
北京农业产业化龙头企业协会	秘书长	谢磊	Beijing Association of Agricultural Industrialization Leading Enterprise	Secretary General	Xie Lei
北京厦门企业商会	会长	蒋清林	Xiamen Enterprise Chamber of Commerce in Beijing	President	Jiang Qinglin
北京市国际服务贸易事务中心	常务副主任	梁惊原	Beijing International Service Trade Service Center	Executive Vice Director	Liang Jingyuan
北京市通州区科技创新企业商会	会长	孟磊	Beijing Tongzhou Chamber of Technology Innovation Enterprises	President	Meng Lei
北京顺义区投融资业商会	会长	刘战均	Beijing Shunyi Chamber of Investment and Finance Industry	President	Liu Zhanjun
北京住宅房地产业商会	执行会长	戚敬东	Beijing Residential Estate Chamber of Commerce	Executive President	Qi Jingdong
北欧湖南农业产业园管委会	主任	唐勇	North Europe-Hunan Agriculture Industrial Park Management Committee	Director	Tang Yong
波兰福建商会	荣誉会长	丁建志	Fujian Chamber of Commerce in Poland	Honorary President	Ding Jianzhi
成都市中小企业协会	执行会长	苏非	Chengdu Association of Small and Medium Enterprises	Executive President	Su Fei
东莞江西兴国商会	秘书长	刘祚全	Jiangxi Xingguo Chamber of Commerce in Dongguan	Secretary General	Liu Zuoquan
东莞市河南洛阳商会	秘书长	郭晓峰	Henan Luoyang Chamber of Commerce in Dongguan	Secretary General	Guo Xiaofeng

东莞市寮步青年企业家协会	会长	钟锦扬	Dongguan Association of Liaobu Young Entrepreneurs	President	Zhong Jinyang
鄂尔多斯工商联	秘书长	王晓东	Erdos Federation of Industry and Commerce	Secretary General	Wang Xiaodong
鄂尔多斯河南商会	会长	陈解放	Erdos Chamber of Commerce	President	Chen Jiefang
法中经济文化教育交流协会	主席	段贺恩	France-China Association of Economy, Culture and Education Communication	Chairman	Duan Heen
佛山市跨境电子商务协会	会长	黄永坤	Foshan Cross-Border E-Commerce Association	President	Huang Yongkun
佛山市顺德区家居五金协会	秘书长	薛蓉	Association of Home Furnishing Hardware Shunde Foshan	Secretary General	Xue Rong
佛山市卫浴协会	秘书长	刘文贵	Foshan City Sanitary Ware Industry Association	Secretary General	Liu Wengui
福建省民宿协会	秘书长	吴水金	Fujian Home Hotel Association	Secretary General	Wu Shuijin
福建省模特文化产业协会	会长	何国鑫	Fujian Model Culture Industry Association	President	Ren Guoxin
福建省信息消费协会	秘书长	陈少华	Fujian Information Consuption Association	Secretary General	Chen Shaohua
甘肃物流学会	秘书长	谭克东	Gansu Logistics Profession Association	Secretary General	Tan Kedong
刚果（金）中华总商会	会长	张琪	China General Chamber of Commerc in Congo	President	Zhang Qi
广东省产业园区协会	秘书长	田虹	Guangdong Industrial Park Association	Secretary General	Tian Hong
广东省工贸发展促进会	常务副秘书长	梁翠华	Guangdong Province Industry Trade Development Association	Executive Vice Secretary General	Liang Cuihua
广东省河南商会	副秘书长	张海卿	Henan Chamber of Commerce, Guangdong	Vice Secretary General	Zhang Haiqing
广东省河南周口商会	秘书长	刘吉宇	Henan Zhoukou Chamber of Commerce, Guangdong	Secretary General	Liu Jiyu
广东省黑龙江鹤岗商会	秘书长	王嘉庚	Heilongjiang Hegang Chamber of Commerce, Guangdong	Secretary General	Wang Jiageng
广东省湖南商会	副会长	邵灿辉	Guangdong Hunan Chamber of Commerce	Vice President	Shao Canhui
广东省机器人协会	执行会长	任玉桐	Guangdong Robotics Association	Executive President	Ren Yutong
广东省跨境电子商务行业协会	会长	吴春梅	Guangdong Cross-border E-commerce Industry Association	President	Wu Chunmei
广东省跨境电子商务协会	执行会长	李凤国	Guangdong Cross-border E-commerce Association	Executive President	Li Fengguo
广东省民营企业金融服务协会	秘书长	黄晓辉	Guangdong Financial Association	Secretary General	Huang Xiaohui
广东省女企业家商会	秘书长	刘宗瓒	Women Entrepreneurs Chamber of Guangdong Federation	Secretary General	Liu Zongzan
广东省皮具创意文化协会	秘书长	汤艳星	Guangdong Leather Chamber of Association	Secretary General	Tang Yanxing
广东省企业诚信建设促进会	常务副会长	谢显华	Guangdong Province Enterprises Integrity of the building Association	Executive Vice President	Xie Xianhua
广东省企业品牌建设促进会	秘书长	王满平	Guangdong Enterprise Brand Construction Promotion Association	Secretary General	Wang Manping

《一带一路中小企业合作·重点项目推介手册》顾问
Consultants of *Belt and Road SME Cooperation · Key Project Promotion Handbook*

单位	职务	姓名	Organization	Title	Name
广东省商业联合会	执行会长	刘穗龙	Guangdong General Chamber of Commerce	Executive President	Liu Suilong
广东省社会学学会健康专委	主任	郭俪蕓	Guangdong Sociology Society Health Committee	Director	Guo Liyun
广东省小商品协会、深圳市小商品协会	执行会长	陈晓宁	Guangdong Small Commodity Association Shenzhen Small Commodity Association	Executive President	Chen Xiaoyu
广东省制造业协会	常务副秘书长	王宏伟	Guangdong Manufacturers Association	Executive Vice Secretary General	Wang Hongwei
广东营销学会	会长	杨洪	Guangdong Marketing Association	President	Yang Hong
广西农业产业行业协会	会长	郎传东	Guangxi Agriculture Industrial Association	President	Lang Chuandong
广州市发改委	原副巡视员	陈权斌	Guangzhou Municipal Development and Reform Commission	Former Associate Inspector	Chen Quanbin
广州外商投资企业协会	副秘书长	敖少华	Guangzhou Association of Enterprises with foreign Investment	Vice Secretary General	Ao Shaohua
贵州企业知识产权保护促进会	会长	黄强	Guizhou Association of Enterprise Intellectual Property Protection Promotion	President	Huang Qiang
贵州省水电行业商会	会长	叶行地	Guizhou Chamber of Commerce for Hydropower Industry	President	Ye Xingdi
贵州省文化传媒企业联合会	秘书长	朱磊	Guizhou Federation of Cultural and Media Enterprises	Secretary General	Zhu Lei
贵州省物流行业协会	秘书长	张愈江	Guizhou Logistics Industry Association	Secretary General	Zhang Yujiang
贵州省小微企业商会	秘书长	马晓春	Guizhou Chamber of Commerce for Small and Micro Enterprises	Secretary General	Ma Xiaochun
贵州省智慧产业技术研究院	院长	杨敢	Guizhou Intelligent Industry Technology Research Institute	President	Yang Gan
呼伦贝尔环保志愿者协会	会长	代守扬	Hulun Buir Environmental Protection Volunteers Association	President	Dai Shouyang
哈尔滨市高科技产品发展促进会	执行会长	胡艳丽	Harbin High-tech Association of Industrial Development	Executive Chairman	Hu Yanli
海南省诚信企业协会	秘书长	孙秀山	Hainan Credible Enterprises Association	Secretary General	Sun Xiushan
海南省电商物流行业协会	秘书长	孟庆余	Hainan E-commerce Logistics Association	Secretary General	Meng Qingyu
海南省中小企业服务中心	部长	赵丽影	Hainan Public Service Platform for SME	Departmental Director	Zhao Liying
杭州市温州商会	副会长	林茂顺	Wenzhou Chamber of Commerce in Hanzhou	Vice President	Lin Maoshun
杭州市物联网行业协会	常务副秘书长	明振东	Hangzhou Internet of Things Industry Association	Executive Vice Secretary General	Ming Zhendong
杭州余杭湖南商会	会长	彭中云	Hunan Chamber of Commerce In Yuhang	President	Peng Zhongyun
河北省产学研合作促进会	常务副会长	赵鹏	Hebei Industry, Education and Research Cooperation Promotion Association	Executive Vice President	Zhao Peng
河北省文化产业协会	秘书长	史勇	Hebei Cultural Industry Association	Secretary General	Sun Yunxia
河北省资本运营协会	执行会长	师志书	Hebei Capital Operation Association	Executive President	Shi Zhishu
河南省装备制造业协会	执行会长	王峰	Henan Equipment Manufacturing Association	Executive President	Wang Feng

机构	职务	姓名	Organization	Title	Name
河南豫商文化促进会	会长	徐军昌	Henan Culture Promotion Association	President	Xu Junchang
荷兰中国友好协会	主席	顾坚明	Netherlands China Friendship Association	Chairman	Gu Jianming
黑龙江女企业家协会	执行会长	吴炳荣	Heilongjiang Women Entrepreneurs Association	Executive President	Wu Bingrong
黑龙江省女创业者协会	会长	张成莲	Heilongjiang Association of Women's Startups	President	Zhang Chenglian
黑龙江省商务合作促进会	秘书长	申志国	Business Cooperation Association of Heilongjiang Province	Secretary General	Shen Zhiguo
黑龙江省商业投资商会	会长	王景艳	Heilongjiang Business Investment Chamber of Commerce	President	Wang Jingyan
黑龙江省特产产业协会	会长	徐飞丰	Heilongjiang Association of Special Local Products	President	Xu Feifeng
湖北模具制造商会	秘书长	金波	Hubei Mold Manufacturers Chamber of Commerce	Secretary General	Jin Bo
湖北省汽车流通协会	秘书长	杨克武	Hubei Automobile Dealers Association	Secretary General	Yang Kewu
湖南省电子商务协会	执行会长	张新亮	Hunan Electronic Commerce Association	Executive President	Zhang Xinliang
湖南省礼品业商会	秘书长	夏勋立	Hunan Gift Chamber of Commerce	Secretary General	Xia Xunli
湖南省软装行业商会	会长	聂楚南	Hunan Soft Decoration Chamber	President	Nie Chunan
湖南省移动互联网协会	会长	王稳行	Hunan Mobile Internet Association	President	Wang Wenxing
华沛集团	董事长	李晓平	Huapei Group	Chairman	Li Xiaoping
吉林省黑龙江商会	会长	张加昕	Hei Longjiang Chamber of Commerce Jilin Province	President	Zhang Jiaxin
济南市企业家协会	秘书长	王宝岭	Jinan Entrepreneurs Association	Secretary General	Wang Baoling
济南市现代职业经理人协会	会长	尚衍伟	Jinan Association of Modern Professional Managers	President	Shang Yanwei
加拿大国际中国商会、义乌市时尚创意产业协会	会长	陈庆文	Canada International Chinese Chamber of Commerce	President	Chen Qingwen
建瓯市网络创业协会	会长	蔡文华	Jian'ou Network Entrepreneurship Association	President	Cai Wenhua
江西省物流行业协会	会长	张新辉	Jiangxi Logistics Industry Association	President	Zhang Xinhui
焦作民建驻会	副主委	焦崇奎	Jiaozuo CDNCA	Vice Chairman	Jiao Chongkui
金华中科智能技术研究所	副所长	苗六	Jinhua Zhongke Intelligent Technology Research Institute	Vice Director	Miao Liu
辽宁省总商会	部长	陈华	Liaoning General Chamber of Commerce	Departmental Director	Chen Hua
聊城市工商联互联网商会	秘书长	贾岩	Liaoning Chamber of Commerce	Secretary General	Jia Yan
卢旺达中国和平统一促进会	会长	尹晴日	Rwanda China for the Promotion of Peaceful National Reunification	President	Yin Qingri
马来西亚深圳社团总会	创始人	赖宜蹀	Federation of Malaysia Shenzhen Association	Founder	Lai Yirou
美国华侨联总会	主席	王铁夫	US Chinese-Overseas Trade Union Genral Association	Chairman	Wang Tiefu

《一带一路中小企业合作·重点项目推介手册》顾问
Consultants of *Belt and Road SME Cooperation · Key Project Promotion Handbook*

机构	职务	姓名	Organization	Title	Name
美中经贸文化交流协会	中方会长	刘波	US - China Economic and Trade Exchange Association	Chinese President	Liu Bo
蒙东电力工程协会	会长	马国文	East Inner Mongolia Power Engineering Society	President	Ma Guowen
蒙古国晋商总商会	会长	史光荣	Shanxi General Chammber of Commerce in Mongolia	President	Shi Guangrong
民革山西省委	副主委	张湘君	RCCK Shanxi Province Committee	Vice Director	Zhang Xiangjun
民建惠州市经济委	副主任	廖焕光	CDNCA Guizhou Municipal Committee of Economy	Vice Director	Liao Huanguang
民建茂名市委	副主委	王燕	CDNCA Maoming Municipal Committee	Vice Chairman	Wang Yan
南宁市青年电子商务协会	秘书长	王晟合	Nanning Youth Electronic Commerce Industry Association	Secretary General	Wang Shenghe
南通民营企业家商会	副会长	李建军	Nantong Chmaber of Commerce for Private Entrepreneurs	Vice President	Li Jianjun
内蒙古北京企业家商会	会长	水恩海	Inner Mongolia Chamber of Commerce in Beijing	President	Shui Enhai
内蒙古地理标志产业协会	会长	韩强	Inner Mongolia Geographical Indication Industrial Association	President	Han Qiang
内蒙古金融行业协会	会长	张学珊	Inner Mongolia Internet Banking Association	President	Zhang Xueshan
内蒙古品牌建设促进会	执行会长	胡松	Inner Mongolia Brand Promotion Association (IBPA)	Executive President	Hu Song
内蒙古企业管理科学促进会	秘书长	张海波	Inner Mongolia Enterprise Management Science Promotion Association	Secretary General	Zhang Haibo
内蒙古企业管理咨询协会	会长	郭万富	Management Consulting Association of Inner Mongolia	President	Guo Wanfu
内蒙古汽车玻璃商会	会长	云天妮	Inner Mongolia Automotive Glass Chamber of Commerce	President	Yun Tianni
内蒙古山西商会	副会长	王爱平	Shanxi Chamber of Commerce in Inner Mogolia	Vice President	Wang Aiping
内蒙古食品商会	常务副秘书长	赵哲睿	Inner Mongolia Food Chamber of Commerce	Executive Vice Secretary General	Zhao Zherui
内蒙古医药商会	主任	马亚骋	Inner Mogolia Medical Chamber of Commerce	Director	Ma Yapin
内蒙古中小微企业发展协会	会长	郭子辰	Inner Mongolia Small and Medium Micro Enterprise Development Association	President	Guo Zichen
内蒙古人力资源协会	会长	那钰菲	Inner Mongolia Human Resources Association	President	Na Yufei
宁夏诚信企业联合会	秘书长	马学林	Ningxia Integrity Business Association	Secretary General	Ma Xuelin
宁夏经济发展促进会	执行会长	赵建平	Ningxia Organization for the Promotion of Economic Development	Executive President	Zhao Jianping
宁夏辽宁商会	会长	杨东洪	Ningxia Liaoning Chamber of Commerce	President	Yang Donghong
宁夏市场营销促进会	秘书长	张梅琴	Ningxia Marketing Association	Secretary General	Zhang Meiqin
黔南州小微企业商会	会长	韦德吉	Qiannan Small & Micro Enterprise Chamber of Commerce	President	Wei Deji
青岛市咖啡协会	秘书长	孙骁勇	Coffee Association Qingdao China (CAQD)	Secretary General	Sun Xiaoyong

组织	职务	姓名	Organization	Title	Name
青岛市名优商品流通协会	会长	林连兴	Qingdao Quality Product Communication Association	President	Lin Lianxing
青岛市烟台商会	秘书长	孙资凯	Qingdao Yantai Chamber of Commerce	Secretary General	Sun Zikai
全国内蒙古商会联席会	执行秘书长	宋和平	All-China Inner Mongolia Chamber of Commerce Joint Association	Executive Secretary General	Song Heping
全国商报联合会	秘书长	姜尚源	China General Association of Commercial Newspaper （CGACN）	Secretary General	Jiang Shangyuan
全国县委书记网理事会	秘书长	任振兴	National Councile for County Secretary Website	Secretary General	Ren Zhenxing
瑞中合作促进会	执行主席	刘芳	CSBC	Executive Chairman	Liu Fang
厦门市诚信促进会	副秘书长	许捷立	Xiamen Honesty Promotion Association	Vice Secretary General	Xu Jieli
山东省黑龙江商会	执行秘书长	胡连举	Shandong Heilongjiang Chamber of Commerce	Executive Secretary General	Hu Lianju
山西临汾市尧都区政协	主席	鲁立波	Shanxi Linfen Yaodu CPPCC	Chairman	Lu Libo
山西省农商联合会	秘书长	程旭刚	Shanxi Federation of Agriculture and Industry	Secretary General	Cheng Xugang
陕西省工业经济联合会	副会长	郑勇	Shaanxi Federation of Industrial Economics	Vice President	Zheng Yong
陕西省南阳商会	秘书长	仝照印	Shaanxi Nanyang Chamber of Commerce	Secretary General	Tong Zhaoyin
上海东北经济文化发展促进会	副主任	李禹宏	Shanghai Northeast Economic and Cultural Development Promotion Association	Vice Director	Li Yuhong
上海三海互联网金融信息服务有限公司	董事长	邱奥雷	Shanghai 3 High Internet Financial Information Service Co.Ltd Chairman	Director	Qiu Aolei
上海市苏州商会	秘书长	茅志杭	Suzhou Chamber of Commerce in Shanghai	Secretary General	Mao Zhihang
上海太原商会	秘书长	赵重伟	Taiyuan Chamber of Commerce in Shanghai	Secretary General	Zhao Chongwei
上海物流企业家协会	会长助理	汤静	Shanghai Logistics Entrepreneur Association	President Assistant	Tang Jing
深港投资联合会	会长	王希常	SZ and HK Investment Federation	President	Wang Xichang
深圳电子商务商会	会长	江红辉	Shenzhen Electronic Commerce Association	President	Jiang Honghui
深圳金融居间服务专业委员会	会长	黄妙英	Shenzhen Intermediate Financial Service Committee	President	Huang Miaoying
深圳市湖南商会	副会长	凌俊猛	Hunan Chamber of Commerce in Shenzhen	Vice President	Ling Junmeng
深圳市互联网学会	秘书长	梓炎	Shenzhen Association of Internet	Secretary General	Zi Yan
深圳市绵阳商会	秘书长	苏湛森	Mianyang Chamber of Commerce in Shenzhen	Secretary General	Su Zhansen
深圳市女性创业促进会	会长	刘淑琴	Shenzhen Council for the Promotion of Women's Startups	President	Liu Shuqin
深圳市企业信用管理协会	秘书长	刘利华	Association of Credit Management of Entreprises Shenzhen City	Secretary General	Liu Lihua
深圳市中小企业投融资商会	会长	陈振丰	ShenZhen SME Finance Association	President	Chen Zhenfeng

《一带一路中小企业合作·重点项目推介手册》顾问

Consultants of *Belt and Road SME Cooperation · Key Project Promotion Handbook*

机构	职务	姓名	Organization	Position	Name
石家庄市中小企业家协会	副会长	杨凤虎	Shijiazhuang SME Entrepreneur Association	Vice President	Yang Fenghu
四川省产业经济发展促进会	副秘书长	刘彬	Sichuan Industry Economic Development Promotion Committee	Vice Secretary General	Liu Bin
四川省微电影艺术协会	会长	肖建兵	Sichuan Micro - Film Arts Association	President	Xiao Jianbing
四川省众扶慈善基金会	秘书长	肖军	Sichuan Province Zhongfu Foundation	Secretary General	Xiao Jun
四川蜀商会	副会长	黄海庭	Sichuan Chamber of Commerce	Vice President	Huang Haiting
台湾农特精品跨岸交流协会	名誉会长	李子宏	Taiwan Cross-Strait Quality Farm Produce Exchange Association	Honorary President	Li Zihong
台湾品牌农业推广协会海西分会	会长	许景云	Taiwan Brand Agriculture Promotion Association, Haixi Branch	President	Xu Jingyun
太原市宝鸡商会	会长	孟柯成	Baoji Chamber of Commerce in Taiyuan	President	Meng Kecheng
太原市民营经济发展促进会	秘书长	张正业	Taiyuan Private Economy Promotion Association	Secretary General	Zhang Zhengye
太原市西安商会	会长	孟洪志	Xi'an Chamber of Commerce inTai yuan	President	Meng Hongzhi
泰安市商会	秘书长	戚桂东	Taian Chamber of Commerce	Secretary General	Qi Guidong
泰国湖南商会	执行会长	杜威逸	Hunan Chamber of Commerce in Thailand	Executive President	Du Weiyi
泰国际贸易商会	秘书长	陈铁君	International-Thai Business Association	Secretary General	Chen Tiejun
天津工商联邯郸商会	秘书长	陈宏	Tianjin Association of Industry and Commerce, Handan Chamber of Commerce	Secretary General	Chen Hong
天津市福建茶业商会	会长	阮祚清	Fujian Tea Chamber of Commerce in Tianjin	President	Ruan Zuoqing
天津市木业协会	会长	陈庆洪	Tianjin Wood Industry Association	President	Chen Qinghong
天津市商务服务行业协会	常务副会长	马振勇	Tianjin Association of Commercial Service Industry	Executive Vice President	Ma Zhenyong
铁岭龙山商会	会长	曹明亮	Tieling Longshan Chamber of Commerce	President	Cao Mingliang
威海市韩国商品经销协会	会长	姜秀利	Weihai Korean Product Sales Association	President	Jiang Xiuli
温州市市场营销协会	会长	徐良溪	Wenzhou Marketing Association	President	Xu Liangxi
武汉职业经理人协会	秘书长	吴先庚	Wuhai Professional Manager Association	Secretary General	Wu Xiangeng
西安岐山商会	秘书长	王建国	Xi'an zones chamber of commerce	Secretary General	Wang Jianguo
西安市中小企业协会	会长	刘钊	Xi'an Federation of Small & Medium Businesses	President	Liu Zhao
西班牙中西合作发展基金会	主席	徐孟彬	Fundacion Hispano China para Cooperacion y Desarrollo	Chairman	Xu Mengbin
锡金商会	会长	蔡建华	Sikkim Chamber of Commerce	President	Cai Jianhua
香港珠宝总商会	會長	卓启灿	HK General Chamber of Jewelry	President	Zhuo Qican
新加坡BSE企业家协会	会长	李建福	The Society of BSE Management Singapore	President	Li Jianfu
匈牙利中国和平统一统促会	副会长	李润颖	China Peaceful Reunification Promotion Union in Hungary	Vice President	Li Runying
徐州市现代物流与产业服务协会	常务副会长	梁卫东	Xuzhou Modern Logistics and Industrial Service Association	Executive Vice President	Liang Weidong

中文机构	中文职务	中文姓名	Organization	Title	Name
亚欧非贸易投资促进会	会长	苏军平	Asia-Europe-Africa Trade and Investment Promotion Association	President	Su Junping
延安民营企业家商会	名誉会长	张正伟	Yan'an Private Entrepreneur Chamber of Commerce	Honorary President	Zhang Zhengwei
义乌市建筑行业协会	会长	陈士进	Yiwu Construction Industry Association	President	Chen Shijin
印中贸易促进会 (TICTA) 中国	会长	马龙	Indo-China Trade Promotion Council	President	Ma Long
长沙市新邵商会	副秘书长	屈意民	Shaoyang Chamber of Commerce in Changsha	Secretary General	Qu Yimin
浙江省机器人协会	执行会长	姜名泓	Zhejiang Robotics Association	Secretary General	Jiang Minghong
浙江省民营投资企业联合会	会长	周德文	Zhenjiang Private Enterprise Federation	President	Zhou Dewen
郑州市盐城商会	秘书长	袁仁锁	Yancheng Chamber of Commerce in Zhengzhou	Secretary General	Yuan Rensuo
中非友好经贸发展基金会	理事长	张仪	China-Africa Friendly Economic and Trade Development Foundation	President	Zhang Yi
中非友好经贸发展基金会	副理事长	朱兴虹	China-Africa Friendly Economic and Trade Development Foundation	Vice President	Zhu Xinghong
中关村成长型科技企业互助促进会	秘书长	张冉静	Zhongguancun Growing Business Mutual Technology Assistance Promotion Association	Secretary General	Zhang Ranjing
中关村国投县域科技经济发展促进会	常务副主席	柴仁生	Zhongguancun State Invested County Technology and Economy Development Promotion Association	Executive Vice Chairman	Chai Rensheng
中关村科技企业促进会	会长	万力	Zhongguancun Technology Enterprise Promotion Association	President	Wan Li
中国 CEO 联盟	秘书长	张良	Chian CEO Alliance	Secretary General	Zhang Liang
中国传统文化促进会	副主任	马玉君	Chinese Traditional Culture Promotion Society	Vice Director	Ma Yujun
中国东北中小企业公共服务平台	主任	初征	China Northeast SME Public Information Service Platform	Director	Chu Zheng
中国国际经济技术合作促进会海联会	副秘书长	常芃	China Overseas Innestment Union of China Association for Promoting International Economic and Technical Cooperation	Vice Secretary General	Chang Peng
中国联合国采购促进会政府采购与服务分会	秘书长	李鹏	China UN Procurement Promotion Association Government Procurement and Service Branch	Vice Secretary General	Li Peng
中国特产采购协会	副会长	杨开武	China Specialty Purchase Association	Vice President	Yang Kaiwu
中国湘商联合会	秘书长	谢作钦	China Federation of Hunan Business	Secretary General	Xie Zuoqin
中国新园区网	主任	马立明	China New Park	Director	Ma Liming
中国杨凌示范区众创空间	主任	上官金辉	China Yangling Demonstration Area for Mass Creation	Director	Shangguan Jinhui
中国中小商业企业协会四川会员服务中心	主任	周兵	China Association of Small & Medium Enterprise Sichuan Member Service Center	Director	Zhou Bing
中华自驾联盟	总会长	龙涌	Road Trip Alliance,	General President	Long Yong

机构	职务	姓名	Organization	Title	Name
中南大学深圳青年商会	会长	任恩邦	Central South University Shenzhen Youth Chamber of Commerce	President	Ren Enbang
中山市江西赣州商会	常务副秘书长	王根茂	Jiangxi Chamber of Commerce in Zhongshan	Executive Vice Secretary General	Wang Genmao
中山市罗定商会	秘书长	梁汉朝	Zhongshan Luoding Chamber of Commerce	Secretary General	Liang Hanzhao
中山市企业管理咨询协会	副会长	周葵敏	Zhongshan Enterprise Management Consulting Association	Vice President	Zhou Kuimin
中山市自行车电动车行业协会	秘书长	周安明	Zhongshan Bicycle Industry Association	Secretary General	Zhou Anming
中商会国际旅游促进会	会长	倪伟	Commerce Economy Association of China Tourism Promotion Association	President	Ni Wei
重庆民营企业家协会	会长	黄益荣	Chongqing Private Entrepreneurs Association	President	Huang Yirong
重庆伸爱养老服务有限公司	总裁	林俊明	Chongqing Shen'ai Pension Service Co., Ltd.	President	Lin Junming
重庆市百货纺织商业协会	会长	王京	Chongqing Department of textile Commercial Association	President	Wang Jing
珠海市社会团体会长协会	执行会长	杨少华	Zhuhai Social Organization Manager Association	Executive President	Yang Shaohua
珠海市生态协会	会长	黄海洋	Association of Environmental Protection and Ecology in Zhuhai City	President	Huang Haiyang
遵义市农村青年致富带头人协会	会长	李显彬	Zunyi Young Rural Leader Association	President	Li Xianbin

在 2017"一带一路"沿线国家中小企业合作论坛开幕式上的讲话
Addresses to the Opening Ceremony of 2017 SME Cooperation Forum among the "Belt and Road" Countries

（代序言）
(Preface)

顾秀莲，第十届全国人大常委会副委员长
Gu Xiulian, Vice Chairman of 10th NPC Standing Committee
中国关心下一代工作委员会主任
Director of China Cares for the Next Generation Working Committee

2017年6月14日•北京雁栖湖国际会展中心
June 14, 2017 • Beijing Yanqi Lake International Convention & Exhibition Center

各位嘉宾、女士们、先生们，朋友们：
Ladies and gentlemen, my friends,

大家好！我对中国中小商业企业协会主办的2017"一带一路"沿线国家中小企业合作论坛的召开，表示热烈祝贺！

First of all, I would like to give all my congratulations to the opening of 2017 SME Cooperation Forum among the "Belt and Road" Countries hosted by China Association of Small & Medium Commercial Enterprise!

"一带一路"倡议是党中央主动应对全球形势深刻变化、统筹国内国际两个大局作出的重大战略决策，对于进一步扩大中国对外开放格局、促进地区经济繁荣、推动中华民族伟大复兴，具有重要的战略意义。从理念到蓝图，从现实到未来，以实现"政策沟通、设施联通、贸易畅通、资金融通、民心相通"为主要内容，四年来，"一带一路"上的中小企业，是拓路的先行者、创新的实践者、开放的合作者、成果的收获者。

The "Belt and Road Initiative" is an important strategic decision by CPC in active response to the profound global changes and in overall considerations of situations both inside and outside China. It is of great strategic significance to the further development of Chinese opening policy, local prosperity and the great rejuvenation of Chinese nation. From idea to blueprint and from reality to future, the "Belt and Road Initiative" aims to realize "policy exchange, infrastructure connection, smooth trade and capital flow as well as civil communication". In the past 4 years, small and medium enterprises along the Belt and Road had become exploring pioneers, innovation practitioners, open cooperators and reapers of great success.

下面，我也就中小企业参与"一带一路"建设，提几点建议，仅供参考：
Now, I will share some of my opinions on small and medium enterprises and the "Belt and Road Initiative":

第一，要借船出海。在"一带一路"设想下，企业走出去应具有充分的自信。因为，在"一带一路"建设框架下，民营企业及中小企业有着广阔的市场空间。尽管在"一带一路"建设项目中，具有优势的央企和国企是主力军，承担基础设施建设、高铁、核电等大型项目建设。但是，民企也要善于"借梯登高"，与国家队"混搭"形成叠加优势，在市场化领域担当参与者、合作者。

First, the shoulders of giants. With the "Belt and Road Initiative", enterprises must be confident in exploring foreign markets. This is because under the framework of "Belt and Road Initiative", private and small and medium enterprises are facing vast markets and opportunities. Although central and state enterprises are the main forces in the "Belt and Road Initiative" and are undertaking large projects, such as the construction of infrastructures, high-speed railway and nuclear power plants, private enterprises may also stand on the shoulders of giants by cooperating with the giant state enterprises, and therefore are able to cooperate and participate in economic activities in specific market sectors.

第二，要差异化发展。对于民营企业及中小企业来说，"一带一路"建设绝不是简单地转移自己落后产能或者粗放地获取市场、资源，而要在科学理念引导下，做好公司技术、标准的安排，真正做好差异化选择与竞争。

发达国家的中小企业在管理、技术、产品方面具有优势，但市场相对饱和；而中国中小企业在这些方面则相对落后，但中国有巨大的市场，二者具有广阔的合作空间。

Secondly, develop by differentiation. To private and small and medium enterprises, the "Belt and Road Initiative" is definitely more than transfer of outdated production capacity or occupation of market share and resources by extensive expansion, but is to win via differentiation and competition through technologies and standard arrangements under scientific guidelines. SMEs in developed countries have their advantages in management, technology and products however are trapped in the saturated market, on the contrary, SMEs in China, though left behind in these aspects, are facing vast market in China. Therefore, there is large space for cooperation between those SMEs inside and outside China.

第三，要充分评估。"走出去"和国际化一定要有长远战略考量，充分考虑复杂的法律、经济和文化环境，要建立全面、灵活、长效的评估机制。同时主动引导市场换资源、换技术，你中有我，我中有你，由此形成商业模式、盈利模式和可持续发展模式。打铁还需自身硬，中小企业"走出去"应做好"强身健体"。企业本身要提升经营管理水平，注意打造品牌竞争优势。在国际市场上，也应向价值链的中高端迈进，主动融入当地竞争环境，熟悉当地文化、法律法规、宗教、风土人情等。要本土化、国际化相结合。

Thirdly, sufficient assessments are important. Steps of "going global" and globalization must be taken with long-term and strategic considerations of the complicated law, economic and cultural backgrounds, and an all-round, flexible and long-term assessment mechanism must be established. Besides, we should take active guidance over the exchange of market share for resources and technologies, involve both sides in economic activities and build up our business and profit models and sustainable development pattern. To compete in market, SMEs need to strengthen their own competitiveness, in order to win in foreign markets. SMEs must keep improving their management and build their brand strengths. In international markets, SMEs must make all efforts to seize the middle and high-end positions in the value chain, by active adaption to the local conditions and learning about local culture, laws and regulations, religions and traditions. Localization must be combined with internationalization.

第四，政府要积极搭台。各级政府应加强对为中小企业提供融资服务的金融机构的扶持力度，建立并完善各级地方政府与当地中小企业以及当地银行等金融机构的信息沟通机制，有效加强政银企合作。各级政府要着力支持中小企业扩大在国际产能合作、产业园区合作、跨境经济合作等方面的项目和规模。只有如此，才能在"走出去、引进来"中分享"一带一路"这一国家战略所带来的红利。

Fourthly, governments should work actively to build platforms. Governments at all levels must strengthen supports to financial institutions providing financing services to SMEs. They must reinforce the cooperation among governments, banks and enterprises, by establishing and continuous improvement of the communication and information exchange mechanism with local SMEs and banking institutions. Governments should support SMEs in winning projects and expanding their scales in international production capacity cooperation, industrial park cooperation and cross-border cooperation. Only in this way can SMEs share the benefits brought about by the "Belt and Road Initiative" strategy in the process of "going abroad and bringing in".

召开本次论坛，共同探讨和展望"一带一路"建设带给中小企业的发展机遇，是一件具有历史性意义的盛举。千百年来，丝绸之路承载的和平合作、开放包容、互学互鉴、互利共赢精神薪火相传。这种精神是我们中华民族的伟大精神，也是孕育我们中国企业的深厚底蕴。梦想在远方，成功在路上。中国政府将为支持中小企业发展而不惮前行，为创造大美丝路而努力奋斗！

This Forum that aims at discussions and outlooks of the development opportunities to SMEs by the "Belt and Road Initiative" is a grand event of historical significance. For thousands of years, the Silk Road has passed on the valuable spirits of peace and cooperation, opening and inclusive, mutual learning and benefiting. This is the great spirit of our Chinese nations and has built the profound basis for Chinese enterprises. We are on our way heading for our dreams. Chinese governments will spare no efforts to assist SMEs in fighting their future along the Silk Road!

谢谢大家！

Thank you!

序 言
Preface

　　6月14日，由中国中小商业企业协会牵头主办的"2017一带一路沿线国家中小企业合作论坛"受到了国内外政商各界的高度关注和积极响应。论坛期间，应与会各方的要求，中国中小商业企业协会启动了《一带一路中小企业合作·重点项目推介手册》编撰工作，成立了编委会邀请国内外官产学研组织相关负责人参与推荐和编撰；在手册的编撰过程当中国家有关部委和沿线相关国家驻华机构也给予了政策指导和鼎力支持。在手册即将成稿付印之际，谨向各方表示诚挚的感谢！

　　On June 14, the "2017 SME Cooperation Forum among the 'Belt and Road' Countries" hosted by CASME won extensive attentions and active responses from political and business societies at home and abroad. During the forum and at requests of participants, CASME launched the compilation of *Belt and Road SME Cooperation · Key Project Promotion Handbook*, for this purpose an editorial board has been established, inviting experts and scholars from governmental, industrial, educational and research institutions inside and outside China for recommendations and compilation. In the compilation process of the Handbook, we have received policy guidance and supports from related Chinese ministries as well as foreign institutions in China. As the Handbook is now completing and getting printed in short time, we must give all our earnest thanks to all participators for their generous contribution!

　　本手册，按照现在已有和未来可能开辟的路径推想出的"丝绸之路经济带"路线图和"21世纪海上丝绸之路"路线图，对沿线国家的基本国情、政治、经济和人文环境，以及节点城市和中小企业项目合作情况作了较为基本的介绍，对于我们选取的首批推荐项目和企业进行了可行性分析，希望能够对关心"一带一路"建设的读者和研究者提供一些参考。需要指出的是，本手册对"一带一路"中小企业合作项目和推荐的描述部分是建立在以本会会员和合作机构推荐企业基础之上的，难免会有错误乃至谬误之处，敬请读者批评与指正。"一带一路"建设是一个渐进的过程，随着建设的进展，其所涵盖的范围会不断扩展，路径也会不断调整，中小企业寻找合作伙伴，寻找项目机遇的步伐也在不断加快。

　　The Handbook, according to the road maps of "Silk Road Economic Belt" and "21st Century Maritime Silk Road" based on existing and potential routes, gives basic introductions to the national situations, political, economic and cultural environments of countries and the node cities and ongoing projects along the road. Besides, it also provides feasibility analysis on the first recommended projects and enterprises, and expects to provide some helpful information to readers and practitioners of the "Belt and Road Initiative". It must be noted that the description of SME cooperation projects in this Handbook is based on the recommendations by CASME members and cooperators, so there might likely be some errors in this Handbook. Luckily, the "Belt and Road Initiative" is a gradual process, as the construction comes to new stages, it may cover more aspects and has the development course modified continually. SMEs should also accelerate their paces in looking for cooperators and opportunities of new projects.

　　我们认为，"一带一路"沿线不少国家还处于工业化初期阶段，在工程基建、建筑建材、交通运输、旅游餐饮、跨境电商等很多细分市场，相关产品、设备和劳务输出的市场巨大。作为中国最具创新精神的群体，中小企业的发展是"一带一路"未来社会价值的重要方向。中小企业的项目具有开发周期短、创新见效快的优势，还有长期对外贸易的经验，打开"一带一路"沿线国家的细分市场，中小企业沿线国家合作前景十分辉煌。

　　We believe that many countries along the "Belt and Road" are still at their early stages of industrialization, which means there are huge markets for related products, equipment and labor services in many market segments, such as infrastructure construction, building materials, transportation, tour and catering services and cross-border E-commerce. As the most creative and initiative group in China, SMEs are important contributors to future social values with the "Belt and Road Initiative". SMEs have advantages in shorter project development cycle, faster innovation application and long-term experiences in foreign trades. As countries along the "Belt and Road" open their market segments, there will be very promising future for those SMEs.

我们相信,"一带一路"建设是一个大舞台,希望通过本手册系列版本的推出,能够不断加深"一带一路"沿线国家中小企业合作,在共建共享、共同受益的舞台上跳出华美的"舞蹈",谱写出绚丽的篇章。

We believe that the "Belt and Road Initiative" has provided a huge stage, With the publication of this Handbook and its amendments, we are hoping to enhance the cooperation between SMEs in countries along the "Belt and Road", so that they can have their most elegant dances on the stage and open up their splendid chapters.

王 民
Wang Min
2017 年 10 月
October 2017

中国中小商业企业协会法人代表、执行会长,中国商业联合会常务副会长兼秘书长,《一带一路中小企业合作·重点项目推介手册》编委会主任

Legal Representative and Executive President of China Association for Small & Medium Commercial Enterprises; Executive Vice President and Secretary General of China General Chamber of Commerce; Director of Editorial Board of *Belt and Road SME Cooperation • Key Project Promotion Handbook*.

序言 / Preface

当今世界，经济全球化是不可阻挡的历史潮流。正如习近平主席所指出的："经济全球化是社会生产力发展的客观要求和科技进步的必然结果，不是哪些人、哪些国家人为造出来的。"尽管目前一些国家和地区还有形形色色的保护主义，甚至出现所谓的"逆全球化"，但那样做终究是站不住脚的。大家知道，"一带一路"建设遵循的是共商、共建、共享的理念，顺应了沿线国家和人民谋求共同发展、过上幸福生活的美好愿望，因此也就具有强大的生命力和广阔的发展前景。本次论坛作为落实"一带一路"峰会共识的具体行动，把各位企业家、政府部门、金融机构和参与国家大使代表邀请在一起，共商参与合作、技术对接大计，这本身就可以提供很多商机。

In the world today, economic globalization has become an irreversible trend. As pointed out by Chairman Xi Jinping, "economic globalization is the inexorable outcome of social productivity development and scientific and technological progress, and is not created by any person or any country." Although trade protectionism still exists in various forms in many countries and regions and even some so-called "reverse globalization" has been found, they can never stand a chance. As we know, the "Belt and Road Initiative" is built on the philosophy of negotiation, mutual efforts and shared benefits, and therefore agrees with the good wishes of countries and people along the "Belt and Road" for development and happy lives. As such, it gains great vitality and promising future. As a concrete action to implement the common sense of "Belt and Road" Summit, this Forum gathers entrepreneurs, governmental authorities, financial institutions and ambassador and representative of participating countries in discussions on cooperation and technical transfer, and therefore it provides many business opportunities.

正如鲁迅先生所讲，世上本没有路，走的人多了就变成了路。作为发展中大国的中国，正是鉴于世界经济复苏缓慢、发展分化、国际和地区形势发生深刻变化，以及中国发展所面临的新形势、新任务，出于责任和担当提出了"一带一路"倡议，而这一倡议，四年来，得到了一百多个国家和国际组织的积极响应和支持，可以说"一带一路"已经成为中国新理念引领世界新发展之路。近年来"一带一路"建设在探索中前进、在发展中完善、在合作中成长，成效远远超出预期。商务部最新数据显示，仅今年一季度，中国与"一带一路"沿线国家（地区）的进口、出口值在同期全国总额中的占比均接近三成。高速增长的数据背后，是广阔的市场和无限的商机，而市场和商机带来的正是企业的发展机遇。随着新亚欧大陆桥、中蒙俄、中国—中亚—西亚、中国—中南半岛等国际经济合作走廊的打造，中巴、孟中印缅两个经济走廊的建设等，中国企业在"一带一路"建设中成了真正的受益者。

As Mr. Lu Xun once said, for actually the earth had no roads to begin with, but when many men pass one way, a road is made. China, as a large developing country, proposed the "Belt and Road Initiative" in the context of slow global economic recovery, diverse development trends, profound changes to international and regional situations as well as the new situations and new missions encountered by China in its path of development. Through the past 4 years, the Initiative had received active response and supports from over 100 countries and international organizations. In a word, the "Belt and Road" is leading the world development with the Chinese new philosophies. In recent years, the "Belt and Road" kept progressing in explorations, improving in development and growing in cooperation. Its achievements has gone far beyond world's expectations. According to latest data of the Ministry of Commerce, the total value of imports and exports from and to countries (regions) along the "Belt and Road" in the first quarter of this year accounted nearly 30% of total national values in the same period. Behind the fast growing data, there are broad markets and endless business opportunities which facilitate the development of enterprises. With the construction of New Eurasian Land Bridge, China-Mongolia-Russia economic corridor, China-Central Asia-West Asia corridor and China-Indo-China Peninsula corridor, together with the China-Pakistan and Bangladesh-China economic corridors, Chinese enterprises will benefit from the "Belt and Road Initiative".

何丕洁，全国政协副秘书长、2017"一带一路"沿线国家中小企业合作论坛共同主席
He Pijie, Vice Secretary General of Chinese People's Political Consultative Conference, Co-Chairman of 2017 SME Cooperation Forum among the Belt and Road Countries

"一带一路"建设就是以"和"为贵的最好例子。俄罗斯《导报》这样评价:"对中国来说,'一带一路'与其说是路,更像是中国最重要的哲学范畴——'道'。"何为"道"?英国思想家罗素曾说:"中国人摸索出的生活方式已沿袭数千年,若能够被全世界采纳,地球上肯定会比现在有更多的欢乐祥和。"他所说的"生活方式",其实质正是中国人所说的"道",生生不已、和而不同的"道"。"一带一路"不是中国一家的独奏,而是沿线国家的大合唱,大家一起发展才是真发展,可持续发展才是好发展,可大可久之业才是万国安宁、和谐共处的伟大事业。"一带一路"凝聚了几千年的东方智慧,承载着沿线各国的发展梦想,迈出了共建人类命运共同体的坚实步伐。

The "Belt and Road Initiative" is a good example of cooperation. The Russian *Messenger* remarked that "To China, 'Belt and Road' is more of 'Tao' than road, it is a most important philosophical concept." Then, what is "Tao"? Bertrand Russell, a British philosopher, once said that "the Chinese has lived their way for thousands of years which, if accepted worldwide, will lead to a more joyful and peaceful world than it is now." The Chinese way in his remarks is actually the "Tao" of the Chinese people which values evolution and harmony in diversity. The "Belt and Road Initiative" is not a solo of China, but a chorus of all countries along the "Belt and Road". World development requires that all countries develop at their own paces and in a sustainable way. Only in this way, there will be prolonged international peace and harmony. The "Belt and Road Initiative" coheres the oriental wisdom throughout thousands of years and carries the dreams of all countries along its path and is a great step to the community of common destiny.

叶小文,中共中央委员、全国政协文史和学习委员会副主任、中国中小商业企业协会专家咨询委员会主任
Ye Xiaowen, Member to CPC Central Committee; Vice Director of Chinese People's Political Consultative Conference Literature, History and Learning Committee; Director of CASME Expert Board

* * *

改革开放30多年来,中国中小企业"走出去"取得了可圈可点的成绩。在"一带一路"倡议下,中小企业要乘势而上,积极作为,在实现沿线国家互联互通中当好积极力量,聚焦合适项目、关键城市、重要产业,发挥自己'船小好调头'和细分市场的优势,善于"借梯登高",与国家队"混搭"形成叠加优势,在市场化领域担当参与者、合作者,为支持沿线国家建设方面发挥重要作用,推动陆上、海上、天上、网上四位一体的联通;在推进新兴产业、互联网、商业服务业、人工智能等合作中当好中坚力量,发挥资金、技术、人才等优势,推动相关技术和标准走出去,开展中小企业产业园区经营,促进集群发展;曙光愿意借助《一带一路中小企业合作•重点项目推介手册》走向世界。

In the past 30 years since Chinese reform and opening, SMEs have made remarkable achievements in their "going abroad" process. With the "Belt and Road Initiative", SMEs must take all opportunities and active actions, and focus on appropriate projects, key cities and important industries in countries that have joined the Initiative. They should take full advantages of their flexibility in operation and strengths in specific market segments, and gain extra advantages by cooperating with large state enterprises. SMEs should actively participate and cooperate in the market and thus play important roles in supporting the construction of countries along the "Belt and Road" and realize interconnection on land, over sea, in air and via Internet. SMEs should be the core supporters in promoting emerging industries, Internet, commercial service industry and Artificial Intelligence, and should make best use of their advantages in capital, technology and talents to facilitate the application and adoption of related technologies and standards. A number of industrial parks will be established for SMEs to improve their aggregation. We are expecting to go global with *Belt and Road SME Cooperation • Key Project Promotion Handbook*.

汪官蜀,中国中小商业企业协会产业园区工作委员会主任、重庆曙光都市工业园管委会主任
Wang Guanshu, Director of CASME Working Committee for Industrial Parks; Director of Chongqing Shuguang Urban Industrial Park Management Committee

序言
Preface

* * *

当然，目前我们在"一带一路"的产业开发、产能合作和品牌建设方面基础还都比较薄弱，还都处于起步阶段。"一带一路"的市场机会还没有完全成熟。中小企业要改变思路，抓住机遇。中小企业走出去不是一蹴而就的，企业要冷静，不要一哄而上，要做好调研，规避沿线国家的政治、汇率等风险。企业在走出去的过程中要特别加强自主品牌的建设，这样有利于中国信誉的提升，也有助于企业经济效益的提升。总之，要充分利用好《一带一路中小企业合作·重点项目推介手册》，达到精准对接项目，深入调研、防范风险之间的平衡。

Of course, we are now still very weak in industrial development, production capacity cooperation and brand building under the "Belt and Road Initiative". We are still at the starting stages. Market opportunities under the "Belt and Road Initiative" are not fully developed yet. SMEs must change their ways of thinking and master all opportunities. The process of going global for SMEs is never smooth, and therefore they must stay calm and avoid rash actions. They must study the opportunities carefully and thoroughly to avoid political and exchange rate risks in countries along the "Belt and Road". In the process of going global, enterprises must strengthen their brand building efforts, because this helps to improve both the reputation of China and economic benefits of enterprises. In all, we must make good use of *the Belt and Road SME Cooperation • Key Project Promotion Handbook* to build up connections with foreign projects, to carry out in-depth investigations and to avoid potential risks.

牛华勇，北京外国语大学商学院院长
Mr. Niu Huayong, President of International Business School, Beijing Foreign Studies University

* * *

时至今日，这一倡议逐渐步入务实合作的新阶段。如何以新战略抓住新机遇，成为摆在沿线各个省市甚至各个国家面前的重要问题。随着"一带一路"国家战略的深入推进和"互联网+"国家战略的实施，如何科学地结合本地实际状况完成产业升级、推动中小企业"走出去"、参与沿线国家项目合作已然成为广大中小企业关注的焦点。"大智兴邦，不过集众思"。

So far, the Initiative has come to a new stage of practical cooperation. A major issue before provinces, cities and even countries along the "Belt and Road" is how they can make new strategies and grasp the new opportunities. With the promotion of "Belt and Road Initiative" and "Internet$^+$" strategy, SMEs have focused their attentions to how they can complete the industrial upgrading by scientifically combining with the local conditions and how SMEs can access foreign markets and participate in national projects in countries along the "Belt and Road". "A great leader draws on the wisdom of the masses to prosper the country."

刘怡，工信部中小企业局副巡视员
Liu Yi, Vice Inspector of MIIT SME Bureau

* * *

"一带一路"倡议为古老的"丝绸之路"符号嵌入新的时代内涵，是实现"中国梦"、"亚洲梦"乃至"世界梦"的伟大畅想，彰显了中华民族的天下观和义利观；"一带一路"倡议是宏伟的蓝图，展示了中华民族的博大胸怀与豪迈气魄。中医药必将在"一带一路"中发挥独特作用，也将承担起光荣使命，希望《一带一路中小企业合作·重点项目推介手册》为推进中医药产业合作做出贡献。

The "Belt and Road Initiative" has attached modern meanings to the symbols of ancient "Silk Road" and is a great vision of the "Chinese Dream", "Asian Dream" and even "World Dream" and it has demonstrated the Chinese view of the world and moral and profits. The "Belt and Road" Initiative is a great blueprint and has fully manifested the great minds and spirits of Chinese nation. Traditional Chinese medicine will play its unique roles in the "Belt and Road Initiative", and will also undertake its glorious missions. We hope that *Belt and Road SME Cooperation • Key Project Promotion Handbook* will contribute to cooperation of the traditional Chinese medicine industry.

刘力，陕西中医药大学校长
Liu Li, President of Shaanxi University of Chinese Medicine

* * *

"一带一路"倡议是党中央主动应对全球形势深刻变化、统筹国内国际两个大局作出的重大战略决策，对于进一步扩大中国对外开放格局、促进地区经济繁荣、推动中华民族伟大复兴，具有重要的战略意义。包商银行始终以服务中小企业、建设国际化好银行为己任，紧抓"一带一路"战略性历史机遇，突出服务重点，强化资源配置，扎实推进综合化、国际化发展战略，为"一带一路"建设提供金融动力。

The "Belt and Road Initiative" is an important strategic decision by CPC in active response to the profound global changes and in overall considerations of situations both inside and outside China. It is of great strategic significance to the further development of Chinese opening policy, local prosperity and the great rejuvenation of Chinese nation. Baoshang Bank always strives to serve SMEs and to become an international bank. We will take all strategic opportunities brought about by the "Belt and Road Initiative", focus our efforts on key services and improve the resources allocation to promote our international development and to contribute financial supports to the "Belt and Road" strategy.

强化顶层设计和持续推动。早在2015年，包商银行就根据国家"一带一路"建设规划，制定了《包商银行落实"一带一路"建设的实施意见》，成立了专项工作领导小组，画好"规划图"、"施工图"、"作战图"、"火线图"，推动"一带一路"倡议在银行落地。服务重点上，将"一带一路"中小企业合作和产业发展、基础设施互联互通、能源资源投资合作、经贸合作等客户和项目作为支持重点；政策配套上，统筹做好机构布局、客户拓展、产品创新、制度流程等政策安排，不断提升客户响应度和服务效能；资源保障上，着力将财务、信贷、资本、人力等经营资源向"一带一路"倾斜。

Top-level design and continuous promotion. Early in 2015, Baoshang Bank worked out its *Baoshang Bank Opinions on Implementation of "Belt and Road Initiative"*. For this purpose, a special leading panel was established to make overall plans, detailed actions, task plans and job arrangement plans, in order to implement the "Belt and Road Initiative" in the bank. In terms of key services, special supports will be provided to "Belt and Road" SME cooperation and industrial development, interconnection of infrastructures, energy and resources investment and cooperation and trade cooperation. In terms of supporting policies, overall plans will be made to guide the organizational arrangements, customer development, product innovation and procedure arrangements, to improve the service response and service efficiency. In terms of resources, priorities in financial, credit, capital and labor resources will be granted to the "Belt and Road" projects.

李镇西，包商银行董事长、中国中小商业企业协会执行会长、亚洲金融合作联盟监事长
Li Zhenxi, Chairman of Baoshang Bank; Executive President of China Association for Small & Medium Commercial Enterprises; Chief Supervisor of Asia Financial Cooperation Association

* * *

"一带一路"倡议有很多合作领域，但是最重要的就是两个领域，一是基础设施的互联互通，二是投资合作。欧亚大陆这些主要的"一带一路"沿线国家，文化差异很大，发展水平和程度不一样，诉求也完全不一样，但是他们有共同的一点是欠发达，所以改善民生、发展经济的诉求非常的强烈。"这个时候，有一个国家说我有意愿，而且我有能力，我们一起来发财，来致富，当然深得大家的欢迎，所以这也是为什么能够得到这些国家响应的很重要的原因"。

序言
Preface

The "Belt and Road Initiative" covers cooperation in diverse fields, of which the two most important fields are interconnection of infrastructures and investment and cooperation. Despite the distinct cultures, development levels and demands in countries along the "Belt and Road" on the Euro-Asian continent, they share a common feature of less development. As such, they have strong expectations for economic growth. "At this time, a country expressed its interest and capability. Since this initiative brings shared opportunities of wealth and fortune, it becomes very popular and widely supported by many countries."

"一带一路"提出来以后,得到了国际社会的普遍响应。两个很重要的时间节点,去年11月17号联合国大会做出决定,关于"一带一路"的国际参与,推进"一带一路"。今年3月17号联合国安理会做出决定,希望"一带一路"等国际合作在参与解决阿富汗问题上发挥更大的作用。这说明中国的"一带一路"倡议在国际上完全形成了势头,下一步要把这样的势头保持住,同时要在各方面具体的合作中取得实实在在的进展。

After the "Belt and Road Initiative" is proposed, it has received extensive supports in the international community. One of two important time is November 17th of last year when the UN Assembly approved the decision on international participation in "Belt and Road Initiative", which was an action to promote the "Belt and Road Initiative". The other important time was March 17th of this year when the UN Security Council decided that international cooperation under the "Belt and Road Initiative" may play more roles in solving Afghanistan issues. This means that the Chinese "Belt and Road Initiative" has won its international position and next step is to maintain its positions while make concrete achievements in specific cooperation projects.

欧晓理,国家发改委西部司巡视员
Ou Xiaoli, Inspector of NDRC West China Division

* * *

感谢中国中小商业企业协会搭建这个平台,我相信它能够为我们铺建未来发展的道路,让中小企业能够更好地发展,帮助发展中国家尤其是"一带一路"沿线国家更好的发展。

I would like to give my thanks to China Association for Small & Medium Commercial Enterprises for this platform. I believe that it will pave the road for our development, so that SMEs can develop better and help developing countries, especially those along the "Belt and Road" to achieve better development.

如果我们有机会跟中国及其他的"一带一路"沿线国家进行合作,定会有助于我们的中小企业得到更好的发展,我们也希望我们的中小企业能得到相关的金融支持,增强国际化技能,并从中学习全球化的相关知识,伴随双方共同发展的美好愿望,我们也能扩大我们的视野,并赢得更好的发展机遇。

If we have the opportunity to cooperate with China and other countries along the "Belt and Road", it will help our SMEs to achieve better development. We hope that our SMEs can receive related financial supports to reinforce our international skills and have better knowledge of the globalization. With the good wishes for mutual development, we can broaden our vision and win our opportunities.

尼泊尔驻华大使利拉·马尼·鲍德尔
Leela Mani Paudyal, Ambassador of Nepal to P.R.C

* * *

中国和西班牙有着非常友好的双边关系,我们的总统也出席了一个月前举行的"一带一路"高峰论坛,是28位元首中的一位。我觉得我们的双边关系棒极了,中国是我们最大的贸易伙伴,目前一共有1.5万家企业向中国出口商品。

China and Spain have very good bilateral relations, and our President also attended the "Belt and Road" Summit held one month ago, and was one of the 28 presidents to the Summit. I feel that our bilateral relations are great. China is our largest trade partner. We have 15 thousand enterprises currently exporting products to China.

我们期待更多的中小企业间的合作，我们经济的 99% 主要是来自于中小企业。我们有很多 5-150 人的这样的企业，它们经济增长贡献最大。中国有很多的中小企业，还有行业协会，是双边关系的主要推动者，对于他们来说这就是我们进行合作的一种方式，我们也积极地参加合作，在电商平台上我们希望进行更好的合作，我们已经和阿里巴巴、京东以及敦煌网签署了合作协议，它们是中国很重要的电商平台。

We expect more cooperation between SMEs. 99% of our economy is contributed by SMEs. We have many enterprises with 5-150 employees that made the largest contribution to our economic growth. China also has many SMEs and industrial associations. They are the main promoters of our bilateral relations. To them, this is a way we can work together. We also actively participate in the cooperation and on the E-commerce platform, we expect more cooperation. We have signed a cooperation agreement with Alibaba, Jingdong and DHgate. They are all important E-commerce platforms in China.

西班牙驻华大使馆一等经济商务参赞裴思乔做主题演讲
Keynote speech by Sergio PrezSaiz, Head Spanish Economic and Commercial Counselor

* * *

可能你知道匈牙利是一个比较小的欧洲国家。匈牙利位于欧洲的中心，政治和经济都很稳定，相比其他的欧洲国家增长非常稳定非常高。失业率是 5.1%，外商投资率是 78%，是一个非常受欢迎的投资目的地。

You might know that Hungary is a small country in the heart of Europe and is very stable both in politics and economy. Hungary is growing steadily and at high rate when compared with other European countries. Hungary has an unemployment rate of 5.1% and foreign investment rate of 78%, which makes Hungary a popular destination of investment.

关于中小企业之间的合作，中国银行在匈牙利已经设立了分行。匈牙利是全球最佳投资目的地，对中国的 SME 来说也是一个非常好的机会，同时我们政府也会提供尽可能多的支持，比如说企业税收最低，大概是 9%，这使得匈牙利也成为了一个非常有吸引力的投资目的地。匈牙利的优势包括政府的资助是非常大的，大概占到投资的 50%，所以你每投资一块钱，就可以得到政府的补贴 2.5 块钱，你还可以创造更多的就业，如果在欠发达地区进行投资，会有更多的优惠政策。

As for cooperation between SMEs, Bank of China has established a branch bank in Hungary. Hungary is the world's best destination of investments and also a good opportunity for Chinese SMEs. Besides, our governments will provide as much support as possible. For example, we have the lowest business tax which is about 9%. This makes Hungary an appealing destination of investment. Hungary advantages lie in that our government has very extent of autonomy which is about 50% of the total investment. As such, for each dollar invested, you will receive 2.5 dollars allowance. You can create more job opportunities. If you invest in less developed areas of Hungary, you will have more policy privileges.

匈牙利驻华使馆商务处副处长戴彼得作主题演讲
Keynote speech by DEÁK Péter, Vice Director of Commerce Office of Hungary Embassy to China

目 录
CONTENTS

加美节能环保润滑油
Jama Energy-saving and Environmental-protection Lubricants ·· 001

自动化砌块成型机
Automated Block Making Machine ·· 004

新型载药平台及材料
New Drug Loading Platform and Materials ··· 006

买灯网
Buylamps.cn ··· 008

皇宫锦绣
Splendid Palace ·· 010

泰远汽车自动防撞器
TaiY Auto Automatic Bumper ·· 012

汽车真空泵
Automobile Vacuum Pump ·· 014

广大众利新零售系统
Guangda Zhongli New Retail System ·· 016

安盛农业树莓时代科技产业园
Ansheng Agricultural Raspberry Times science and Technology Industrial Park ··· 018

智慧水务系统
Smart Water System ··· 020

建筑装饰内外墙涂料
Architectural Decoration Coating for Interior and Exterior Walls ·· 022

富沃斯（FOC）珠宝数字资产
Foc Jewelry Digital Assets ··· 024

裕康高弹强力环保防水涂料
Yukang High Elastic Strong Environmental Protection Waterproof Paint ·· 026

PIIPIINOO 皮皮诺换面鞋
PIIPIINOO Face-changing Shoes ·· 028

中文名称	英文名称	页码
大家社区	Dajia Community	030
金凤凰家具	Gold Phoenix Furniture	032
中华江旗袍	China's Jiangqipao	034
贝姆燃气采暖热水炉	Beamo Gas Heating Water Heater	036
大基地·大麦青苗粉	Big Base· Young Crops Powder of Barley	038
乾坤汽车紧固件	Qiankun Auto Fasteners	040
晚乐福养老平台	Wanlefu Pension Platform	042
浪度家居	Nondo Furniture	044
有害生物专业防治	Professional Pest Control	046
土壤固化建筑材料	Soil Solidified Building Material	048
霸王寨农业生态观光园	Bawangzhai Agriculture Ecological Tourist Garden	050
南电电力施工安装项目	Nandian Electrical Installation Project	052
信息化科技创新产业互联平台建设	Construction of Interconnection Platform of Information Science & Technology Innovation Industry	054
洞宫葬 + 互联网	Hole Palace Funeral + Internet	056
舒理他纯益生菌发酵酸奶	Cherita Pure probiotic Fermented Yogurt	058
智慧社区·智慧停车	Wisdom Community · Wisdom Parking	060
蒙古国矿业投资开发	Mongolian Mining Investment and Development	062
中医养生百家秘方	Hundreds of Secret TCM Recipes of Health Maintenance	064

赛益德民族特色产品
Saiyide Products with National Characteristics ··· 066

YESO 国际赛事高定品牌
YESO Haute Couture for International Events ··· 068

沂脉山泉饮用天然苏打水
Yimai Mountain Spring Drinking Natural Soda Water ··· 070

滋养臻品 – 松露酒
Good Nutritious Product-Truffle Wine ·· 072

校贝通云教育平台
Xiaobeitong Cloud Education Platform ··· 074

中药材仓储物流基地
Traditional Chinese Medicine Warehousing and Logistics Base ··· 076

嘎仙洞旅游
Gaxian Cave Tourism ·· 078

共价型多核强化絮凝除磷
Covalent Polynuclear Enhanced Flocculation Dephosphorization ··· 080

云章
Cloud Sign ·· 082

室内外艺术雕塑及构件
Indoor and Outdoor Art Sculptures And Components ··· 084

尚雨轩 – 连锁管理新模式
Shangyuxuan - Chain Management Model ·· 086

水基型灭火器
Water - based Fire Extinguisher ··· 088

室内外照明工程
Indoor and Outdoor Lighting Engineering ··· 090

信合义乌小商品
Xinhe Yiwu Commodity ·· 092

柯赛德尖端润滑科技
Kroneseder Sophisticated Lubrication Technology ·· 094

节能环保装饰工程
Energy Conservation and Environmental Protection Decoration Project ·· 096

阳明养生养老中心
Yangming Health and Old-age Care Center ·· 098

乾承机械磨损修复技术
Qiancheng Mechanical Wear Repair Technology ··· 100

移动环保公厕	
Mobile Environmental Protection Public Toilet	102
富蓝特酒店	
Friends Hotel	104
大气新能源	
Atmospheric New Energy	106
VR 手机助手 & 易企炫	
VR Mobile Phone Assistant & Yiqixuan	108
海陆空运输	
Maritime, Land and Air Transport	110
嘉佑－贝吉塔饰材	
Jiayou- Vegeta Decorative Material	112
防腐保温工程	
Anti-corrosion and Heat-preservation Project	114
阳光照明、光热发电及供热系统	
Solar Lighting, Solar Thermal Power Generation and Heat Supply System	116
太阳能灯具及储能产品	
Solar Lamps and Energy Storage Products	118
室内空气污染治理	
Indoor Air Pollution Treatment	120
高新技术产权交易所	
High-tech Intellectual Property Exchange	122
黑背景显微镜	
Black Background Microscope	124
智能安防、智能交通	
Smart Security Control, Smart Traffic	126
建筑供应链平台	
Building Supply Chain Platform	128
水溶性高分子产品	
Water-soluble Polymer Products	130
种群耘平台	
Zhongqunyun Platform	132
凤凰中药材花卉种植基地	
Phoenix TCM and Flower Plantation Base	134
安全社区智能管理平台	
Secure Community Intelligent Management Platform	136

目录 / CONTENTS

"手机控"养生产品
Health Products for "Phone Freaks" ·· 138

妈妈安 – 小儿推拿连锁加盟
Mamaan - Infant Massotherapy Chain Store ·· 140

流量计
Flow Meter ··· 142

中药材种植与深加工
Cultivation and Deep Processing of Chinese Medicinal Herbs ··· 144

雲山椿山茶油
Yunshanchun Camellia Oil ··· 146

光伏太阳能景区道路指示牌
Photovoltaic Solar Road Sign in Scenic Areas ·· 148

译境语言服务平台
Project E-ging Language Service Platform ·· 150

乐居公社
Leju Community ·· 152

企业 SP 集合服务商
Enterprise SP Integrated Service Provider ·· 154

沙发、汽车座套革
Sofa and Car Seat Cover Leather ··· 156

豪运盈发汽车
Haoyun Yingfa Auto ··· 158

纯滚动轴承
Pure Rolling Bearing ·· 160

液晶书画板
LCD Sketchpad ··· 162

阳光赛赛公司绩效价值管理系统
Sunshine Saisai Performance & Value Management System for Company ·· 164

高精度标准齿轮
High-precision Standard Gears ··· 166

阀门
Valves ··· 168

篆刻艺术·皇家珍藏品
Art of Seal Cutting·Imperial Collection ··· 170

中药生态旅游观光庄园
Traditional Chinese Medicine Ecological Tourism Manor ·· 172

天伦网·一站式服务
Tianlunwang·One-stop Service ··· 174

自然之诺自然活酒
Promise of Nature Natural Live Wine ··· 176

宜速家
Yisujia ·· 178

大健康公共服务平台
Great Health Public Service Platform ·· 180

新尼燕窝饮
Xinni Bird's Nest Drink ·· 182

聚氨酯及热缩材料
Polyurethane and Pyrocondensation Materials ··· 184

凤英·智慧外交 APP 平台
Fengying· Smart Diplomatic App Platform ··· 186

传统艺术推广平台
Traditional Art Promotion Platform ·· 188

元古页岩画艺术
The Art of Proterozoic Shale Painting ··· 190

泉龙佛像雕塑工艺
Quanlong Buddha Statue Sculpture Craft ··· 192

蒙古族根雕及旅游商品
Mongolian Root Carving and Tourism Commodity ······································· 194

营养型奶酒
Nutrition-type Milk Wine ··· 196

首铝铝材
Shoulv Aluminum ··· 198

风机
Blowers/Fans ··· 200

加美节能环保润滑油
Jama Energy-saving and Environmental-protection Lubricants

一、项目公司名称：江苏加美润滑油有限公司
I. Project Company Name: Jiangsu Jama Lubricant Co., Ltd.

二、项目公司介绍：
II. Project Company Introduction：

加美出身欧美，但根扎在中国，时刻牢记发展重任和社会责任。从20世纪70年代初开始，经过近半个世纪的励志与沉淀，早已集研发、生产、销售和服务四大功能于一体。在不断前行与发展中，于2003年跨越太平洋，进入中国。是年6月，加美中国在香港成立，次年5月加美厦门公司成立。2005年3月，江苏加美成立。2010年，在厦门建成年产量5万吨以上的优质润滑油生产基地。2011年，设立加美润滑油（天津）有限公司。2012年9月，上海加美实业有限公司诞生。至此，加美石油在中国的战略格局已经形成。

Found in Europe and America and taking root in China, Jama always has the development and social responsibility in mind, and has integrated R&D, production, sable and service after nearly half a century of encouragement and accumulation since the early 70s of last century. During the continuous progress and development, Jama came into China in 2003 across the Pacific. Jama (China) was found at Hong Kong in June 2003 and Jama (Xiamen) was found in May 2004. Jama (Jiangsu) was found in March 2005. A high-quality lubricants production base was set up in 2010, with annual output more than 50,000 tons. Jama Lubricants (Tianjin) Co., Ltd. was found in 2011, and Shanghai Jama Industrial Co., Ltd. was set up in September of the next year. At this point, Jama Petroleum has been distributed in China.

三、负责人介绍：
III. Responsible Person Introduction:

叶文贤先生，福建师范大学经济系毕业，后就读于牛津大学国际金融系；
Mr. Ye Wenxian, studied in the Department of International Finance in Oxford University after graduated from the Department of Economics in Fujian Normal University;

1999年6月参加工作；
Started to work in June 1999;

2005年到江苏昆山开辟加美华东市场，成立江苏加美润滑油有限公司；
Opened up the Jama market of East China in Jiangsu Kunshan 2005 and set up Jiangsu Jama Lubricants Co., Ltd.;

2009年10月加入中国共产党；
Joined the Communist Party of China in October 2009；

2014年当选昆山市青年企业家协会常务副会长；
Acted as the Executive Vice President of Kunshan Youth Entrepreneurs Association in 2014;

2016年7月被浙江大学聘为创业顾问；
Hired by Zhejiang University as an Entrepreneurial Consultant in July 2016;

2016年获颁国家创新创业导师资格证书；
Awarded with the Qualification Certificate for National Innovation and Enterprise Tutor in 2016;

2016年5月荣获"昆山市十大杰出青年"称号；
Won the title of one of "Kunshan Ten Outstanding Young Persons" in May 2016;

2016年中共昆山市第十五届政协委员。
Acted as the Fifteenth CPPCC Member in Kunshan CHC.

四、项目名称：加美节能环保润滑油
Ⅳ. Project Name: Jama Energy-saving and Environmental-protection Lubricants

五、项目概况：
Ⅴ. Project Profile:

高速发展的加美润滑油正在进行第二轮的产业大布局，努力加快身处长三角的这个战略高地建设，全面辐射两岸三地的润滑油市场。本次规划的项目由"年产10万吨的加美公司第二座优质润滑油生产基地、立体仓储中心和一座五星级形象店"重头组合而成，实现加美润滑油公司的生产制造、仓储物流与品牌形象"三大功能"再提升。建设中的第二座加美润滑油生产基地和华东地区仓储中心，引进领先行业的全套自动人工智能设备，实现生产制造、封装测试、物流配送等方面的产业升级，增强加美品牌团队的快速反应能力。项目建成后，加美润滑油在安全生产、环境保护、员工关怀、市场服务方面的社会责任落实更加完善，搏击市场的能力进一步增强，为股东、为社会创造财富的能力进一步提高。

Jama Lubricants which has been developed rapidly is undergoing the second round of the industrial layout, strives to speed up the construction in the Yangtze River Delta that is its strategic highland, and occupies the lubricants market in Mainland China, Taiwan and Hong Kong. This project consists of "the second high-quality lubricants production base with annual output of 100,000 tons, 3D storage center and 1 five-star image shop of Jama Company" to re-improve the production, warehousing logistics and brand image. A complete set of industry-leading automatic artificial intelligence equipment was introduced in the second Jama Lubricants production base and East China Storage Center in the construction to update the industry in the production, package test, logistics distribution and other aspects to improve the rapid response capability of Jama Brand Team. After completion of the Project, Jama Lubricants is more perfect in the social responsibility implementation of safe production, environmental protection, staff care and market services, and further enhances the competitive capacity, to create more social wealth.

六、项目优势：
Ⅵ. Project Advantage(s):

作为润滑油行业十大品牌之一的加美，在中国两岸三地的战略布局已经形成，目前已经进入事业升级再次腾飞的二次发展阶段。加美在中国拥有两个生产基地、一个呼叫中心、30余家营销公司，以及遍及全国的经销商网络和销售团队；

As one of the top ten brands of lubricants industry, Jama has been distributed in Mainland China, Taiwan and Hong Kong, and it has been re-developed at present for industry update. Jama contains 2 production bases, 1 call center, more than 30 marketing companies, and country-wide dealer network and sales teams in China.

1．加美研发能力具备了世界级的实力，在中国建设了高规格的产品研发中心两个、中心实验室一个，拥有自主知识产权的各类专利技术，包括国际专利在内多达几十项，已经广泛运用到加美的110多项产品之中；

First, Jama has the world-class strength in R & D, set up 2 high-standard product R & D centers and 1 central laboratory, and possesses dozens of patented technologies of independent knowledge industry including the international patents. All of these technologies have been widely used in more than 110 Jama products；

2．加美产品被经济强省江苏省的政府机构认定为高新技术产品；

Second, Jama products are identified as high-tech products by the provincial government agencies in Jangsu which is a powerful economic province；

3．加美被中国质量检验协会认定为"全国润滑油行业质量领军企业"、"全国产品和服务质量诚信示范企业"。

Third, Jama is identified as the "Quality-leading Enterprise in the National Lubricants Industry" and the "Integrity Model Enterprise in National Product and Service Quality" by the China Association for Quality Inspection.

七、项目需要：
Ⅶ. Project Demand(s):

致力于绿色润滑油和"一带一路"产业布局的加美面向全球招商，欢迎海内外有志者携手加美润滑油，在车用领域与工业领域两大项目中开展多种形式的合作，投身加美事业阵线，共同开创未来，实现共赢，为中华民族的伟大复兴努力奋斗！

Committed to green lubricants and industrial layout of the "Belt and Road", Jama Institutional Organization is for global investment, and the aspiring at home and abroad is popular to cooperate with Jama to put forward a variety of cooperation ways in the automotive industrial fields. Let's devote into Jama Lubricants to create the future jointly and achieve win-win situation and work hard for the great rejuvenation of the Chinese nation!

自动化砌块成型机
Automated Block Making Machine

一、项目公司名称： 保定市泰华机械制造有限公司

I. Project Company Name: Baoding Taihua Machinery Manufacturing Co., Ltd.

二、项目公司介绍：

II. Project Company Introduction:

公司已有 20 多年的发展历程，主要产品为全自动化砌块成型机生产线。资产雄厚、设备齐全、质量控制体系完善，具有独立的产品研发和制造能力，设有机械加工厂、热处理厂、研发中心、节能环保的新型墙材示范基地、建筑垃圾资源化处理厂等多元化综合服务体系。

The Company has been developed for more than 20 years, and it mainly produces the fully-automated block making machine production line. With the abundant assets, complete equipment and improved quality control system, it has the independent product research and development and manufacturing capacity, and it has the diversified comprehensive service system including the mechanical professing plant, heat treatment plant, research and development center, energy-saving and environment-friendly new-type wall material demonstration base and construction waste recycling plant.

泰华先后荣获"河北省科技型中小企业"、"中国中小企业科技创新 100 强"、"十二五全国墙材革新创新标杆企业"等荣誉称号，为中央电视台科技标榜企业。

Taihua successively won the honorary titles such as "Hebei Provincial Small and Medium-sized Enterprise of Science and Technology", "China Top 100 Small and Medium-sized Enterprises in Science and Technology Innovation" and "'The 12th Five-year Plan' National Wall Material Renovation and Innovation Benchmarking Enterprise", and it has been the science and technology advertised by CCTV.

三、负责人介绍：

III. Responsible Person Introduction:

郭春玲，保定市泰华机械制造有限公司董事长，目前担任中国中小商业企业协会副会长职务，先后获得"全国优秀中小企业家金钻奖"、"中国优秀创新企业家"、"全国巾帼建功标兵"、"全国三八红旗手"等荣誉称号。

Guo Chunling, President of Baoding Taihua Machinery Manufacturing Co., Ltd., serves as Vice Chairman of China Association of Small & Medium Commercial Enterprise, and she successively won the honorable titles such as "Gold Diamond Prize in National Excellent Small & Medium Entrepreneurs", "Chinese Excellent Innovative Entrepreneur", "National Contribution Woman Pacemaker" and "National Woman Pace-Setter".

四、项目名称： 自动化砌块成型机

IV. Project Name: Automated Block Making Machine

五、项目概况：

V. Project Profile:

泰华现有 THQM6-15、THQM8-15、THQM10-15、THQM12-15、THQM15-15、THQM18-18 等几十种拥有自主知识产权的全自动化模振砌块成型机系列组合配置的生产线，以满足不同客户需求。独创的悬挂式模振技术，采用机、电、液一体化技术，PLC 智能控制，配备数据输出装置，实现人机对话。在控制系统中还包括了先进的安全逻辑控制及故障诊断系统，它可以根据客户要求配置具有远程控制功能的装置，用全自动化装置完成自动回板与接板、机械手码垛，使整机程序实现了智能化无人操作。产品遍布全国各地，赢得了广大用户的一致好评，提高了我国砌块成型机在国际市场的竞争力，引领砌块机的新潮流。

Taihua has tens of fully-automated production lines of mold vibration block making machine series combination configuration having the proprietary intellectual property right, including THQM6-15, THQM8-15, THQM10-15, THQM12-15, THQM15-15 and THQM18-18, to meet the demands of different clients. Its unique suspension-type mold vibration technology adopts the machine-electricity-liquid integrated technology and PLC intellectual control and is equipped with the data output device to realize man-machine interaction. The control system also includes the advanced safety logic control and fault diagnosis system, and it can configure the devices with the remote control function according to the clients' requirements and complete the automatic plate returning, plate connecting and robotic palletizing with the fully-automated devices to enable the complete machine procedure to realize intelligent unmanned operation. Its products have spread over all the country, have been praised by the users, have improved the competitiveness of China's block making machines in the international market and have guided the new trend of the block machines.

泰华自动化砌块成型机，可选用水泥、石渣、粉煤灰、陶粒、炉灰渣、钢渣、矿渣、建筑垃圾等为原材料，通过更换模具即可生产出混凝土实心标砖、多孔砖、空心砌块、植草砖、彩色路面砖、复合自保温砌块等100多种新型建材制品。所生产的建材产品满足中国国家标准《复合保温砖和复合保温砌块》GB/T29060 要求，符合国家新版《建筑设计防火规范》，达到国家建材行业标准，实现建筑节能75%，广泛应用于商住、公建、路面等工程建设。

The cement, rock ballast, fly ash, ceramsite, furnace ash and slag, steel slag, mineral waste residues, construction waste and others can be used as the raw materials of Taihua automated block making machine. More than 100 kinds of new-type building material products such as standard solid concrete brick, porous brick, hollow block, grassing brick, color pavement brick and composite self-insulation block can be produced by the replace of molds. All the building material products produced meet the requirements in the national standard *Composite Insulation Bricks and Composite Insulation Blocks* GB/T29060, conform to the national new version of *Specification for Design of Building Fire Protection* and reach the national building material industry standards, and they realized 75% building energy efficiency and are widely used in the commercial and residential, public, road and other engineering constructions.

六、项目优势：
Ⅵ. Project Advantage(s):

1．节能，泰华 THQM 模振砌块成型机与其他台振机相比，节能 40% 以上；
Energy conservation; compared to other vibration machines, Taihua THQM mold vibration block making machine saves the energy of more than 40%；

2．成型周期短、生产效率高；
Short molding cycle, high production efficiency;

3．布料均匀，所出产品达强度等级和密度等级双控标准；
Uniform cloth; the products produced reach the double-control standards of strength level and density level;

4．超大台面设计，产品产量高；
Oversized table design, high product yield;

5．整机噪音低、寿命长。
Low noise and long life of complete machine.

七、项目需求：
Ⅶ. Project Demand(s):

产品推介：泰华模振砌块成型机品质优良，在国际市场有独特的竞争力，愿乘"一带一路"之风，将产品推向沿线国家。

Product promotion: Taihua mold vibration block making machine has the high quality and has the unique competitiveness in the international market. The Company hopes to promote our products to the countries along with the help of the "Belt and Road".

新型载药平台及材料
New Drug Loading Platform and Materials

一、项目公司名称： 南京生矶坊生物工程有限公司

I. Project Company Name: Nanjing Shengjifang Bioengineering Co., Ltd.

二、项目公司介绍：

II. Project Company Introduction:

公司于2012年12月成立，坐落在南京经济技术开发区红枫科技园，自有厂房面积7000平方米，其中实验室1000平方米。公司致力于提供难溶性药物解决方案及载药系统。已经独立研制成功新型载药系统及新材料，并已获得美国和欧盟多国的专利授权。主要的产品为：难溶药物载药系统及材料，自主开发的新制剂药物、全新药物的增溶技术。

Established in December 2012, the company is located in Hongfeng Science and Technology Park of Nanjing Economic and Technological Development Zone. Its own plant area is 7,000 m^2, of which the laboratory is 1,000 m^2. The company is committed to providing insoluble drug solutions and drug-loading system. It has independently developed new drug-loading systems and new materials, and has obtained patent licensing of the United States and many countries of European Union. The main products are insoluble drug-loading system and materials, self-developed new formulation drugs, and new drug solubilization technology.

三、负责人介绍：

III. Responsible Person Introduction:

胡工，董事长，具备25年以上丰富的商业经验，独特的视角和领导力，学习能力强大，对行业市场趋势敏感度高，搭建跨国跨区域高科技合作平台，带领团队专注于创新药物和新制剂的研发、生产与销售，并且将中国研发、制造带入世界市场，使公司快速进入成长阶段。

Hu Gong, board chairman, has more than 25 years of rich business experience, unique perspective and leadership, strong learning ability and high sensitivity to market trends. He builds transnational cross-regional high-tech cooperation platform, leads the team to be devoted to the development, production and sales of innovative drugs and new formulations, and brings China's R&D and manufacturing into the world market so that the company quickly enters the growth stage.

孙晓东，总经理，生物工程硕士，20年研发药物及其行业质量标准的控制与管理经验，带领技术团队完成超分子材料及国际领先水平新材料的研制，设定药品、生物制品、植物制剂的安全质量标准，为公司取得多项国际专利及中国专利。

Sun Xiaodong, general manager, master of bioengineering, has 20 years of research and development experience in R&D drugs and control and management experience of the industry quality standards. He leads the technical team to complete the development of supramolecular materials and new materials of international leading level, and sets up safety and quality standards of drugs, biological products and plant preparations to obtain a number of international patents and Chinese patents for the company.

四、项目名称： 新型载药平台及材料

IV. Project Name: New Drug Loading Platform and Materials

五、项目概况：

V. Project Profile:

增溶技术介绍：公司技术团队以技术成熟的磺丁环糊精为起点，研究多种类型的药物增溶技术，申请组合物专利十余项，其中多西他赛注射剂已经通过美国FDA审核，正在进行生产验证，稳定性合格后即可上市销售。

Solubilization technology: With mature sulfo-butyl cyclodextrin as a starting point, the company's technical team studies a variety of types of drug solubilization technologies, and applies for more than 10 composition patents, of which docetaxel injection has been approved by the US FDA, is in the ongoing production verification, and can be sold in the market after the stability is qualified.

以多西他赛的研制及美国报批为基础，公司完成了实验室的仪器设备及实验规范改造，全部研发数据获得美国FDA认可，为后面的研究工作铺平了道路。后续再研同类产品20余个，其中4-6个已经完成立项，准备开展报批工作。

Based on the development of docetaxel and the approval of the United States, the company has completed the laboratory equipment and experimental specifications transformation, and all R&D data are approved by the US FDA to pave the way for the subsequent research work. The follow-up similar products are more than 20, of which 4-6 have been completed the project approval, and are ready to report for approval.

载药系统介绍：经过大量的增溶药物研发发现，由于磺丁环糊精的乙醇溶解度很低，导致易水解药物难以通过该技术实现制剂改进。公司经过长时间研究，成功研制了新一代新型载药材料，实现了乙醇及水共溶，不但解决了多数药物的溶解问题，而且极大优化了制剂工艺，实现了过程简化，质量可控，同时降低了生产周期及成本。

Drug-loading system: After a lot of solubilization drug research and development, it is found that Sulfobutylether-β-Cyclodextrin ethanol solubility is very low, leading to the hydrolytic drugs are difficult to achieve the technology improvement of the preparation. After a long period of research, the company has successfully developed the next generation of new drug-containing materials to achieve the ethanol and water co-solubility, which not only solves the dissolution problem of the majority of drugs, but also greatly optimizes the preparation process to achieve a simplified process, and controllable quality, meanwhile reduces the production cycle and cost.

六、项目优势：
Ⅵ. Project Advantage(s):

全新超分子技术和新材料，将新药或畅销药进行低成本，低风险剂型改进。基于此技术的新型载药系统平台，可以收购前期研发成功的难溶性药物，进行后期开发。独具产业延展特性，应用范围广泛，技术平台优势明显，促进产业创新和竞争能力的自主知识产权，科学规范管理，持续发展动力强劲。

Brand-new supramolecular technology and new materials have low cost and low risk so that the company carries out dosage form improvement of the new drugs or best-selling drugs. Based on the new drug-loading system platform with this technology, we can acquire insoluble drugs of early successful research and development to carry out the late development. It has unique industry extension characteristics, a wide application range, and obvious advantages of technical platform to promote industrial innovation and competitiveness of independent intellectual property rights, scientific and standardized management and strong sustainable development momentum.

七、项目需求：欢迎药品研发、药品生产机构合作及投资。
Ⅶ. Project Demand(s)：Welcome cooperation and investment of drug research and development and drug production enterprises.

买灯网
Buylamps.cn

一、项目公司名称：西安广鑫灯饰有限责任公司

Ⅰ. Project Company Name：Xi'an Guanxin Lamps Co., Ltd.

二、项目公司介绍：

Ⅱ. Project Company Introduction:

公司成立于 1998 年，是集照明工程规划设计、照明产品生产制造、销售、服务及施工安装于一体的专业化大型照明公司，具有城市及道路照明工程专业总承包壹级资质。公司于 2015 年 1 月在上海股权托管交易中心挂牌上市，被中国中小商业企业协会评为"企业信用评价 AAA 级信用企业"，先后荣获"中国建筑电气名优产品奖"、"中国建材流通行业名优产品奖"、"3.15 消费者放心首选品牌"、"中国著名品牌"，企业被评为"国家建材 AAA 级质量服务信用企业"、"中国照明工程百强企业"、"中国照明工程施工五十强企业"、"灯饰行业十强单位"等。

Established in 1998, Guangxin Lamps is now a large supplier of lighting devices, lighting planning and designing, lighting device manufacturing sales, service and installation, and has been licensed for Class-I urban and road lighting engineering. The company was listed at Shanghai Equity Exchange in January 2015. Guangxin is chosen by CASME as a "AAA Credit Company", and won a number of prizes, including "Famous Quality Product Prize for Building Construction", "Famous Quality Product Prize in Building Material Industry", "3.15 Customer Trusted Brand", "China Famous Brand" and titles, including "National AAA Quality and Credit Enterprise", "China Top 100 Lighting Enterprise", "China Top 50 Lighting Engineering Enterprise" and "Top 10 Lamp Manufacturer".

三、负责人介绍：

Ⅲ. Responsible Person Introduction:

杨林科，买灯网创始人、国家一级注册照明设计师、国家二级建造师、电气工程师、西北大学 MBA、西安交通大学 EMBA、西安外事学院创业导师、陕西省照明学会理事、西安市电子商务协会常务理事、西安设计师联合会会员。

Yang Linke: Founder of buylamps.cn; National Certified Lighting Designer Grade-I; Associate Constructor; Electrical Engineer; MBA from Northwest University; EMBA from Xi'an Jiaotong University; Enterprise Mentor at Xi'an International University; Member to Illuminating Engineering Society of Shaanxi Province; Managing Director of Xi'an Electronic Commerce Association; member to Xi'an Design Union.

四、项目名称：买灯网

Ⅳ. Project Name：Buylamps.cn

五、项目概况：

Ⅴ. Project Profile:

公司位于西安市高新技术产业开发区高新路，自 2011 年开始，打造中国灯饰行业垂直电商综合平台——买灯网，把灯具灯饰工厂搬到网上，把灯具灯饰卖向全球，让客户买灯就上买灯网，使买灯省时、省力、省钱。深入挖掘电商运营的价值，采用层层合伙机制，寻找优秀有资质的设计师以及品牌灯具厂家合作，预计在 2018 年达到产值 2 亿，2019 年产值 6 亿，2020 年产值 20 亿，2021 年产值 60 亿，2022 年产值 100 亿，IPO 上市。

The company is situated in Gaoxin Road, Xi'an High-Tech Industrial Development Zone. The company invested and established buylamps.cn a comprehensive vertical E-commerce platform, by which the lamps are made available to consumers directly online to save their energy, time and money. Based on in-depth study of the values of E-commerce operation, buylamps.cn adopted two-level partnership and cooperated with qualified designers and brand owners and manufacturers. It is expected that the total output value will be CNY 200 million in 2018, CNY 600 million in 2019, CNY 2 billion in 2020, CNY 6 billion in 2021 and CNY 10 billion in 2022. Then the company will go public.

融资方案：

Financing plan：

1．融资方式：债权融资、股权融资

Financing method：debt, equity

2．退出机制：A．上市转让　B．公司回购

Withdrawal mechanism：A. Public transfer B. Redemption

六、项目优势：

Ⅵ. Project Advantage(s)：

1．拥有自主品牌

Proprietary brand

2．一支十九年行业经验的团队

A team with 19-year experiences in the industry

3．上万种照明产品，专业化的咨询顾问

Over ten thousand lighting product series, professional consultants

4．具有专业资质的安装及售后服务队伍

Qualified installation and service team

5．省、市、县三级市场及合理的配送体系

Reasonable delivery system covering provinces, cities and counties

6．做到线上线下结合，设计师、灯具生产厂家及施工安装企业联合，形成透明的供应链和及时的售后服务体系。

Combination of online and offline operation. Designers, lamp manufacturers and installation service providers will cooperate with each other to build a transparent industrial chain and timely after-sales service systems.

七、项目需求：寻找合伙人及资本注入或相关资源对接。

Ⅶ. Project Demand(s)：The company is looking for potential partners and capital investments or related resources.

皇宫锦绣
Splendid Palace

一、项目公司名称：苏州市沈寿刺绣艺术研究中心

I. Project Company Name: Suzhou Shen Shou Embroidery Art Research Center

二、项目公司介绍：

II. Project Company Introduction：

位于苏州高新区镇湖街道绣品街，是目前国内专门研究中国传统刺绣工艺及传承发扬沈寿仿真绣技艺的专业性刺绣研究机构，也是中国丝绸非遗手工艺研究、传承、发展、总结及创新的重要研究单位。中心主要研究任务：苏绣历史传承，中国刺绣的演变、发展和脉络，中国刺绣在社会发展中的作用和意义，中国刺绣的艺术成就和社会贡献，中国刺绣对社会经济的发展意义，苏绣在提升人文素养中的重要作用。

Located at Xiupin Street, Zhenhu Subdistrict, Suzhou High-tech Zone, it is a professional embroidery research institution specializing in the research of Chinese traditional embroidery art and inheriting and carrying forward Shen Shou emulational embroidery artistry and also a key research organization for research, inheritance, development, summary and innovation of Chinese silk crafts as intangible cultural heritage. The Center undertakes the main research tasks as follows: historic inheritance of Suzhou Embroidery, evolution, development and skeleton of Chinese embroidery, and role of Chinese embroidery and its significance in social development, artistic achievement and social contribution of Chinese embroidery, significance of Chinese embroidery to social and economic development, and the key role of Suzhou Embroidery in enhancing humanity qualities.

三、负责人介绍：

III. Responsible Person Introduction

濮惠菊：沈寿刺绣艺术研究中心主任、苏绣·仿真绣创始人沈寿第四代门人、泼墨绣创始人、研究员级工艺美术师、江苏省工艺美术名人、世界非物质文化遗产代表性传承人、国礼指定艺术家、中华文化大使。

Pu Huiju: Director of Shen Shou Embroidery Art Research Center, successor of the fourth generation of Shen Shou – the founder of emulational embroidery under Suzhou Embroidery, Founder of embroidery in paint-splashing style, researcher-level craft artist, a celebrity of crafts and arts in Jiangsu Province, representative successor of World Intangible Cultural Heritage, approved national ceremony artist, Ambassador of Chinese Culture.

1966年出生于苏州西华（西华即镇湖镇），一个世代办私塾的先生人家。在浓郁的家族传统文化氛围中熏陶和沉淀，从小机智聪慧，靠自己特有的天赋与悟性从上辈人手中接过绣花针，俗话说："一根绣花针没有三钱重，拿起来根根筋骨动。"几十年来，濮惠菊熔古铸今、传承与创新，成功探索多元化的刺绣表现技法，无论虚、静、隐逸、仿真等，每幅刺绣作品她都赋予中国传统文化艺术的风骨与现代艺术的丰韵。自创"泼墨绣"，1991年绣成了梁楷的《泼墨仙人》，获国际美术书道文化一等赏奖。熟识中国传统绘画文化神似的境界，佛心禅境。为了刺绣艺术，濮惠菊把自己的毕生都献给了手中的神针，刺绣如同一种气息洋溢着爱的力量和热情，都早已渗入濮惠菊的生命之中，融为血脉太湖的山灵水秀，江南的人文底蕴成就了濮惠菊的刺绣艺术。

She was born in Xihua (Zhenhu Town), Suzhou in 1966 to a tutor family running a private school from generation to generation. Influenced and immersed in the rich traditional culture atmosphere in the family, Ms. Pu was intelligent and witty. She took over the embroidery needle from her ancestors with unique gift and perception. As an old saying goes, "an embroidery needle is not heavy in weight, but it would be laborious when using it." For decades, Pu Huiju has blended the ancient and the modern and achieved both inheritance and innovation, successfully exploring the diversified embroidery presentation techniques. In every piece of the embroidery work, she has granted the spirit of Chinese traditional culture and art and the essence of modern art, irrespective of virtue, motionlessness, recluse or emulation. With the birth of the "embroidery in pain-splashing style", she completed *the Paint-Splashing Immortal* by Liang Kai in 1991 which led her to be awarded the first prize for international fine art and calligraphy art culture. Pu has devoted all her life to the miraculous needle. Embroidery is filled with the power and passion for love as scent and has infiltrated to Pu's life and fused with her veins. The beautiful landscape scenery by Taihu Lake and gathering of talents in regions south of the Yangtze River make Pu's embroidery art.

四、项目名称：皇宫锦绣
IV. Project Name：Splendid Palace

五、项目介绍：
V. Project Introduction：

"皇宫锦绣"项目，是苏州市沈寿刺绣艺术研究中心深入开展的传统文化技艺抢救性复制研究项目，通过对中国种桑、养蚕、缫丝、织布、刺绣等资料的全面整理研究，向世人展现我们东方传统手工艺术的辉煌成就，让更多的人了解"刺绣"对中国社会经济有着非常重要的作用和意义。中心通过搜集各类资料，研究中国刺绣的重要发展体系，复制完成了自春秋以来的部分刺绣艺术作品，展现了各时期人民的生活审美和文化内涵。该中心自成立以来，博采众长，推陈出新，总结、汇集了60多种传统针法，刺绣作品更是凝聚了两千多年历史的技艺和精华，并通过贸易、文化交流、非遗展演与世界各国发生了良好的交流作用，建立起了团结友好的国际关系。

The "Splendid Palace" project is a rescuing reproduction research project for traditional cultural artistry developed by Suzhou Shen Shou Embroidery Art Research Center in a deep-going way. Full sorting and research of the information on mulberry planting, silkworm breeding, silk reeling, weaving and embroidery in China reveals the dazzling and brilliant traditional crafts and arts in the East and enables more people to understand the role and significance of "embroidery" in Chinese social economy. The Center has researched the major development system of Chinese embroidery by collecting various data. It reproduces a portion of the embroidery art works in the Spring and Autumn period and afterwards and shows the connotations of aesthetics culture in the life of people of different periods. Since its establishment, the Center has learnt the advantages of others and made innovation to summarize and collect over 60 kinds of traditional needling methods. The embroidery works consolidates the key and essential art over the history of more than two thousand years. It plays a positive role in exchanging with countries around the world by trading, cultural exchange and intangible cultural heritage exhibition and performance, thus establishing neighboring relations of unity and friendship.

六、项目优势：
VI. Project Advantage(s)：

苏州市沈寿刺绣艺术研究中心已成为中国刺绣艺术之乡-镇湖当代苏绣艺苑中的领军者，具有不可替代的龙头地位，于2013年被授予"中华老字号"，并被中国商业联合会评为"2016年度百年功勋企业"。

Suzhou Shen Shou Embroidery Art Research Center has been leading the contemporary Suzhou Embroidery circle in Zhenhu – the town of Chinese embroidery art and gained an irreplaceable leader position. In 2013, the Center was awarded "China Time-honored" Brand title and was rated "2016 Top 100 Meritorious Enterprise" by China General Chamber of Commerce.

七、企业需求：
VII. Enterprise Demand(s)：

希望通过"一带一路"活动，用刺绣本身所传承的中国传统文化的吸引力，积极开拓海外市场，为扩大市场打下基础。

The Center wishes to develop overseas markets and lay foundation for market expansion through the "Belt and Road" activities and with the appeal of Chinese traditional culture inherited by embroidery.

泰远汽车自动防撞器
TaiY Auto Automatic Bumper

一、项目公司名称：北京泰远汽车自动防撞器制造有限公司
I. Project Company Name: Beijing TaiY Auto Automatic Bumper Manufacturing Co., Ltd.

二、项目公司介绍：
II. Project Company Introduction:

公司于 2001 年成立，是一家集智能交通等多项高新技术领域相关产品的技术研发、参数验证、标准制定、生产制造（委托其他公司生产，泰远公司监制）以及市场开发、产品销售于一体的专业公司。产品于 2004 年被确定为"国家级重点新产品"，2005 年确定为"国家火炬计划"项目，2011 年通过中国人民解放军的权威部门认证。拥有完全独立的知识产权。

Our company was established in 2001, which is an integrated professional company for technical research & developing, data verification, standard preparation, manufacture & production (subcontracted to other companies with our supervision), marketing and selling for relative intelligent transportation products in several hi-tech fields. We gained "National Key New Product" in 2004 and awarded "the National Torch Program" in 2005. We are qualified authority from the People's Liberation Army of China in 2011. We have owned fully independent intellectual property.

三、负责人介绍：
III. Responsible Person Introduction:

发明人刘泰远先生，现任泰远时代（北京）技术研究院院长、北京泰远汽车自动防撞器制造有限公司董事长，汽车自动防撞器发明人，2006 年"中国十大科技英才"。

Inventor, Mr. Liu Taiyuan, the dean of TaiY Time (Beijing) Technology Institute, chairman of Beijing TaiY Auto Automatic Bumper Manufacturing Co., Ltd., and inventor of automatic bump-shielded device of automobile, has won "Top 10 Scientific & Technical Talent in China" in 2006.

主要科技成果先后被编入《中国专家大辞典》《中国世纪专家》等书籍。

Mr. Liu's major scientific & technical achievements are compiled in *Chinese Expert Dictionary* and *Chinese Century Expert*.

四、项目名称：泰远汽车自动防撞器
IV. Project Name: TaiY Auto Automatic Bumper

五、项目概况：
V. Project Profile:

"泰远汽车自动防撞系统"源自泰远研究院多年研究成果，汽车防撞技术结合了多学科，包括机械、电子、计算机、信息、生理学、心理学和社会科学技术等领域，是实现人与系统耦合与接口的现代新科技，它集汽车、人、主动防撞系统于一体，实现汽车主动安全智能化，弥补人和车的弱点，变被动为主动，变人动为自动，达到人和防撞系统共同判断、共同决策和协调统一，构建了人与系统合作互补的"伙伴"关系。它赋予汽车以灵魂，全程保护驾乘人员安全。

TaiY Auto Automatic Bumper System sources from research achievements for years from TaiY Time (Beijing) Technology Institute. Automobile bumper technology integrates the knowledge of multi subjects and technical fields, including mechanics, electronics, computer, information, physiology, psychology and social science and so on, which is modern technology to achieve coupling and interface for human and system. This technology is integrated by automobile, human and active bump-shielded system, realizing activeness, safety and intelligence of automobile. Disadvantages of human and automobile are remedied, negativeness turns to activeness and the control mode is changed from manual to automatic. Common judgment, common determination and unified coordination between human and bump-shielded system are fulfilled. Corporation, complementation and "Partnership" between human and system are formed. Soul is granted to automobile. Drivers and passengers' safety are guaranteed all the way.

六、项目优势：
VI. Project Advantage(s)：

30多年来，我们更专注于高速、大车的、主动安全。

We have been focusing on safety of large vehicle in high speed for more than 30 years.

1．120迈以上遇到危险自动刹车！避免群死群伤！

Automatic brake in case of hazard, higher than 120km, to avoid mass death and casualty!

2．30多年来大国工匠精神智造！责任和使命的担当！挽救生命为己任！

Intelligent creation with the spirit of craftsman for over 30 years! Undertaking responsibility and mission! Our mission is to save life!

3．30多年来大量的实验数据积累，掌握关键核心算法，领先于同行的2-3年以上！

能够检测原刹车系统是否正常！

不改变原车结构，任意车型都能够安装！

Abundant accumulation of experimental data for more than 30 years. We master critical and core algorithm, maintaining the leading position in the field for 2 to 3 years.

Be able to monitor original braking system's status!

Installed to any type of car without structure changed!

七、项目需求：
VII. Project Demand(s)：

合作模式：前装市场（和汽车整机厂合作），后装市场（在已经出厂的汽车上安装使用）

Mode of Corporation：factory-installed products (corporation with automobile manufacturer) and aftermarket installed products (installed and used in manufactured automobile)

人才引进：对产品升级、生产自动化、售后服务APP软件开发人才的进入

Introduction of Talent：introductions of talents for product update, manufacture automation and APP software developing for after-sale service

宣传推广：品牌效应，广泛宣传，国内外各大城市推广

Propagating and Advertising：brand effect, wide range of propagation and advertising in domestic and foreign cities

汽车真空泵
Automobile Vacuum Pump

一、项目公司名称： 江苏梅花机械有限公司
I. Project Company Name: Jiangsu Meihua Machinery Co., Ltd.

二、项目公司介绍：
II. Project Company Introduction:

公司是"汽车真空泵"国家行业标准制定单位、省级高新技术企业，拥有多台套真空泵泵体精加工专用数控设备和进口全自动化专用加工中心，技术力量雄厚。目前拥有专利19项，实用型专利16项，发明型专利3项。获国家工业和信息化部批准，负责制定的"汽车真空泵性能要求及台架试验方法"行业标准已于2014年3月1日正式实施。国内首创国际领先的全套汽车真空泵检测试验设备的启用与运行，填补了国内汽车真空泵行业的空白。

The company is a national industry standard setting unit for "automobile vacuum pump", and a high-tech enterprise at provincial level. It possesses multiple vacuum pump finish machining CNC equipment and imported full-automatic machining center, with strong technical force. It now possesses 19 patents, including 16 utility patents and 13 invention patents. It has obtained the approval of the Ministry of Industry and Information Technology, and the industrial standard of "Automobile Vacuum Pump Performance Requirements and Bench Test Methods" prepared by it was implemented on March 1, 2014 formally. The launching and running of the first international leading complete set of automobile vacuum pump test equipment in China, has filled the blank in domestic automobile vacuum pump industry.

三、负责人介绍：
III. Responsible Person Introduction:

韦梅芳，公司创始人，自1985年开始从事机械制造液压系统研究，于2000年创办民营独资企业，2009年担任"汽车真空泵性能要求及台架试验方法"行业标准起草专家组组长，先后获得过江苏省第四届"创业之星"、中国杰出创新人物、中国汽车真空泵行业品牌建设十大领军人物、中国优秀创新企业家等荣誉称号。

Wei Meifang, founder of the company, who has been engaged in the research of mechanical manufacturing hydraulic system since 1985, and created the privately operated sole-source investment enterprise in 2000. In 2009, acted as the leader of industrial standard drafting expert group for "Automobile Vacuum Pump Performance Requirements and Bench Test Methods". She was awarded with honorary titles of the 4th "Star of Start-ups" of Jiangsu Province, China's Outstanding Innovation Figures, Top Ten Leading Figures in Brand Building of China's Automobile Vacuum Pump Industry, China's Outstanding Innovative Entrepreneurs etc.

四、项目名称： 汽车真空泵
IV. Project Name: Automobile Vacuum Pump

五、项目概况：
V. Project Profile:

本公司主要生产机械刮片式、电子和电动汽车真空泵三大系列产品320多个品种，分别配套商用汽车、乘用汽车以及新能源汽车，主要配套北汽、一汽、通用、江铃、五十铃、丰田、三菱、江淮、长城等国内外知名品牌的汽车上。机械刮片式真空泵具有结构简单、性能可靠、泵油与机油互用、维修简单等特点，整体外形较小，成本低，效率高，功率消耗低，油流量低，重量轻。

The company is engaged in producing more than 320 types of three major series of products namely mechanical wiper, electronic and electric automobile vacuum pumps, which are used in commercial vehicles, passenger vehicles and new energy vehicles, mainly for well-known brands at home and abroad such as BAIC, FAW, GM, JMC, ISUZU, Toyota, Mitsubishi, JAC, Great Wall etc. The mechanical wiper vacuum pump is simple in structure and reliable in work, with pump oil and engine oil exchangeable, making easy maintenance. The overall dimension is small, which is low in cost, high in efficiency, low in power consumption, low in oil flow and light in weight.

电子真空泵适驱纯电动汽车，采用有刷和无刷电机驱动设计，优化容腔轮廓型线的真空泵，能够在排量最大化的同时，尽可能地减少摩擦和振动噪音，提供程序控制开关功能，减少能耗和碳排放，在极限温度范围内能提供稳定的真空性能。新能源电驱动真空泵采用自控、自吸和永磁直流电机驱动，具有体积小、重量轻、耗油少和环保安全等特点。

The electronic vacuum pump is suitable for blade electric vehicles. By adopting vacuum pumps with brush and brushless motor drive design optimized cavity profile lines, it could reduce friction and vibration noise as far as possible, while maximizing displacement, promote program control switch function, reduce energy consumption and carbon emission, and could provide stable vacuum performance within the scope of extreme temperature. The new energy electric vacuum pump adopts self-control, self-priming and permanent magnet DC motor drive, and possesses characteristics of small volume, light weight, small oil consumption, energy conservation and environment protection, safety etc.

六、项目优势：
VI. Project Advantage(s)：

公司负责汽车真空泵国家行业标准的制定，并已于2014年3月1日正式实施，拥有国内首创国际领先的加工检测设备和填补国内空白的"汽车真空泵试验评价中心"。

The company is responsible for the preparation of national industrial standards for automobile vacuum pumps, which was formally implemented on April 1, 2014. It possesses the first international leading machining and testing equipment in China and the "Testing and Evaluating Center for Automobile Vacuum Pumps" which fills the domestic blank.

七、项目需求：
VII. Project Demand(s)：

根据汽车真空泵的发展趋势，结合实际情况，公司通过融资和适放股权或股份制合作的模式，预计融资6000万元（技改投入），解决目前流动资金困难和加大部分技改投入，制定短期、中期和长期的发展规划。

According to the development trend of automobile vacuum pumps, and combining actual situation, the company plans to finance with 60 million Yuan (technical modification investment) by means of financing and releasing equity or cooperative shareholding system, to solve the current difficulty in liquidity and part of investment on technical modification, so as to establish development planning on a short-term/mid-term/long-term basis.

广大众利新零售系统
Guangda Zhongli New Retail System

一、项目公司名称: 深圳前海金泰丰实业有限公司

I. Project Company Name: Shenzhen Qianhai Jintaifeng Industries Co., Ltd.

二、项目公司介绍:

II. Project Company Introduction:

深圳前海金泰丰实业有限公司携手福建广大众利商贸有限公司,旨在寻找当下中国茶业发展的动力,为茶产业贡献思想,传播和普及茶业知识,拉动茶业相关消费,带来以茶为主体的传统中国符号以及生活方式的复兴,通过茶生活营造和输出中国价值。

Shenzhen Qianhai Jintaifeng Industries Co., Ltd. has joined hands with Fujian Guangda Zhongli Trading Co., Ltd. with the aim to find some impetus for the development of existing Chinese tea industry, contribute to the concepts of tea industry, spread and popularize knowledge about tea industry, stimulate tea industry-related consumption and bring a renaissance to tea-led traditional Chinese symbols and lifestyle as well as create and export Chinese value through tea life.

三、负责人介绍:

III. Responsible Person Introduction:

易广大出生在安溪,世代茶农之家,从出生那一刻起,茶一直陪伴着他长大,从小为人就慷慨大方,喜欢与人交朋友。13岁的时候就在安溪县《山茶花》杂志刊登了诗歌作品,被县文化馆干部誉为诗神童。20世纪90年代初,易广大在安溪县一家国有企业任书记兼董事长,落户福州开发区免税市场。亦因此,2012年中央党刊《求是》杂志社中国茶小康专刊特约了易广大,代表中国7万家茶企就关于中国茶的现状及出路进行了采访。为了茶乡人民改变命运,造福社会,于2015年在福建自贸区注册成立了以自主品牌、自创产品、跨境电商为一体的省级综合智能现代化企业——福建广大众利公司。用三年时间成功研制出咖啡红、芽韵红、观音袍、蟹香红四种茶叶,其中咖啡红荣获2015年世界工夫茶王双金奖,同时在美国和马来西亚开设分公司,进军国际市场。

Mr. Yi Dali was born in an Anxi-based tea-growing family that has passed on from generations to generations. Since his birth, he has grown up with tea. He has been generous from childhood and likes making friends. At the age of 13, Mr. Yi published his collected poems on an Anxi-based magazine named *Camellia*, for which he was regarded as a "genius" by the county culture center. In the early 1990s, Yi served as the Secretary and Chairman of state-owned enterprise in Anxi and settled in the tax-exempt market of Fujian development zone. For this reason, China Tea Well-To-Do column under *Seeking Truth* magazine as a party journal of the Central Government contacted and interviewed Mr. Yi representing 70,000 tea enterprises in China on current situation and the way-out of Chinese tea. To change the fate of the people in the tea county and benefit the society, he incorporated a provincial integrated intelligent modern enterprise – Fujian Guangda Zhongli Company Limited that specializes in proprietary brand, OBM and cross-border E-commerce in China (Fujian) Pilot Trade Zone. Within three years, he successfully developed "*Kafei* Hong", "*Yayun* Hong", "Guanyin Pao" and "Xiexiang Hong" as four kinds of tea. "Kafei Hong" received the Double Gold Medal on 2015 World King Kungfu Tea Competition. Mr. Yi settled his foot on the global stage by establishing branches in America and Malaysia.

四、项目名称: 广大众利新零售系统

IV. Project Name: Guangda Zhongli New Retail System

五、项目概况:

V. Project Profile:

我们团队走遍全国、美国、加拿大、南美洲、东南亚并生根发芽,在各国开办公司。茶是中国的国饮,茶之于民生是第一等重要的价值,在青海湖边,我们重温了昔年10万人饮茶的盛景(文章详见《海峡茶道》2013年头条文章《探茶边疆》);在江西,我们看到数量庞大的清饮茶馆出现,以茶为主导的雅集每日都在上演;在

厦门，我们看到安溪人一年为茶业贡献了25亿的产值；在安徽，我们看到数以亿万的资金流向茶产业；在云南，这个季节，数以万计的人正在茶山奔走，铁观音茶名重天下的局面正在重现，在武夷山，茶文化旅游已经成为支柱产业。

Our team could be seen throughout the nation and in the America, Canada, South America and Southeast Asia where we take root and grow by establishing branches in these countries. Tea has been the national drink in China. Tea has the value of capital importance to people's livelihood. By the side of Qinghai Lake, we review the spectacular event where 100,000 people drunk tea in the past days (for more information, see the Headline News *Exploring Tea in the Border Area, Strait Tea Philosophy*, 2013). In Jiangxi, we see the occurrence of a vast number of light drinking houses, and elegant tea-led meetings were on in each day. In Xiamen, we learn that Anxi businessmen contributed an amount of RMB 2,500 million to the output value of tea industry. In Anhui, we witness the flow of billions of capital to tea industry. And in Yunnan, thousands of people are moving to the tea mountain in this season. *Tieguanyin* tea is regaining its global fame. Tea cultural tourism has been a pillar industry in Wuyi Mountain.

茶与旅游的结合，"一带一路"将会拉动茶产业、文化产业以及旅游产业多重聚合效应。公司发展茶文化以及以茶为主体的中国式生活方式。探索茶消费新零售模式，运用快销方式开拓年轻时尚茶饮消费，整合商业文化立体运营。而与茶密切相关的水产业、陶瓷产业、旅游产业、健康茶业、服饰产业、养老产业亦会促进本公司茶叶产业提升。

With the combination of tea and tourism, the "Belt and Road" will drive the effect from multiple convergences of tea, culture, tourism and handmade tea industries. The Company develops tea culture and tea-led Chinese lifestyle. Efforts should be made to explore a new retain mode for tea consumption. Comprehensive commercial and cultural operation should be integrated by using fast moving consumer goods (FMCG) approach and based on the tea drinking habit of the young fashionable people. The water, ceramics, tourism, healthy tea, apparel and pension industries with a close relation to tea will also contribute to the improvement of the Company's tea industry.

六、项目优势：
VI. Project Advantage(s)：

从种植、制作、包装、品饮、科研等层面着手，提升中国茶叶整体生产水平。本公司自创新品安溪铁观音咖啡红（黑茶），获得世界工夫茶大赛普洱类金奖、铁观音炭焙金奖，号称"中国茶界煮不烂泡不开的黑茶"。响应"一带一路"号召，推广促进新零售销售模式，造福广大人民群众。

The work will begin with planting, manufacturing, packaging, tasting and research to improve the overall production level of Chinese tea. Being awarded the Gold Prizes for *Puer* Tea and for Roasted *Tieguanyin* Tea on the World Kungfu Tea Competition, Anxi *Tieguanyin* "*Kafei Hong*" (black tea) as OBM of the Company has been known as "the black tea that will be neither boiled out nor over-brewed in Chinese tea circle". The Company releases and promotes the new retail sales pattern as a response to the call of B&R and with an aim to benefit the masses.

七、项目需求：
VII. Project Demand(s)：

投资兴办茶园茶场基地10万亩，茶农慈善养老基地1000亩，自助茶饮设备10000台，"一带一路"实体茶饮时尚连锁店2000家。招募有限合伙人50人，需要资金1000万。

The Company has invested to set up a 100,000-mu tea garden & farm base of the Company, a 1,000-mu tea grower charitable pension base covering and provide 10,000 sets of self-servicing tea equipment and opens 2,000 B&R fashion chain stores. 50 limited partners are recruited. The funds required will be RMB 10 million.

安盛农业树莓时代科技产业园
Ansheng Agricultural Raspberry Times science and Technology Industrial Park

一、项目企业名称：安徽安盛农业科技发展有限公司

Ⅰ. Project Company Name：Anhui AnSheng Agricultural Science and Technology Development Co.,Ltd.

二、项目公司介绍：

Ⅱ. Project Company Introduction：

公司于 2014 年 9 月成立，是以发展树莓为主的现代企业。

The company was founded in September 2014, which is a modern enterprise engaged in developing raspberry.

我国是全球树莓三大出口国之一，是国际树莓组织（IRO）中具有影响力的核心成员。随着人们对树莓价值认识的逐步提高及我国居民生活水平的提高，树莓的营养保健价值越来越被人们所认可，国人的消费观念也将逐步转变，我国树莓产业也将逐步由出口主导型向内销主导型转变。树莓产品将成为人们普遍消费的新一代健康保健食品。安盛农业科技发展有限公司引进树莓产业，是为推进农业结构调整，发展高效、创汇农业。实现"做强树莓产业，成就企业员工，福佑一方百姓，健康一个民族"的伟大夙愿。

China is one of the top 3 exporters of raspberries in the world, and the core member with influence in the International Raspberry Organization (IRO). With gradual improvement in the recognition of the value of raspberries among people and the improvement in living standards of Chinese citizens, the nutrition and health value of raspberries is becoming more and more accepted by people, and the consumption concept of them is also changing. The raspberry industry in China is also converting from export-oriented to domestic sale-oriented. Raspberry products will become a new generation of healthcare food with popular consumption among people. The introduction of raspberry products of Ansheng Agricultural Technology Development Co., Ltd. is to promote agricultural structure adjustment, develop high efficiency and gain foreign exchange income for agriculture. Realize the grand ideal of "enhancing raspberry industry, accomplishing enterprise employees, benefiting people, and making a healthy nation".

三、负责人介绍：

Ⅲ. Responsible Person Introduction：

盛月勤，女，热爱共产党、热爱祖国、热爱社会主义。

Sheng Yueqin, female, in favor of the Communist Party, in favor of China, and in favor of socialism.

2011 年被推荐为民建亳州市企业家联谊会副理事；

Recommended as Deputy Director of Bozhou Entrepreneurs Association of China Democratic National Construction Association in 2011;

2012 年被推荐为谯城区第十四届政协委员；

Recommended as the 14th CPPCC member in Qiaocheng District in 2012;

2015 年被聘为"中国爱心事业联合会副会长"；

Hired as the "Vice President of China Love Heart Business Association Limited" in 2015;

2015 年被授予"中国百名杰出女企业家"及"返乡创业能人"等荣誉称号；

Awarded with honorary titles of "One Hundred Chinese Outstanding Women Entrepreneurs" and "Homecoming Entrepreneur" in 2015;

2016 年被选为亳州市第四届人民代表大会代表。

Elected as the Bozhou representative of the 4th Session of the National People's Congress in 2016.

其负责经营的公司也多次被国家部委、省、市、区行业及政府部门评为"放心消费单位"、"重合同守信用单位"、"质量、服务、信誉 AAA 级信用单位"荣誉称号。

The company managed by her has also been evaluated as "Reassurance Consumption Unit", "Contract and Accredit Honoring Unit" and "Quality, Service and Credit Level AAA Credit Unit" by national ministries and commissions, provincial, municipal and district industrial and governmental departments.

四、项目名称：安盛农业树莓时代科技产业园

Ⅳ. Project Name: Ansheng Agricultural Raspberry Times science and Technology Industrial Park

五、项目概况：

Ⅴ. Project Profile：

1．公司自建树莓种植示范基地3000亩。采取公司＋基地＋农户（合作社）的模式，通过基地的示范作用，推广带动合作社和农户种植，逐步实现种植面积10万亩以上，树莓年产鲜果量120000吨规模。形成育苗、种植、冷藏、加工、贸易一条龙的产业链。

The company has established a raspberry planting demonstration base of 3,000 mu. By adopting the mode of company + base + farmers (cooperative), via demonstration function of the base, the company leads cooperatives and farmers to plant, and realizes a planting area above 100 thousand mu gradually, reaching an annual output of fresh raspberries of 120,000 ton. It has formed a coordinated industrial chain of seedlings, planting, refrigerating, processing and trading.

2．2015年8月启动万吨级冷库建设，作为树莓的收购、冷藏、加工基地，同时为树莓的深加工提供原料保障。

In August 2015, it launched its 10-thousand-ton cold storage construction, as the purchase, refrigerating and processing base, meanwhile, providing raw material guarantee for deep processing of raspberries.

3．2017年下半年启动脱毒树莓种苗繁育基地，其中建设生物"组织培养室"2000平方米，配套建设炼苗温室大棚150亩，形成年培育2000万株脱毒树莓种苗的能力。为树莓的推广种植提供高品质的种苗保障。

In the second half of 2017, it launched the detoxification raspberry seed breeding base, including the biological "tissue culture room" of 2,000 m^2 equipped with acclimatization greenhouse of 150mu, forming a capacity of cultivating 20,000 thousand detoxification raspberry seedlings. Providing high quality seedling guarantee for promotion and planting of raspberries.

4．引进树莓系列产品生产线，逐步形成树莓饮料、果酱、树莓酒、树莓叶茶、口服液及药品和化妆品等树莓产品加工生产链。

Introduced production line of raspberry series, forming a processing and producing chain for raspberry products such as raspberry drinks, jam, raspberry wine, raspberry leaf tea, oral liquids and medicines as well as cosmetics etc.

六、项目优势：

Ⅵ. Project Advantage(s)：

树莓产业不仅可以加快农业产业升级，有效增加农民收入，同时在从种苗繁育、种植、冷储、产品加工、出口贸易形成的一条龙的产业链中，能够实实在在促进地方经济发展，完全有希望在较短的时间内，成为支撑地方经济的支柱型产业，是一项极具发展前景，利国、利民、富民、富政的优质项目。

The raspberry industry could not only accelerate the upgrade of agricultural industry, but could increase farmers' income effectively. Meanwhile, based on the coordinated industrial chain involving seedling breeding, planting, cold storage, product processing, exporting and trading, it could promote local economic development essentially. It is hopeful to become a pillar industry supporting local economy in a short period of time, which is a high quality project with developing prospects, which is beneficial to the nation and its citizens, enriching citizens and government.

七、项目需求：

Ⅶ. Project Demand(s)：

公司为发展树莓深加工产品，需要大量树莓果原材料，寻找种植合作伙伴，项目重点需求是树莓系列产品的加工技术及国内外市场的拓展。

In order to develop deep processing products of raspberries, the company needs lots of raspberries, and seeks for partnership for planting. The project demand is to process technology of raspberry series and market expansion both at home and abroad.

智慧水务系统
Smart Water System

一、项目公司名称： 江苏中科君达物联网股份有限公司
I. Project Company Name: Jiangsu Zhongke Kingda IOT Co.,Ltd.

二、项目公司介绍：
II. Project Company Introduction:

公司股票代码：835051，2010年成立，注册资本3700万元，位于宿迁市经济开发区，是北京中关村科技园区团队君达集团投资建设的国家级高新技术企业，主要立足于仪器仪表、物联网传感器及软件技术领域，针对工业智能测控、智慧水务、物联网智能家居、节能环保产业不断开发设计一体化解决方案。目前公司与国内外众多知名企事业单位形成长期战略合作关系，产品遍布亚洲、美洲、欧洲、南非等区域，其中服务的世界五百强企业就有20多家。

Established in 2010, the company (stock code: 835051), is located in Suqian Economic Development Zone, Jiangsu, China and has the registered capital of RMB 37 million. We are a national level high technology enterprise invested by Kingda Group located in Zhongguancun Science and Technology Park, Beijing, and we are mainly engaged in development and design of integrated solutions for industrial smart measurement and control, smart water, Internet of Things (IoT) smart home, energy conservation and environmental protection industry based on the technology fields of instruments, Internet of Things (IoT) sensor and software. At present, we have established long-term strategic cooperation relations with numerous well-known enterprises and public institutions home and abroad. Our products are sold to Asia, Americas, Europe, South Africa and Southeast Asia, etc., and we have provided services to more than 20 of Fortune Top 500 Enterprises.

三、负责人介绍：
III. Responsible Person Introduction:

刘健，董事长，1976年8月出生，汉族，中共党员，工业管理博士，国家科技创业创新推进计划人才、"国家万人计划专家"，具有多年创业经历和参与大型项目研发的丰富经验，先后主持和参与开发科研成果十多项，并成功实现科技成果转化；对智能控制和计算机软件的实现有较深入的研究与实践，一直跟踪信息化领域的最新发展，擅长把各项科研成果通过创业实现成果转化以及科技型现代化企业的运作管理。

Liu Jian, Chairman of the board, born on August 1976, the Han nationality, a member of Communist Party of China, a Ph.D in Industrial Management, a talent of National Technology Entrepreneurship and Innovation Promotion Program and an expert of "National High-level Talent Support Special Program"; many years of entrepreneurship experience and abundant large project R&D experience; successively presided over and participated in developing more than ten items of scientific research achievements, and successfully achieved the commercialization of such scientific research achievements; in-depth research and practice on implementation of smart control and computer software, always keeps abreast with the latest development of informatization field, good at achieving commercialization of various scientific research achievements through entrepreneurship and managing the operation of scientific and technologic type modern enterprise.

四、项目名称： 智慧水务系统
IV. Project Name: Smart Water System

五、项目概况：
V. Project Profile:

智慧水务项目是我国水资源紧缺形势及国家对环保的日益重视等因素的推动下，我公司在近十年的物联网传感技术经验基础上开发的一项新的项目。本项目是通过将传统水利与现代信息化技术进行深度融合，来提高水务的管理和服务水平。系列产品涉及智能远传水表、智能卡表系统、智慧水务RTU系列、管网GIS、SCADA系统、调度平台等。

Smart water project is a new project developed based on our recent ten years of Internet of Things (IoT) sensor technology experience, driven by factors of water resource shortage situation in China and Chinese increasing attention on environmental protection, etc. The project aims to improve the water management and service level through deeply integrating the traditional water conservation and modern informatization technology. The series products include smart remote water meter, smart card meter system, smart water RTU series, pipe network GIS, SCADA system and dispatching platform.

目前中科物联智慧水务项目能够分析处理供水管网监测设备及其他系统回传的数据，并能进行功能强大的供水计算，为水务公司的供水规划、合理运行、漏损分析和应急服务等高层次的决策和优化调度提供强大的基础数据和技术支撑，帮助水务公司改善管理作业，及时发现供水异常，降低运行维护成本。通过调度中心，还能够及时准确地把握城市的供水状况，实现故障的及时排查，提出解决预案，还能指导新建城区的管网铺设。

At present, the IoT smart water project of China Sciences Group can analyze and process the data transmitted by the water supply pipe network monitoring equipment and other systems and perform powerful water supply calculation, providing powerful basic data and technical support for the high-level decision and optimized dispatching of the water companies such as water supply planning, reasonable operation, leakage analysis and emergency service to help water companies improve management, timely find water abnormality and reduce the operation and maintenance costs. Through the dispatching center, the urban water supply conditions are timely and accurately grasped to timely clear faults, set forth solutions and also guide the pipe network laying of newly built urban area.

利用智慧水务项目系统，可在水质安全、供水调度、漏损控制、智能抄表、系统整合方面提高效率。水质安全方面，在供水现场使用视频采集，实时监控水质传感器的数据，并设置报警；供水调度方面，系统会分析水量和流量计口径匹配的合理性，分析峰谷值水量对管网负荷的影响，实时监测管网末梢压力，合理调度，降低成本；漏损控制方面，能够提供水表选型依据，及时发现管网漏点，分区计量数据拓扑图，实时分析产销差；智能抄表方面，实行民用水表智能化改造，能够远程水表数据抄收，提高抄见率，降低人工成本。综合系统整合了压力监控、水厂运行、大用户监控管理、居民小区二次加压、居民供水远程抄表收费等系统，方便运行。

Meanwhile, with the smart water project system, efficiency will be improved in water quality and safety, water supply dispatching, leakage control, smart meter reading and system integration. In water quality and safety, video capture is applied at the water supply site to real-timely monitor the data of water quality sensor mounted and set alarm; in water supply dispatching, the system will analyze the matching reasonability of water volume and flowmeter caliber as well as the influence of peak-valley water volume on the pipe network load, to real-timely monitor the end pressure of pipe network, reasonably dispatch water and reduce costs; in leakage control, the system can provide basis for water meter selection, timely detect the pipe network leakage points, provide metering data topological graph of zones and real-timely analyze the difference between water production and sale real-timely; in smart meter reading, the intellectualized renovation of domestic water meter will be implemented to remotely read the water meter data, improve the reading rate and reduce labor costs. The comprehensive system integrates systems of pressure monitoring, water plant operation, large user monitoring and management, residential quarter second pressure and remote water meter reading and charge, to facilitate the operation.

六、项目优势：
VI. Project Advantage(s)

1．可形成"城市水务物联网"，将海量水务信息进行及时分析与处理，实时感知城市供排水系统的运行状态；

We can establish "Urban Water IoT" to timely analyze and process mass water information and real-timely sense the operation state of urban water supply and drainage system；

2．让供水企业利用物联网技术管理业务；

We enable the water supply enterprises to manage business through IoT technology；

3．有效控制管网漏损，节约水资源；

We effectively control the leakage of pipe network and save water resources；

4．有效地实现城市的智慧供水。

We will effectively achieve the smart water supply of smart city.

七、项目需求：
VII. Project Demand(s)：

希望通过"一带一路"中小企业平台为公司的智慧水务项目给予一定的国家政策扶持，协助公司完成智慧水务产品的国内外市场拓展和产品推广。

We hope The "Belt and Road" SME Platform will support our smart water project with certain national policy and assist us in domestic and foreign markets development of smart water products and products promotion.

建筑装饰内外墙涂料
Architectural Decoration Coating for Interior and Exterior Walls

一、项目公司名称： 中军创发展集团北京九龙士涂料有限公司

I. Project Company Name: Beijing Jiulongshi Coating Co., Ltd. of China's Soldier Entrepreneurship & Development Group

二、项目公司介绍：

II. Project Company Introduction:

中国建设九龙装饰集团成立于2002年，同年在香港成立香港九龙装饰集团，是建筑装饰一体化、墙体保温装饰一体化新材料的研发、设计、生产、销售、施工、服务于一体的高科技企业。在北京、天津、青岛等地建立了绿色建材生产基地。"九龙士"漆畅销香港、澳门及东南亚等国家和地区，受到广大用户的认可。其中内外墙乳胶漆、真石漆被评为"中国好建材"。公司获住建部全国保障性住房建设用材料优秀供应商等荣誉。

China Architecture Jiulong Decoration Group was established in 2002 and launched Hong Kong Jiulong Decoration Group in Hong Kong in the same year. It is a high-tech enterprise which integrates R&D, design, production, sales, construction and service of new materials for integration of architectural decoration and wall heat preservation decoration. The Group has built green architectural materials production bases in Beijing, Tianjin, Qingdao, etc. The paint named "Jiulongshi" sells well in Hong Kong, Macao and other countries and regions in South East Asia. Emulsion paint for interior and exterior walls and stone-like coating were evaluated to be "good architectural materials made in China", and the Group was awarded the honor of one of the excellent suppliers of materials for nationwide affordable houses by the Chinese Ministry of Housing and Urban-Rural Development.

三、负责人介绍：

III. Responsible Person Introduction:

顾正军，山东青岛即墨人。1982-2000年，任黑龙江省兴隆林业局人造板厂厂长。2007年至今，任中国建设九龙装饰集团董事长，中军创发展集团董事长，北京九龙士涂料有限公司董事长，中国中小商业企业协会理事。

Gu Zhengjun, born in Jimo, Qingdao, Shandong. In 1982-2000, factory manager of the Artificial Board Factory of Heilongjiang Xinglong Forestry Bureau. From 2007 to now, chairman of board of directors of China Architecture Jiulong Decoration Group, chairman of board of directors of China's Soldier Entrepreneurship & Development Group, chairman of board of directors of Beijing Jiulongshi Coating Co., Ltd., and director of China Association of Small & Medium Commercial Enterprise.

四、项目名称： 建筑装饰内外墙涂料

IV. Project Name: Architectural Decoration Coating for Interior and Exterior Walls

五、项目概况：

V. Project Profile:

公司以"绿色革命，环保先锋"为科研理念，致力于高端绿色材料产品的研发、生产，倡导企业的规模化、专业化，产品功能明确化，公司不断引进专业的技术、管理人才，组建业内领先的技术研发中心和标准化实验室。

With "green revolution and environment protection pioneer" as its scientific research ideas, the Group is dedicated to research, development and production of high-end green materials, initiates its scale, profession and product function definition, constantly introduces professional technical and management talents and builds a technical R&D center and a standard laboratory which take the lead in the industry.

公司不断创新研发新产品，"九龙士"漆畅销香港、澳门及东南亚等国家和地区，受到广大用户的认可。其中内外墙乳胶漆、真石漆被评为"中国好建材"。公司获"住建部全国保障性住房建设用材料优秀供应商"等荣誉。

The Group makes constant innovation, research and development of new products. The paint named "Jiulongshi" sells well in Hong Kong, Macao and other countries and regions in South East Asia. Emulsion paint for interior and exterior walls and stone-like coating were evaluated to be "good architectural materials made in China", and the Group was awarded the honor of one of "the excellent suppliers of materials for nationwide affordable houses" by the Chinese Ministry of Housing and Urban-Rural Development.

公司拥有建筑总承包一级、建筑装修装饰一级资质，能独立承揽大中型建筑外墙装饰、建筑节能保温、内外墙涂装、防水、真石漆、仿石漆工程以及大理石安装工程。

The Group has obtained the qualifications of the first-class architecture main contractor and the first-class architectural fitment and decoration. We are able to independently undertake the decoration of exterior walls for large- and middle-sized architectures, energy conservation and heat insulation of buildings, coating for interior and exterior walls, water prevention, stone-like coating and stone-like paint works, and marble installation work.

公司先后收购和投资组建了九大公司，产品涉及五大类上百个品种。

The Group established nine companies successively through acquisition and investment, whose products cover five categories and more than 100 varieties.

六、项目优势：
VI. Project Advantage(s)：

公司不断创新研发新产品，"九龙士"漆畅销香港、澳门及东南亚等国家和地区，受到广大用户的认可。公司为适应国家发展需要和市场需求，利用更高端的技术生产出更优质的产品，"九龙士负氧离子生态涂料"对人体能产生更好的作用，更有益于环保。公司拥有建筑总承包一级、建筑装修装饰一级资质，能独立承揽大中型建筑外墙装饰、建筑节能保温、内外墙涂料、防水、真石漆、仿石漆工程以及大理石安装工程。公司自成立20年来，曾先后获得"中国建筑装饰行业AAA信用单位"、"国家建筑幕墙专项工程设计甲级"、"国家建筑装饰装修专项工程设计甲级"等荣誉。

The Group makes constant innovation, research and development of new products. The paint named "Jiulongshi" sells well in Hong Kong, Macao and other countries and regions in South East Asia. To adapt to China's development needs and market demand, the Group produces better products by using more sophisticated technologies. "Jiulongshi negative oxygen ion ecological coating" has a better effect on human body and is more beneficial to environmental protection. The Group has obtained the qualifications of the first-class architecture main contractor and the first-class architectural fitment and decoration. We are able to independently undertake the decoration of exterior walls for large- and middle-sized architectures, energy conservation and heat insulation of buildings, coating for interior and exterior walls, water prevention, stone-like coating and stone-like paint works, and marble installation work. Since its founding for more than 20 years, the Group has successively obtained "AAA Credit Unit of China Building Decoration Industry", "Class A Special Engineering Design of China Building Curtain Wall", "Class A Special Engineering Design of China Building Decoration and Fitment" and the like.

七、项目需求：
VII. Project Demand(s)：

希望更多的专业设计师、技师、销售等优秀人才加入。公司需要与房地产开发商和建筑总包深度合作。另外，公司的发展实行股东制，也需求在社会上有一定人脉、资源，有共同理想，志同道合的有志之士共谋发展。

we hope that more excellent talents such as professional designers, technicians, salesmen, etc. to join us, because talents are the root of the Group's development. We want in-depth cooperation with real estate developers and building main contractors. Besides, we adopt a stockholder system for our development and need those persons who have some contacts and resources and cherish the same ideals and follow the same path.

富沃斯（FOC）珠宝数字资产
Foc Jewelry Digital Assets

一、项目公司名称：四川富沃斯珠宝有限公司

Ⅰ. Project Company Name: Sichuan FOC Jewelry Co., Ltd.

二、项目公司介绍：

Ⅱ. Project Company Introduction:

公司 2013 年成立于深圳前海，2015 年迁至成都。公司顺应国家提出的共享经济，及消费金融结合互联网+大数据，推出珠宝"免费"戴模式，创未来新的差异化项目：以全球不可再生的等值增值的稀有珠宝作为信用背书，采用实物加赠送的数字资产，达到消费分红，帮助老百姓抵御人民币贬值、经济下滑的风险。

The Company was founded in 2013 at Qianhai of Shenzhen, and was moved back to Chengdu. Complying with the sharing economy, consumer finance combining Internet plus big data proposed by the country, the Company raised the mode of free wearing jewelry, and created future differentiated new Project. Take the World's non-renewable rare jewelries of equivalent and increasing value as the credit endorsement, adopt material objects adding digital assets presented to achieve profits sharing of consuming, assist the ordinary people to defense the risks of depreciation of RMB and economic depression.

三、项目负责人：

Ⅲ. Responsible Person Introduction:

张思诗，公司创始人兼董事长，早期从事过六年的金矿开采、冶炼和十八年珠宝原矿石采购，珠宝批发与零售的等工作，后担任四川省新闻中心地方部领导，调任北京从事城镇化建设工作调研，对货币政策有深度研究。在改革创新的新一轮政策下，她为了让珠宝货币化，抵制经济下行给老百姓带来的风险，实现老百姓增值增收，联合专家、学者、企业家等带领创始团队经过三年的模式设计与优化、两年的实体运营测试，FOC 珠宝"免费"戴模式于 2015 年 10 月成功落地运营。

Zhang Sishi, the founder and chairman of the Company, has six years experiences of gold mining, smelting and eighteen years of jewelry ore purchasing, jewelry wholesaling and retailing, and then took charge of Local Department of Sichuan New Center, then transferred to Beijing for urbanization researches, therefore has deep researches for monetary policies. Under the new round of policy for reformation and innovation, she jointed experts, scholars and entrepreneur to lead founding team for three years' model design and optimization in order to monetize the jewelry, to prevent risks to ordinary people due to economic downturn as well as to achieve value and income increasing for ordinary people, carried out entity operation test for two years, and finally implemented operation for FOC jewelry "free" wearing mode in October of 2015.

四、项目名称：富沃斯（FOC）珠宝数字资产

Ⅳ. Project Name: Foc Jewelry Digital Assets

五、项目概况：

Ⅴ. Project Profile:

富沃斯拿出珠宝交易、原材料上下游投资以及买方信贷等项目上赚的钱，自愿分享给消费者，使得我们的消费分红会员成为极具归属感的群体，在创互联网珠宝项目的道路上培养锁定一大批未来的共同利益合作者。

FOC voluntarily share profits obtained from jewelry trade, raw materials and downstream investment as well as buyer's credit to consumers, therefore our consumption sharing members become a group of extremely loyalty. Cultivate a group of future partners with common interests on the way of creating Internet jewelry Project.

富沃斯要做深做透珠宝金融领域的业务，建成互联网珠宝项目后，除了现在的原材料采购和投资、设计和生产，珠宝商买方信贷等业务外，我们可以开展原矿收购、珠宝回购、珠宝贷款、珠宝租赁、珠宝保险、珠宝抵押、珠宝保理等各种业务。

To deepen the business in jewelry finance sector, after establishing the Internet jewelry Project, FOC would start various businesses such as raw ore purchasing, repurchasing jewelries, jewelry loans, jewelry leasing, jewelry insurances, jewelry mortgages, jewelry factoring in addition to the raw material purchasing, investment, design and production.

所有的消费会员和储户都可以是未来项目的"股东",除了"免费"带珠宝和分红,更可以享受低息贷款、私董会项目分享,真正享受到差异化合作信用项目的巨大利益!

All consuming members and depositors may be the "shareholders" of future Project, besides the "free" jewelry wearing and profits sharing, they may also enjoy cheap money, dividends from private advisory board projects and really enjoy the great profits from differentiated cooperative credit Project.

六、项目优势:
VI. Project Advantage(s):

公司以全球不可再生的等值增值的稀有珠宝作为信用背书,采用实物加赠送的数字资产达到消费分红,帮助老百姓抵御人民币贬值、经济下滑的风险。

The Company takes the World's non-renewable rare jewelries of equivalent and increasing value as the credit endorsement, adopts material objects adding digital assets presented to achieve profits sharing of consuming, assists the ordinary people to defense the risks of depreciation of RMB and economic depression.

公司的模式可以跨界到房产、旅游、教育、金融、美容、摄影等各个行业中。

The Company mode may transfer to all sectors such as real estates, tourism, education, finance, cosmetology, photograph and alike.

七、项目需求:跨界合作、诚招代理。
VII. Project Demand(s): Cross-border cooperation, agent wanted.

裕康高弹强力环保防水涂料
Yukang High Elastic Strong Environmental Protection Waterproof Paint

一、项目公司名称： 长沙裕康建材科技股份有限公司

I. Project Company Name: Changsha YuKang Building Materials Science & Technology Co., Ltd.

二、项目公司介绍：

II. Project Company Introduction:

公司是一家由湖南大学教授发起组建，以中国建材研究院、湖南大学等著名院校为依托的高科技（集团）公司，成立于 2010 年，注册资本 2130 万元，以致力于打造中国大型的绿色、环保型高科技建材航母为己任，专业从事高科技防水涂料的科研、生产与销售以及防水工程的施工。公司自组建以来，短短几年时间，已发展成为高科技防水材料及防水施工的综合型公司。

The company is a high-tech (group) company organized by professors in Hunan University, relying on famous universities and academies such as China Building Materials Academy, Hunan University etc. It was founded in 2010, with a registered capital of 21.3 million Yuan. It devotes itself in creating a large green and environmental protective high-tech carrier for building materials in China, and is engaged in the scientific R&D, production and sales of high-tech waterproof paints as well as construction of waterproof works. Since its establishment, in just two years, the company has developed into a comprehensive company engaged in high-tech waterproof materials and waterproof construction.

三、负责人介绍：

III. Responsible Person Introduction:

邓菊初中国共产党党员、湖南大学教授，曾担任湖大党委办主任，长沙裕康建材科技有限公司董事长、湖南大学房地产公司董事长、总经理，长沙归一建材公司常务副总等职。

Deng Juchu member of the Communist Party of China, professor of Hunan University, and the former Director of Party Committee Office of Hunan University; Chairman of Changsha Yukang Building Materials Science & Technology Co., Ltd., Chairman and General Manager of Real Estates Company of Hunan University; Executive Vice President of Changsha Guiyi Building Materials Company etc.

四、项目名称： 裕康高弹强力环保防水涂料

IV. Project Name: Yukang High Elastic Strong Environmental Protection Waterproof Paint

五、项目概况

V. Project Profile:

公司专利产品 RG 防水涂料，是目前国内顶级的防水涂料，其防水有效期长，可在背水面防水，耐酸碱盐、环保、黏结能力强等特性，被广泛地应用于防水要求极高的项目中，比如自来水厂、垃圾填埋场、蓄水池等。

The RG waterproof paint, the patent product of the company, is the first class waterproof paint in China, with characteristics such as long waterproof duration, acid, alkali and salt resistance, environment protection, strong bonding capacity etc., and is widely used in projects with high requirements on waterproof, such as water works, refuse landfill, impounding reservoir etc.

六、项目优势

VI. Project Advantage(s)

产品相比传统防水产品有很大的优势。目前用得最多的防水产品是防水卷材，而防水卷材有以下缺点：对施工面要求高，搭接缝容易进水，漏水点难找，处理异性基面能力差等。而本公司的专利产品 RG 防水涂料解决了传统防水材料的难点、痛点，是防水领域革命性的产品。

Compared with traditional waterproof product, the product possesses great advantages. At present, the most frequently used waterproof product is waterproof coiled material, but it has the following defects: High requirements on construction surface, water ingress at lap seams, difficult finding of water leakage points, poor treatment of anisotropic base plane etc. However, the patented product, RG waterproof paint of the company solves difficulties and problems of traditional waterproof materials, which is a revolutionary product in waterproof field.

它的以下特点，都是同类产品不具备的：

The following characteristics of the product are those not possessed by products of the same kind：

1．黏结性非常强，可牢固粘结在任何基面，甚至玻璃陶瓷；

Extremely strong bonding, makes the product firmly stick on any base plane, even glass ceramic;

2．抗紫外线、抗老化，可直接在屋顶受日晒雨淋；

The product is anti-ultraviolet, anti-aging, and could be directly used on the roof subject to sunshine or rains;

3．耐候性能好，可耐零下40摄氏度和150摄氏度高低温；

The product has good weather resistance, and could resist low temperature down to minus 40 degrees and high temperature up to 150 degrees.

4．安全环保、耐水浸泡，可用于自来水池、游泳池的防水。

The product is safe and environmentally friendly, resistant to water immersion, and could be used for waterproof in tap pools and swimming pools.

七、项目需求：

Ⅶ. Project Demand(s)：

寻求海外渠道，将中国好的防水产品推向全世界。

The company is seeking for overseas channels to promote this excellent waterproof product of China to all over the world.

PIIPIINOO 皮皮诺换面鞋
PIIPIINOO Face-changing Shoes

一、项目公司名称：厦门市旺普利商贸有限公司

Ⅰ. Project Company Name：Xiamen Wangpuli Trading Co., Ltd.

二、项目公司介绍：

Ⅱ. Project Company Introduction：

厦门市旺普利是PIIPIINOO控股集团下全球换面鞋中国发明专利持有者，是换面鞋全球唯一供应商。旗下拥有换面鞋多个品牌和商标，历经十多年的发展，已从单纯的换面鞋出口型公司升级为换面鞋全球供应商，拥有的换面鞋种类有换面童鞋、换面帆布鞋、换面休闲鞋、换面增高鞋、换面商旅鞋等产品体系。旺普利向全球自营换面鞋品牌，授权贴牌和全球供应。

Xiamen Wangpuli Trading Company holds the patent for face-changing shoes which have been invented by PIIPIINOO Holdings Group. As it is the only global supplier, it has multiple brands and trademarks of the face-changing shoes. Through 10 years of development, it has been upgraded to the global supplier from the pure exporting company of the face-changing shoes. Till now, it has operated the following types of the face-changing shoes, such as face-changing child's shoes, face-changing canvas shoes, face-changing casual shoes, face-changing elevator shoes, and face-changing travel shoes. Moreover, it has supported the self-operation of face-changing shoe brands to the whole world, authorization of Original Equipment Manufacturer (OEM), and global supply of face-changing shoes.

三、负责人介绍：

Ⅲ. Responsible Person Introduction：

品牌创始人Cheery Xu，一位从国家211工程大学英语老师转型为中国创意PIIPIINOO换面鞋的文化传播者和品牌推广者，代表"中国制造"于2015年参加美国巴菲特股东大会，是中国唯一被美方邀请的创意品牌创始人。她的情怀和激情全部倾注于中国创意换面鞋，如今已经将PIIPIINOO在国际上打造为换面鞋鼻祖和换面鞋第一供应商品牌地位，PIIPIINOO换面鞋已经推向世界十多个国家。

PIIPIINOO皮皮诺换面鞋产品在2017全球华人春节联欢晚会获得全球最具竞争力品牌奖。

Cheery Xu, a college English teacher who has graduated from National "211 Project" University, has created the brand of PIIPIINOO face-changing shoes, and subsequently transformed to the cultural spreader and brand promoter of Chinese creative PIIPIINOO face-changing shoes. On behalf of "Made in China", she has been invited to go to the United States and participate in Buffett Shareholders Meeting in 2015, which is the only creative brand founder invited by the Buffett Shareholders Meeting in China. She has devoted her feelings and passion to the Chinese creative face-changing shoes. Nowadays, the PIIPIINOO brand has been built as the originator and first supplier brand of the face-changing shoes. This brand of face-changing shoes has been promoted to over 10 countries all over the world.

In addition, the PIIPIINOO face-changing shoes have been awarded "The World's Most Competitive Brand" prize in 2017 Global Chinese Spring Festival Gala.

四、项目名称：PIIPIINOO皮皮诺换面鞋

Ⅳ. Project Name：PIIPIINOO Face-changing Shoes

五、项目概况：

Ⅴ. Project Profile：

换面鞋也叫拆组鞋，顾名思义，鞋面与鞋底可自行拆装。一个鞋底可搭配多个鞋面，易于清洗，鞋子拆下后，里里外外都可以洗得焕然一新，可除臭、除菌、抗汗，解决了很多人穿运动鞋、休闲鞋等极易出现的一系列脚部问题，同时还节省空间，出差旅行，随身携带几款鞋面即可，随着心情随时换面，百变由我，想换就换。即方便了"懒人"，又迎合了"潮人"。真正意义上改变了人类百年来传统制鞋、买鞋、穿鞋的观念，做到经济，时尚，个性兼具的神奇换面鞋。

The Face-changing Shoe is also called Split Shoe. As the name suggests, the vamp and sole can be split freely. A sole can be used for multiple vamps, which makes the shoe easy to clean; after the shoe is split, the vamp and sole can be cleaned wholly, and deodorization, degerming, and sweat resistance can be performed to the shoe. These features possessed by the face-changing shoes have helped to solve a series of foot problems which occur easily after many people wear sport shoes and casual shoes. Moreover, the face-changing shoe can help to save space. When people go for business trips, the people only need to carry a sole and several types of vamps. The vamps can be changed at any time freely according to people's mood. This does not only facilitate "the lazy", but also cater for "the street people". In other words, the magic face-changing shoes which combine economic, fashionable, and individual features has really changed hundreds of years' traditional concepts of human beings in making, buying, and wearing shoes.

六、项目优势：
VI. Project Advantage(s):

1．拥有全球范围的销售权和换面鞋供应权，是世界上第一个拥有换面鞋专利的公司并进入国际专利PCT保护体系。

Possess worldwide sales and supply rights of the face-changing shoes: Xiamen Wangpuli Trading Company is the world's first company to possess the patent of the face-changing shoes, and joins in Patent Cooperation Treaty (PCT) protection system.

2．弥补并占领了换面鞋行业的空隙：一鞋多用，健康时尚，个性自由。

Make up and occupy the gap for the face-changing shoe industry: One pair of shoe is for multiple purposes, which have healthy, fashionable, and individual features.

3．换面鞋解决的是人们便利出行，携带鞋子和搭配衣服的多选性，以及保护脚部健康的问题。解决了几百年来传统鞋子所不能解决的一些问题，给鞋子同质化市场增添了亮色和活力。也是未来人们追求便利、健康、环保和个性化生活的需要，是一个新型的朝阳产业。

Help to solve the problems on convenience of travel, carry of shoes, multiple choices of clothes matching, and protection of foot health: The face-changing shoes have helped to solve the shoe problems that cannot be solved for hundreds of years, and added bright color and vitality to the shoe homogenization market. Meanwhile, the face-changing shoes are also required by the people to pursue convenient, healthy, green, and individual lives. It is a new type of sunrise industry.

七、项目需求：
VII. Project Demand(s):

在信息碎片化时代，旺普利公司将用独特的商业模式和营销模式（个性化定制＋文化创意跨界结合）的方式来展现换面鞋文化，并以此来征服全球各国消费市场。为了应对日益扩大的订单的需求，公司致力于引进志同道合的合作伙伴，共同做大皮皮诺事业。

In the information fragmentation era, Xiamen Wangpuli Trading Company will adopt the unique business model and marketing model (Individual Customization + Cross-border Combination between Culture and Creativity) to show the face-changing shoe culture, and conquer the global consumer markets. To cope with increasing demands of orders, the company is committed to introducing like-minded partners and expanding PIIPIINOO business together.

大家社区
Dajia Community

一、项目公司名称： 北京慧友云商科技有限公司
I. Project Company Name: Beijing Huiyou Could Business Technology Co., Ltd.

二、项目公司介绍：
II. Project Company Introduction:

公司成立于 2015 年，是卓越的移动服务平台提供商，为传统企业提供基于社群的客户经营平台。

The company was founded in 2015, which is an excellent mobile service platform provider, providing a customer management platform based on community for traditional enterprises.

慧友云商拥有国内领先的架构、模块、存储、运维等技术，让政企客户快速拥有个性化、一云多端、多层级、易拓展的移动服务平台，并提供后续运营维护、升级迭代等一站式服务，让无任何技术的传统企业即刻完成向互联网的初步转型。

Huiyou Could Business possesses national leading technologies such as architecture, module, storage and operation & maintenance etc., to make government and enterprise customers quickly possess a personalized, one-cloud-multi-ends and multi-hierarchy mobile service platform easy to expand, and provides one-stop services such as subsequent operation maintenance, updating etc., to make traditional enterprises achieve the instant transformation to internet without needing any technology.

慧友云商核心团队，有来自微软、SAP、Gartner、阿里、思科、用友等知名企业的精英，也有曾经多次参与互联网创业的达人和草根组成，阵容堪称业内豪华。

In the core team of Huiyou Cloud Business, there're elites from famous enterprises such as Microsoft, SAP, Gartner, Ali, Cisco, Yonyou etc., as well as talents and grassroots participating in Internet Startup Bootcamp for multiple times, which could be rated as a luxury lineup of the industry.

目前，慧友云商已帮助近 3000 家企业完成互联网转型，终端使用客户超过 700 万人。同时，已有 10+ 企业在大家社区的帮助下成功上市或融资。

By far, Huiyou Cloud Business has helped nearly 3,000 enterprises to complete the internet transformation, with end users exceeding 7 million. Meanwhile, 10+ enterprises have been listed or conducted financing successfully under the help of Dajia Community.

三、负责人介绍：
III. Responsible Person Introduction:

文杰，北京慧友云商科技有限公司创始人 /CEO。毕业于北京大学，新加坡国立大学博士，曾在贝尔实验室、微软、SAP、用友等国内外顶级互联网企业担任技术研发、产品规划总负责人，并在 2004 年作为前期主要的设计者，参与了 SAP 有史以来投资最为巨大的 SaaS 云管理软件 SAP Bydesign，拥有两次成功的创业经验，是全球最早探索云计算 SaaS 资深专家，中国 SaaS 领军人，荣获多项业界大奖，拥有国内外五项专利。

Wen Jie, founder/CEO of Beijing Huiyou Could Business Technology Co., Ltd. Graduated from Peking University, Doctor of National University of Singapore, former responsible person for technical research and development in top class internet enterprises both at home and abroad such as Bell Labs, Microsoft, SAP, Yonyou etc., the main designer at earlier stage in 2004, once participated in the SaaS cloud management software SAP Bydesign enjoying the biggest investment in the history of SAP. He has two successful entrepreneurial experiences. Senior SaaS expert exploring cloud computation at the earliest time, and leader of SaaS in China, he has obtained multiple grand awards of the industry, and possesses 5 patents both at home and abroad.

著作《站在云端的 SaaS》在两岸同时出版，现任商务部中小企业创业创新培训导师、中国声谷创业导师、授渔计划公益促进中心理事。

His works *SaaS Standing on the Cloud* has been published in Taiwan and mainland, and currently acts as tutor for

E&I Training on Middle and Small-sized Enterprises of the Ministry of Commerce, enterprise tutor for China Speech Valley, and Director of Public Welfare Promotion Center for Showyes Project.

四、项目名称：大家社区
Ⅳ. Project Name：Dajia Community

五、项目概况：
Ⅴ. Project Profile：

大家社区——基于社群的客户经营平台，为企业提供全流程的移动客户经营平台（APP、移动网站、二维码、微信公众号、小程序），涵盖吸引流量、流量经营、用场景化电商实现流量变现、会员管理、大数据分析五大功能模块，实现增加新客户、提升老客户活跃度、提升复购率、提高市场投入回报率，让企业成功完成互联网＋转型。

Dajia Community——A customer management platform based on community, provides a full-process mobile customer management platform for enterprises (APP, mobile website, QR code, Wechat public account and small apps), which covers flow attraction and flow management. It utilizes scenario e-commerce to achieve five major function modules such as flow cashing, member management, big data analysis etc., and realize increasing new customers, promoting activeness of old customers, promoting repurchase rate, and improving market investment return rate, so as to make enterprises complete internet + transformation successfully.

六、项目优势：
Ⅵ. Project Advantage(s)：

1．领先的企业社区机制：
Leading enterprise community mechanism：
可配置的门户、有主题的互动、有层级的结构、带权限的应用、可管理的社区、可统计的数据。
Configurable portal, interactions with subject, hierarchical structure, application with permission, manageable community and statistical data.

2．领先的可靠技术优势：
Leading and reliable technical advantages：
高并发：支持百万级用户在线；海量数据存储：大数据分析挖掘；企业级数据安全保障：基于微软 SDL 安全体系打造；稳定高可用：五星级电信云平台。
High concurrency：Support online users of one million, massive data storage：Big data analysis and mining, enterprise-level data security：Built based on Microsoft SDL security system, stable and highly available：Five-star telecom cloud platform.

3．领先的平台开放保障：微信式开放接口：快速集成，学习成本极低；页面快速挂接：无需编码，有 html 页面就能整合；数据唾手可得：全流程数据打通，与业务系统无缝对接。
Leading platform opening guarantee：Wechat opening interface：Fast integration, extremely low learning cost, fast page hooking：No coding is needed, just html pages is enough for integration, making data easy to get：Full-process data getting through, and seamless joint with business system.

七、项目需求：
Ⅶ. Project Demand(s)：

向希望互联网转型，希望做消费升级、新零售新门店、社群经济，但缺乏互联网技术和经验的传统企业，推广大家社区产品。跨界合作，寻求渠道伙伴。
Transform to desired internet, and expect to be engaged in consumption upgrade, new retails and new shops, as well as community economy, while promote products of Dajia Community to traditional enterprises lack of Internet technology and experience. Seek for cross-boundary cooperation and channel partners.

金凤凰家具
Gold Phoenix Furniture

一、项目公司名称：深圳市金凤凰控股家具有限公司

Ⅰ. Project Company Name：Shenzhen Gold Phoenix Furniture Holding Co.,Ltd

二、项目公司介绍：

Ⅱ. Project Company Introduction：

金凤凰家具（国际）集团是一家与意大利家具制造商联合创办，集设计、研发、生产、销售于一体的大型跨国家具集团，专业生产豪华酒店家具、别墅家具、航空家具、邮轮家具及总裁办公家具、装饰材料，年总产值 23 亿元，其中酒店家具产值 12 亿元，民用家具产值 11 个亿元。

Gold Phoenix Furniture (International) Group is a large international furniture group company with joint investments from Italian furniture manufacturers and its business lines currently cover designing, development, production and sales. The company manufactures and supplies furniture for luxury hotels, villas, airplane and passenger liners as well as office furniture and decoration materials. We have a yearly output value of CNY 2.3 billion, of which CNY 1.2 billion is from hotel furniture and CNY 1.1 billion is from household furniture.

三、负责人介绍：

Ⅲ. Responsible Person Introduction：

黄鸿燕担任企业法人七年，成功完成豪生、凯悦、际丰、凯宾斯基、希尔顿、香格里拉、半山半岛、威斯汀等高端酒店及国内外多个国宾馆的系统家具配置，并得到高度赞誉。

Huang Hongyan has been acting as legal representative of the company for the past seven years, during which period the company successfully completed furniture configuration for a number of high-end hotels inside and outside China, including Howard Johnson, Hyatt Hotels, Gfour Hotel, Kempinski Hotels, Hilton Hotel, Shangri-La Hotel, Serenity Coast Resort Sanya, and Westin Hotel, and won their praises.

四、项目名称：金凤凰家具

Ⅳ. Project Name：Gold Phoenix Furniture

五、项目概况：

Ⅴ. Project Profile：

1. 品牌：金凤凰

Brand：Gold Phoenix

2. 产品：豪华酒店家具、别墅家具、航空家具、邮轮家具及总裁办公家具、装饰材料。

Products：Luxury hotel furniture, villa furniture, aviation furniture and passenger liner furniture as well as president office furniture and decoration materials.

3. 技术、服务：各类高端家具生产配置。

Technology and Service：High-end furniture production configuration.

4. 拓展：国内市场部分：立足深圳、东莞，覆盖广东，延伸全国，影响世界，打造直营团队，建立完善体系，面向全国，精准定位高品质客户群体，承担别墅、豪宅及会所的整体配套项目，同工厂直营团队实现从商务接洽谈判到设计制造、交付安装及售后的一体化服务。国际市场部分：从原来的封闭状态转为主动走出国门，通过开发更为精准的客户群体，如中东、东南亚等，从原来的酒店产品、民用产品延伸到金凤凰整体配套家居产品，加强国际市场的规范化操作流程，以国际化的视野来发展国际市场部，加强与国际化公司的战略方向及多元的合作方式，成就"中国制造、国际品牌"。

Development：China：based on Shenzhen and Dongguan, the company seeks to extend its business to cover Guangdong Province, entire Chinese markets and international markets. The company has built up its direct sales team and a complete system that helps to precisely identify high-quality customers. The company supplies constructs entire furniture for villas and luxury houses and provides one-stop services integrating customer approaching, negotiation, design, delivery, installation and after-sales services. International markets：The company makes active efforts to extend its business in international markets by developing targeted customer groups, such as customers in Mid-east and Southeast Asia. It also extends its business lines from traditional hotel supplies to complete furniture and household products under the brand Gold Phoenix. The company strove to standardize its international operation procedures and develop with international vision and by strengthening the company strategies and diverse cooperation forms. Through these efforts, the company practiced the goals of "International Brand Made in China".

5．合作：与各知名装饰公司、设计公司、原材料公司紧密合作。

Cooperation：The company established close cooperation with famous decoration companies, design companies and raw material companies.

六、项目优势：
Ⅵ. Project Advantage(s)：

1．专业：从事酒店设计装修十年，具备二十年的高档酒店家具工程设计、装修施工、制造经验。

Professional strengths：The company has been engaged in hotel design and decoration for over 10 years and has 20-year experiences in hotel furniture design, decoration engineering and manufacturing.

2．设计：集团拥有专业酒店家具设计师200人，并为重点项目设立由设计总监带头的设计小组，确保每件家具都是艺术品。

Design：The company has 200 professional hotel furniture designers and establishes design groups led by the Design Director for key projects, to ensure that each piece of furniture is an art.

七、项目需求：
Ⅶ. Project Demand(s)：

推广产品：豪华酒店家具、别墅家具、航空家具、邮轮家具及总裁办公家具、装饰材料；
市场拓展：立足深圳、东莞，覆盖广东，延伸全国。

Product promotion：Furniture for luxury hotels, villas, airplanes, passenger liners and president offices, decoration materials.

Market development：Based on Shenzhen and Dongguan, the company seeks to cover entire Guangdong Province and Chinese markets.

中华江旗袍
China's Jiangqipao

一、项目企业名称：江旗袍服饰设计有限公司

I. Project Company Name：Jiangqipao Apparel Design Co., Ltd.

二、项目公司介绍：

II. Project Company Introduction：

江旗袍品牌由意大利留学归来的江欣芸女士创办，是集开发、设计、制作、销售及售后服务于一体的高端纯手工旗袍专属定制品牌。江旗袍时尚、性感、高端，以让国服成为行走世界的时尚为设计理念，用现代风格结合国服古韵展现旗袍新魅力，成为女企业家和名媛明星的时尚新宠。

Jiangqipao brand is established by MS Jiang Xinyun returned from studying in Italy, and is a brand for high-end pure manual tailored cheongsam. Jiangqipao insists the design concepts of fashion, attractive, high-end as well as letting China's national clothing joining the world, utilizing the modern style to combine the archaic rhyme of traditional Chinese clothing so as to show the new attraction of cheongsam which may become the fashion favorite for successful female entrepreneurs, ladies and stars.

2013年以来江旗袍组织了大量文化交流活动，包括：2014中泰服饰文化交流，2014中韩服饰文化交流，2015法国凡尔赛宫、卢浮宫旗袍秀，2015意大利米兰女企业家旗袍秀，2016中美旗袍大赛，2016中美国际电视节旗袍文化交流，2016中美蜀韵走天下旗袍文化交流，2016中澳旗袍国际文化交流周等，为中国的传统服饰文化海外推广做出巨大贡献，也奠定了江旗袍成为中国时尚旗袍第一品牌的行业地位。

Jiangqipao has organized lots of cultural exchange activities since 2013, including 2014 Sino-Thailand clothing cultural exchanges, 2014 China - South Korea clothing cultural exchanges, 2015 cheongsam show in French Versailles Palace and Louvre, 2015 Milan Italy cheongsam show for women entrepreneurs, 2016 Sino-US cheongsam contest, 2016 Sino-US international TV festival cheongsam cultural exchange, 2016 Sino-US Su-style cheongsam cultural exchange, 2016 Sino-Australia cheongsam week of international cultural exchange, etc., which have made a great contribution to promotion of China's traditional costume culture in overseas, and also laid a Jiangqipao the first brand of fashion cheongsam industry in China.

三、负责人介绍：

III. Responsible Person Introduction：

江欣芸出生于旗袍世家，祖母和姨妈都是经验老到的旗袍裁缝。2000年回国后，江欣芸开始从事旗袍事业，因为她的专注和差异化产品，很快在成都开起了12家成品旗袍专卖店。2007年，和供应商在上海共同成立了旗袍高定代加工厂，专门为高定旗袍品牌生产高品质旗袍。2013年，她以自己的姓氏命名成立了"江旗袍"品牌，致力于打造中国本土奢侈品品牌。2014年荣获成都榜样女性，2015年荣获创业中国杰出女性，2016年荣获世界杰出华人奖。

Jiang Xinyun as born in a cheongsam family, and her grandmother and aunt were experienced cheongsam tailors. After returning to China in 2000, Jiang Xinyun began a career in cheongsam, because of her focus and differentiated products; she quickly opened 12 opened cheongsam stores in Chengdu. In 2007, she established the cheongsam high tailored processing plant jointly with suppliers in Shanghai, specifically for producing high quality cheongsam for high-end tailored cheongsam brand. In 2013, she founded "Jiangqipao" brand by using her surname, to be committed to creating local Chinese luxury brand. In 2014, she was awarded with Chengdu's Example Female, in 2015, she was awarded with China's outstanding female in entrepreneurship, in 2016, she was awarded with the World's outstanding Chinese.

四、项目名称：中华江旗袍

IV. Project Name：China's Jiangqipao

五、项目概况：
Ⅴ. Project Profile：

江旗袍风格定位：时尚生活、经典复古、高雅礼服三个系列。公司全新的理念打破了人们对于旗袍的传统思想和固定思维的束缚，相比市场上的旗袍走自身差异化的路线，在款式、面料、工艺、色彩等方面做大胆创新和改良，让追求时尚性感的女性、想要优雅端庄的名媛、需要自信、气场的女企业家都能找到属于自己的魅力旗袍。

Jiangqipao's styles position in three serials of fashion life, classic and elegant dresses. The new ideas of the Company break the constraints of people to traditional thoughts and fixed thinking for cheongsam, and practice a differentiated route for cheongsam in market. Carry out adventurous innovation and reformation in style, fabric, processes and color, so as to let the female pursuing fashion, ladies wanted to be elegant and female entrepreneur needing confidence and gas field to finding their own charming cheongsam.

六、项目优势：
Ⅵ. Project Advantage(s):

1．时尚设计：江旗袍把国际上最流行的色彩，最流行的图案和设计运用在旗袍的设计上，达到结合古今，融汇中西。

Fashion design：Jiangqipao applies the most popular color in the World, most popular patterns and design in cheongsam design to achieve combining ancient and modern as well as integrating west and Chinese style.

2．精准量体：一件江旗袍的制作需要测量女性38处尺寸进行制作。

Accurate body measuring：one Jiangqipao production needs to measure 38 sizes for female body.

3．专人专版：根据每位顾客独特的身材特点和体型专属打版，达到衣衬人。

Special cheongsam for special client：according to each client's figure characteristics and body type, design the cheongsam to achieve the most fitted.

4．面料选择：采用顶级的重磅真丝，确保面料的亲肤、护肤性。

Fabric selection：adopt the top heavy-weight silk to ensure the fabric skin-friendly and skin caring.

5．专属设计：保证客户的专属性和唯一性。

Exclusive design：ensure client's exclusive and unique properties.

6．传承和收藏价值：手工高级定制的旗袍具有传承和收藏价值！

Inheritance and collection value：manually advanced tailored cheongsam has inheritance and collection value!

七：项目需求：
Ⅶ. Project Demand (s):

2013年以来，公司已经在九个国家和地区建立了江旗袍销售定制中心，在国内外拥有了一定的知名度和影响力。公司希望在2017年至2019年进一步扩大招商加盟规模，希望更多热爱传统文化事业的企业家加入到江旗袍的大家庭，把江旗袍开到不同的省市和不同的国家和地区，真正做成中国最具影响力的时尚旗袍品牌。

Since 2013, the Company has established Jiangqipao tailoring and sales center in 9 countries and regions, and has built certain reputation and influence. The Company wants to further expend the join investment from 2017 to 2109, want more entrepreneurs loving the traditional cultural sectors to join Jiangqipao, spread Jiangqipao in different cities, provinces as well as different countries and regions, therefore really build China's most influential fashion cheongsam brand.

贝姆燃气采暖热水炉
Beamo Gas Heating Water Heater

一、项目公司名称： 北京贝姆热能科技有限公司
I. Project Company Name： Beijing Beamo Heat Energy Technology Co., Ltd.

二、项目公司介绍：
II. Project Company Introduction：

公司注册资金5028万元，集研发、生产、销售、服务于一体，在家电之都——广东广州市市设立分公司，建立生产研发基地，引领国际一流工艺，专业生产"贝姆"牌燃气壁挂炉、电壁挂炉、空气源热泵、燃气热水器等系列产品，在京设立北京贝姆热能科技有限公司作为中国区域营销中心，打造国际化销售服务平台。"Beamo贝姆"壁挂炉是我司自主研发生产的产品，公司拥有多项技术专利，是国家高新技术企业和中关村高新技术企业，取得AAA级诚信企业。公司通过ISO 9000质量管理体系、OHSAS18000职业健康管理体系和ISO14000环境管理体系，获得了英国BM认证机构颁发的UKAS证书，成功入围北京市政府折子工程"老楼通气"、"还首都蓝天"计划、"煤改气"项目等。

The company, with a registered capital of RMB 50.28 million, combines R&D, production, sales and service into one. It set up a branch and a production and R&D base in Guangzhou (the City of Household Appliances), Guangdong, leads the world-class process and specializes the production of a series of "Beamo" brand gas wall-mounted heater, electric wall-mounted heater, air source thermal pump, gas heater and the like. Besides, the company set up a Beijing Beamo Heat Energy Technology Co., Ltd. in Beijing as a regional marketing center in China, creating an international sales service platform. The "Beamo" wall-mounted heater is a product independently researched and developed by our company, owning multiple technical patents. We are one of Chinese national high-tech enterprises and one of the high-tech enterprises in Zhongguancun and has obtained an AAA-class honest enterprise title. We have passed the certification of ISO 9000 (Quality Management System), OHSAS18000 (Occupational Health Management System) and ISO14000 (Environmental Management System), obtained a UKAS certificate issued by BM in the United Kingdom, and successfully undertaken "Old Building Ventilation", "Beijing Blue Sky" Plan, "Coal to Gas" and the like included in compulsory works carried out by Beijing Municipal Government.

三、负责人介绍：
III. Responsible Person Introduction：

李志军，北京贝姆热能科技有限公司、北京市海达设备安装有限责任公司、北京众义佳和科技有限公司的法定代表人和总经理，现任北京市燃气集团燃气具专家委员会委员、民建党派燃气工程专业委员，荣获2015全国优秀中小企业家"金钻"奖章。

Li Zhijun, the legal representative and general manager of Beijing Beamo Heat Energy Technology Co., Ltd., Beijing Haida Equipment Installation Co., LLC, and Beijing Zhongyi Jiahe Technology Co., Ltd., now is the member of the Gas Appliance Expert Committee of Beijing Gas Group and the member of the Gas Engineering Committee of China Democratic National Construction Association, and won a "Golden Diamond" prize for 2015 Chinese Excellent Small- and Medium-sized Entrepreneur.

四、项目名称： 贝姆燃气采暖热水炉
IV. Project Name： Beamo Gas Heating Water Heater

五、项目概况：
V. Project Profile:

1. 案例名称：宁夏永宁县李俊小城镇棚户改造二期
Case Name：Renovation Phase II of Shantytowns in Lijun Town, Yongning County, Ningxia, China
主要内容：宁夏永宁县李俊小城镇棚户改造二期煤改气，安装贝姆燃气采暖热水炉1600台，项目投资额

800万元，型号：BM9，功率20KW。

Main items: gas was used to replace coal; 1,600 Beamo heating water heaters (model：BM9; power：20kW) installed; RMB 8 million invested.

这款产品采用超静音风机、水泵、燃烧系统、卫浴、供暖独立系统，适应性更强；轻触式按键，精确操作每一步；LED动态显示界面，运行过程一目了然；省气节能，热效率高达90.2%。

This product has strong adaptability because it uses an ultra-quiet blower, a water pump, a combustion system and an independent bathroom and heating system; each step is precisely operated by using lightly touched keys; A LED screen displays interfaces, making the operation process clear at a glance; both gas and energy are saved, and thermal efficiency is up to 90.2%.

2．案例名称：2016年大兴区魏善庄镇农村接入天然气工程燃气采暖炉具采购项目

Case Name：2016 Purchase Project of Gas Heaters Installed in Weishanzhuang Town, Daxing District

主要内容：2016年大兴区魏善庄镇农村接入天然气工程燃气采暖炉具采购项目，安装贝姆燃气采暖热水炉300台，项目投资额180万元，型号：BM15，功率28KW。

Main items：For the Purchase Project, 300 Beamo gas water heaters were installed (model：BM15; power：28kW) and RMB 1.8 million invested.

这款产品低噪音运行，安装快捷，操作简便；大屏幕蓝屏显示器定时显示壁挂炉运行状态；内置八段定时、恒温采暖功能，舒适节能；轻触式按键，精确操作每一步；省气节能，热效率高达90.2%。

The product is characterized by in-operation low noise, fast installation and easy operation; a blue display with a large screen displays the operating conditions of the wall-mounted heater at a specified time; an 8-section timer is built in the heater with constant temperature heating, comfort and energy saving; each step is precisely operated by using lightly touched keys; and both gas and energy are saved, and thermal efficiency is up to 90.2%.

六、项目优势：
Ⅵ. Project Advantage(s)：

产品使用舒适灵活、技术先进、智能化程度高、操作方便，节能环保，能够24小时提供生活热水，还可以实现分户供暖方式，它可以与各种式样的散热器、地暖系统配套，满足了老百姓多样化的消费需求。

The product is characterized by comfort, flexibility, advanced technology, high intelligence, easy operation, energy saving and environmental protection, and can supply hot water 24 hours a day. By using the product, household heating is realized. Besides, the product can be used together with various kinds of radiators and floor heating systems, meeting diversified consumption demands of people.

七、项目需求：
Ⅶ. Project Demand(s):

推广产品、招商融资、市场拓展，希望中外合作、股份合作。城市道路，桥梁工程，给排水、燃气和热力工程，以及工业和民用建筑的设备、线路、管道的安装，煤改气、煤改电项目、锅炉低氮改造项目均可合作。

Promote products, attract investment and financing, expand markets and hope Chinese-foreign cooperation and stock cooperation. Able to undertake urban roads, bridge engineering, water supply and discharge, gas and thermal engineering; the installation of equipment, lines and pipelines for industrial and civil buildings; coal to gas, coal to electricity, and boiler low nitrogen renovation.

大基地·大麦青苗粉
Big Base · Young Crops Powder of Barley

一、项目公司名称： 酒泉西部农业股份有限公司

Ⅰ. Project Company Name: Jiuquan Western Agriculture Co., Ltd

二、项目公司介绍：

Ⅱ. Project Company Introduction:

公司成立于1996年，注册资金壹亿元，是中国西部集蔬菜种植、加工、贮藏、出口为一体的规模化农业产业化国家重点龙头企业、国家级高新技术企业和国家级"守合同、重信用"企业。公司不仅担负着当地农民科技培训、新产品新技术研发、推广的重任，而且承担着国家的高科技农转资金项目、星火计划项目、重点新产品开发项目和国家的高技术产业化（西部专项）、948科技研发等重点高新项目。

Founded in 1996, with the registered capital of 100 million yuan, the company is a scale agricultural industrialization national key leading enterprise which integrates vegetable planting, processing, storage and export in the west of China, and national high-tech enterprise and national "valuing the contract, defending the credit" enterprise. It not only undertakes the scientific and technological training on local farmers, and research & development and promotion of new products and new technology, but also undertakes the national high-tech agriculture transfer capital project, spark plan project and key new product development project as well as the national high-tech industrialized project (special project in the west) and "948" technical research and development project.

三、负责人介绍：

Ⅲ. Responsible Person Introduction:

赵云博士，长期从事农产品精深加工技术开发工作，经验丰富，在创办企业的过程中，不断创新，锐意进取，以科技创新为动力，为当地的农民增收和农业产业化发展做出了积极的贡献。

Dr. Zhao Yun, engaged in agricultural products deep processing technology development work for long time, has rich experience. In starting a business, Zhao Yun continuously innovates, forges ahead, and takes the technological innovation as the power to positively contribute to increasing the local farmers' income and agricultural industrial development.

四、项目名称： 大基地·大麦青苗粉

Ⅳ. Project Name: Big Base · Young Crops Powder of Barley

五、项目概况：

Ⅴ. Project Profile:

鉴于麦绿素巨大的生产和开发价值以及当地的大麦资源优势，公司为积极适应国际保健食品的发展趋势，促进西北地区农业及农村经济结构调整，加快企业发展，公司对筛选适宜甘肃河西地区种植的大麦品种、生长期进行研究，开展有机大麦麦绿素提取工艺研究及关键技术护色保绿技术和低温干燥技术的研究。

In view of huge production and development value of barley green and local barley resources advantages, in order to actively adapt to the development trends of international health food products, promote agricultural and rural economic structure adjustment in northwest China, and accelerate the development of enterprises, the company studies the screening of barley variety and growth period suitable for being cultivated in Hexi area of Gansu, and carries out the extraction process research on barley green of organic barley and the research on the key color-protecting green-keeping technology and low-temperature drying technology.

为扩建大麦青苗粉生产线，年处理大麦嫩苗原料500吨；根据生产线要求，建设相应的生产车间、公用辅助工程、厂区工程、服务工程，购进大麦青苗辅助设备286台/套及仓储和相关配套设施；加大大麦青苗基地建设投入，基地种植面积5000亩。

In order to expand the production line of green crops powder of barley, the company processes 500 tons of young crops materials of barley annually, builds the corresponding production workshop, public auxiliary works, plant engineering and service works according to requirements for production line, purchases 286 sets of barley green crops auxiliary equipment as well as warehousing and related facilities, and adds the construction investment of barley green crops base, covering the base planting area of 5,000 mu.

该项目建设期为两年：2017年6月至2019年6月。项目总投资为5841.95万元，其中，建设投资4671.50万元，建设期利息96.00万元，铺底流动资金1074.45万元。项目资金来源：企业自筹资金1841.95万元，银行贷款1000万元，计划融资5000万元人民币。项目建成后，正常年营业收入为22000万元，平均年总成本为17000万元，正常税后年利润总额为5000万元，财务（税前）内部收益率19.42%，项目财务上可行。

The project construction period is two years：from June 2017 to June 2019. The project total investment is 58,419,500 yuan, including the construction investment of 46,715,000 yuan, construction interest of 960,000 yuan and circulating funds of 10,744,500 million yuan. Source of project fund：enterprise self-raised funds of 18,419,500 million yuan, bank loans of 10 million Yuan, planned financing of 50 million yuan. After the completion of the project, the normal annual business income is 220 million Yuan, the average annual total cost is 170 million Yuan, the normal after-tax annual profit is 50 million Yuan, and the financial (pre-tax) internal rate of return is 19.42%. Therefore, the project is financially feasible.

六、项目优势：
VI. Project Advantage(s)：

1．从事大麦青苗麦绿素技术综合开发研究工作较早，拥有自主知识产权。

Work on technical overall development and research in barley green of young crops of barley early, and own proprietary intellectual property rights.

2．产品原料均源于祁连雪水滋润的河西走廊无污染自有备案基地，原料供应充足，产品利润空间大。

Product raw materials come from non-polluting proprietary filing base of Hexi Corridor of Qilian, with moist snow water, so supply of raw materials are sufficient and product profit space is big.

3．产品销售渠道广阔，采取线上＋线下的O2O销售模式。

Vast product sales channel, adopting online+offline O2O sales model.

七、项目需求：
VII. Project Demand(s)：

为实现发展计划，公司计划融资5000万元，资金用于产品原料种植基地、生产设备增扩与产品宣传推广。若该融资到位可实现两年内创业板和五年内主板的上市目标。

In order to realize the development plan, the company plans to raise 50 million yuan and put funds in the production equipment expansion and product promotion of product raw material planting base. If funds are in place, the goals of being listed in the second-board market within 2 years and main-board market within 5 years can be achieved.

乾坤汽车紧固件
Qiankun Auto Fasteners

一、项目公司名称：河南乾坤汽车零部件有限公司
I. Project Company Name：Henan Qiankun Auto Parts Co., Ltd.

二、项目公司介绍：
II. Project Company Introduction:

公司创建于 2001 年，位于河南省武陟县东辰园区内，占地面积 77.18 亩，是郑州日产汽车有限公司优秀的一级供应商，现一期厂房 15000 平方米已经正常投产使用三年多。现有员工 120 多人，有专业的技术人员及优秀的员工队伍。拥有各类进口螺母冷镦机、螺栓多工位冷镦机及各类专用设备等 80 余台设备。专业生产各种规格汽车用高强度螺栓、螺母，可根据客户要求加工生产各类国标件、非标类零件。

The company was founded in 2001, located in the Dongchen Park, Wuzhi County, Henan Province, covering an area of 77.18mu. It is an excellent tier-one supplier of Zhengzhou Nissan Motor Co., Ltd., and its phase I plant of 15,000 m^2 has been put in the production for more than three years. It possesses more than 120 employees, as well as professional technicians and excellent staff team. It possesses more than 80 devices such as various imported nut cold heading machines, bolt multi-station cold heading machines and various special devices etc. It is specialized in producing high strength bolts and nuts of various specifications for vehicles. It could produce and process various national standard parts, and non-standard parts according to customer requirements.

三、负责人介绍：
III. Responsible Person Introduction:

沙志卫，男，汉族，江苏江阴人，现任河南乾坤汽车零部件有限公司董事长，焦作市政协委员。从一名下岗职工，到实现自主创业，凭着一股坚韧不拔的精神和不屈不挠的意志，闯出一条发展创新之路，成为当地有名望的企业家。

Sha Zhiwei, male, Han, born in Jiangyin, Jiangsu, now the Chairman of Henan Qiankun Auto Parts Co., Ltd. Jiaozuo municipal CPPCC member. He was once a laid off worker, who set up his own business later and now becomes an honorable entrepreneur depending on persistent efforts and indomitable will.

四、项目名称：乾坤汽车紧固件
IV. Project Name：Qiankun Auto Fasteners

五、项目概况：
V. Project Profile:

公司于 2014 年 7 月获 ISO/ TS16949：2002 美国质量认证（AQA）国际标准的证书。目前根据汽车标准（Q）、国家标准（GB）生产的各类产品已通过 TS16949:2009 国际质量体系认证，本着"追求零缺陷、达到顾客满意"的质量方针，产品交付准时率 100%、顾客满意度大于 88 分的质量目标取得了良好的市场信誉。近年来，始终坚持把质量和客户放在第一位，业绩每年以超过 5% 的比例增长，连年创新高！

The company obtained the ISO/ TS16949：2002 American Quality Assessors (AQA) international standard certificate in July, 2014. At present, various products produced according to automobile standards (Q) and national standards (GB) have passed the TS16949:2009 international quality system certification. Based on the quality policy of "seeking for 0 defect and achieving customer satisfaction", and the quality objective of "product delivery punctuality of 100%, and customer satisfaction greater than 88", it has obtained a sound market reputation. In recent years, it adheres to putting quality and customer to the first place, with performance growing at a rate of 5% on a yearly basis, creating new high in consecutive years!!

六、项目优势：

VI. Project Advantage(s):

河南乾坤位于河南武陟县，地处中原腹地，离郑云高速路出口仅2公里，地理位置佳，交通便捷。

Qiankun, Henan is located in Wuzhi County, Henan, which is in the hinterland of the central plains. It is only 2km from Zhengzhou-Yuntaishan Expressway intersection, enjoying a sound geographical location, and convenient traffic..

企业标准化管理：严格技术标准、工作标准，对于某些规格产品进行合理的归纳，控制多样化和差异化，对工艺流程合理简化，从而提高产品的生产批量，以减少单位产品的劳动消耗、降低成本，通过使生产过程中的每一道工序，每一道操作步骤标准，避免操作过程和步骤上的混乱，达到标准化的要求，从而使生产更加安全高效，保障操作人员的人身安全、设施的安全，提高生产效率。

Enterprise standardization management：For technical standards and work standards, conduct reasonable conclusion on products of certain specification, control diversification and differentiation, and simplify process reasonably, so as to improve production batch of products, thus to reduce labor consumption of unit product, and reduce cost. Via standardizing each procedure and each operating step in production process, avoid chaos in operation process and steps, and meet standardization requirements, so as to make production safer and more efficient, guarantee personal safety of operators, and safety of equipment, and improve production efficiency.

七、项目需求：

VII. Project Demand(s) :

希望与国内国外企业（投资公司）合作，从而达到做大做强市场、可以股份合作、带动国外标准件产品"本土化"。

It is expected to cooperate with national and international enterprises (investment companies), so as to enlarge and enhance markets, while share cooperation is allowed, to promote "localization" of international standard products.

晚乐福养老平台
Wanlefu Pension Platform

一、项目公司名称：重庆伸爱养老服务有限公司
Ⅰ. Project Company Name：Chongqing Shen'ai Pension Service Co., Ltd.

二、项目公司介绍：
Ⅱ. Project Company Introduction:

公司是以护理养生为主题的智慧养老服务公司，主要从事养老看护服务及老年产业。公司秉承"以人为本，心德为先"的企业宗旨，致力于将养老行业标准化，做中国专业的居家养老平台，为已进入老龄化社会的中国尽绵薄之力。

The company is a wisdom pension service company focusing on nursing and regimen, which is mainly engaged in the nursing service for the aged and old-age industry. The company inherits the enterprise tent of "human-oriented and putting moral values in the first place", and devotes itself to the standardization of pension industry, so as to become a home-based care platform in China, and make contributions to the aging society of China.

三、负责人介绍：
Ⅲ. Responsible Person Introduction:

高小兰女士是重庆伸爱养老服务有限公司的法人代表，在新加坡经商多年，积累了丰富的营销经验，通过大量数据分析，对未来养老市场充满信心，全力开发晚乐福APP平台，优化软件设计及服务内容并制定相关品牌推广战略。

Ms. Gao Xiaolan is the legal representative of Chongqing Shenai Pension Service Co., Ltd., who has many years of experience in business in Singapore, and accumulated abundant marketing experience. Via a large amount of data analysis, she is very confident with the pension market in future, and decides to develop the Wanlefu platform, optimize software design and service content, as well as prepare related brand promotion strategies.

四、项目名称：晚乐福养老平台
Ⅳ. Project Name：Wanlefu Pension Platform

五、项目概况：
Ⅴ. Project Profile:

晚乐福APP于2016年初启动顶层设计，2017年2月建立市场运营团队，8月初以重庆为试点平台正式上线。晚乐福APP以儒道居家式养老为核心，为康复期老人提供专业的护理服务，通过大数据整合反馈老人健康状况，从身体和心理帮助老人实现生活独立，解决当下独生子女、双职工家庭常见4:2:1的家庭结构所面临的工作与"孝道"难两全的矛盾。

The top-level design of Wanlefu APP was launched at the beginning of 2016, the mark management team was established in February, 2017, and the platform was launched formally at the beginning of August taking Chongqing as the pilot. The Wanlefu APP takes rudaor home-based care as the core, provides professional nursing service for the aged in recovery period, integrate and feed back health conditions of the aged via big data, and help the aged to realize independent living from physical and physiological aspects, which solves the contradiction between the work faced by the common 4:2:1 family structure such as only child family and two-earner family etc. and the "filial piety".

现经过晚乐福技术人员的不断优化，客户端新增史册功能、看护评分功能等功能。服务端优化看护流程，进一步的确保服务质量。用户可以通过客户端实现自主预约、下单，看护员通过服务端可以实现接单、上传汇报老人情况。晚乐福平台的医疗专家会根据回传数据运用专业知识为老人健康评级，并推荐最适合老人的生活方式等，客户能通过推送信息及时了解老人健康状况并得到相应反馈建议。

At present, via constant optimization by technical personnel of Wanlefu, new functions such as history function and nursing score etc. have been added to client. The nursing process has been optimized at server, which further guarantees service quality. Users could realize automatic-reservation and ordering at client, and nursing administrator could realize accepting orders and reporting situation of the aged at server. Medical experts of Wanlefu platform will utilize professional knowledge to rate the health situation of the aged according to returned data, and recommend the most suitable life style for them etc., while customers could understand health situation of the aged and obtain corresponding suggestions via push messages.

现今，晚乐福进入市场后，得到大众一致好评，平台看护员招募及培训持续进行中，同时晚乐福还同诸多从事养老服务的企业达成合作协议，共同谋划养老业的发展，解决时代痛点，让老人在家里度过幸福晚年。

Nowadays, since Wanlefu entering the market, it has won unanimous applause from the public. The recruitment and training of platform nursing administrators is undergoing, meanwhile, Wanlefu has also cooperated with numerous enterprises engaged in pension service industry, to jointly plan the development of pension industry, and to solve the problems of the era, so as to make the aged have a happy time at home.

六、项目优势：
Ⅵ. Project Advantage(s):

1．创新三联网"物联网＋护联网＋互联网"的综合标准化服务模式。

A comprehensive and standardized service mode of innovative three networks namely "IoT + Care Network + Internet".

2．解决4:2:1家庭结构中年轻人工作生活与孝顺老人之间的时间矛盾。

Solve time contradiction between work/life and filial piety among mid-aged and young people in 4:2:1 family structure.

3．养老行业标准化、平台价格透明化、专业服务人性化。

Standardization of pension industry, transparency of platform price, and humanization of professional service.

4．居家养老，维护家庭情感维度。

Home-based care, maintains family emotional dimension.

七、项目需求：
Ⅶ. Project Demand(s):

公司正处于大力推广阶段，欢迎热爱养老市场的营销专业人士以及各界投资人的加盟，为中国养老事业做出一份贡献。同时针对居家养老方面国家出台的政策较少，希望各地政府给予相关支持。

The company is under vigorous promotion stage, and welcomes marketing professionals and investors from all walks of life in favor of the pension market to join us, thus to make contributions to the pension undertaking in China. Meanwhile, policies for home-based care formulated by the nation are very few, so we hope governments around the nation could give relevant support.

浪度家居
Nondo Furniture

一、项目公司名称：成都浪度家私有限公司
I. Project Company Name: Chengdu Nondo Furniture Co., Ltd.

二、项目公司介绍：
II. Project Company Introduction:

公司成立于1998年，坐落于成都市新都经济开发东区，拥有现代化的企业管理理念和专业的人才队伍，现有员工3000余人，生产厂房15万平方米。2005年顺利通过ISO9001:2008质量管理体系认证，并获得"中国驰名商标"、"四川家居出口五强"等多项殊荣。历经20年创新发展，目前公司已在全国各地开设了1000余家专卖店及双厅标准化旗舰店，是西部地区集研发、设计、生产、销售于一体的综合型家具制造业之一。

The company was founded in 1998, located in the Eastern District of Xindu Economic Development Zone in Chengdu, and possesses modern enterprise management ideology and professional talent team. The company has more than 3,000 employees and production plant of 150 km². It passed the certification of ISO9001:2008 quality management system in 2005, and obtained multiple honors like "China's Well-known Trademark" and "Top Five Furniture Exporters in Sichuan" etc. Via 20 years of innovation and development, at present, the company has set up more than 1,000 exclusive agencies and double-hall standard flagship stores throughout the nation, which is among comprehensive furniture manufacturers integrating R&D, design, production and sales.

三、负责人介绍：
III. Responsible Person Introduction:

公司营销总经理张小涛先生，曾先后供职于中石油、联想等国企及沿海企业，拥有先进的企业管理理念，加入浪度以来，以先进、科学的创新经营模式，使浪度家居广受市场追捧和消费者好评。

Mr. Zhang Xiaotao, General Marketing Manager of the company, once worked in some state-owned enterprises such as CNPC and Legend etc., as well as in coastal enterprises, possessing advanced enterprise management ideology. Since his participation in Nondo, he has made Nondo Furniture sought after by the market and highly appraised by consumers, based on his advanced and scientific innovation management mode.

四、项目名称：浪度家居
IV. Project Name: Nondo Furniture

五、项目概况：
V. Project Profile:

浪度家居产品体系齐全，涵盖沙发、板木（板式）家具、软床、餐桌、茶几等30多个系列、4000余款式，丰富的产品矩阵满足不同消费者需求，其中，温馨布艺沙发、环保板实木、睡眠中心、全屋定制、精致桌几、格调真皮等产品系列深受消费者喜爱。浪度家居从德国引进豪迈全自动家具生产线等一流设备，运用了国际领先的SAP信息管理系统，拥有实力强大的研发中心和来自国际的顶尖设计师团队，充分把握国际潮流趋势，洞察国内消费者偏好，以高质平价的产品和完善优质的服务，受到广大消费者的青睐和商家的追捧。随着公司国外战略的布局，目前产品已远销美国、德国、英国、法国、日本、澳大利亚等数十个国家和地区。

Nondo Furniture is complete in product system, covering more than 30 series such as sofa, wooden (plate) furniture, soft bed, dining table, tea table etc. of more than 4,000 styles, so its abundant product matrix can meet the demand of different consumers. Among them, product series such as fabric sofa, environmental protection solid wood plate, sleep center, whole house customization, delicate stool, elegant leather etc. are very popular among consumers. Nondo Furniture introduces first class equipment such as Homag full-automatic furniture production line etc. from Germany, utilizes international leading SAP information management system, possesses a powerful R&D Center and a top class designer group from international world, grasps international trend, investigates preferences of domestic consumers, and obtains favor and appraisal of wide consumers with its products of high quality and average price and its perfect services of high quality. With the strategic layout in foreign countries of the company, its products have been sold to several countries and regions such as the United States, Germany, England, France, Japan, Australia etc.

六、项目优势：
VI. Project Advantage(s):

浪度家居产品荣获多项国家专利，是四川家具出口前三名，产品远销全球20余国家，是四川家具原创设计5强品牌，曾两次获国际家具展览会银奖。浪度沙发享有"中国十大真皮沙发"荣誉，被中国中轻质量保证中心评为"中国著名品牌"。

Nondo Furniture has won multiple national patents, which is among the top 3 furniture exporters in Sichuan. Its products have been sold to more than 20 countries of the globe; it is among the top 5 brands for original design of furniture in Sichuan, and has won 2 Silver Awards in the International Furniture Exhibition. Nondo sofa enjoys an honor of "Top 10 Leather Sofas in China", and is evaluated as the "Chinese Famous Brand" by the China Light Industry Products Quality Guarantee Centre.

七、项目需求：
VII. Project Demand(s):

品牌推广、市场拓展及产品推广，目前浪度家居的市场布局正从三四线城市发展到一二线城市。

Brand promotion, market expansion and product promotion. At present, Nondo's market layout has transferred from tie-3 and tie-4 cities to tie-1 and tie-2 cities.

有害生物专业防治
Professional Pest Control

一、项目公司名称：桂林市科迅白蚁害虫防治有限公司

Ⅰ. Project Company Name: Guilin Kexun Termite and Pest Prevention and Control Co., Ltd.

二、项目公司介绍：

Ⅱ. Project Company Introduction:

桂林市科迅白蚁害虫防治有限公司是一家专业从事白蚁防治、环境消杀、灭四害工程及相关药械销售的综合型 PCO 服务企业，是目前桂林市最具专业化，服务级别最高的 PCO 公司，旗下创办了广西媒美文化传媒有限公司、广西富强广告有限公司、桂林通祥物业服务有限公司、桂林市科迅有害生物研究院、桂林清湘书画艺术研究院等。企业于 2017 年 3 月 16 日获得中国有害生物防制服务 A 级资质，是中国有害生物防制协会会员，是专业鼠虫害控制及管理的综合型鼠虫控技术企业。

Guilin Kexun Termite and Pest Prevention and Control Co., Ltd. professionally engages in comprehensive PCO services, such as termite prevention and control, environmental disinfection, pests killing engineering and related medical instrument sales. Currently, it is the most professional PCO company with the highest service level in Guilin. Guangxi Meimei Culture Media Co., Ltd, Guangxi Fuqiang Advertising Co., Ltd., Guilin Tongxiang Property Service Co., Ltd., Guilin Kexun Institute of Pest Research, Guilin Qingxiang Institute of Painting and Calligraphy Art Research and etc. are subordinates of this company. On March 16th, 2017, it won the A-class qualification of China pest control service. It is the member of China Pest Control Association. It is a professional pest control and technology integrated management enterprise.

三、负责人介绍：

Ⅲ. Responsible Person Introduction:

石树长于 2006 组建了一支专业有害生物防制团队。在 2007 年桂林市总工会举办的"绝招绝活"展示中，石树长以独特的诱除老鼠的绝招征服众评委，被市政府授予"特殊技能人才"荣誉；2013 年加入中国民主建国会；2014 年当选为桂林市秀峰区人大代表；2015 年担任中国民主建国委员会秀峰总支二支部副主委及桂林市秀峰区工商联执委；2016 年当选为民建秀峰区副主委、桂林临桂区政协常委、临桂区工商联副主席及桂林市收藏家协会副会长；2017 年当选为桂林市社科联行业委员及桂林市秀峰区工商联执委。

In 2006, Shi Shuzhang established a professional pest controlling team. In 2007, during the "Unique Skills" Exhibition held by Guilin City Federation of Trade Unions, Shi Shuzhang astonished all the judges by luring and disinfesting mice with unique skills, and was awarded as "talent with special skills"; in 2013, he joined in China Democratic National Construction Association and became a member of China Democratic National Construction Association of Guilin; in 2014, he was elected as NPC member of Xiufeng District, Guilin City; in 2015, he served as deputy co-chairman of the second branch team of the Xiufeng general branch team of Committee of China National Democratic Construction Association, and committee of Federation of Industry and Commerce in Xiufeng District, Guilin City; in 2016, he was chosen as co-chairman of China Democratic National Construction Association of Xiufeng, member of Standing Committee of the CPPCC of Lingui District in Guilin City, vice-chairman of Federation of Industry and Commerce of Lingui District, and Vice President of Collectors Association; in 2017, he was chosen as member of industry of Federation of Humanities and Social Sciences in Guilin City and member of Federation of Industry and Commerce in Guilin City.

四、项目名称：有害生物专业防治

Ⅳ. Project Name: Professional Pest Control

五、项目概况：

Ⅴ. Project Profile:

按照《广西壮族自治区爱国卫生管理办法》第十六条"由其经营者或者管理者负责"的规定，机关、企事

业单位、营业场所、村（居）委、有物业住宅小区及居民住户，鼓励病媒生物预防控制服务机构（专业消杀公司）为单位和个人提供符合质量安全要求的有偿服务。按照中华人民共和国建设部第72号、130号令规定，凡白蚁危害地区的新建、改建、扩建、装饰装修的房屋必须实施白蚁预防处理。我公司以"注重环保、追求健康"为经营理念，在对数百个单位实施PCO服务过程中，确立了一条"政府组织、部门负责、群众参与，专业公司参与实施，疾控中心监督测评"的"统一战线"，获得了政府、专家及群众的高度评价。在服务过程中我们不仅能为客户提供有效的白蚁及鼠虫害防治程序，而且还能帮助客户提供有效的、合理的、可操作性的建议来改善客户存在的建筑结构缺陷以及卫生条件等，从而达到更好的白蚁及鼠虫害控制效果。

According to the sixteenth item of *Guangxi Zhuang Autonomous Region Patriotic Health Management Measures*, namely the regulation of "the business operators or managers should be responsible", organs, enterprises and institutions, business premises, village (neighborhood) committees, residence community with Property Management and residents, should encourage pests prevention and control services agent (professional disinfection company) to provide paid and qualified service which meets safety requirements for units and individuals. According to the No. 72 and 130 orders of the Ministry of Construction of the PRC and termite prevention shall be carried out in all the newly built, rebuilt, expanded and decorated houses in areas with termite threat. In the implementation of PCO services for hundreds of units, the company treated "pay attention to environmental protection, and approach to health" as the business principle, and has established a "United Front" of "government organization, department responsibility, public participation, professional company implementation and CDC supervision and assessment" which was highly praised by the government, experts and the masses. During the service, the company can not only provide an effective pest control program of termites and rats for customers, but also help customers to provide effective, reasonable and feasible suggestions to improve the defects of existing structures and other sanitary conditions, so as to achieve better control effect of termite and rodent pest.

六、项目优势：
VI. Project Advantage：

桂林市科迅白蚁害虫防治有限公司是桂林本土首个也是目前唯一获得有害生物防制（PCO）服务机构能力A级资质的消杀公司，消杀业务可面向全国，是目前桂林市最具专业化，服务级别最高的PCO公司。

Guilin Kexun Termite and Pest Prevention and Control Co., Ltd. is the first local and the only company coping with disinfection that currently owns the A-level qualification of PCO service ability in Guilin. Its disinfection business is oriented toward the whole country and it is the most professional PCO company with the highest severs level in Guilin.

七、项目需求：
VII. Project Demand：

公司秉承"质量第一，信誉为重"的服务宗旨，承接有害生物防制服务、物业管理服务、传媒业务、广告印制业务、名家字画交流。

Adhering to the "quality is the first and reputation is the heaviest" service tenet, the company undertakes pest control services, property management services, media business, advertising printing business, and well-known calligraphy and painting exchanges.

土壤固化建筑材料
Soil Solidified Building Material

一、项目公司名称：北京磊土鑫生态科技有限公司

I. Project Company Name：Beijing Leituxin Ecology & Technology Co., Ltd.

二、项目公司介绍：

II. Project Company Introduction：

本公司主要经营生态环保科技项目的开发与应用，产品有"磊土鑫胶泥粉（固土王）"、"高效砂浆增稠粉"、"环保免烧砖"、"雕刻粉"、"植物纤维泥土板材"、"纳米防水技术的开发与应用"，承接道路工程、软基处理、水利工程、生态旅游项目工程、园林及生态农业综合开发工程、仿古砖制造等就地取材的专利技术的开发与应用。2008年7月时任国务院副总理王岐山在考察四川省北川灾区震后的重建工作时，对本产品制作的建筑材料给予了高度赞誉，指出："这个项目好，要在全国大力推广"。

The company is mainly engaged in the development and application of science and technology projects of ecological environmental protection, the products include "Leituxin Clay Powder (solid earth king)", "High Performance Mortar Thickening Powder", "Environmental Protection Baking-free Brick", "Carved Powder", "Plant Fiber Soil Plank" and "Development and Application of Nano Waterproof Technology". And the company undertakes the development and application of the road engineering, soft foundation treatment, water conservancy engineering, ecological tourism project engineering, landscape and ecological agriculture comprehensive development engineering as well as the antique brick manufacturing and other local patent technology. In July 2008, Vice Premier of State Council, Wang Qishan, has given high praise for the construction materials manufactured by the product in the investigation of the reconstruction work of the disaster area of Beichuan in Sichuan after the earthquake, and pointed out: "This project is good and should be vigorously promoted throughout the country".

三、负责人介绍：

III. Responsible Person Introduction：

董事长李成敏先生，毕业于广西建筑工程学院，从事建筑行业30多年，在建筑技术、经营管理等方面有丰富的经验。公司技术负责人谢盈庭先生，是"磊土鑫胶泥粉"等五项科技成果专利发明人，曾获国家多项"专利证书"和"国家突出贡献奖"、"国家管理科学研究院2016年度十佳杰出创新人物"及"香港国际博览会金牌奖"、"世界科学技术发展成就奖"等殊荣。

Mr. Li Chengmin, the Chairman of the company, graduated from Guangxi Architectural Engineering College, and has been engaged in the construction industry for more than 30 years, and has rich experience in construction technology, management and other aspects. Mr. Xie Yingting, in charge of the technical director of the company, is the patent inventor of "Leituxin Clay Powder" and other 5 technological achievements, and has won a number of national leading "Patent Certificate" and "National Outstanding Contribution Award", "2016 Top Ten Outstanding Innovators of National Management Science Institute" as well as "Hong Kong International Exposition Gold Award", "World Science and Technology Development Achievement Award" and other awards.

四、项目名称：土壤固化建筑材料

IV. Project name：Soil Solidified Building Material

五、项目概况：

V. Project Profile：

经历了十多年来实践检验，土壤固化建筑材料用于2001年广西玉林福绵区水利工程、2004年广西扶绥弄谷总干渠修复工程、2009年四川泸州市安宁石材园区道路硬化工程、2009年四川宜宾明威乡道路、2010年重庆江津区架平镇公路、2010年四川泸州安齐道路、2013年重庆江津区水坝工程、2010年泸州市江阳区江北镇金马湖大坝、2010年在泸州市江金马镇修筑的水坝、2014年重庆江津区嘉平镇公路等诸多成功案例，经多年使用，质

量可靠，效果良好，均得到当地政府及相关专业权威部门的认可和赞誉。

The material has been used for the water conservancy engineering of Fumian district in Guangxi in 2001 after more than 10 years of inspection; The restoration engineering of Nong Gu main canal of Fusui in Guangxi in 2004; The road hardening engineering of Anning Stone Park of Luzhou in Sichuan in 2009; Mingwei township road of Yibin in Sichuan in 2009; Jiaping town highway of Jiangjin District in Chongqing in 2010; Anqi road of Luzhou in Sichuan in 2010; The dam engineering of Jiangjin district in Chongqing in 2013; Jiangbei town jinma lake dam of Jiangyang district in Luzhou in 2010; The dam built in Jiang Jinma town in Luzhou in 2010; Jiaping town highway of Jiangjin district in Chongqing in 2014 and many successful cases. After many years of use, the quality is reliable and the effect is well. All of these engineering have been recognized and praised by local authorities and relevant professional authorities.

磊土鑫胶泥粉的发明专利是世界首创，拥有国家知识产权局颁发的专利发明证书和自主创新的品牌商标，这项专利技术成果对于缺少砂、石料的地区和交通不便的山区道路与农田水利建设具有特殊价值意义。本项目取材方便，节省材料、人工，可减轻劳动强度30%，比使用水泥节约成本减少30%-40%，并能保护生态环境。

The patent invention, "Leituxin Clay Powder", is the first in the world, and has the patent invention certificate issued by the "State Intellectual Property Office" and the brand trademark innovated independently. The patent technical achievement has special value for the area lack of sand and stone as well as the water conservancy construction of the road and farmland of the mountain area where the traffic is inconvenient. The patent invention can realize the convenient drawing, save materials and labor, reduce labor intensity by 30% and the cost by using cement by 30%-40%, and protect the ecological environment.

六、项目优势：
VI. Project Advantage(s)

与普通土混合，配水搅拌，经七天晾干后可达到水泥硬度。可代替水泥，用于房屋建设、公路、山体护坡、防渗漏工程、鱼塘水池防渗，制作免烧砖等。已通过广西科技厅组织的专家鉴定。

Mixed with the ordinary soil and stirred with the water, and the cement hardness can be achieved after air-drying for 7 days. The material can replace cement for the housing construction, highway, mountain slope protection, seepage prevention engineering, fish pond seepage prevention and the production of unburned brick, etc. The material has been identified by the experts organized by the Guangxi Science and Technology Department.

七、项目需求：
VII. Project Demand(s)

推广与应用，投资少、见效快、能耗低、无污染，按国家节能环保政策可申请减免增值税。企盼有识之士投资融资，将本科技成果造福全人类。

Project Demand(s) Promotion and application, with low investment, quick effect, low energy consumption and no pollution, the exemption of VAT can be applied in accordance with national energy conservation and environmental protection policies. Our company is looking forward to the investment financing from the people of insight to benefit all mankind through the scientific and technological achievement.

霸王寨农业生态观光园
Bawangzhai Agriculture Ecological Tourist Garden

一、项目公司名称： 汉中市碧云天农业发展有限公司
Ⅰ. Project Company Name: Hanzhong Biyuntian Agriculture Development Co., Ltd.

二、项目公司介绍：
Ⅱ. Project Company Introduction:

公司主营乡村旅游观光系列服务，农业种植、果蔬采摘、畜禽养殖等服务，农业种植技术的信息咨询、技术培训、技术研发及技术转让服务以及农业优质品种引进、实验、研发。目前大力推出的汉中市城固县霸王寨农业生态观光园，是以自然生态环境综合利用和发展高科技生态农业循环经济为主导，以生态开发为宗旨，集高效农业、种植、养殖、旅游、休闲、环保为一体的绿色生态园。

The main businesses of the Company include serial services for rural tourism, services for farming, fruits and vegetables picking, livestock breeding, services for information consultation, for agricultural technology, technique training, technology researches and technology transfer as well as introduction, test and R&D for quality agricultural varieties. The current vigorously launched Chenggu Bawangzhai Agriculture Ecological Tourist Garden is an integrated green ecological garden guided by comprehensive utilization of natural ecological environment and development of recycling economy for high-tech ecological agriculture, taking ecological exploitation as the purpose and integrating high-efficiency agriculture, planting, tourism, leisure and environment protection as a whole.

三、负责人介绍：
Ⅲ. Responsible Person Introduction:

秦旭红，汉中市碧云天农业发展有限公司董事长，有多年养殖、种植的工作经验，为人实在，工作认真，学习能力强，追求快乐健康的人生。

Qin Xuhong, the President of Hanzhong Biyuntian Agriculture Development Co., Ltd., has many years of work experiences in cultivation and implantation. He is honest, hard-working, good learning capacity and seeking happy and healthy life.

四、项目名称： 霸王寨农业生态观光园
Ⅳ. Project Name: Bawangzhai Agriculture Ecological Tourist Garden

五、项目概况：
Ⅴ. Project Profile:

按照国家相关标准建设，占地500亩，其中，生态种植区50亩，项目观光路两边3.7公里的白沙枇杷果树种植，生态蔬菜种植体验区2亩，荷花塘景观观赏区10亩，四沟翻水坝景观带。四沟水产生态养殖观光路：

Built according to relevant national standards, occupying an area of 500 mu, with an ecological planting area of 50 mu. There is 3.7 km Baisha lute fruit tree planting at both sides of project tourist road, 2 mu of experience area for ecological vegetable planting, 10 mu of wing area for lotus pond landscape, and landscape belt of Sigou turnover dam. Landscape road of ecological breeding for aquatic products:

1. 农业生态养殖区15亩，其中包括生态林地放养鸡场、天鹅、孔雀观赏区。

Agricultural ecological farming areas of 15 mu, including ecological forest chicken farm, swan and peacock viewing area.

2. 水产生态养殖区、娃娃鱼养殖观赏区0.5亩（农家乐区内水系观光）。娃娃鱼仿生态养殖区1200平方。生态土鳖养殖区1200平方（荷花池及景观鱼观赏区）。

Ecological breeding area for aquatic products and aquaculture viewing area for giant salamander of 0.5 mu (water sightseeing within agritainment). Imitation ecological farming areas for giant salamander of 1,200 m^2. Ecological woodlouse aquiculture area of 1,200 m^2 (viewing area for lotus pond and landscape fish).

3．生态畜牧业养殖区：骑马场 5 亩（林地内）。

Ecological livestock breeding area：riding stable of 5 mu (within woods).

4．农业生态养殖区的配套设施：4 亩。

Supporting facility for ecological livestock breeding area：4 mu.

生产储物间、蓄水池、泵房、办公室、养殖区房、生产资料库房、农家乐操作间、形成生态农业和观光旅游、休闲运动健身、观光度假为一体的好去处。

Production storage, reservoir, pump room, office, cultivation area room, warehouse, production goods warehouse, preparation room for agritainment form a destination integrated ecological agriculture and tourism, and leisure sports fitness.

六、项目优势：

Ⅵ. Project Advantage(s):

1．项羽庙址即在今霸王寨。它南依青山，北望汉水，青松叠翠，登高远望，美丽的城固县一览无余，五百余亩梯地形成在农业生态观光园，种植有杨梅、大樱桃、白沙枇杷、牡丹花、玫瑰花等名贵花木。

Xiangyu Temple is current Bawangzhai. It lays at the south side of green mountain, faces to Hanjiang River at north, and grows with pines. You can view the beautiful Chenggu County on its top, five hundred mu terrace land forms agriculture ecological sightseeing garden, plant wax berries, large cherries, Baisha loquat, peony, roses and other rare flowers and trees.

2．依托农业开发的汽车露营、木屋度假、爬山徒步、花海徜徉、果树采摘、生态蔬菜、果木认养等体验活动，更有映月荷塘、生命绿地、四沟塘水库、激情红枫、松林听涛、特色美食能充分让你及家人在工作、生活之余享受霸王寨带来的快乐和惬意。

Relied on agricultural development, auto-camping, holiday in log cabin, climbing the mountain on foot, wandering in flowers, picking fruits, ecological vegetables, fruit tree adoption and such experience activities, lotus pond reflecting moon, life green land, Sigou reservoir, passion red maple, listen to pine woods and special food can fully let you and your family to enjoy the happiness and leisure at Bawangzhai after work and city life.

3．与陕甘、宁川、渝鄂旅游新区域毗邻，丝路文化、汉水文化底蕴深厚，休闲娱乐项目丰富，是大众观光的理想之地。

Adjoin to new tourist area such as Shaanxi-Ganshu, Ningxia-Sichuan, Chongqin-Hubei, silk road culture and Hanjiang River culture have profound foundation, with aboudant leisure and entertainment items, which is an idea place for public tourism.

4．交通便利发达，汉中市城固县地处中国中西部两大经济区域的结合部，是汉中地区通往西南、中原、西北、华东和华北的门户和交通枢纽。汉中铁路站是我国连接西南和西北重要的铁路枢纽，联结西康、成西、阳安等铁路线。

Convenient traffic, Chenggu of Hanzhong is located at the joint part of two economy for China middle and west part, is the door and transportation junction for Hanzhong to Southwest, Central Plains, Northwest, East and North China. Hanzhong railway station is the important railroad junction to connect Southwest and Northwest of China, and joins Xi'an to Ankang, Xi'an to Chengdu and Yangpingguan to Ankang railways.

七、项目需求：

Ⅶ. Project Demand (s):

该项目建设周期长，回收期较慢，目前属于筹建初期，投资成本大，企业流动资金短缺。希望能争取到政府的补助来缓解流动资金的不足。

The project has a long building period, slow payback period, currently the project is at the initial stage, needing big amount of investment while the Company is short of flowing capital. Therefore hope to get the government financial subsidy to relieve the flowing capital insufficient.

南电电力施工安装项目
Nandian Electrical Installation Project

一、项目公司名称： 广东南电建设集团有限公司

I. Project Company Name: Guangdong Nandian Construction Engineering Co., Ltd.

二、项目公司介绍：

II. Project Company Introduction:

公司成立于2004年，具备房屋建筑总承包二级、输变电工程专业承包三级、城市及道路照明工程专业承包三级，同时取得由国家能源局南方监管局核发的承装类三级、承修类三级和承试类四级电力设施许可证。公司集建筑、电力施工双重资质，房屋建筑、构筑物工程房屋建筑、构筑物工程可承担110kV及以下输电、供电、受电电力设施的安装、维修及试验以及可经营电力销售。集团公司分别在北京市以及广东省内广州市、珠海市设立了分公司，并且在清远本土也设立了清远城建建材贸易有限公司、清远（南电）园林建设有限公司、南电（清远）售电有公司、富银通宝企业信息咨询有限公司，在广东省内获得一定知名度和影响力。

The company was founded in 2004. It possesses house building general contract second grade, power transmission and distribution specialized contract third grade, urban and road lighting specialized contract third grade, meanwhile it has obtained installation class third grade, repair class third grade and commissioning class fourth grade power facilities permit issued by South China Energy Regulatory Bureau of National Energy Administration of P. R. C.. The company integrates double qualifications of building and power construction. House construction, structure engineering house building and structure engineering could undertake installation, maintenance and test as well as operational power sales of power transmission, power supply and electric power facilities under 110kV. The group company sets up branch companies in Beijing as well as in Guangzhou and Zhuhai in Guangdong Province, set up Qingyuan Urban Construction Building Material Trading Co., Ltd., Qingyuan (Nandian) Landscape Construction Co., Ltd., Nandian (Qingyuan) Electricity Industry Co., Ltd. and Fuyin Tongbao Enterprise Information Consultancy Co., Ltd. in Qingyuan, and has obtained certain fame and influence in Guangdong Province.

三、负责人介绍：

III. Responsible Person Introduction:

董事长林国荣现任中国投资协会城镇化专业委员会基础设施中心主任、清远市政协委员、清远市工商业联合会（总商会）执委会常务委员、广东省能源协会副会长、清远市建筑业协会副会长，资深电气工程师，经常在《城市建设》等书刊中发表一些专业学术论文。

Lin Guorong, Chairman, is now the Director of Infrastructure Center of Urbanization Professional Committee, China Investment Association, CPPCC member of Qingyuan, standing committee member of executive committee of Qingyuan Chamber of Commerce and Industry (General Chamber), Vice President of Guangdong Energy Association, and Vice President of Qingyuan Construction Association. Senior electrical engineer, with frequent publication of professional academic papers in periodicals such as *Urban Construction* etc.

四、项目名称： 南电电力施工安装项目

IV. Project Name: Nandian Electrical Installation Project

五、项目概况：

V. Project Profile:

公司启用"客户的需求是我们关注的焦点"的服务模式，坚持对投产以及竣工后的项目跟踪维护服务。目前已竣工品质工程有深圳华星光配电工程、君安大厦高低压供配电工程、中央首座、东方天城以及城市百合雅居高低压配电工程、沥头安置区、凤凰安置区等一大批优质工程。

The company launches the service mode of "customer demand is our focus", and insists on tracking maintenance service for projects which have been completed and put into production. At present, completed projects of high quality include Shenzhen Huaxing Optical Distribution Project, Jun'an Building High/Low Voltage Power Supply Project, High/Low Voltage Power Distribution of Central First, Oriental City and Urban Baihe Residential Quarters, Litou Settlement Area, Phoenix Settlement Area etc.

鉴于"坚持创新、负责守信、回馈社会"的理念获得了卓越的社会信誉,于2007年度荣获"广东省诚信示范企业"、2008年荣获"线路施工、变电施工技能过硬企业"、2009年荣获全国首批"青年就业创业见习基地"、2007-2014年荣获"守合同重信用企业"、2012年荣获"首批省级电力应急救援队伍"、2014年荣获"扶贫帮困,回馈社会"单位、2016年被清远市中小企业协会授予"优秀会员单位"。

It adheres to the concept of "insisting on innovation, responsible and hones, feeding back to society", and obtains outstanding social reputation. It obtained "Guangdong Good Faith Demonstration Enterprise" in 2007, obtained "Skilled Enterprise for Line Construction and Substation Construction" in 2008, obtained "Youth Employment and Entrepreneurship Probation Base" 2009, obtained "A-level Enterprise of Credit" between 2007-2014, obtained the "First Batch of Provincial Electric Power Emergency Rescue Teams" in 2012 and obtained "Help and Support the Poor and Feed Back to Society" in 2014 respectively. It was awarded as the "Excellent Member Unit" by Qingyuan Small and Medium-sized Enterprise Association in 2016.

六、项目优势:
VI. Project Advantage(s):

电力施工安装,具有人才配备多元化、技能专业化、高学历化、人员结构年轻化、集团管理人性化的特点。多年来"以管理求效益,以质量求发展,以安全为保障,以人才为基础,以客户为上宾"的企业精神,着力于"和谐南电"的企业文化建设,使企业更加充满生机和活力。

Power construction installation, with characteristics of diversified talent configuration, professional skills, high education background, young personnel structure, and humanized group management. Over the years, the company seeks for efficiency based on management, seeks for development based on quality, and takes safety as guarantee, while regards talent a basis, focusing on the enterprise spirit of "customer oriented", and focusing on the enterprise culture construction of "harmonious Nandian", to make the enterprise filled with vitality and vigor.

七、项目需求:
VII. Project Demand(s):

希望在电力施工安装领域能与各地更多企业携手合作,共同创造一个崭新的未来。

It is expected to cooperate with more enterprises throughout the nation in power construction installation field, to jointly create a brand new future.

信息化科技创新产业互联平台建设
Construction of Interconnection Platform of Information Science & Technology Innovation Industry

一、项目公司名称：北京软道科技有限公司
I. Project Company Name：Beijing Ruandao Technology Co., Ltd.

二、项目公司介绍：
II. Project Company Introduction:

软道取名自"探索软件行业的良性发展之道"，立足企业信息化建设及其衍生领域。软道专门为科研院所、高等院校、资深专家、企事业单位、咨询公司、创新个人等具有行业和专业特长的单位和个人提供科技创新产品孵化服务，提供专业和精准的高技术支持及产品孵化整体解决方案。

Ruandao obtains its name from "exploring benign development way of software industry", and is based on enterprise informatization construction and its derivative field. Ruandao provides science and technology innovation product incubation service for units and individuals with industrial and professional expertise such as scientific research institutions, institutions of higher learning, senior experts, enterprises and public institutions, consulting firms, innovative individuals, and provides professional and accurate high-tech support and overall product incubation solution.

软道定位在TOB的信息化产业互联平台建设，借助实现具有业务深度创新和市场高价值的创新型项目形成行业创新产品群，通过联合行业既有渠道和高级资源形成行业的信息化产业互联合作，快速占领行业市场并引领新时代背景下的行业信息化发展。

Ruandao focuses on TOB's informative industrial interconnection platform construction, forms industrial innovative product groups by realizing innovative projects with deep business innovation and high market price, forms informative industrial interconnection and cooperation via combining existing channels and senior resources of the industry, occupies industrial market quickly and leads industrial information development under the background of new era.

三、负责人介绍：
III. Responsible Person Introduction:

李岗，企业信息化产业互联模式及方法的创始人，从事企业信息化规划和建设近20年，主持研发并推广了多款大型企业级应用平台产品和工业化开发工具级产品，参与和承担了多个国家十二五规划、十三五规划重点项目的信息化建设工作。

Li Gang, founder of interconnection mode of enterprise information industry. Engaged in enterprise information planning and construction for nearly 20 years, led research and development and promoted multiple large application platform products at enterprise level and industrial products at development tool level. Participated and undertook information construction for multiple key projects of the Twelfth Five-year Plan and the Thirteenth Five-year Plan of the nation.

四、项目名称：信息化科技创新产业互联平台建设
IV. Project Name：Construction of Interconnection Platform of Information Science & Technology Innovation Industry

五、项目概况：
V. Project Profile：

通过建立为企业信息化建设服务的线上和线下模式，充分发挥"产业互联云服务"和"本地化服务"不同的优势，帮助企业做好持续的信息化建设工作，支撑起企业信息化建设的刚需。

Via establishing online and offline modes for enterprise information construction, give full play to the different advantages of "industrial interconnection cloud service" and "localization service", help enterprises to conduct sustaining information construction, and support the rigid demand for enterprise information construction.

1. 机制：在送炭网上建立虚拟企业协作机制，在虚拟企业间建立"互信协作机制"。

Mechanism：Establish a virtual enterprise collaboration mechanism on carbon feed, and establish a "mutual trust and collaboration mechanism" between virtual enterprises.

2．联系：虚拟企业内部、项目合作双方及监理方的沟通交流服务。

Contact：Communication service inside virtual enterprise, between cooperative parties and supervisor of the project.

3．对接：双创项目和送炭项目的对接匹配服务。

Docking：Docking and matching service between E&I project and carbon feed project.

4．技术：联合中间件合作伙伴提供低价或免费的中间件产品支持服务。

Technology：Joint middleware partners, and provide middleware product support service of low price or free of charge.

5．人才：为虚拟企业提供人才库及匹配推荐服务，帮助刚起步的双创团队建立社会人才和高校人才相结合的可成长型协作组织。

Talent：Provide talent pool and matching recommendation service for virtual enterprises, and help E&I team at initial stage to establish a growth collaborative organization combining social talents and high school talents.

6．市场：为企业和项目合作提供创新产品库，帮助虚拟企业开展市场推广和对接企业需求服务。

Market：Provide innovative product library for enterprises and projects, and help virtual enterprises to develop market promotion and dock with enterprise demand.

六、项目优势：
VI. Project Advantage(s)：

采用线上和线下相结合的方式，线下整合技术采用拥有独创并历经八年实践验证的运行期模型驱动设计方法和技术，结合不同中间件技术的特点建立互联互通机制，连接世界中间件产品。本项目模式紧密结合当下科技创新、创新创业、产业互联、资源整合、长板效应的核心思想，同行难以模拟复制。

Adopt a method of combination of online and offline. The offline integration technology adopts an exclusive and running model drive design method and technology which has been verified by eight years of practice, establishes an interconnection mechanism by combining characteristics of different middleware technologies, and connects world middleware products. The mode of this project combines the core idea of current technology innovation, E&I, industrial interconnection, resource integration and long board effect, which is hard to be simulated or copied by counterparts.

七、项目需求：
VII. Project Demand(s):

规划每年联合研发，孵化一批科技创新产品并推向市场，同时联合多路渠道和资源快速发展壮大，脚踏实地、有规划地逐步建立起新时代背景下信息化产业支撑平台，目前正在积极寻求科技创新项目投资方向，且对企业信息化建设事业有情怀的优秀资金合作。

Plan to research & develop and incubate a batch of science and technology innovation products and promote to the market on a yearly basis, meanwhile joint multiple channels and resources to develop quickly, stand on solid ground, and establish an information industrial platform under the ground of the new era in a planned manner. At present, it is seeking for investment direction for science and technology innovation projects in an active stance, as well as excellent fund cooperation interested in enterprise information construction cause.

洞宫葬 + 互联网
Hole Palace Funeral + Internet

一、项目公司名称： 厦门大易孝德文化产业有限公司

I. Project Company Name: Xiamen Dayixiaode Cultural Industry Co., Ltd.

二、项目公司介绍：

II. Project Company Introduction:

公司是民政部中国殡葬协会会员单位，成立于 2015 年，注册资本金为 1 698 334 元人民币。公司首创 "洞宫葬 + 互联网" 模式，即地下洞宫葬 + 地面主题文化公园 + 互联网远程祭祀，真正实现节地生态安葬和文明祭祀，开创智能陵园建设先河，立志成为中国节地生态安葬标准的创建者。

The Company is the member unit of China Funeral Association of Ministry of Civil Affairs, founded in 2015, with a registered capital of RMB 1,698，334. The Company initiates the mode of hole palace funeral + Internet, i.e. underground hole palace funeral + ground theme cultural park + Internet remote sacrifice, therefore really realizes the land-saving ecological burial and civilized sacrifice, creates the intelligent cemetery construction pioneer, and resolves to be the creator of China's land-saving ecological burial.

2016 年 11 月 11 日 "洞宫葬式 + 网视祭奠" 创新项目，通过了国家科技部、工信部共同委托的第三方专业评价机构论证，作为国家科技成果，正式入选国家科技成果数据库，成为我国民生领域的重大创新科技项目。国家发改委《中国改革报》以 "优秀企业技术创新重点项目" 为标题，刊发了专题报道，进行全国推介。

On November 11, 2016, innovation project "hole palace funeral + Internet visual sacrifice" passed the argumentation by third party professional assessment agent entrusted by Ministry of Science and Technology and Ministry of Industry and Information Technology, and was selected into the national scientific and technological achievement database as the national technological achievement, and the project became the important innovative technology project in people's livelihood of China. *The China Reform Daily* of NDRC published special report in title of Major Project for Technology Innovation by Outstanding Enterprise to carry out national wide promotion.

大易孝德在我国推行的树葬、草坪葬、花坛葬、海葬等生态葬式的基础上提出了 "洞宫葬 + 互联网" 模式，可真正实现节地生态、入土为安、一存千古、文明祭祀的目标，得到政府与百姓的普遍认可，或将成为 21 世纪人类殡葬祭祀模式的主流。

Dayixiaode raised mode of "hole palace funeral + Internet" on basis of promoting tree burial, grassland burial, flower bed burial and such ecological burial national wide, which can really realize goals of land saving, bones buried, storage through the ages, resolving the current problems and eliminating the root causes and civilized sacrifice, and acquired wide acceptance by government and ordinary people, and may become the main mode for twenty-first century human funeral and sacrifices.

三、负责人介绍：

III. Responsible Person Introduction:

沈杰斌，字炫旭，号大易山人，资深周易文化研究专家、民俗师、风水专家，主攻寺庙、陵园、古建、旅游景区的风水策划，廿年从业经验，操盘湘西凤凰古城、衡阳双水湾、万石千骨葬、海沧石峰岩寺、南靖紫云寺、龙岩龙华寺等风水策划，在业界享有盛誉。经过八年的苦心钻研，反复论证，携自主研发的二十几项专利技术，形成 360° 完整行业壁垒。

Shen Jiebin, also named Xuanxu or called Dayishanren, is an experienced expert for the Book of Changes study, folk-custom expert and geomancy specialist. He assaults the main targets in geomancy planning for temple, cemetery, ancient architecture and tourist attractions, has 20 years experiences in this field. He operated the geomancy planning for Fenghuang of Southwest of Hunan, Henyang Shuangshuiwan, Wanshi Qianguzang, Haicang Shifeng temple, Nanjing Ziyuan Temple, Longyan Longhua Temple and alike, with high reputation in the field. After eight-year's study, through repeatedly demonstration, formed 3600 completed industry barrier with over 20 patent technologies.

四、项目名称：洞宫葬+互联网

Ⅳ. Project Name：Hole Palace Funeral + Internet

五、项目概况：

Ⅴ.Project Profile:

把传统几千年的山体表层孤坟造墓模式，转变为利用自然山体挖洞穴、隧道，在洞穴、隧道内建设多层次架体集约式安放骨灰盒，降低成本、利国惠民。同时，真正把陵园从地上转化为地下，既顺应入土为安民俗，又保护青山绿水、节地环保。

Change the mode of grave building on mountain surface for thousands of years to place cremation urn collectively on multilayer frame in caves and tunnel by utilizing caves and tunnels excavated on natural mountain body, to reduce costs, seeking both temporary and permanent solutions and benefiting both country and the people. Simultaneously, transfer the cemetery from ground to underground, which not only follow the bones buried customer, but also protect green mountains and rivers as well as save land and protect environment.

结合互联网、物联网实现点对点多功能祭祀。依托墓地刚性需求，配合"金灵台、远程祭祀、长明灯、孝心元宝"等互联网产品，形成长期用户沉淀和线上高频消费，构筑全球最大的殡葬祭祀O2O全价值链服务平台。

Combine Internet and Web of Things to realize point-to-point multifunction sacrifice. Relied on rigid demands for cemetery, acting in concert with Internet products such as gold Lingtai, remote sacrifice, incandescent light and filial Yuanbao, form long-term user precipitation and online high frequency consumption, build globally largest O2O full value chain service platform for funeral and sacrifice.

六、项目优势：

Ⅵ. Project Advantage(s):

1．模式得到普遍认可，受邀考察项目36个。已筛选优质项目六个，确定样板示范项目两个，正在完善相关手续，计划年内开工建设。

In investigating 36 projects through invitation, the mode is commonly accepted. Selected 6 quality projects, confirmed 2 model projects, which are currently in process of perfecting the procedures and will be started within half year.

2．寻求以PPP模式与各地政府合作，目前完成意向合作项目五个。

Sought PPP mode to be cooperated with local governments, and completed 5 intentional cooperation projects.

3．已与民政部一零一研究所形成战略合作，争取2018年下半年样板工程示范项目获民政部授牌，同时召开研讨会和现场会，"洞宫葬+互联网"确定为行业标准，以点带面，在全国推广。

Reached strategic cooperation with 101 Research Institution of Ministry of Civil Affairs, we are striving to acquire the award for example demonstration project in second half of 2018, simultaneously call for seminar and site meeting to confirm the industrial standards for "hole palace funeral + Internet" so as to let point promoting whole as well as promote nationwide.

4．成立专业团队实施"一城一园"战略，实现"促项目、融资金、布渠道"目标。

Establish professional team to implement strategies of "One-city and One Cemetery", and realize the goals of "promoting project, capital raising and building channels".

七、项目需求：项目开发、专利授权、区域加盟。

Ⅶ. Project Demand(s)：Project development, patent licensing, region franchising.

舒理他纯益生菌发酵酸奶
Cherita Pure probiotic Fermented Yogurt

一、项目公司名称：北京颐和村科技有限公司

I. Project Company Name：Beijing Yihecun Tech.Ltd

二、项目公司介绍：

II. Project Company Introduction：

公司成立于2004年，由专业从事生物、食品技术开发人员组成，首家推出"酸奶直投式发酵剂"产品替代进口，获教育部科技进步奖。应用鼠李糖乳杆菌LGG发酵酸奶获得国家发明专利，每100克"舒理他酸奶"含有1000亿LGG菌株，是益生菌酸奶的旗舰产品，获北京市新技术新产品证书。

The Company, founded in 2004, consists of developers engaging in biology and food technologies, firstly launched the directed vat set (DVS) for yogurt to replace the imported similar products which awarded with technology advancement award by Education Ministry of Education. Fermented yogurt with lactobacillus rhamnosus (LGG) acquired national patent for invention, every 100 g Cherita yogurt includes 100 billion LGG bacterial strains, which is the flagship product for probiotic yogurt and gained the Beijing new technology & new product certificate.

三、负责人介绍：

III. Responsible Person Introduction：

董事长凌凡先生(人民大学EMBA)主持"旺季蔬菜保鲜技术"在三北地区和部队推广，主持"纯益生菌发酵酸奶"产品获国家发明专利和北京市新技术产品证书，曾任北大绿色科技公司董事、香港佛教杂志撰稿人。协同技术总监凌海波女士（北京大学生物系毕业）主持开发"直投式发酵剂"产品填补国内空白。

Chairman Mr Lin Fan (EMBA of People's University) directed the promotion of preservation technology for peak season vegetables in North China, Northeast China and northwest China as well as in PLA, directed the pure probiotic fermented yogurt product which acquired the national patent of invention and Beijing new technology & new product certificate, was the director of Beida Green Technology Co., Ltd., the writer of Buddhist in Hong Kong, cooperated with MS Lin Haibo, the Technology Director (graduated in Department of Beijing University) in directing the development for DVS products which filled the domestic gap.

四、项目名称：舒理他纯益生菌发酵酸奶

IV. Project Name：Cherita Pure probiotic Fermented Yogurt

五、项目概况：

V. Project Profile:

普通酸奶的乳酸菌不耐胃酸，不能活着抵达肠道，对人体健康的功效有限。北京颐和村科技有限公司经过十年研发，采用耐受胃酸且功效明确的超级益生菌"鼠李糖乳杆菌LGG"经过24小时深度发酵制成酸奶，不添加香精，自然发酵风味，已取得中国发明专利，是益生菌酸奶的旗舰产品。"舒理他"品牌取自"鼠李糖乳杆菌"的谐音，舒理他益生菌具有增强人体免疫、治疗肠道疾病、预防呼吸道疾病等明显功效。

The lactic acid bacteria of common yogurt is not resist to gastric acid, cannot actively reach the intestines, therefore has limited efficiency to health. Through 10-year's R&D, Beijing Yihecun Technology Co., Ltd. adopts lactobacillus rhamnosus (LGG), the super probiotics resisting to gastric acid and with confirmed efficiency, to prepare the yogurt through 24 h deep fermentation without adding essence. It has the natural fermentation flavor, acquired the national patent of invention, and is the flag product of probiotic yogurt. Brand "Cherita" is so called from the Chinese partial tone of lactobacillus rhamnosus. Cherita probiotics has the confirmed functions of improving the human immunity, treating intestines problem and preventing respiratory diseases.

研究表明，肠道健康影响着生命健康，在日常饮食中补充益生菌已经被越来越多的人采纳，健康饮食显得愈发重要。利用舒理他益生菌开发有益于中老年人、减肥人士、年轻女士、成长期儿童的营养功效酸奶，有巨

大的市场潜力。

The studies indicate that the intestinal health impact the life health, more and more people adopt the method of supplementing probiotics in daily diets as the diet healthy becoming more and more important. The nutritious yogurt developed for middle aged and elderly people, people losing weights, young ladies and growing children by utilizing Cherita probiotics has huge marketing potential.

六、项目优势：
VI. Project Advantage(s):

舒理他酸奶的发酵菌株不是普通的嗜热链球菌和保加利亚乳杆菌，而是健康人体自有的超级益生菌，在全球已有上百篇临床报告证明对人体的健康作用，其功效被几十个发达国家所公认，在我国也被列入允许婴幼儿食用的益生菌目录，百度"鼠李糖乳杆菌"可查阅健康功效。舒理他酸奶出厂时，检测活菌益生菌数量达到了100克含1000亿活菌以上，远高于国家标准。

The fermentation strain for Cherita yogurt is not the common streptococcus thermophilus or Lactobacillus bulgaricus, is the super probiotics benefiting the human body, over 100 clinic reports throughout the World have evidenced the healthy function to human body, its efficiency has been recognized by dozens of developed countries, it also listed to the probiotics content for infant food permitted by our country. For healthy functions, you can search "actobacillus rhamnosus" in Baidu website. In factory test for Cherita yogurt, the number of live bacteria probiotics tested is 100 billion live probiotics per 100 g, which is higher than the national standards.

七、项目需求：推广产品、项目融资、市场拓展。
VII. Project Demand(s)：Marketing products, project financing and market expending.

智慧社区·智慧停车
Wisdom Community · Wisdom Parking

一、项目公司名称：江阴星光文化传媒有限公司
Ⅰ. Project Company Name：Jianyin Star Culture Communication Co., Ltd.

二、项目公司介绍：
Ⅱ. Project Company Introduction:

公司成立于 2010 年，主营媒体领域投资以及"智慧社区"、"智慧停车"项目投资与建设。团队组建于 2009 年，2011 年经由相关部门审批成功入驻高新区创意产业园，2014 年上海股权交易中心挂牌，2015 年被评为"一级广告资质企业"，2016 年被评为"江苏省科技型中小企业"，同年，公司媒体板块"道闸广告媒体"与"江阴电台"共同被评为"商会推荐媒体"，中国广告协会会员，江阴广告商会副会长单位。

The company was founded in 2010, which is mainly engaged in the investment on media field as well as investment and construction of "Wisdom Community" and "Wisdom Parking" projects. The team was founded in 2009, successfully entered the Creative Industrial Park in the High-tech Zone via approval of related department in 2011, listed into Shanghai Stock Exchange in 2014, evaluated as "Grade I Advertising Qualification Enterprise" in 2015, and evaluated as the "Jiangsu Province Middle and Small-sized Technology-based Enterprises" in 2016, in the same year, the company's media blocks of "Gate Advertising Media" and "Jiangyin Radio" were jointly evaluated as "Media Recommended by the Chamber of Commerce". It is also the member of China Advertising Association and Vice President Company of Jiangyin Advertising Chamber of Commerce.

三、负责人介绍：
Ⅲ. Responsible Person Introduction:

梅刚，公司董事长，生于 1988 年，中国广告协会会员，江阴广告商会副会长。2009 年一手创立星光传媒公司，公司主营媒体领域投资以及"智慧社区"、"智慧停车"项目投资与建设。经过七年的建设发展，星光传媒共服务于本土企业 1700 家，外来企业 200 家，上市公司 53 家，服务过江阴本土上市公司超八成。江阴星光文化传媒公司是目前江阴最大、行业最强的广告传媒公司。

Mei Gang, Chairman of the company, born in 1988, member of China Advertising Association, and Vice President of Jiangyin Advertising Chamber of Commerce. He founded Star Media Company in 2009, managing the investment on media field as well as investment and construction of "Wisdom Community" and "Wisdom Parking" projects. Over construction and development of 7 years, Star Media has provided services for 1,700 local enterprises, 200 external enterprises, and 53 listed companies, among which local listed companies in Jiangyin exceed 80%. At present, Jiangyin Star Culture Media Co., Ltd. is the biggest and strongest advertising media company of the industry in Jiangyin.

四、项目名称：智慧社区·智慧停车
Ⅳ. Project Name：Wisdom Community · Wisdom Parking

五、项目概况：
Ⅴ. Project Profile:

道闸媒体项目是江阴星光文化传媒有限公司独家专利设备，基本覆盖全市各小区、停车场、乡镇，占据 95% 市场份额。智慧社区、智慧停车项目实现了"车位预约"、"车位共享"、"在线支付"等功能。

The Gate Media project is the exclusive patent of Jiangyin Star Culture Communication Co., Ltd., almost covering all communities, parking lots, villages and towns, and accounting for 95% mark share. The Wisdom Community and Wisdom Parking projects realize functions such as "parking reservation", "parking space sharing" and "online payment" etc.

1．与江阴银行（江阴农村商业银行）联名银行卡"星光慧通"停车补贴与优惠。
The co-branded card "Star Huitong" for parking subsidies and preferential jointly developed with Jiangyin Bank (Jiangyin Rural Commercial Bank).

2．加强物业线上管理体系，提升社区整体安保。
It enhances online property management system, and promotes the overall community security.

3．全自动识别、手动进出无牌车、交接班记录、车辆信息记录与查询、多元化抬杆规则、手持设备管理远程抬杆等功能。
It possesses functions such as full-automatic identification, manual access for vehicles without license, shift recording,

vehicle information recording and query, diversified bar lifting rules, handheld equipment management, remote bar lifting etc.

4．职能界定清晰，岗亭端和管理端拥有不同权限，双方各取所长，避免传统平台的缺陷。

Function definition is clear, while watch box and management have different permissions, and both parties could take advantages of each, to avoid defects of traditional platforms.

5．停车场管理方无纸化办公，财务报表、信息记录需求均由系统集成。

Paperless office for parking lot management, while financial statements and information records need system integration.

6．手机APP能一键寻找车位、提供最新的出行资讯、提供便捷的交管服务、车位预订及线路导航、公布停车场实时车位及收费信息等。

Mobile APP could find parking space by pressing one key, provide latest travel information, provide convenient traffic management service, parking space reservation and route navigation, publicize parking lot real-time parking space and charge information etc.

7．多元化线上支付：市名卡支付、二维码扫码支付、线上APP支付、线上微信公共平台支付。

Diversified online payment：Citizen card payment, QR code scanning payment, online APP payment, online Wechat payment, and public platform payment.

8．汽车后市场合作：在线预约洗车、电子停车券、在线二手车评估交易、电子车牌功能等。

Automobile post-market cooperation：Functions such as online car wash reservation, electronic parking coupons, online second-hand car evaluation and trade, and electronic license plate etc.

六、项目优势：

Ⅵ. Project Advantage(s):

1．政策优势

Policy Advantage(s)

公司位于国家高新区创业园内，是国内首批认证高新科技项目资质企业，享受国家十三五期间科技创新规划政策，并积极参与"中国制造2025"、"互联网＋"的科技创新型企业申报，同时智慧社区项目得到了省委省政府的高度重视及认可。

The company is located in the Innovation Park of National High-tech Zone, and is among the first batch of certified high-tech project qualification enterprises in China. It enjoys the national technology innovation planning policies during the period of the 13th National Five-year Plan. Besides, it takes an active stance in participating the declaration of scientific and technological innovation enterprises of "Made in China 2025" and "Internet ＋". Meanwhile, the Wisdom Community project has attracted high attention and has been highly recognized by provincial committee and government.

2．人才优势

Talent Advantage(s)

智慧社区、智慧停车项目拥有21人技术开发团队，团队成员均是国内外知名大学研究生以上学历。

The Wisdom Community and Wisdom Parking projects possess a technical development team composed of 21 persons, and team members are postgraduates or above from domestic and foreign famous universities.

3．资本优势

Capital Advantage(s)

智慧社区、智慧停车项目，与江阴银行（江阴农村商业银行，股票代码：002807）密切合作，2017年7月28日，星光传媒与江阴银行联名信用卡——"星光慧通"发行，隆重推向市场。

As for the Wisdom Community and Wisdom Parking projects, under close cooperation with Jiangyin Bank (Jiangyin Rural Commercial Bank, share code：002807), in 28th July, 2017, the co-branded credit card jointly developed by Star Media and Jiangyin Bank - "Star Huitong" was issued, and introduced to the market grandly.

七、项目需求：

Ⅶ. Project Demand(s):

政策需求：项目科技成果专利申请。

Policy demand：Patent application for project scientific and technological achievements.

人才需求：软件技术开发人才APP研发团队的引入。

Talent demand：Introduction of software technology developers and app R&D teams.

资本需求：IPO。推广需求：科技众筹，城市推广。

Capital demand：IPO. Promotion demand：Science and technology crowd funding, and city promotion.

蒙古国矿业投资开发
Mongolian Mining Investment and Development

一、项目公司名称：蒙古国晋华集团
Ⅰ. Project Company Name：Mongolia Jin Hua Group

二、项目公司介绍：
Ⅱ. Project Company Introduction:

2004年在蒙古国注册成立，集团总部在蒙古国首都乌兰巴托，旗下有六家公司，另在中国首都北京、香港特区设有分公司。集团业务涉及五大板块，包括能源、矿产、环保、金融、国际贸易。能源方面，有总投资近300亿元的坑口电厂，拥有3000兆瓦的机组，此电厂可以称得上蒙古国最大的电厂。矿业方面，涉及投资有19个矿。环保方面，与江苏博大共同开发蒙古国污水厂项目。金融方面，晋华集团还收购了一家俄罗斯在蒙古国开的银行。该银行的收购保障了中国商人在蒙古国生意投资的安全性。如今，晋华集团旗下的所有涉及行业，每年可为蒙古国创造人民币约七八百万的税收。

Incorporated in Mongolia in 2004, the group headquarters is in Ulan Bator, the capital of Mongolia, and six companies are subordinate to it; additionally, it has branches in Beijing, the capital of China, and Hong Kong SAR. The group's business involves five sectors including energy, mineral products, environmental protection, finance and international trade. In terms of energy, it has a coal mine mouth power plant with the total investment of nearly RMB 30 billion, which has the 3,000 MW set, and this power plant can be considered as the largest power plant in Mongolia. In terms of mining industry, it is involved in the investment of 19 mines. In terms of environmental protection, it has developed Mongolian sewage plant project with Jiangsu Boda, and in terms of finance, Jin Hua Group has also purchased a Russian bank in Mongolia. Acquisition of this bank has guaranteed safety of the Chinese businessmen's business investment capital in Mongolia. Nowadays, all the related industries subordinate to Jin Hua Group can create the tax of about RMB seven or eight million for Mongolia.

三、负责人介绍：
Ⅲ. Responsible Person Introduction:

史光荣，汉族，中共党员，现担任蒙古国晋华集团有限公司董事长、蒙古国晋商总商会会长。1990年踏上蒙古土地，根据市场向导和需求与蒙古商人共同成立了中蒙双马公司（合资），迈开了国际贸易商路。随着业务发展的良好态势，借助蒙古的有利条件、有利资源、有效人脉，在2004年8月27日成立了属于独资的皮制加工厂进行经营，2007年开始介入矿产和能源的开发与利用，目前已拥有矿产资源的探矿证和开采证，项目有铬矿、萤石矿、钨矿、铅锌矿、铁锌矿、煤矿等多金属矿。

Shi Guangrong, Han nationality, member of the Communist Party of China, serves as President of Mongolia Jin Hua Group Co., Ltd. and Chairman of Mongolian Shanxi Merchants Chamber of Commerce currently. He set foot on Mongolia in 1990 and according to the market guide and demand, founded Sino-Mongolian Double Horse Company (joint venture) with Mongolian businessmen to start the international trade. With the good situation of business development and by virtue of the advantages, favorable resources and effective contacts in Mongolia, he immediately founded a solely-invested leather processing plant to conduct business on August 27, 2004; in 2007, he began to get involved in the development and utilization of mineral products and energy; currently, he has had the prospecting and mining permits of the mineral resources, and there are the polymetallic ores such as chrome ore, fluorite ore, tungsten ore, lead-zinc ore, iron-zinc ore and coal mine in his project.

四、项目名称：蒙古国矿业投资开发
Ⅳ. Project Name：Mongolian Mining Investment and Development

五、项目概况：
Ⅴ. Project Profile:

晋华集团在蒙古国以独立或合作形式分别投资开发了东方省马塔德苏木8亿吨储量褐煤矿（动力煤）、中戈壁省戈壁乌塔尔苏木和东戈壁省乌日根苏木萤三石矿、中戈壁省温德苏木锰矿、戈壁阿尔泰省阿尔泰市铬铁矿、中戈壁省戈壁沃物苏木锌矿、铁矿、金矿等十多个探矿权和采矿权，目前已完成上述矿权的普查、详查以及开采前相关准备工作。未来主要以多种方式联合境内外具有资源优势、资金优势及人才优势的企业共同开发，建立国内、国际矿业投资基地。

Jin Hua Group has invested and developed more than 10 prospecting and mining rights including the brown coal mines (steam coals) of 800 million tons in Matad cyM of Dornod Province, fluorite ore in Govi-Ulttal cyM of Dundgovi Province and Wuenigr cyM of Dornogovi Procine, manganese ore in Wind cyM of Dundgovi Province, chrome iron ore in Altay City of Govi-Altai Province, zinc ore, iron ore and gold ore in Govi-Waugh of Dundgovi Province respectively in the independent or cooperative form in Mongolia, and the general survey, detailed survey and the relevant preparations before mining have been completed for the mineral rights above. In the future, the domestic and overseas enterprises of the resource advantages, capital advantages and talent advantages will be mainly united in multiple ways to conduct the joint development and establish the domestic and international mining industry investment bases.

六、项目优势：
VI. Project Advantage(s):

1．拥有权威专业的矿产专家，是国内民营企业进入蒙古国投资的先行者，对蒙古国的法律法规风土人情有深入全面的了解。

It has the authoritative and professional mineral experts, and as the pioneer of the domestic private enterprises entering Mongolia to make investment; it has the thorough and comprehensive understanding of the laws and regulations as well as local customs and practices in Mongolia.

2．矿产资源种类繁多，比如褐煤矿、萤石矿、铁矿、金矿、铬矿、铜矿、铜锌矿、锡矿等。

There is a great variety of mineral resources, such as brown coal mine, fluorite ore, iron ore, gold ore, chrome ore, copper ore, copper-zinc ore and tin ore.

3．公司旗下有蒙古国政府批准的蒙古信贷银行，可为国内企业的投资资金以及投资收益提供资金安全保护。

The Company has a Mongolian credit bank approved by the Government of Mongolia, which can protect the domestic enterprises' investment capitals as well as investment incomes.

4．公司依托蒙古国晋商商会，为国内的企业家提供全方位的项目咨询，项目考察，项目立项，项目施工等服务。

Depending on the background of Mongolian Shanxi Merchants Chamber of Commerce, the Company provides the services including the all-round project consulting, project investigation, project approval and project construction for the domestic entrepreneurs.

5．晋华集团现已成为蒙古国矿业企业环境保护、共同发展的典范。

Jin Hua Group has become a model of environmental protection and joint development among the Mongolian mining enterprises at present.

七、项目需求：
VII. Project Demand(s):

在公司日益扩大的今天，公司希望与各国投资商以共同开发矿业项目的方式来进行投资并开发，共同把蒙古国的矿业开发利用起来。

Today when the Company is expanding day by day, the Company hopes to conduct investment and development in the way of developing the mining project together with the investors from all countries to jointly develop and utilize the mining industry in Mongolia.

中医养生百家秘方
Hundreds of Secret TCM Recipes of Health Maintenance

一、项目公司名称：重庆少善世家生物科技有限公司
I . Project Company Name：Chongqing SSAF Biotechnology Co., Ltd.

二、项目公司介绍：
II . Project Company Introduction:

少善世家是一家致力于健康养生产业的多元化股份制民族企业，横跨医疗、中草药、保健品、中医药化妆品、健康养生教育等诸多领域，拥有一批精干的管理人员和一支高素质的专业技术团队。公司搭建全新的健康养生产业平台、关联健康数据、融汇健康养生项目、打造全球无界联盟O2O健康服务平台，未来将在全国布局263家地级市分公司，36000家社区服务点，同时建立公益中医院，

SSAF is a diversified joint-stock national enterprise devoted to the health maintenance industry, which is involved in many fields such as medical treatment, Chinese herbal medicine, health care products, TCM cosmetics and health maintenance education. It has a batch of capable management staffs and a high-quality professional technical team. It has set up the brand-new health maintenance industry platform, has associated the health date and integrated the health maintenance projects, and has created the global unbounded union O2O health service platform. In the future, it will arrange 263 branches in the prefecture level cities, 36,000 community service points and establish the TCM hospitals for public interest across the country.

三、负责人介绍：
III . Responsible Person Introduction:

徐文睿，公司董事长，旗下公司有重庆信沐科技有限公司、重庆龙越汇商贸有限公司、重庆顺通报关有限公司、重庆飞米科技有限公司，曾任某知名互联网农业公司总经理，有多年品牌推广和产品运营经验，精于管理，善于用人。

Xu Wenrui, President of the Company, was former General Manager of a well-known Internet agricultural company, and his subsidiary companies include Chongqing Xinmu Technology Co., Ltd., Chongqing Longyuehui Trading Co., Ltd., Chongqing Shuntong Customs Clearance Co., Ltd. and Chongqing Feimi Technology Co., Ltd., with the brand promotion and production operation experience for many years. He is proficient in management and knows how to make proper use of personnel.

四、项目名称：中医养生百家秘方
IV . Project Name：Hundreds of Secret TCM Recipes of Health Maintenance

五、项目概况：
V . Project Profile：

1．依托国家"一带一路"相关政策，结合公司相关健康养生文化，通过现有会员健康大数据，收集民间药食同源专利处方，建立"健康养生大课堂"，覆盖全国社区服务养生体验店，创立"健康养生联盟"，努力发展公益事业，创办"中医福利医院"，造福社会。

Relying on the national policies related to the "Belt and Road" and combined with the Company's relevant health maintenance cultures, it has collected the folk medicine-and-food homologus patent prescriptions; established Health Maintenance Class; covered the community service health maintenance experience stores nationwide and founded Health Maintenance Union; made efforts t to develop the public good and found Welfare Hospital of TCM to benefit the society by the existing big data of member health.

2．战略合作伙伴重庆中医少林堂，经过一百多年的发展，现已成为最具规模化、现代化和专业化的民间医药研发机构之一，其研发的产品包含了千年传承下来的上千副独家秘方，并获得38项国家专利和国家非物质文化遗产证明，主要涵盖营养保健产品、自然医学产品、草本护理日用系列产品、家庭养生护理品、节能环保产

品以及中草药等诸多方面。

Its strategic partner Chongqing TCM Shaolintang has become one of the most scalable, modern and professional folk medicine research and development institutions after the development of more than one hundred years. The products, which are researched and developed by it, include thousands of unique recipes inherited for thousands of years, and they have obtained 38 national patents and national intangible cultural heritage certificates. They mainly cover many aspects such as the nutrition and health care products, natural medical products, herb care products of daily series, family health maintenance and nursing products, energy saving and environment-friendly products as well as Chinese herbal medicine.

3．现拥有"五行膏"、"掌灸"、"汉式咖啡"三款主打产品，经近十年的临床实验，均为独家秘方配制，专注于改善人类亚健康状态，如：颈椎病、腰椎病等症状。

It has three main products including "Wuxing Cream", "Palm moxibustion" and "Chinese-style Coffee", which have been for the clinical use for nearly ten years. All of them are prepared according to the unique secret recipes and focus on improving the human's sub-health status, such as：cervical spondylosis, lumbar spondylosis and other symptoms.

4．拥有近800平米会员体验馆，为人们提供经络养生、经道养生、健康保养、中医预防养生、减压放松等服务。

It has a nearly 800 m^2 member experience hall to provide the services such as meridian health maintenance, meridian vessel health maintenance, health care, TCM prevention health maintenance and stress relaxation.

六、项目优势：
Ⅵ. Project Advantage(s):

有最具规模化、现代化和专业化的民间医药研发机构——少林堂的助力，中医文化底蕴更加深厚。部分产品配方获国家专利与国家非物质文化遗产证明，更加权威。产品来源有据可查，真实可靠。

Assisted by the most scalable, modern and professional folk medicine research and development institution – Shaolintang, it has the more profound cultural deposits. Some product recipes have obtained the national patents and national intangible cultural heritage certificates and have been more authoritative. The product sources are well documented, and are true and reliable.

七、项目需求：
Ⅶ. Product Demand(s):

推广产品及市场拓展。在医疗保健市场供需失衡、健康知识缺乏的情况下，许多人无法找到适合自己的健康管理方法，如何摆脱"亚健康"状态，成为人们最为关注的焦点。望通过产品的推广以及市场的拓展，满足人们所需。

Product promotion and market expansion. In the case of the supply and demand imbalance in health care market and the lack of health knowledge, many people cannot find the health management methods suitable for themselves. How to get rid of the "sub-health" status becomes the focus that people are most concerned about. It expects to meet the people's demands by the product production and market expansion.

赛益德民族特色产品
Saiyide Products with National Characteristics

一、项目公司名称：青海赛益德民族服饰有限公司

I. Project Company Name: Qinghai Saiyide National Clothing Co., Ltd.

二、项目公司介绍：

II. Project Company Introduction:

公司位于青海省海东市高铁新区中关村，注册资本为15000万元人民币，是一家中外合资企业。公司自成立以来，一直秉承"信誉至上、质量第一、绿色环保"的经营理念，引进国外现代化管理技术。公司主要经营民族服饰、民族用品、民族工艺品、床上用品、针纺织品加工及销售，经营国家禁止和指定公司经营以外的进出口商品，经营进出口代理业务。

Located in Zhongguancun, Gaotie New District, Haidong City, Qinghai Province, the Company is a sino-foreign joint venture with the registered capital of RMB 150,000,000. Since its establishment, the Company has always adhered to the operation idea of "Reputation First, Quality First, Green and Environmental Protection", and has introduced the foreign modern management technology. The Company is mainly engaged in the processing and sales of the national clothes, national articles, national crafts, beddings and knitgoods, engaged in the import and export commodities in addition to those banned by the state or operated by the companies designated and engaged in the import and export agent services.

三、负责人介绍：

III. Responsible Person Introduction:

公司董事长魏福忠为当地民营企业家，其名下青海建渊房地产开发有限公司在当地有多处房地产开发项目，在征地拆迁、解决下岗职工再就业方面起到了至关重要的作用。公司副董事长ELSAID拥有先进的国际管理经验及多年的国际营销策略。

President of the Company Wei Fuzhong is a local private entrepreneur, and Qinghai Jianyuan Real Estate Development Co., Ltd., under his name, has many real estate development projects in the local place, and it has played the crucial role in land demolition and reemployment of the laid-off workers; Vice President of the Company ELSAID has the advanced international management and operation experience and the international marketing mode for years.

四、项目名称：赛益德民族特色产品

IV. Project Name: Saiyide Products with National Characteristics

五、项目概况：

V. Project Profile:

公司地处"一带一路"经济带，沿线多为少数民族国家，多数地区为藏、回、蒙古、撒拉族等53个少数民族聚集地，具有丰富的民族文化底蕴，在推广民族服饰、民族用品、民族工艺品领域具有先天的优势和市场。公司具有丰富的进出口贸易和国际化销售经验，产品均符合国际"绿色环保"要求，在原料、生产加工、运输环节严格把关，杜绝不达标产品投入市场，推广民族服饰及用品符合"一带一路"促进共同发展实现共同繁荣的框架思路。

The Company is located in the economic zone of the "Belt and Road" along which most are the minority countries; as the gathering place of 53 minorities such as the Tibetan nationality, the Hui nationality, the Mongol nationality and the Salar nationality and this zone has the rich national cultural deposits and has the congenital advantages and market in promoting the national clothes, national articles and national crafts; the Company has the rich import and export trading and international sales experience. All the products conform to the international requirements of "Green and Environment-friendly" and are strictly controlled in the links of raw materials, production and processing and transportation, and the substandard products are completely eradicated to be put into the market. Promotion of the national clothes and articles conforms to the framework thought of promoting the common development and realizing the common prosperity of "the Belt and Road".

六、项目优势：

VI. Project Advantage(s):

公司所在地为藏、回、撒拉、蒙古族等聚集地，具有丰富的民族文化底蕴。公司产品在保留原有民族特色的基础上，应用国际化设计理念和印花技术，趋向于方便、快捷、商务等时代潮流，产品有生活装、商务装、宗教职业装等。

The place where the Company is located in the gathering place of the Tibetan nationality, the Hui nationality, the Salar nationality, the Mongol nationality and other nationalities, and it has the rich national cultural deposits; based on retaining the original national characteristics, the Company's products apply the international design idea and printing technique and tend to the age trend of convenience, fastness business, etc. and the products include the life wear, formal wear, religious occupational wear and so on.

七、项目需求：

VII. Project Demand(s):

在借助"一带一路"沿线国家中小企业合作平台推广本公司民族服饰、民族用品的同时，希望致力于发展民族文化特色产品的合作者加入。

The Company expects that the partners devoted to developing the products with the national characteristics join while promoting the Company's national clothes and articles by virtue of the platform of Cooperation Between the Small and Medium-size Enterprises in the Countries along the "Belt and Road".

YESO 国际赛事高定品牌
YESO Haute Couture for International Events

一、项目公司名称：厦门伊说品牌管理有限公司

I. Project Company Name：Xiamen Yishuo Brand Management Co., Ltd.

二、项目公司介绍：

II. Project Company Introduction：

公司旗下品牌YESO，拥有品牌多品类商标知识产权，主营户外运动和生活休闲系列产品及赛车装备包袋产品，如车手专业用具包装物，赛事机构专用包装用品。YESO在为各大赛事机构及厂商队服务中，将赛车的高标准和对安全的严苛要求融入其经营理念中，并为各著名赛事机构提供经典的外观设计，辅以功能性和人体工程学设计为辅的质造产品。

The brand YESO subordinate to the Company has the brand multi-category trademark intellectual property right, and its main products include the outdoor sports and life and leisure series of products and the racing equipment bag products, such as drivers' professional equipment packaging materials and the event organizations' special packing materials. YESO has blended the racing's high standards and strict requirements on safety in its operation idea while serving the event organizations and manufacturers' teams, and it has provided the famous event organizations with the classic appearance design, supplemented with the quality products assisted by the function and human engineering design.

三、负责人介绍：

III. Responsible Person Introduction：

陈景城，YESO品牌创始人，首席设计师，厦门大学美术系毕业，戛纳电影节首邀华人手袋设计师，提倡创新及梦想驱动无限可能的原则，促成YESO从产品研发生产开始走向平台的链接。

Graduating from Department of Fine Arts, Xiamen University, Chen Jingcheng is founder and chief designer of YESO and has been the first Chinese handbag designer invited by Cannes Film Festival. He advocates the principles of innovation and dream driving the infinite possibilities and has made YESO begin to move toward the platform link from the product research & development and production.

阮惠君，公司总经理、YESO品牌负责人，曾为某上市公司总裁助理，人力行政中心代总经理，营销中心副总经理，厦门大学创业导师，多家企业战略顾问。擅长品牌推广落地及民族品牌推动，布局品牌IP产业链授权及合作，品牌运营。

Being President Assistant of a listing company, Acting General Manager of its Administrative Center and Deputy General Manager of its Marketing Center in the past, Ruan Huijun is General Manager and responsible person of YESO of the Company, and he is an entrepreneurship tutor of Xiamen University and strategy consultant of several enterprises. He is good at brand promotion and implementation as well as national brand promotion, arrangement of the brand IP industry chain authorization and cooperation, and brand operation.

四、项目名称：YESO国际赛事高定品牌

IV. Project Name：YESO Haute Couture for International Events

五、项目概况：

V. Project Profile：

YESO由一个设计师品牌一跃成为赛事文化IP品牌，专为国际赛事机构提供赛事装备、赛事纪念品，及戛纳红毯女星高端手袋定制。YESO主张以赛车的专注为原念和以赛车级别的品质为标准，以至简、超耐磨损、功能性超强以应不时之需为唯一诉求，成功用中国制造和品牌叩开向法国各大拉力赛、摩洛哥拉力赛及世界拉力锦标赛（WRC），并于2015年正式成立YESO老爷车国际文化中国事业部，成为国际汽车赛事文化在中国区的主要传播者。目前YESO已成为赛事IP品牌，集合赛事鞋帽各品类的IP授权，赋能中国制造体育IP在国际市场推动作用。15年间YESO用产品和追求产品高品质的坚持和态度，与各国际机构建立起了链接和信任，

并逐步拓开国际赛事服务商合作的品类，YESO 奠定了中国制造在国际高端赛事运动品牌服务商的地位，践行"一带一路"的精神，

YESO has become an IP brand for events and cultures from a designer brand to specially provide the event equipment and event souvenir for the international event organizations as well as the high-end handbag customization for the female stars walking the red carpet in Cannes. Advocating taking the racing concentration as intention and the racing-level quality as the standard as well as coping with the needs which may arise any time in the future with extreme simpleness, super wear-resistance and super-function as the only appeal, YESO successfully became a brand entering and being stationed in major French rallying, Moroccan rallying and WRC with the products made in China, and it formally founded YESO Vintage Car International Culture Chinese Business Unit in 2015 and became the main communicator of the international automobile event cultures in China. Currently, YESO has become an event IP brand gathering the IP authorization of event shoes and hats and enabled the promotion role of made-in-China sports IPs in the international market. During the past 15 years, YESO has built the link and trust with the international institutions with the products and its insistence in and attitude toward the products, and gradually expanded the categories that are cooperated with the international event service providers. YESO has laid the position of made-in-China products in the international high-end event sports brand service providers, and it is practicing the spirit of the "Belt and Road".

六、项目优势：
VI. Project Advantage(s):

YESO 创立于 2002 年，以匠心品牌频频打动国际高端机构，收获认可，并成为中国制造担任国际众多赛事机构服务商的先例。各大赛事活动品牌频繁曝光，品牌识别度较高，已成为各大赛事冠军车手明星御用品牌及推广品牌。

Established in 2002, YESO frequently touched the international high-end institutions with the originality brand and gained recognition, and became the precedent of made-in-China product acting as the service provider of numerous event institutions. The brand has been frequently exposed in the event activities so it has had the high brand identity, and it has become the exclusive brand and promotion brand of the championship drivers in the major events.

两次受邀戛纳电影节及金手腕晚宴。

It was invited to Cannes Film Festival and Gold Wrist Party for twice.

多次组织国外艺术家及明星车手从法国巴黎重走丝绸之路，沿途考察不同国家设计元素，推广中国民族品牌及 YESO 品牌 IP 运用。

It organized the foreign artists and star drivers to re-walk the Silk Road from Paris, France for many times to investigate the design elements of different countries along the way, promote the Chinese national brands and conduct YESO brand IP application.

七、项目需求：
VII. Project Demand(s)：

YESO 面向各大时尚、运动、户外鞋、帽、服、眼镜、赛车游戏、赛道旅游线路，共享国际赛事广告位置等进行招商，IP 授权合作及返采，IP 品类开发、IP 买断、分授权的商业模式，及 YESO 综合品类线下门店招商等。同时也需政府提供更大的平台机会或政策支持，发力中国品牌招商融资创造更为有利的条件。

YESO faces to the fashion, sports, outdoor shoes, hat, clothes, glasses, racing games, racing track travel routes, sharing international event advertising positions and so on to conduct investment attraction and YESO comprehensive category offline store investment attraction by adopting the business models such as IP authorization cooperation and, IP category development, IP buyout and sub authorization. Meanwhile, it also needs the greater platform opportunities or policy support to be provided by the government to strive to create the more favorable conditions for China's brand investment attraction and financing.

沂脉山泉饮用天然苏打水
Yimai Mountain Spring Drinking Natural Soda Water

一、项目公司名称： 临朐山旺泉矿泉水有限公司

I. Project Company Name: Linqu Shanwangquan Mineral Water Co., ltd.

二、项目公司介绍：

II. Project Company Introduction:

公司位于山东临朐甘石沟，2013年9月27日取得全国工业产品生产许可证（QS认证），是一家专门从事高端水产品生产的国有企业，天然苏打水，水源地覆盖面积14平方千米，水资源储量60多万立方米，注册资金2000万元，总投资8600万元。公司通过山东省卫生厅备案，具备生产、包装和检验能力执行"食品安全国家标准——包装饮用水"标准，引进目前国内灌装能力最大、自动化程度最高、配套合成最强的一体化生产线和先进的水处理设备系统，现拥有三条灌装生产线。公司利用优质天然苏打水，坚持天然健康的理念，开发出"沂脉山泉"、"水米粒"等高端饮用水和养生水系列。

Located in Ganshigou, Linqu county of Shandong province, the company, which has gained the national industry production license (QS certification) on September 27, 2013, is a state-owned enterprise specialized in the high-end water product production. It's a natural soda water, with a water source coverage of 14 km^2 and a storage volume of 600,000 m^3; The registered capital is RMB 20 million and a total investment is RMB 86 million. Put on records by Shandong Province Health Department, it's qualified in the production, the package, the inspection and the implementation of "Food Safety National Standards- Packaged Drinking Water" standards; By bringing in the integration production line, biggest in the filling capacity, highest in the automation degree and strongest in the support and the advanced water treatment equipment system, it has three filling production lines at present. Making use of the qualified and natural soda water, the company insists in the nature and health concept and develops a series of high-end drinking water and health maintenance water, such as Yimai Mountain Spring and Shuimili.

三、负责人介绍：

III. Responsible Person Introduction:

白兴港，男，46岁，中共党员，本科学历，现任公司总经理，企业法人，从事饮用水企业生产管理九年，具备良好的专业知识和组织领导能力，熟练掌控生产、新产品开发、现场管理、采购管理、品质管理、产品销售等公司系统。在总经理的带领下，公司目前开发生产出的"沂脉山泉"、"水米粒"等高端饮用水和养生水系列，受到广大客户的一致好评。

Bai Xinggang, male, 46 years old, CCP member, bachelor degree, the present general manager, the legal person of the enterprise, working on the drinking water production and management for 9 years, he has excellent professional knowledge and organization leading capacity, and masters the production, new product development, the site management, purchase management, quality management, and product sales. Under the leading of the general manager, the company has developed a series of high-end drinking water and health maintenance water, such as Yimai Mountain Spring and Shuimili, which are highly and consistently appreciated by the clients.

四、项目名称： 沂脉山泉饮用天然苏打水

IV. Project Name: Yimai Mountain Spring Drinking Natural Soda Water

五、项目概况：

V. Project Profile:

天然苏打水是一种稀缺的珍贵自然资源。沂脉山泉饮用天然苏打水的水源隐藏于地下深层碱性橄榄玄武岩层中，独特的地质构造使得水源中碳酸氢钠（$NaHCO_3$）平均含量达到420-460mg/L，高于340mg/L的国际标准，且PH酸碱度在7.5-8.5之间，富含锶、偏硅酸等30多种微量元素和矿物质，兼具矿泉水标准。沂脉山泉饮用天然苏打水无色无味、清澈透明，甘洌爽口，能中和人体内酸素，水中稀有活跃的小分子团，有利于人体吸

收，能够传输氧气，调节新陈代谢，有效缓解尿酸过高、痛风、胃酸过多、胃痛等症状，排除酸性废物和预防疾病，其中多种微量元素呈动态平衡状态，能促进人体器官健康生存，增强体质，给身体一个健康的环境。沂脉山泉饮用天然苏打水是国际天然苏打水中罕见的珍品。

The natural soda water is a rare and valuable natural resource. The water source of Yimai Mountain Spring Drinking Natural Soda Water is hidden deep in the alkaline olive basalt layer, whose geologic structure has made the average content of the Sodium Bicarbonate ($NaHCO_3$) in the water source reach 420-460mg/L higher than the international standard 340mg/L. What's more, its PH value is between 7.5-8.5, while it also has more than 30 trace elements and minerals like strontium and metasilicic acid. It meets the mineral water standards. Yimai Mountain Spring Drinking Natural Soda Water is clean and transparent in color and flavor but tastes sweet. It can neutralize the oxygen inside the human body. With the rare and active micro cluster, it's easy for the human body to absorb. It can deliver the oxygen, so it can adjust the metabolism. It's efficient in relieving the high uric acid, gout, hyperacidity and stomachache. It can rule out the acidic waste and prevent diseases. The trace elements are in a dynamic equilibrium state that it can promote the health operation of the human organs, strengthen the physique and offer a healthy environment for the body. Yimai Mountain Spring Drinking Natural Soda Water is a rare treasure in the international soda water products.

六、项目优势：
VI. Project Advantage(s):

1．沂脉山泉饮用天然苏打水中多种微量元素呈动态平衡，更易被人体吸收，尤其是锶和偏硅酸的含量较高，品质高于一般苏打水；

The trace elements inside Yimai Mountain Spring Drinking Natural Soda Water are in a dynamic equilibrium state, so it's easy to absorb by the body. The contents of strontium and metasilicic acid are high, so its quality is better than the common soda；

2．独有的地质条件保证水源不受污染，从广州达意隆引进先进高端的生产设备，引进美国先进的紫外线杀菌处理系统，运用严谨的生产工艺，高标准的生产流程，直接从深层火山岩层中取水，采用无空气接触一次性灌装生产技术；

The unique geological conditions have guaranteed no pollution to the water source. The advanced high-end production equipment brought in from Guangzhou Tech-Long, the ultraviolet sterilization processing system brought in from America, the strict production craft, the high-standard production process, and the water fetching from the deep volcanic layer, and the no-air contact one-time filling production technology；

3．更有效地缓解人体尿酸过高、痛风、胃酸过多、胃痛等症状，改善酸性体质等。

More efficient in relieving the high uric acid, gout, hyperacidity and stomachache, and promoting the acidic physique.

七、项目需求：
VII. Project Demand(s)：

推广产品，打造沂脉山泉品牌，开拓市场，树立良好口碑，让各界人士认识和深入了解我们的产品。

Promote the product, create the Yimai Mountain Spring brand, expand the market, build up the good reputation, make the people recognize and understand our products.

滋养臻品－松露酒
Good Nutritious Product-Truffle Wine

一、项目公司名称：北京能合碳氢化学研究所有限公司（楚雄州百草岭药业发展有限公司）
Ⅰ. Project Company Name: Beijing Nenghe Institute of Hydrocarbon Chemistry Co., Ltd. (Chuxiong Baicaoling Pharmaceutical Develop Co., Ltd.)

二、项目公司介绍：
Ⅱ. Project Company Introduction:

公司以北京石油化工学院、燃料清洁化及高效催化减排技术北京重点实验室为技术开发平台，拥有知名教授专家团队，与北京化工大学、中国矿业大学（北京）、中国农业大学、中国科学研究院等研究机构建立紧密合作关系。

With Beijing Institute of Petrochemical Technology and Beijing Key Laboratory of Fuel Cleaning and High Efficiency Catalytic Reduction Technology as the technology development platform, the Company has a group of well-known professors and experts, and has built the close cooperation relationship with the research institutions such as Beijing University of Chemical Technology, China University of Mining and Technology (Beijing), China Agricultural University and Chinese Academy of Sciences.

公司是楚雄州农业产业化经营龙头企业，国家绿色食品 A 级认证企业，云南省科技型中小企业，国家高新技术企业，集天然植物药物种植、推广、技术研究、提取加工、产品开发于一体。

It is the leading enterprise of the industrialization of agriculture in Chuxiong Prefecture, national green food Class-A certification enterprise, Yunnan Province small and medium-sized enterprise of science and technology and national new high-tech enterprise integrated with natural plant and herb planning, promotion, technology research, extracting and processing and product development.

三、负责人介绍：
Ⅲ. Responsible Person Introduction：

罗林军，北京能合碳氢董事长，北京化工大学硕士研究生毕业，长期从事产品开发拓展领域，对于产品创新、改进有丰富的经验和非凡的创意，致力于贯通融合科技与健康生活形态。

Graduating as a postgraduate student from Beijing University of Chemical Technology, President of Beijing Nenghe Hydrocarbon, Luo Linjun has been engaged in the product development and expansion. He has rich experience and extraordinary creativity in product innovation and improvement, and is devoted to integrating science and technology with the healthy lifestyle.

四、项目名称：滋养臻品－松露酒
Ⅳ. Project Name：Good Nutritious Product – Truffle Wine

五、项目概况：
Ⅴ. Project Profile：

北京能合碳氢化学研究所有限公司（楚雄州百草岭药业发展有限公司）联合研发制作松露高端养生酒，选料考究，精心生产。产品结合了时下全世界流行的松露文化，将贵族和名士的华贵、知理、守信、荣耀的精神文化加以发扬壮大，一樽优雅极致的松露酒，亦是表现了尊贵、信誉的人生态度，符合当代人们对于礼仪信用方面的需求。

Beijing Nenghe Institute of Hydrocarbon Chemistry Co., Ltd. (Chuxiong Baicaoling Pharmaceutical Develop Co., Ltd.) has jointly developed and produced the high-end truffle wine for health maintenance with the well-chosen materials and in the meticulous production way. Meanwhile, combined with the popular truffle culture all over the world at present, the product carries forward the spirit and culture of luxuriousness, sense, honesty and glory of the noble and the celebrity. A glass of elegant truffle wine also presents the life attitudes of dignity and reputation, and it conforms to the peoples' demands on etiquette and credit.

研究报告记载，菌类多糖、多肽、三萜具有增强免疫力、抗衰老、抗疲劳作用等；雄性酮有调理男女内分泌的显著功效；鞘脂类化合物在防止老年痴呆、动脉粥样硬化以及抗肿瘤、抗细胞毒性方面有明显活性。松露中含有虫草酸和腺苷，是冬虫夏草的主要成分，对预防和治疗脑血栓、脑出血、心肌梗死有显著疗效。药理研究证明，黄精能提高机体免疫功能，增强人体抗病能力，还有抗菌、降压、抗衰老、丽容颜、强精力的作用。

According to the research repot, polysaccharides, peptides and triterpenes of fungus have the role of increasing immunity, resisting aging, resisting fatigue and so on; male ketone has the significant effect of conditioning men and women's endocrine; and sphingolipid has the significant activity in preventing senile dementia and atherosclerosis as well as resisting tumor and cytotoxicity. Cordycepic acid and adenosine contained in truffle are the main ingredients of cordyceps sinensis, which have the significant effect of preventing and treating cerebral thrombosis, cerebral hemorrhage and myocardial infarction. Proved by pharmological study, polygonatum can increase the human immune function so it can strength human resistance to diseases and it also has the role of resisting bacteria, reducing blood pressure, resisting aging, beautifying appearance and increasing energy.

本款松露酒除了满足人们一般饮用的基础要求之外，在产品质量和功能方面还具有其他酒不可比拟的优势，产品具有特殊的味道，不断挑战您的味蕾，让松露几千年以来的味觉冲击在您身上延续。松露以及其他物料中积存的营养物质转变为小分子物质，融入血液中，滋养全身。本款松露酒属于稀缺高端产品，从品质、原料以及满足人们健康需求、文化诉求方面均有非常好的契合点。

In addition to the base of meeting the people's general drinking requirements, this Truffle Wine separately has the advantages which other wines cannot compare with in product quality and function. The product's special taste will continue to challenge your taste bud so that the taste impact of truffle wine for thousands of years will continue in you. The nutrients deposited in the truffle and other materials will transform to the small molecules and blend in flood to nourish your whole body. This Truffle Wine belongs to the rare high-end product, and it has the good corresponding points from the quality, materials as well as meeting the people's health demands and culture appeals.

六、项目优势：
Ⅵ. Project Advantage(s)：

本款产品不仅是一款保健养生产品，同时也是一款赋予历史文化和精神需求的文化作品，产品具有非常高的国际认可度，市场巨大。目前在中国生产厂家很少，本产品具有原材料产地优势、产品质量和先进工艺方面的技术优势。

this Product is not only a health maintenance product but also a literature work endowed with the historical culture and spiritual demands. The product has been highly approved in the world and has the huge market. Currently, there have been few manufacturers in China. This product has the advantages in the origin place of raw materials, product quality and advanced process.

七、项目需求：
Ⅶ. Project Demand(s):

寻求合作方共同打造知名品牌，同时寻求市场推广方。

to seek the partners to create the well-known brands together and need the market promoters.

校贝通云教育平台
Xiaobeitong Cloud Education Platform

一、项目公司名称: 福建省新泽尔资讯科技有限公司

I. Project Company Name: Fujian Newzer Information Technology Co., Ltd.

二、项目公司介绍:

II. Project Company Introduction:

新泽尔公司是一家集软、硬件产品设计、研发、销售、安装、服务为一体的物联网系列产品解决方案提供商,以物联网核心技术为平台,成功推出"智慧校园"、"智慧能源"、"智慧园区"、"手机支付一卡通"等物联网系统整体解决方案。公司以过硬的产品和先进的解决方案在行业中异军突起,独树一帜,同时不断完善,持续创新,不断改进系统产品的性能,以高质量的产品,先进的技术和良好的服务取信于用户。

Newzer Company is a provider of solutions to the products of IoT series, which is integrated with the software and hardware product design, research and development, sales, installation and service; with the IoT core technology as the platform, it has successfully launched the integrated solutions to the IoT systems, such as "Intelligent Campus", "Intelligent Energy", "Intelligent Park" and "Mobile Payment One-card". The Company suddenly rose and has been unique in the industry with the high-quality products and advanced solutions; meanwhile, it has continuously perfected, continued to innovate and continuously improved the performance of system products. It has won the confidence of the users with the high-quality products, advanced technology and good serviced.

三、负责人介绍:

III. Responsible Person Introduction:

苏彩通,毕业于福州大学计算机系计算机应用专业,现就读江西财经大学EMBA,新泽尔公司创始人,目前就任公司董事长兼CEO,主要负责公司战略发展及市场运营。2006年6月创立的福建省新泽尔资讯科技有限公司,主要致力于为客户提供物联网整体解决方案,并建立环境及能耗监测平台、校园平安校园云平台等多个物联网平台,被评选为"中国优秀创新企业家"、"时代功勋感动中国年度优秀人物"、"2010年度中国优秀企业家"金钻奖章等荣誉称号。

Su Caitong: graduating from Computer Application Major in Department of Computer, Fuzhou University, he is now studying EMBA in Jiangxi University of Finance and Economics. He is founder of Newzer Company and serves as President and CEO of the Company, and he is mainly responsible for the Company's strategic development and market operation. In June 2006, he established Fujian Newzer Information Technology Co., Ltd., mainly devoted to providing the IoT integrated solutions for the clients, and established the multiple IoT platforms such as the environment and energy consumption monitoring platform and campus safety cloud platform. He won the honorary titles such as "Chinese Excellent Innovative Entrepreneur", "Annual Excellent Figures Touching China of Age Feats" and Gold Diamond Prize of "2010 Annual Chinese Excellent Entrepreneur".

四、项目名称: 校贝通云教育平台

IV. Project Name: Xiaobeitong Cloud Education Platform

五、项目概况:

V. Project Profile:

公司的校贝通产品依托强大的研发实力,推出以移动便携设备为载体、采用云计算、结合校园一卡通生活场景,以校园安全为抓手,实现家校实时互动沟通,进而提升校园安全以及辅助提升校园信息化和智能化建设。

Depending on the strong research and development capacity, with the mobile portable equipment as the carrier and with the campus safety as the starting point, the Company's Xiaobeitong product adopts cloud computing, combines with the campus one-card life scene and realizes the real-tem interactive communications between the parents and the school so as to promote the campus safety as well as assist in promoting the campus information and intelligence construction.

通过校贝通云平台＋大数据＋智能硬件的综合解决方案，可以实现全面保障学生人身安全，生理卫生健康及心理健康，帮助教委职能部门和学校进行快捷高效的政务校务管理，架起家长与学校的沟通桥梁，实现"家校智能互动"的智能应用。

The comprehensive solution of Xiaobeitong Cloud Platform + big data + intelligent hardware can comprehensively safeguard the students' personal safety, physiological health and psychological health, help the functional departments of Education Commission and the schools to conduct the rapid and efficient administration and school affairs management, erect the communication bridge between the parents and the schools to realize the intelligent application of "Parent-School Intelligent Interaction".

我们将为学校及学生家长免费提供校贝通云教育管理平台和APP，并与运营商合作，推出不同的套餐模式，供学生家长选择。

We will provide the Xiaobeitong Cloud Education Management Platform and APP for free, and will cooperate with the operator to launch different package modes for the schools as well as the students and parents to choose from.

未来，校贝通将继续深度开发家校互动平台，培养新的市场和用户习惯，为用户提供更专业、更深度以及更高效的定制化服务，为用户创造价值，也为公司赢得客户的信赖和良好的口碑，增强核心竞争力，把校贝通打造成教育行业的龙头品牌。

In the future, Xiaobeitong will continue the in-depth development of the parent-school interaction platform, cultivate the new market and user habits, provide the users with the more professional more in-depth and more efficient customized services, create the value for the users, and also win the clients' trust and good reputation and strengthen the core competitiveness for the Company, and create Xiaobeitong into the leading brand in the educational industry.

六、项目优势：
VI. Project Advantage(s):

1．完美整合校园考勤、校园消费、交通出行等物联网运用。

Perfectly integrate the IoT applications such as campus attendance, campus consumption and transportation.

2．采用大数据技术，对学生、老师、家长所记录的数据进行分析。

Adopt the big data technology to analyze the data recorded by the students, teachers and parents.

3．语音、视频、多媒体等沟通方式让信息更直观。

The communication modes such as voice, video and multi-media enable the information to be more visual.

4．为孩子在德、智、体方面提供更多的内容服务。

Provide more content service for the children in terms of virtue, wisdom and sports.

七、项目需求：
VII. Project Demand(s)：

推广校贝通云教育平台、智能可穿戴设备，招募城市合伙人或代理商，对接资本。

to promote Xiaobeitong Cloud Education Platform and intelligent wearable equipment, to recruit the city partners or agents, and to conduct capital connection.

中药材仓储物流基地
Traditional Chinese Medicine Warehousing and Logistics Base

一、项目公司名称：甘肃琦昆农业发展有限公司
Ⅰ. Project Company Name：Gansu Qikun Agricultural Development Co., Ltd.

二、项目公司介绍：
Ⅱ. Project Company Introduction：

公司成立于2015年12月，主营中药材以及"甘肃琦昆中药材仓储物流基地"项目的投资与建设。2015年12月28日成功加入中国仓储与配送协会，并被评为"常务会员理事单位"，2016年被宕昌县工信局评为"扶贫工作示范企业"。

Founded in December 2015, Qikun is now mainly engaged in the industry of traditional Chinese medicine and the investment and construction of "Gansu Qikun Traditional Chinese Medicine Warehousing and Logistics Base" project. On December 28, 2015, Qikun became a member of the China Association of Warehousing and Distribution. In 2016, it was awarded by Dangchang County Bureau of Industry and Information Technology as a "Demonstrative Enterprise of Poverty Relief".

三、负责人介绍：
Ⅲ. Responsible Person Introduction：

高建军，公司董事长，生于1970年，民建兰州市城关基层委副主委，城关政协常委，陇南市政协委员，2015年创立琦昆公司，有多年从事商业工作的经验，目光敏锐，思维超前，敢于开拓创新。

Gao Jianjun, Chairman of Qikun, born in 1970, once worked as Vice Director of CNDCA Lanzhou Chengguan Primary Committee, Standing committee member of Chengguan CPPCC, and Longnan CPPCC member. In 2015, Gao established Qikun. He has profound experiences in commerce industry and has sharp insight and proactive thinking and strong ambitions.

四、项目名称：中药材仓储物流基地
Ⅳ. Project Name：Traditional Chinese Medicine Warehousing and Logistics Base

五、项目概况：
Ⅴ. Project Profile：

甘肃琦昆中药材仓储物流基地项目位于宕昌县哈达铺镇召藏村，一期工程占地97亩已通过招拍获得土地使用权证，总投资51376万元。该项目紧紧围绕县委、县政府建设"药材大县"的奋斗目标和"园区带动、基地支撑、科技引领、加工增值、提质增效"的总体思路开展各项工作。该宗地处于宕昌县药材种植大镇，也是红色旅游重点乡镇，经报批审核通过，项目已开始施工建设。

Gansu Qikun Traditional Chinese Medicine Warehousing and Logistics Base is located in Zhaocang Village, Hadapu Town of Dangchang County. The company has purchased the land use rights to 97-Mu land piece for the Phase-I project, with a total investment of CNY 513,760 thousand. The project is mainly focused on the goals of a "Major TCM County" set up by the local government and CCP committee and the overall planning of "Led by industrial parks, supported by bases, guided by science and technology, adding value by processing and increasing profitability by quality improvement". Hadapu Town is a major TCM town in Dangchang County and also an important town for red tourism. The project has been approved by related authority and commenced construction.

六、项目优势：
Ⅵ. Project Advantage(s)：

1. 区位优势
Location

一是项目坐落于有着"千年药乡"美誉的药材种植大县宕昌县。据统计，野生及人工种植药材有690种，

其中有收购量的就有142种，这大大提升了公司在中药材市场的占有率和竞争力；二是项目建设地位于兰渝铁路和渭武高速的交汇处，交通便利。

The project is located in Dangchang County which is praised as "Village of Medicine of Thousand Years" and known for large-scale plantation of traditional Chinese medicine materials. According statistics, there are 690 species of TCM materials including both wild and family grown materials, among which 142 species of TCM materials are purchased in large volume. This greatly improves the market shares and competitiveness of the company. Secondly, the project is located at the intersection of Lanyu Railway and Weiwu Expressway and thus enjoys very convenient traffic conditions.

2．政策优势

Policies

甘肃琦昆中药材仓储物流基地项目是宕昌县第二十二届兰洽会签约的重点招商引资项目，同时也作为甘肃六个中药材物流基地之一，已纳入全国91个中药材物流基地的布局规划。项目建成后将全面带动全县药农增产增收。一是解决了全县1.4万多户贫困户药材的产销问题；二是有效解决我县中药材产地加工与包装、仓储设施分散落后，现代种植技术落后等问题；三是促进当地就业率。该项目得到了省委省政府的高度重视和认可。

Gansu Qikun Traditional Chinese Medicine Warehousing and Logistics Base is a key investment project signed on the 22nd Lanzhou Trade Fair and it is also one of the 6 major TCM logistics bases in Gansu and has been included in the overall planning and arrangement for 91 TCM logistics bases throughout China. After completion of the project, it will help TCM farmers in the county to increase their income. Firstly, it solved the production and sales problems of 14,000 impoverished farmers; secondly, it has effectively solved the problem of less developed local processing, packaging and warehousing capacity in the county and backward technology in modern plantation. Thirdly, it can effectively promote the local employment. The project has won high attentions and recognition of the provincial government and CCP committee.

3．资本优势

Capital

甘肃琦昆中药材仓储物流基地项目，作为扶贫产业已依据相关政策向甘肃银行申请了扶贫产业专项贷款。

Gansu Qikun Traditional Chinese Medicine Warehousing and Logistics Base, as a poverty relief action, has applied to Gansu Bank, in accordance with related policies, for special loans for poverty relief.

七、项目需求：

Ⅶ. Project Demand(s):

1．政策需求：加大政策支持及配套资金补贴。

Policy：More policy supports and supporting fund allowance.

2．人才需求：引入专业经济经营相关人员，共同打造现代化仓储物流体系。

Talents：Introduce professionals of economy and operation, to build a modern warehousing and logistics system.

3．推广需求：得到更多药材企业的关注，达到合作共赢。

Promotion：Win attentions of more TCM enterprises to realize cooperation and mutual benefits.

嘎仙洞旅游
Gaxian Cave Tourism

一、项目公司名称：赛程假期（北京）旅游咨询有限公司
I. Project Company Name: Saicheng Holiday (Beijing) Tourism Consultation Co., Ltd.

二、项目公司介绍：
II. Project Company Introduction:

公司于2014年4月16日正式成立，是以助力客户事业发展为主题的旅游咨询公司，公司与东南亚境外旅游地接资源及泰国和港澳台的各商协会组织平台实现资源共享，同时，公司细节化个性化差异化服务、持续不断的创新力成为专业领域典范。

Established in 2014, the company is engaged in tourism consultation with the theme of boosting the customers' business development. We have achieved the sharing of overseas tourism guiding resources in Southeast Asia and platform resources of business organizations in Thailand, Hong Kong, Macao and Taiwan. Meanwhile, we provide detailed and individualized differentiated services and our continuous innovation has become the model of professional field.

三、负责人介绍：
III. Responsible Person Introduction:

刘佳琪，公司创始人，草根创业者，从基层干起，凭借创新创意打造了自有旅行服务品牌，2015年在北京人民大会堂被授予"全国中小商业企业系统首届五四青年创业创新标兵"奖项，相继担任中国策划学院旅游研究院秘书长、BIF国际品牌联盟CBO（首席品牌官）、香港中华工商总会常务会董，荣获"中国优秀诚信企业家"、"第八届创业中国年度人物大众创业奖"、"中国中小企业家金钻奖章"、"2016百杰女性创业人物"等荣誉称号和奖项。

Liu Jiaqi, the founder of the company, a grass roots entrepreneur, created the self-owned tourism service brand by virtue of innovative idea starting at the bottom, awarded with the model prize of First National SME system May Fourth Youth Entrepreneurship and Innovation at Great Hall of the People in 2015, successively served as the Secretary General of Tourism Research Institute of China Plan Institute, CBO of International Brand Federation (BIF), Managing Director of The Chinese General Chamber of Commerce and won titles of "Chinese Excellent Good Faith Entrepreneur", "the Mass Entrepreneurship Award of 8th China Entrepreneur Person of the Year" and "Golden Diamond Medal of Chinese SME Entrepreneur" and "Excellent Female Entrepreneur 2016", etc.

四、项目名称：嘎仙洞旅游
IV. Project Name: Gaxian Cave Tourism

五、项目概况：
V. Project Profile:

嘎仙洞为天然大型山洞，离地面25米。洞口向西南，略呈三角形。洞内南北长90余米，东西宽约28米，穹顶最高处20余米，略分为前、中、后三室（现只开放前室），面积约2000平方米。洞内幽暗深邃，石壁平整。嘎仙洞是鲜卑人的祖庭，鲜卑人是炎帝的支裔，是通古斯（东胡）语各族的祖先，因此嘎仙洞是通古斯诸语族的祖庭、发祥地，他们领有整个西伯利亚、中亚、西亚、欧洲的古丝绸之路，位于丝绸之路的东北亚的沿长点上，与大兴安岭、漠河形成我国北疆战略安全保障带。洞内堆积有较丰富的文化层，对于研究拓跋鲜卑的早期历史，具有重要科学价值。

Gaxian Cave is a large natural cave and 25 meters from the ground. The cave entrance is southwestward and lightly triangle. The cave is more than 90 meters in length, about 28 meters in width internally with the maximum height to dome of over 20 meters. With an area of about 2,000 square meters, the cave is slightly divided into three parts: front, middle and rear parts (now, only the front part is opened to the public). The cave is dark and deep internally and contains flat stone walls. Gaxian Cave is a birthplace of Xianbei people who were a branch of Yan Emperor and ancestors of

Turgus (Donghu) language nationalities. Therefore, Gaxian Cave was the birthplace and cradleland of Turgus language nationalities who occupied the ancient Silk Road of Siberia, Central Asia, West Asia and Europe. Located at the extension point of Northeast Asia on the Silk Road, Gaxian Cave forms the strategic safety guarantee belt on the northern boundary of China with Greater Khingan Mountains and Mohe River. With bundant cultural layer accumulated internally, the cave has significant scientific value for study on early history of Tuoba Xianbei.

六、项目优势：
VI. Project Advantages:

独有的通古斯语族民族民俗文化，内蒙古与东北三省联合开发的地缘优势。嘎仙洞遗址保护工程的实施是一项功在当代、利在千秋的宏伟业绩，对于研究发掘鲜卑文化，促进自治旗旅游事业的发展，扩大鄂伦春对外的知名度有着不可估量的促动作用。

The project has unique folk custom culture of Turgus language nationalities and geographical advantage of joint development by Inner Mongolia and three provinces in Northeast China. The implementation of Gaxian Cave Relics Protection is a magnificent project bringing benefits to generations and will remarkably promote the study and exploration of Xianbei culture, development of local tourism and external reputation of Oroqen.

七、项目需求：
VII. Project Demands：

政策支持，资金合作。

Policy support and financial cooperation.

共价型多核强化絮凝除磷
Covalent Polynuclear Enhanced Flocculation Dephosphorization

一、项目公司名称：神美科技有限公司
Ⅰ. Project Company Name: Shenmei Technology Co., Ltd.

二、项目公司介绍：

公司成立于2011年，是一家专注于环保技术开发、生产、工程技术服务、销售于一体的高科技环保领域的新兴高新技术企业，在污水处理、工业水处理、污泥减量资源化等技术领域独辟蹊径，具有多项技术突破。公司总部坐落于北京市顺义区泰达园保税区内，生产基地位于河北省河间市经济技术开发区。公司在华北和华东地区分别设立二级销售服务中心，在贵州设立二级生产中心项目部，销售网络覆盖全国三十多个省、市。公司与中科院及国内顶尖大学形成研发战略合作并紧跟最新科研动向，积极与先进环保企业强强合作、紧密联系，致力于打造污水处理、污泥处置及资源化利用平台，整合、汇集国内外环保处理处置的先进技术，创造国内环保处理领域第一品牌。

Founded in 2011, the company is a high and environment-friendly technology company dedicated to development of environment-friendly technologies, production, engineering technical services and sales. It has unique advantages in sewage treatment, industrial waste water treatment and sludge reduction and recycling and has realized many technological breakthroughs. Backed by headquarters in Taida Bonded Area in Shunyi, Beijing, the company established production bases in Hejian Economic Development Zone in Hebei Province. The company has established second-tier sales and service centers respectively in North China and East China and a second-tier project department in Guizhou and a sales network in over 30 provinces and cities. The company has established strategic development cooperation with Chinese Academy of Sciences and top universities in China. Besides, it keeps up with the latest scientific development and works actively to establish cooperation and close connections with advanced environmental protection enterprises. The company is devoted to sewage treatment, sludge treatment and recycling platform, integrates and aggregates advanced environmental protection technologies at home and abroad, and has built a top brand in Chinese environmental protection industry.

三、项目负责人介绍：

周继柱，应用化学硕士，中国科学院化学研究所研究员，一直深耕于化工行业污水处理，在研究所工作期间作为骨干技术人员参与了国家十一五期间油田水处理领域国家863、973、重大专项等科研项目，在企业工作期间作为项目负责人申报并完成了省级星火计划、中小企业创新基金等应用项目。负责并从事过油田污水、炼化污水、景观水、焦化水等领域几十个水处理项目，具备多年环保企业产品技术研发和生产经验，开发新产品和技术类别设计有几个大类十余种产品，参与申报专利13项，3项为第一发明人。

Zhou Jizhu, Master degree of applied chemistry, Researcher of Institute of Chemistry, Chinese Academy of Sciences. Zhou has devoted himself to industrial wastewater treatment. When he was still a student, he participated in a series of national 863 and 973 oilfield water treatment projects in the 11th Five-Year Plan period. When he worked in enterprises, as the project leader, he applied for and completed a provincial projects under the Spark Program and SME Innovation Fund Program. Through his working experiences, he worked on dozens of water treatment projects including oilfield wastewater treatment, oil refinery wastewater treatment, landscape water treatment and coking water treatment. Armed with the experiences for years in R&D and production of products for environmental protection enterprises, his products and technologies involve over ten species under several major categories. Besides, he participated in the filing of 13 patents and was the first inventor of 3 patents.

四、项目名称：共价型多核强化絮凝除磷
Ⅳ. Project Name: Covalent Polynuclear Enhanced Flocculation Dephosphorization

五、项目概况：
V. Project Profile：

絮凝是饮用水处理、污水处理工艺流程中最常用的处理单元，具有处理效果好、操作简便、建设或升级改造容易等特点。絮凝的效果主要取决于絮凝剂的结构和性能，传统的无机或单纯的有机絮凝剂因其性能上的缺陷已经不能满足当前水和废水处理所面临的原水水质情况日趋复杂、出水水质指标日渐苛刻的现实问题。本公司开发的无机—有机复合多核絮凝剂是一种兼具无机高分子絮凝剂与有机高分子絮凝剂的优点的新型絮凝剂，其可在不增加污水处理综合费用的前提下，大幅度提高了絮凝效果。此絮凝剂可在工程中将多步投加多种絮凝剂变为一步投加，简化了操作程序，大幅度节省了设备投资。其各项性能、技术指标均已超过国内外同类产品，是目前国内效果最好、可应用范围最广的絮凝剂。

Flocculation is a common unit in treatment of potable water and sewage treatment. It is featured by satisfactory treatment effect, easy operation, construction, upgrade and modification to existing facilities. The effect of flocculation depends on the structure and performance of flocculation. Traditional inorganic or simple organic flocculating agents can no longer solve the current problems of complex water quality and demanding requirements in water pretreatment and sewage treatment due to their performance flaws. The inorganic-organic composite polynuclear flocculating agent is a new flocculating agent that combines the strengths of both inorganic polymer and organic polymer flocculating agents. It can significantly improve the flocculation effect without increasing the comprehensive treatment costs. With the flocculating agent, multiple dosing processing is simplified into single dosing step, saving equipment investments. The performance and technical specifications of the flocculating agent is better than similar products available both in Chinese and international markets, and is currently the best and most widely used in China.

六、项目优势：
VI. Project Advantage(s)：

本项目中多核絮凝剂，其无机和有机部分通过化学共价键方式连接。相比于一般的无机有机复合絮凝剂，这种结合方式更为紧密，使得无机和有机组分更充分发挥各自作用，并达到优势互补，相辅相成，处理效果远优于两者单独使用。本项目同时兼具无机絮凝剂廉价实用、无毒高效和有机高分子絮凝剂用量少、浮渣量少、絮凝能力强、絮体易分离、除油及除悬浮物效果好的优点。

For the polynuclear flocculating agent in this project, the inorganic and organic parts are joined by chemical covalent bond. In comparison with common inorganic and organic composite flocculating agents, this bonding method provides securer boding, so that the inorganic and organic components can function completely to realize complementarity effect. The treatment effect is much better than the single use of any single agent. Besides, it also has the advantages of inorganic flocculating agents, including excellent cost effectiveness, toxicity free and good effect, as well as the advantages of organic flocculating agents, including small dose, less scumming, excellent flocculation effect, easy separation and good effect in removing oil and suspended solids.

七、项目需求：
VII. Project Demand(s)：

在未来的研发过程中需要添加的设备有分光光度计、高压灭菌锅、XRD等。需要资金的注入，在产品成型后，投入市场，欢迎有需求的企业共谋合作。

In future R&D process, additional devices will be required, including spectrophotometers, high-pressure sterilizing pot, and XRD, etc. Additional investments will be required after the product development is completed and ready for market promotion. We are looking for cooperation with interested companies.

云章
Cloud Sign

一、项目公司名称：北京爱国小男孩科技有限公司
Ⅰ. Project Company Name: Beijing Patriotic Boy Technology Co., Ltd.

二、项目公司介绍：
Ⅱ. Project Company Introduction:

爱国小男孩科技有限公司成立于2015年2月，以物联网智能产品的研发、应用与技术服务为主营业务，拥有自主知识产权14项、通过三项国家级企业/产品认证，涉及经营、管理、法律、财务、安防等多个专业领域，是一家获得国家级认证高新技术企业。

Beijing Patriotic Boy Technology Co., Ltd. was founded in December 2015, with R&D of IoT intelligent products, application and technical service as its main business. It possesses 14 independent intellectual property rights, and has passed 3 national enterprise/product certification, involving multiple professional fields such as business, management, law, finance and security etc. It is a high-tech enterprise obtaining national certification.

目前公司已与中国联通、中国卫星导航定位协会结成了紧密的战略合作伙伴关系，初步形成了覆盖全国的物联网智能产品的销售与服务网络。

At present, the company has established strategic partnership with China Unicom and GNSS and LBS Association of China (GLAC), taking initial shape of a sales and service network for IoT intelligent products covering the whole nation.

三、负责人介绍：
Ⅲ. Responsible Person Introduction:

卢平山："以前，我是一名军人，保护祖国是我的责任。现在，我是一个创业者，用科技的力量保护政府、企业印章使用安全，推动政府、企业实现网络化、信息化、智能化、数据化的印章管理是我的责任！"

Lu Pingshan, "I was once a military man previously, and protecting my country is my responsibility. Now, I'm an entrepreneur, who uses the power of science and technology to protect safety of government and enterprise seals, so as to promote the government and enterprise to realize seal management on networking, informatization, intelligence and data!"

四、项目名称：云章
Ⅳ. Project Name: Cloud Sign

五、项目概况：
Ⅴ. Project Profile:

云章借助物联网技术实现了印章→客户端→管理者之间的信息交互，便于政府、企业及时、有效的对印章的使用进行监管并形成完善的、系统的印章使用台帐，杜绝了因印章被私盖、盗盖、乱盖的现象，在确保印章使用安全的同时，提升了印章使用效率、降低了印章使用成本。

Cloud Sign realizes information interaction between the seal, client-side and manager in using the IoT technology, which is convenient for the government and enterprise to conduct supervision on the use of seals timely and effectively, and form a compete and systematic seal use book-keeping, eradicating private sealing, stolen sealing and illegal sealing of seals, which promotes use efficiency of seals and reduces cost of seals, while guaranteeing use safety of seals.

截至2017年2月，公司已为全国3万多家法人单位提供了印章智能管理服务或用章规范管理培训服务，涉及公安、工商、税务、民政、林业、港务等政府机构和工程建筑、物流仓储、金融保险、加工制造、科研院所等企业单位，整体推动了中国政府、企业印章管理的网络化、信息化、智能化、数据化体系的建设。

As of February 2017, the company has provided intelligent seal management service or standard seal use and management training service for more than 30 thousand legal person units all over the country, involving government organizations such as public security, industry and commerce, taxation, civil, forest and harbor affairs etc., and enterprises such as engineering construction, logistics & storage, finance & insurance, processing & manufacturing, scientific research institutes etc., which promotes networking, informatization, intelligence, data system construction of seal management in Chinese government and enterprises.

六、项目优势：
Ⅵ. Project Advantage(s):

1．技术领先优势：云章采用最新的物联网和芯片技术，产品通过了北京市新产品新技术认证和国家安全防范报警系统质量监督检测中心检测。

Leading technical advantages：Cloud Sign adopts the latest IoT and chip technology, and the product has passed the certification of Beijing New Product & New Technology Certification Center, and passed the examination of Quality Supervision and Inspection Center of National Safety Alarm System.

2．产品领先优势：在印章智能管理方面，尚未发现与云章相同或相近的产品或服务。第三代云章即将上市。

Leading product advantages：With respect to intelligent management, no product or service identical or similar to Cloud Sign has been found. The third generation Cloud Sign is coming soon.

3．市场领先优势：已在北京、天津、河北、山东、山西、湖北等15个省、市、自治区的县级以上市场全面落地。

Leading market advantages：It has launched in the market above county level in 15 provinces, cities and autonomous regions such as Beijing, Tianjing, Hebei, Shandong, Shanxi, Hubei etc.

4．运营领先优势：爱国小男孩科技发起"中国政府、企业互联网＋印章智慧管理工程"，累计为3万余家政府、企业提供了印章智慧管理服务。

Leading operation advantages：Patriotic Boy has launched the "Chinese Government and Enterprise Internet + Cloud Sign Wisdom Management Project", and has provided Cloud Sign wisdom management service for more than 30 thousand governments and enterprises.

七、项目需求：
Ⅶ. Project Demand(s):

期待更多的从事法律、财务、管理、风控等行业的朋友加入到"中国政府、企业互联网＋印章智慧管理工程"中来，共同推动中国政府、企业印章管理的规范化、信息化、智能化体系的建设，避免政府、企业因印章被私盖、盗改、乱改而造成财产损失、信用损伤。

It is expected that more friends engaged in industries such as law, finance, management, risk control etc. could join the "Chinese Government and Enterprise Internet + Cloud Sign Wisdom Management Project", to jointly promote the construction of standardized, informationized and intelligent system of Cloud Sign management in Chinese governments and enterprises, so as to avoid property loss or reputation damages of governments and enterprises due to private sealing, stolen sealing and illegal sealing.

室内外艺术雕塑及构件
Indoor and Outdoor Art Sculptures And Components

一、项目公司名称：广州图腾美术雕塑厂

Ⅰ. Project Company Name：Guangzhou Totem Art Sculpture Factory

二、项目公司介绍：

Ⅱ. Project Company Introduction:

本厂是集艺术创作、设计、制作、安装及售后服务为一体的专业性艺术工厂，承接定制生产各类型艺术雕塑品及室内外建筑构件，主要材质为GRP/FRP玻璃钢、GRC欧标砂岩、GRG高强钢化石膏、水转印高仿真表面纹理加工等。本厂1999年创建以来，在中外多个城市已有许多案例项目作品鉴。本厂以诚信为本，精益求精的态度、匠心独运的设计，竭诚为国内外客户提供优质的产品和服务，为现代城市公共空间增添生命活力与文化艺术品位。

It is a professional art factory integrating artistic creation, design, manufacturing, installation and after-sales service into one, which undertakes, customizes and produces various art sculptures and indoor and outdoor building components. The main materials are GRP / FRP, GRC Euro-standard sandstone, GRG high-strength steel gypsum and water-transfer-printing high-simulation surface texture processing materials, etc. Since its establishment in 1999, many case projects of it have been reported in many cities and countries in China and abroad. The factory is dedicated to providing the high-quality services and products to customers at home and abroad, and adding vitality and cultural and artistic taste to the modern urban public space with its integrity-based and excelsior attitude and unique design.

三、负责人介绍：

Ⅲ. Responsible Person Introduction:

何运良，早年于广东师范学院美术系进修，广东英德市总工会职业技术学校美术系讲师、广州图腾美术雕塑厂创始人、广东知名雕塑家，2015年获"中国工艺美术大师"称号，2016年被OPC职业鉴定中心评为"雕塑卓越成就奖"，2017年评为国家一级美术师。

He Yunliang, studied in Art Department, Guangdong Normal University in early years, lecturer at Art Department, FTU Vocational School, Yingde, Guangdong, founder of Guangzhou Totem Art Sculpture Factory, famous sculptor in Guangdong, rated as a national-level artist in 2017, awarded the outstanding achievement award for sculpture by International Occupational Planning Certification Center (OPC) in 2016 and won the title of master of Chinese arts and crafts in 2015.

四、项目名称：室内外艺术雕塑及构件

Ⅳ. Project Name：Indoor and Outdoor Art Sculptures And Components

五、项目概况：

Ⅴ. Project Profile:

1．技术材质：玻璃钢FRP(GRP)、欧标砂岩GRC、高强钢化石膏GRG、水转印高仿真表面纹理工艺、无机复合料、金属材质、石材、油漆彩绘、纳米电镀，仿真仿古工艺等。

Technical material：FRP (GRP), Euro-standard sandstone GRC, high-strength steel gypsum GRG gypsum and water-transfer-printing high-simulation surface texture process, inorganic composite material, metal material, stone, painting, nano plating and simulation of antique crafts etc.

2．雕塑工艺品类：城市广场雕塑、园林景观小品、校园及企业文化雕塑、佛寺宗教雕塑、游艺乐园景观设施、楼盘商城景观、浮雕壁画等。

Sculptures and handicrafts：sculpture for urban square, garden and featured landscape, sculpture for campus and corporate culture, religious sculpture for Buddhist temple, landscape facilities in amusement park, landscape in houses and malls, reliefs and murals, etc.

3．室内外装饰构件类：建筑装饰结构体及预制件、异形定制，中欧式梁柱梁托罗马柱、工艺花瓶花盆、艺术花线腰线、喷泉水景、室内壁炉、门套窗套、天花造型、工艺栏杆、背景墙装饰板，凉亭古建等。

Indoor and outdoor decorative components: Structure of agricultural decoration, prefab, special-shaped customization, Chinese and European beam, corbel and roman column, craft vase and flowerpot, art colored thread and string course, fountain waterscape, indoor fireplace, door frame and window frame, ceiling modeling, craft railings, decorative panels of wall and ancient pavilions, etc.

4．应用场所：建筑及园林、城市广场、楼盘商城、市政规划、酒店装饰、娱乐场所俱乐部、学校校园、展厅博物馆等。

Applications : building and garden, urban square, house and mall, municipal planning, hotel decoration, entertainment place, club, school campus, exhibition hall and museum, etc.

我厂的创作理念和灵感源于对生活的感受和理解、对人文地理的关怀和尊重、对科学技术的娴熟与掌握。本厂进行美工、周易、环境、文化等全方位的策划，制作涉及建筑内外环境艺术氛围的营造和空间效果布局设计，探求与实践人文艺术再现等。

Our factory's creative idea and inspiration are from the feeling and understanding of life, the care and respect for human geography, the skill and mastery of science and technology; all-around planning on artwork, Zhouyi, environment and culture, etc., creation of an atmosphere involved in environmental art inside and outside the building, layout design of space effect, reproduction of humanity art and other exploration and practices.

我厂以艺术为根，挟中华文化之传统，偕欧陆艺术之风韵，作品既有现代的雄伟与前卫，也有古代的遗风韵味，追求巴洛克精髓与传统国魂的完美。图腾源于祖先文化栈道。今天再创现代文明艺术所取得的成绩都是承蒙各界客户的鼎力支持与认同。

Our factory takes root in art, relies on the traditional Chinese culture together with the continental art charm, with both majestic and avant-garde modern style and the ancient legacy of charm in the works, and pursues the perfect Baroque essence and traditional spirit. The totem originates from the ancestral culture. Today, the achievements from the arts by recreation of the modern civilization are due to the utmost support and recognition from customers from all walks of life.

六、项目优势：
VI. Project Advantage(s)：

厂区面积约为3000平方米，分为六个制作车间，产品生产各步骤分区分件处理，技术设备齐全，达到国家环保及安装生产要求。我厂拥有高级工艺大师1名，雕塑艺术家4名，美术设计师5名及技术人员48名，并邀请国内著名艺术家作为艺术顾问亲临指导。

The factory covers around 3,000 ㎡, which is divided into six production workshops, with each procedure of product production handled by sections and pieces and with full technical equipment, and meets the requirements for national environmental protection, installation and production. Our factory is provided with 1 senior craft master, 4 sculpture artists, 5 art designers and 48 technicians, and the famous artist in China has been invited as the artistic consultant for personal guidance.

七、项目需求：
VII. Project Demand(s):

在国内外各大城市已有我厂作品供鉴赏，同时也积极与全球各机构成为合作伙伴。

The works from our factory have been appreciated in many cities both at home and abroad, and meanwhile we also actively become the cooperative partners with the organizations all over the world.

尚雨轩－连锁管理新模式
Shangyuxuan – Chain Management Model

一、项目公司名称：北京尚雨轩餐饮管理有限公司
Ⅰ. Project Company Name：Beijing Shangyuxuan Catering Management Co., Ltd.

二、项目公司介绍：
Ⅱ. Project Company Introduction:

公司是一家综合性餐饮连锁管理企业。专注国人，回归本土饮食文化，为中国真正开始的"平民餐饮时代"而来；开创伊始，就以国际化品牌连锁管理思维模式，结合团队多年招商、运维经验，国际视野，为合作加盟者和终端消费群，提供亲民的产品线、跨界创新餐饮模式。从品质管理到落地执行，逐步提升品牌价值。通过标准化、亲民、时尚氛围的优质体验，通过互联网智能化管理手段，为中国百姓餐饮开辟出一条高效盈利管道。

Shangyuxuan is a comprehensive catering chain management enterprise. We focus on services to Chinese customers and local food cultures and aim to accommodate the coming "Era of Commoner Food". Since the foundation, we have integrated the international brand chain management models with our experiences in attracting investments and operation, international insights, to provide our partners and end consumers with friendly product lines and innovative catering models. We pursued brand value promotion by quality management and implementation. With high-quality experiences featured by standardized and friendly service and fashionable settings, further supported by Internet-based intellectual management, Shangyuxuan has opened up a highly profitable channel for catering services.

公司旗下品牌：半兽人、咔悠悠、魔煮三个品牌。
Our brands include Orcish, Kayouyou and Mozhu.

三、负责人介绍：
Ⅲ. Responsible Person Introduction：

董事长张彬先生，新疆建设兵团359旅后代，一位有情怀有梦想的创业者，有着敏锐的商业嗅觉，曾带领企业实现全疆外贸行业进出口多年第一。

Mr. Zhang Bin is a descendant of the Xinjiang Production and Construction Corps Brigade 359. As an entrepreneur with great passion and dreams, Zhang Bin has acute business insight, and under his leadership, the company ranked first in exports in Xinjiang for many years.

主要经历：新疆生产建设兵团工商业联合会副主席；新疆生产建设兵团青年联合会委员；2008年创办新疆海耀贸易有限公司；2015年创办北京尚雨轩餐饮管理有限公司。

Main experiences：Vice Chairman of Association of Industry and Commerce of Xinjiang Production and Construction Corps; Member to the Youth Federation of Xinjiang Production and Construction Corps; Founder of Xinjiang Hailuo Trade Co., Ltd. (2008); Founder of Beijing Shangyuxuan Catering Management Co., Ltd. (2015).

四、项目名称：尚雨轩-连锁管理新模式
Ⅳ. Project Name：Shangyuxuan - Chain Management Model

五、项目概况：
Ⅴ. Project Profile:

1．自主研发中国首家移动端连锁加盟品牌智慧化的"运维管理平台"
China's first intelligent mobile Operation and Management Platform developed independently

目标解决对连锁门店、直营门店从选址开业到日常运营、商品售卖、物流交换等链接问题，让系统化管理更加快捷、高效。

The project is aimed to solve the linkage problems confronted by chain stores, direct stores in location selection, routine operation, product sales and logistics, to realize quick and effective systematic management.

2．建立核心区域孵化中心

Incubation centers in core areas

实现总部功能下移，在大总部与加盟商之间的小总部——即地区孵化中心，实行总部与孵化中心垂直管理，总部顶层设计负责对区域孵化中心培训监管，区域孵化中心保障执行，将彻底解决连锁加盟行业的痛点。

Some functions will be transferred from the head office to local centers of franchisee - the regional incubation center. The project realizes vertical management between the company head office and the incubation centers, by which the head office is responsible for training and supervision of the regional incubation centers, while the incubation centers are responsible for supports and implementation to completely solve the troubles of chain operation industry.

区域孵化中心：第一阶段实现中国金三角——北京、上海、乌鲁木齐北京辐射华北、东北地区，新疆辐射西北地区，上海辐射华东、华南地区。

Regional incubation centers：The Phase-I project aims to realize coverage of the Golden Triangle Area of Beijing, Shanghai and Urumchi. Beijing center is responsible for coverage of North China, Northeast China, Xinjiang Center is responsible for Northwest China and Shanghai center responsible for East China and South China.

六、项目优势：
Ⅵ. Project Advantage(s)：

特许经营连锁模式的优势：连锁合作是前所未有最成功的市场策略，是快速聚合力量，抱团取暖，共同对抗各种经济压力、社会压力的企业优质生存法则；科技技术的优势：聚合支付、APP 运维平台——尚雨轩 – 贴身餐饮运维专家；差异化优势：孵化中心、经营理念、六芒星部署计划；渠道优势。

Advantages of chain franchise：Chain operation is an unprecedented successful market strategy that is able to quickly aggregate idle investors to resist economic and social pressures. Advantages of technologies：Integrated payment, APP operation platform - Shangyuxuan, is a catering expert closest to consumers. Differentiation advantages：Incubation center, operation philosophy, hexagram plan. Besides, the project also enjoys advantages in channels.

七、项目需求：
Ⅶ. Project Demand(s)：

尚雨轩公司自开创伊始，专注国人餐饮，秉持着"吃对、用对、活对"的核心理念，希望人人回归安心健康的生活。建立一个对生产者、消费者环境友善的共好循环。以国际化品牌连锁管理思维模式，结合团队多年招商、运维经验，国际视野，为合作加盟者和终端消费群，提供亲民的产品线、跨界创新餐饮模式。从品质管理到落地执行，逐步提升品牌价值。

Ever since its foundation, Shangyuxuan has focused on catering services to Chinese consumers and under the guidance of the core concepts of "right for live", we hope that customers can go back to a healthy and peaceful life. Shangyuxuan expects to build up a mutually benefiting cycle for producers, consumers and environment. We integrated the international brand chain management models with our experiences in attracting investments and operation, international insights, to provide our partners and end consumers with friendly product lines and innovative catering models. We pursued brand value promotion by quality management and implementation.

水基型灭火器
Water – based Fire Extinguisher

一、项目公司名称： 河北军拓鸿顺安防科技有限公司

I. Project Company Name： Hebei Juntuohongshun Security Technology Co., Ltd.

二、项目公司介绍：

II. Project Company Introduction：

公司设立在河北省唐山市开平区现代装备制造工业区，占地面积30亩，是具有年产200万支水基型系灭火器灌装项目的生产规模型企业，全方位配套产品试验。公司专业生产手提式水基型灭火器、简易式家庭型水基型灭火器，消防水带；水喷淋自动灭火系统、防撞调压栓、消防系统阀门。公司技术力量雄厚、生产设备精良，制造工艺先进，检测设备齐全，有完善的质量保证体系。公司在全国省、直辖市建立了销售和服务机构，做到为客户设计、施工、服务、维保等一条龙服务，业务已经延伸到海外等多个国家和地区，使公司的销售、服务、诚信网络形成了国际化格局。

The company is located in Modern Equipment Manufacturing Industrial Zone, Kaiping District, Tangshan City, Hebei Province, covering an area of 30 mu. It has a production scale of an annual output of 2 million water-based fire extinguishers filling items, and the all-round ancillary product testing. The company specializes in the production of portable water-based fire extinguishers, simple family-type water-based fire extinguishers, fire hose; water spray automatic fire extinguishing system, anti-collision pressure regulation hydrant, and fire system valves. The Company has strong technical force, sophisticated production equipment, advanced manufacturing technology, complete testing equipment, and sound quality assurance system. The Company establishes sales and service agencies in the provinces and municipalities throughout the country to provide a one-stop service of customers design, construction, services, maintenance, etc. Our business has been extended to overseas countries and regions so that the company's sales, service, and integrity network form an international pattern.

三、负责人介绍：

III. Responsible person instruction：

李旭芬，女，现年60岁，河北省唐山市人，拥有唐山中絮工业水处理有限公司、唐山鸿顺科技有限公司，一直致力于环保节能减排行业，为该地区的环保水处理做出了杰出的贡献。

Li Xufen, female, 60 years old, a native of Tangshan City, Hebei Province, has Tangshan Zhongxu Industrial Water Treatment Co., Ltd. and Tangshan Hongshun Technology Co., Ltd. She has been committed to environmental protection and energy saving & emission reduction industry to make an outstanding contribution for the environmental protection for the region.

四、项目名称： 水基型灭火器

IV. Project Name： Water - based Fire Extinguisher

五、项目概况：

V. Project Profile：

水基型灭火器为物理性灭火器原理。灭火剂主要有碳氢表面活性剂、氟碳表面活性剂、阻燃剂和助剂组成。灭火剂对A类火灾具有渗透的作用，如木材、布匹等，灭火剂可以渗透可燃物内部，即便火势较大未能全部扑灭，其药剂喷射的部位也可以有效的阻断火源，控制火灾的蔓延速度；对B类火灾具有隔离的作用，如汽油及挥发性化学液体，药剂可在其表面形成长时间的水膜，即便水膜受外界因素遭到破坏，其独特的流动性可以迅速愈合，使火焰窒息。故水基型（水雾）灭火器具备其他灭火器无法媲美的阻燃性。水基型灭火器不受室内、室外、大风等环境的影响，灭火剂可以最大限度的作用于燃烧物表面。

The mechanism of the water-based fire extinguisher is the principle of physical fire extinguishers. Fire extinguishing agents are mainly hydrocarbon surfactants, fluorocarbon surfactants, flame retardants and additives. The fire extinguishing agent has permeation effect on Class A fire, such as, wood, cloth, etc. The fire extinguishing agent can penetrate the interior of the combustible materials. Even if the big fire is not extinguished fully, the location by the pharmaceutical spray can also effectively block the fire to control the spread of the fire. It has isolation effect on Class B fire, such as, gasoline and volatile chemical liquid. The agent can form a long-time water film on its surface. Even if the water film has been destroyed by external factors, its unique mobility can rapidly heal so that the flame is suffocated. So water-based (water mist) fire extinguishers have the flame retardant other fire extinguishers can not match. Water-based fire extinguishers will not be affected by the indoor and outdoor big wind and so on so that the fire extinguishing agent can maximize the effect on the surface of the combustion materials.

六、项目优势：
Ⅵ. Project Advantage(s)：

项目主要生产国际先进、国内领先的新一代高性能水基型灭火器。是在国家固定灭火系统和耐火构件质量监督检测中心第一个按新规则全项检测通过的合格产品，是国内为数不多的拥有自主知识产权、高效环保、多功能水基型灭火器。伴随着我国农村人口不断流向城镇，城镇化率较快上升。城镇人口的增加使得相应的城市建筑、写字楼、民宅等都需要进行新建、扩建、改建，而消防工程投入会随之进入增长态势，因此未来几年城镇化水平的提升仍是消防行业发展的重要契机。产品还可以广泛应用于石油化工企业、新能源装备配套企业、地铁轨道交通、仓库、油田、车船、码头、机场、计算机房、采油平台等，能满足各类用户的需要。

The project mainly produces the international advanced and the domestic leading new generation of high performance water-based fire extinguishers. It is the first qualified product which went through the whole test according to the new rules and passed the test by a national appointed fire extinguishing system and refractory components quality supervision and inspection center, and is one of the few efficient, environmentally friendly, and multi-functional water-based fire extinguishers with independent intellectual property rights. With the continuous flow of rural population to urban areas, the urbanization rate increases rapidly. The increase in urban population makes the corresponding urban buildings, office buildings, houses newly built, expanded and rebuilt. Therefore, fire engineering investment will continue to enter the growth trend, so in the next few years, the level of urbanization is still the important opportunity of the development of the fire industry. The product can also be widely used in petrochemical enterprises, new energy equipment supporting enterprises, subway rail transportation, warehouses, oil fields, vehicles, wharfs, airports, computer rooms, oil platforms and so on to meet the needs of various users.

七、项目需求：
Ⅶ. Project Demand(s):

根据国内外对水基型灭火器的需求情况，我公司需要融资3000万元，其中1000万元用于根据市场需求研发新产品及技术研发，1000万元用于原料购买和产品生产，1000万元用于市场推广和企业扩大规模。

According to the demand for water-based fire extinguishers at home and abroad, our Company needs to finance 30 million yuan, of which 10 million yuan is used for the research and development of new products and technology based on the demand of the markets, 10 million yuan for raw materials purchasing and product production, and 10 million yuan for marketing and expansion of enterprise scale.

室内外照明工程
Indoor and Outdoor Lighting Engineering

一、项目公司名称：中山市高芯晶光电科技有限公司
Ⅰ. Project Company Name: Zhongshan Gaoxinjing Photoelectric Technology Co., Ltd.

二、项目公司介绍：
Ⅱ. Project Company Introduction:

公司是集室内外亮化工程，照明工程，城市亮化工程，路灯工程及太阳能路灯研发、设计、生产、销售于一体的灯饰企业。公司2013年创办与中国灯都古镇，一直以开拓新品、质量优越、客户认可度高、发展稳健而著称。随着中国内地的改革开放和经济发展，本公司在中山古镇的交通枢纽地段建立总面积40,000多平方米的生产基地。本公司深获客户推崇并带动了众多行业蓬勃发展。经过数载的耕耘，公司先后通过了ISO9001、2000、3C、UL、CE、ROSH等认证，并多次荣获："最受欢迎工程照明品牌"、"消费者最信赖质量放心品牌"、"广东省守合同重信用企业"，被公认为行业十大最具影响力的企业。

The company is a lighting device manufacturer integrating R&D, design, production and sales of indoor and outdoor lighting and illuminating engineering, urban lighting engineering, road lamp projects and solar street lamps. The company was founded in 2013 in the ancient town of lamps. Since its foundation, the company has won reputation for its new products, excellent quality, customer recognition and stable development. With the opening and reform of Chinese inland markets, the company established a 40,000 m² production base at the transportation junction in Zhongshan Town. The company won high praises from customers and promoted the development of many industries. Through efforts for years, the company a series of certification including the ISO9001:2000, 3C, UL, CE and ROSH. Besides, it was granted many titles such as "Most Popular Lighting Brand", "Customer Trusted Quality Brand", "Guangdong Credit Enterprise" and was recognized as the most influential enterprise in the industry.

三、负责人介绍：
Ⅲ. Responsible Person Introduction:

林少军，1995年在中山市胜球集团担任工程总监工作，在珠三角和各个省市设计、统筹、指挥现场的灯饰工程施工。2000年，在非洲苏丹及多个国家承接多个酒店灯饰工程。有着多年的工程灯饰设计、生产制造经验。2003年创办了中山市高芯晶光电科技有限公司，并成功研发设计多款室外灯饰、路灯和太阳能路灯。

Lin Shaojun worked as engineering director in Zhongshan Shengqiu Group, and was responsible for designing, overall management, site management of projects in Pearl River Delta and some other provinces. In 2000, Lin undertook several hotel lamp engineering projects in African countries including Sudan. Lin has profound experiences for years in lamp design and manufacturing. In 2003, he founded Zhongshan Gaoxinjing Photoelectric Technology Co., Ltd. and successfully developed several indoor lamps, street lamps, and solar street lamps.

四、项目名称：室内外照明工程
Ⅳ. Project Name: Indoor and Outdoor Lighting Engineering

五、项目概况：
Ⅴ. Project Profile:

本公司推崇照明与艺术结合，照明与设计的统一。秉承高贵典雅、富丽奢华的法式风格，匠心设计之道，先后创作数万款赏心悦目的艺术灯饰，广为行业内外赞誉。2003年开始打造高质量品牌，在海外购买先进设备，并定期培训相关技术人员。每年委派公司技术人员在美国、韩国等国家学习先进LED技术。并成立优秀的服务团队，定期给客户保养和回访的售后服务。

Our company highly values the integration of lighting and arts and designs. Sticking to the noble, graceful and luxury French style and elaborate design, the company created tens of thousand of lamp products, which won praises throughout the industry. Starting with 2003, the company began to pool its resources in building a high-end brand, by importing advanced equipment from overseas markets and regular training programs to related technical staff. The company sends its technicians to U.S. and Republic of Korea each year to study their advanced LED technologies. Besides, the company established an outstanding service team, providing customers with regular services and visits.

六、项目优势：
VI. Project Advantage(s):

公司拥有一批经验丰富，工艺精湛的优秀设计师、技术人员及管理人员；技术、管理、产品均达到国际认证标准；高芯晶灯饰被公认为灯饰行业最佳配搭和首选目标，向海内外数之不尽的华堂高厦提供了傲世同行的品位、艺术化的经典产品。工程案例遍布五洲四海，全国各大城市的高档会所、五星级宾馆酒店以及国家一级场所等并秉承恒大、富力、德豪润达等上市公司所开发的房地产灯饰。有着多年的灯饰工程经验，对于酒店、道路、墙体的户外亮化有着丰富的安装、设计经验。LED的亮化技术是公司的独家专利，灯饰的光效，效果符合客户的要求率达到100%。

The company has a large number of veteran and skilled designers, technicians, and manager as well as technical, management systems and products certified by international standards. Gaoxinjing was recognized as the ideal and preferred brand in the lamp industry and supplies lamps for various buildings and mansions in Chinese and international markets, which are of finest quality and identified as an artistic symbol. Our history projects cover high-end private clubs, 5-star hotels and national Grade-I premises throughout China. We are also a lamp supplier for real properties developed by famous listed developers such as Evergrande, R&F Properties, Elec-Tech. The company has extensive experiences in lamp engineering and installation and designing of outdoor lighting for hotels, streets and walls. The company is also the exclusive patent owner of LED lighting technologies, and our products can 100% satisfy customer expectations.

七、项目需求：
VII. Project Demand(s):

1．与国际接轨，加强企业品质管理，提高企业效益；
International connections, to enhance quality management and profitability of the company；

2．提升产品品牌国际地位，筑建一流品牌；
Promote brand position in international markets as a first-class brand；

3．寻求产品国际经济合作（金融融资，扩大生产规模）和技术交流（引进国外高端技术人才）；
International product cooperation (financing, expanding production scale) and technical exchanges (introducing foreign high-end talents)；

4．促进企业自我改进能力的提高，满足全球化生产要求；
Company capacity in self-improvement to satisfy the needs for global manufacturing；

5．实现产品满足不同国家差异化生产需求，寻求国外生产合作基地；
Country-specific production needs, foreign production bases；

6．立足国际市场，全球招商合作，建立国际销售团队；
Exploration of international markets, global cooperation, and international sales team；

7．产品融入中国文化和价值观，强化中国元素在国际上的影响力。
Products with Chinese cultures and values, improving Chinese influence in international markets.

信合义乌小商品
Xinhe Yiwu Commodity

一、项目公司名称：山西晋源通能源科技有限公司

I. Project Company Name: Shanxi Jinyuantong Energy Technology Co., Ltd.

二、项目公司介绍：

II. Project Company Introduction:

公司成立于 2010 年 12 月，其前身为位于湖北省武汉市的湖北鹏泰贸易有限公司，是一家以经营煤炭、化肥、钢材等产品为主的专业化铁路物流贸易公司。经过近几年的稳定发展，公司以铁路物流为基业，把经营项目扩展到了矿山机电、房地产开发、大型商场、职业技术培训等大型综合企业。

Established in December 2010, the company, the former Hubei Pengtai Trade Co., Ltd., located in Wuhan, Hubei, is a professional railway logistics trade company which mainly operates coal, chemical fertilizers, steel and the like. After steady development for several years, the company, with railway logistics as a basic business, has expanded its scope of business to mine machinery, real estate development, large markets, occupational technology training, etc. and become a large comprehensive enterprise.

公司现下设四个子公司：

Up to now, the company has four branches:

1．山西信合义乌小商品城批发有限公司，成立于 2012 年，经销批发面向全国市场，年营业额达到 3000 余万元，以科学的管理手段，雄厚的技术力量，靠诚信、实力和产品质量获得业界的高度认可。

Shanxi Xinhe Yiwu Commodity City Wholesale Co., Ltd., founded in 2012, distributes and wholesales goods to the markets across China with an annual turnover of more than RMB 30 million, and is highly approved by the industry through scientific management methods, strong technical power, good faith, strength and product quality.

2．山西欣建建筑工程公司，成立于 2011 年，是一家专门从事建筑工程有着三级资质的建筑企业，公司总部设在晋城市开发区，现已拥有一批高素质管理人才和专业施工队伍。

Shanxi Xinjian Construction Engineering Company, founded in 2011 and with its headquarters in Jincheng Development Zone, is a construction enterprise with three-level qualification specializing construction work, and now has a batch of high-quality management talents and professional construction teams.

3．晋城市沁丹房地产开发有限公司，成立于 2016 年月，公司按照现代企业制度的管理模式，坚持以市场为导向，开发为重点，质量为根本的开发理念，为城市留下了一个个美丽的作品。主营房地产开发、投资咨询、项目投资、项目融资、建材批发、装饰装修、物业管理。

Jincheng Qindan Real Estate Development Co., Ltd., founded in 2016, follows the management mode of modern enterprise system, sticks to market orientation, focuses on development and takes quality as its root, providing many attractive products for cities. The company mainly deals in real estate development, investment consultation, project investment, project financing, building materials, decoration and fitment, and property management.

4．晋城市文苑职业培训学校，是晋城市人社局、财政局定点培训机构，是晋城市安监局安全生产定点培训机构，学校位于晋城市城区，占地 6000 平方米，拥有标准化教室、电子化考场、多媒体教室等。教学设施齐全；校园功能优越，环境幽雅，有浓厚的学习氛围。

Jincheng Wenyuan Occupational Training School, a training institution specified by Jincheng Municipal Human Resources and Social Security Bureau and Finance Bureau, and a safe production training institution specified by Jincheng Administration of Work Safety. The school, located in downtown Jincheng and covering an area of 6,000 m^2, has standard classrooms, electronic examination rooms, multi-media classrooms and the like. It has complete teaching facilities with advanced school functions, peaceful and elegant environment, and strong learning atmosphere.

三、负责人介绍：
III. Responsible Person Introduction:

石勇，男，1966 年月生，汉族，晋城市民进会员，山西省泽州县人，现任山西晋源通能源科技有限公司董事长，兼任山西省晋城市政协委员、晋城市民营经济联合会常务副会长；2016 年在第十六届世纪大采风中被授予"十大诚信企业家"称号。

Shi Yong, male, born in 1966, Han nationality, member of Jincheng Association for Promoting Democracy, and resident in Zezhou County, Shanxi, now is chairman of board of directors of Shanxi Jinyuantong Energy Technology Co., Ltd., Shanxi Jincheng CPPCC committee and standing vice-chairman of Jincheng Private Economy Association; he was awarded "Top 10 Honest Entrepreneurs" title in the 16th Century Dacaifeng in 2016.

四、项目名称：信合义乌小商品
IV. Project Name：Xinhe Yiwu Commodity

五、项目概况：
V. Project Profile:

安全、快速、低成本的现代铁路物流与全国范围内一带一路沿线工业园区实现无缝化衔接；面向"一带一路"沿线各国及国内各地，经销批发各类小商品、提供建筑工程及房地产开发、投资咨询、项目投资、项目融资、建材批发、装饰装修、物业管理、职业技术培训等服务。

Modern railway logistics featuring safety, rapidness and low cost is seamlessly connected with the industrial parks along the "Belt and Road" across China; the company distributes and wholesales various types of petty commodities to all countries along the Belt and Road and regions in China and provides them with services in architectural engineering, real estate development, investment consultation, project financing, building material wholesale, decoration and fitment, property management, occupational technology training and the like.

六、项目优势：
VI. Project Advantage(s):

铁路现代物流基地设施功能齐全，可为企业提供"一条龙服务"，降低综合物流成本。物流中心集仓储、配送、商贸等功能于一体，货物到发能力达到年 350 万吨。该中心远期规划建设 4000 多亩，分为集装箱作业区、板材作业区、仓储库、冷链库等六大功能区，各类产品可通过这里的现代物流服务，运输销售到"一带一路"沿线各地。

The modern railway logistics bases are equipped with complete facilities and able to provide "a whole set of services" for enterprises and reduce comprehensive logistics cost. The logistics center combines warehousing, distribution and business trade into one, reaching delivery and service of 3.5 million tons of goods each year. The center, with a planned future area of 4,000 mu, is divided into six functional areas including a container operation area, a plate operation area, a warehouse, a cold chain warehouse, etc. Various kinds of industrial and agricultural products are transported and sold to all regions along the "Belt and Road" via the modern logistics service in the center.

七、项目需求：
VII. Project Demand(s):

铁路物流、工程建设、房地产开发、建材各类商品批发、装饰装修、物业管理、职业技术等培训合作。

Railway logistics, engineering construction, real estate development, wholesale of various types of building materials, decoration and fitment, property management, occupational technology training cooperation, etc.

柯赛德尖端润滑科技
Kroneseder Sophisticated Lubrication Technology

一、项目公司名称：柯赛德（厦门）投资有限公司
I. Project Company Name：Kroneseder(Xiamen)Investment Co.,Ltd.

二、项目公司介绍：
II. Project Company Introduction：

柯赛德,1948 年在德国创建的润滑油品牌，德国的工业重镇曼海姆是我们的发源地。为客户提供最具竞争力的产品或服务是柯赛德的价值，我们先帮客户创造价值，最后发展成为战略合作伙伴。这样一来，柯赛德就可以精确地了解客户的需求，为客户提供一个极具竞争力的润滑解决方案。如此帮助客户减少了运营成本，为客户带来了更多的利润空间。

Kroneseder is a lubricating oil brand founded in 1948 in Germany. The German industrial city of Mannheim is the birthplace. Providing the most competitive products or services is the value of kroneseder. First, we help our customers to create value and then establish a strategical partner relationship with them. In this way, kroneseder can know the demands of customers precisely and then provides customers with an extremely competitive lubrication solution, to help customers to reduce operation cost and bring more profit space to customers.

三、负责人介绍：
III. Responsible Person Introduction：

vincent 先生从事石油行业 18 年，致力于军工、航空及科技领域的润滑应用，是智能制造润滑处理、供应链平台等项目的引领者，专注于设计协调的润滑油产品组合和相关技术服务，为行业为客户带来更为高效服务。

Mr. Vincent, who has been engaged in the petroleum industry for 18 years, is dedicated to the lubricant application in military, aviation and technological fields and one of the leaders in smart manufacture lubrication treatment, supply chain platform and the like, and focuses on design and coordination of lubricating oil product combination and related technical services so as to bring more efficient services to the customers in the industry.

四、项目名称：柯赛德尖端润滑科技
IV. Project Name：Kroneseder Sophisticated Lubrication Technology

五、项目概况：
V. Project Profile:

柯赛德建立了覆盖全球的生产、销售和服务网络，100 多家柯赛德子公司和众多的产品活动在润滑油服务领域。柯赛德在亚洲的销售与服务地区包括日本、韩国、新加坡等工业领先的国家。2010 年柯赛德来到中国，和中国的企业建立战略合作伙伴关系，建设系统的润滑油服务网络。

kroneseder has set up a network covering worldwide production, sales and service, and more than 100 kroneseder branches work in the lubricating oil service field and various kinds of products are used for the same field. kroneseder has established sales and service offices in industry-leading countries in Asia, including Japan, South Korea, Singapore, etc. In 2010, kroneseder came to China, establishing a strategical partner relationship with Chinese enterprises and setting up a systemic lubricating oil service network.

六、项目优势：
VI. Project Advantage(s):

柯赛德的优势是快速的创新和适应市场需要的产品生产，我们依靠发现和满足客户的市场需求，聚集资源创造关键竞争力的管理观念，不仅专注地去开发世界上最优秀的润滑油产品，同时积极推广新产品来解决客户的经营问题，从而使所有的润滑产品具有真正的意义。所以柯赛德创造出满足客户需要的产品，支持更高的效率和保护设备性能。

The advantages of kroneseder are fast innovation and adaption to production of products needed on the market.

Based on discovery, we meet the demands of customers and collect resources to create key competition power, not only focusing on developing the most excellent lubricating oil in the world, but also actively promoting new products to solve operation problems of customers, thus giving full play to all lubricating products. For these reasons, kroneseder is able to create the products that meet customers' demands, provide more efficient support and protect equipment performance.

七、项目需要：
Ⅶ. Project Demand(s):

对柯赛德而言，技术创新不是闭门造车，柯赛德是一个有机的整体，每个环节都有密切的联系，技术工程师遵循市场导向及客户需求，按照客户使用需要研发新产品，新产品的出现，帮助客户战胜行业面临的挑战。急需新产品迅速进入市场的导入及运用，能够进一步开拓、应用市场，以区域为单位来服务更多客户。

For kroneseder, technological innovation is not working behind closed doors, but an organic entirety：all links are in a close relation with each other；technical engineers follow market orientation and customer demands；research and develop new products based on the use by customers；and the emergence of new products helps customers to overcome. We need urgent introduction of new products into the market and their application, and we are able to further expand the application market to serve more customers in each region.

节能环保装饰工程
Energy Conservation and Environmental Protection Decoration Project

一、项目公司名称： 成都市广田华南装饰工程有限公司

I. Project Company Name: Chengdu Grandland South China Decoration Engineering Co., Ltd.

二、项目公司介绍：

II. Project Company Introduction:

2012年5月公司与深圳广田集团股份有限公司实行强强联合并建立战略合作伙伴关系，广田集团为全国建筑装饰行业中实力雄厚的龙头企业，于2010年9月上市。合作使公司在管理、技术力量、工程质量安全、工程业绩等方面都上了一个新台阶。借助广田集团强大的资金实力、规范管理、品牌价值以及在同行业中领先的技术和团队优势，公司将会为广大客户提供更加优质的服务。

In May 2012, the Company and Shenzhen Grandland Group Co., Ltd. implement a powerful combination and establish a strategic cooperative partnership. Grandland Group is a strong leading enterprise in the construction industry in China, which was listed in September 2010. The cooperation makes the Company get on a new stage in the management, technical strength, project quality and safety, engineering performance and so on. With Grandland Group's strong financial strength, standardized management, brand value and leading technology and team advantages in the same industry, the Company will provide the clients with more quality services.

三、负责人介绍：

III. Responsible Person Introduction:

周玉章，男，毕业于西南交大，现任广田华南总经理，同时任大海川投资有限公司董事长。在其带领下，广田华南近年承接了银川丽人妇产医院、成都雅居乐豪生酒店、岷江普特豪斯国际大酒店、成都希尔顿酒店、峨眉智选假日酒店、重庆朗廷酒店、成都阿玛尼艺术公寓等大型工程。

Zhou Yuzhang, male, was graduated from the Southwest Jiaotong University. Currently he is general manager of Grandland South China, at the same time acts as chairman of the Dahaichuan Investment Co., Ltd. Under his leadership, Grandland South China has undertaken Yinchuan Beauty Maternal Hospital, Howard Johnson Agile Plaza Chengdu, Minjiang Puthouse International Hotel, Chengdu Hilton Hotel, Holiday Inn Express Emei, Chongqing Langham Hotel, Chengdu Armani Art Apartments and other large projects in recent years.

四、项目名称： 节能环保装饰工程

IV. Project Name: Energy Conservation and Environmental Protection Decoration project

五、项目概况：

V. Project Profile:

成都乔治希尔顿酒店位于成都天府大道南沿线上的地标建筑希顿国际广场内。该项目由广田华南精心打造，建筑主体为框剪式结构，地面以上36层、地下4层，标准层高4.5米，施工建筑面积12000平方米。该工程已荣获中国建筑工程装饰奖（国优），是广田华南装饰推广绿色装饰理念，打造节能环保工程的又一典范力作。

George Hilton Grand Hotel Chengdu is located in Heaton International Plaza, a landmark building of Tianfu Avenue South, Chengdu. The project is built elaborately by Grandland South China. The main body of the building is frame-shear structure with 36 floors above ground and 4 floors underground. The standard layer is 4.5m high and the construction area is 12,000 m^2. The project has won the China Construction Engineering Decoration Award (National best). It is another masterpiece for Grandland South China Decoration to promote the concept of green decoration and to create energy conservation and environmental protection project.

在墙体、屋面和地面围护等节能工程方面，使用的保温隔热材料导热系数、密度、抗压强度、燃烧性能均结合当地实际和符合国家要求。通过改造门窗和墙体的保温性能，使得建筑门窗和墙体保温性能加强可节约60%的能源。

In respect of the wall, roof and ground enclosure and other energy-saving works, the thermal conductivity, density, compressive strength and combustion performance of used thermal insulation materials are in accordance with the local reality and meet national requirements. Through the transformation of doors and windows and wall insulation performance, the building doors and windows and wall insulation performance can be strengthened to save 60% of energy.

在配电和照明方面，通过建筑规划充分利用自然光源，合理的设置照明点，在满足光照要求的基础上兼顾设计美观的效果。

In the power distribution and lighting, by the building planning, make full use of natural light source, set lighting points reasonably, and fully consider beautiful design results on the basis of meeting the requirements of light.

六、项目优势：
VI. Project Advantage(s):

项目严格执行建筑节能减排的法律制度和技术规范，按照建筑节能强制性标准进行节能设计、注意施工管理和材料产品选购。工程选用大量的优质材料进行施工，新工艺、新技术、新材料的运用达到80%。其中隔墙制作选择的新型轻钢龙骨材质，具有良好的结构性、防火保温以及隔音性，相较传统的砖砌墙体更加的节能环保。广田华南秉持"绿色、低碳、文化、科技"的发展理念，以技术创新、创意设计为基点，在业内积极推进工业化、一体化、智能化、高技术化、互联网化和节能环保化，致力构筑绿色、健康、舒适、时尚、智慧的美好人居。

The project strictly enforces the legal system and technical specifications of building energy-saving and emission reduction. Carry out the energy-saving design in accordance with the building energy efficiency mandatory standards, and pay attention to construction management and materials products selection. A large number of high-quality materials are selected for construction, and the use of new process, new technology and new materials reaches 80%. A new light steel keel material is chosen for fabrication of partition with good structure, fire insulation and sound insulation. It is more energy saving and environmental protection compared to the traditional brick wall. Grandland South China upholds the development concept of "Green, Low Carbon, Culture, Science and Technology", with technological innovation and creative design as the starting point, actively promotes industrialization, integration, intelligence, high technology, Internet and energy saving in the industry, and is committed to building a green, healthy, comfortable, stylish and intelligent beautiful habitation.

七、项目需求：品牌推广。
VII. Project Demand(s)：Brand Promotion.

阳明养生养老中心
Yangming Health and Old-age Care Center

一、项目公司名称：崇义县阳明旅游实业有限公司

Ⅰ. Project Company Name：Chongyi County Yangming Tourism Industry Co., Ltd.

二、项目公司介绍：

Ⅱ. Project Company Introduction：

公司成立于 2015 年 1 月 13 日，注册资金 2000 万，地址位于江西赣州崇义县国家 4A 级旅游风景区内 – 阳岭国家森林公园阳明湖畔，其旗下子公司有阳明左溪颐园（阳明养生养老中心）、阳明湖酒店、阳岭氧吧山庄。

The Company was established in January 13, 2015 with the registered capital of 20 million, located in Yangming Lakeside of Yangling National Forest Park, a National 4A level tourism scenic area, Chongyi County, Ganzhou, Jiangxi. Its subsidiary has Yangming Zuoxi Emperor Garden (Yangming Health and Old-age Care Center), Yangming Lake Hotel and Yangling Oxygen Bar Villa.

三、负责人介绍：

Ⅲ. Responsible Person Introduction：

肖孟良，男，1973 年 7 月出生，祖籍江西赣州，广州中山大学硕士毕业，现任崇义县阳明旅游实业有限公司董事长。2007 年到今，与北京灵镜医疗净化工程有限公司合作并发展成立自己的企业，主要从事医疗养老事业，企业在行业内市场占有率超过 60%，服务全国 80% 的大型三甲医院，改善医疗服务和医疗水平。被评为"2015 赣州经济年度十大人物"。

Xiao Mengliang, male, born in July 1973, from Ganzhou in Jiangxi Province, master degree of Sun Yat-sen University, is chairman of the board of directors of Chongyi County Yangming Tourism Industry Co., Ltd. at present. From 2007 to this day, he cooperates with Beijing Lingjing Medical Purification Engineering Co., Ltd. and set up his own enterprise, mainly engaged in medical care and old-age care career. The enterprise has a market share of more than 60% in the industry, and serves 80% of the large 3A hospitals to improve medical services and medical care level. In January 2016, Xiao Mengliang won "the Top Ten Figures in 2015 Ganzhou Economic Year".

四、项目名称：阳明养生养老中心

Ⅳ. Project Name：Yangming Health and Old-age Care Center

五、项目概况：

Ⅴ. Project Profile：

以阳明文化为底蕴，遵从"天人合一"的养生思想，以休闲度假、会议培训、健康体检、康复调理、养生养老、观光农业为核心功能。建设各式休闲养生公寓别墅、文化展览馆、会议培训中心、娱乐活动场所、生态观光农业、园林景观、人工湖、医疗体检康复中心。总建筑面积约 5 万平方米。2016 年分别列入江西省及赣州市重点项目。

With Yangming culture as the fundament, comply with the idea of health of "Harmony between man and nature," regard the leisure, conference training, health examination, rehabilitation, health and pension for the ages, tourism agriculture as the core function, and construct various types of leisure health apartment and villas, cultural exhibition hall, conference training center, recreational activities places, ecological tourism agriculture, landscape, artificial lake, and medical examination rehabilitation center. The total construction area is about 50,000m^2. In 2016, they were included in the key projects of Jiangxi Province and Ganzhou City.

六、项目优势：

Ⅵ. Project Advantage(s)：

养生养老、健康体检、康复调理与旅游相结合，实行跨界融合。

Health care and old-age care, health examination, rehabilitation and tourism combination to implement the crossover integration.

七、项目需求：

Ⅶ. Project Demand(s):

本项目为省市重点项目，总投资5亿元，自有资金1.5亿元，项目正在建设中，需融资3.5亿元。

The project is the provincial and municipal key project, a total investment is 500 million yuan, and its own funds are 150 million yuan. The project is under construction, and needs financing of 350 million yuan.

乾承机械磨损修复技术
Qiancheng Mechanical Wear Repair Technology

一、项目公司名称：大连乾承科技开发有限公司
Ⅰ. Project Company Name: Dalian Qiancheng Technology Development Co., Ltd

二、项目公司介绍：
Ⅱ. Project Company Introduction：

乾承技术的研发始于2000年，于2008年、2009年分别申报两项国家发明专利，并在2010年、2013年分别获得批准。

The company started R&D in 2000. Two Chinese national invention patents were reported respectively in 2008 and 2009 and approved respectively in 2010 and 2013.

2011年，在大连成立"大连乾承科技开发有限公司"，注册资本2000万元人民币。

In 2011, the company was established with a registered capital of RMB 20 million.

2016年被认定为"国家高新技术企业"。

In 2016, the company was regarded as a Chinese national high-tech enterprise.

2016年获得硅谷高科技创新创业高峰会（北京）暨全球产业互联网大会颁发的"创新奖"。

In 2016, the company was awarded the "Innovation Prize" issued on the Silicon Valley High-tech Innovation and Entrepreneurship Summit (Beijing) and Global Industry Internet Conference.

2017年5月通过中国科学院文献情报中心获得科技查新结论：在国内外公开的文献中未见相同报道。

In May 2017, the company obtained a sci-tech novelty retrieval conclusion through National Science Library, Chinese Academy of Sciences：no identical reporting in the public literatures at home and abroad.

三、负责人介绍：
Ⅲ. Responsible Person Introduction:

王绪廷先生，内燃机管理专业，曾从业大型航运企业，研究发动机及机械设备维护；曲宝珠女士，材料学、化工学专业，曾在德国马普所摩擦实验室从事研究，研发金属摩擦修复技术17年。他们是两项国家发明专利的所有人和企业创始人。

Mr. Wang Xuting, majored internal combustion engine management, once worked in a large shipping company and is now engaged in engine research and mechanical equipment maintenance. Mrs. Qu Baozhu, majored in materials and chemical engineering, once performed research in the Max Planck Institute, Germany and has researched metal friction repair technology for 17 years. The two persons are the owners of two Chinese national invention patents and the creators of the company.

四、项目名称：乾承机械磨损修复技术
Ⅳ. Project Name：Qiancheng Mechanical Wear Repair Technology

五、项目概况：
Ⅴ. Project Profile:

机械运动的摩擦导致的磨损，使人类承受了巨大的沉没成本！据不完全统计，世界能源的30%-50%消耗于摩擦，而机械零件失效80%的原因是磨损，这是世界难题！

The wear due to mechanical friction of motion makes human suffer huge sunk cost! According to incomplete statistics, 30%-50% of energy in the world is consumed due to friction, while the failure of 80% mechanical parts is caused by wear. This is the difficulty across the world.

长久以来，人们在做的，只是尽可能地提高润滑效果，磨损，无法阻止。

What human have long been doing is to improve lubrication effect as much as possible, but wear cannot be avoided.

乾承科技，创造了世界第一！革命性地改变了克服磨损的路径——即时有效地修复磨损。同时，创造了第三种解决有害尾气排放的方法。

Qiancheng technology creates Number 1 in the world and revolutionarily changes the way to overcome wear and effectively repair wear timely, and creates the third way to solve the problem of harmful exhaust gas emission.

1．修复：持续的磨损，会不断增加能耗、降低效能直至损坏设备。"乾承产品"是修复磨损，而不是简单的提高润滑，这也是与其他各种润滑油添加剂的本质区别。

Repair：Continuous wear increases energy consumption and reduce energy efficiency until equipment damage. "Qiancheng products" repair wear other than simply improvement of lubrication. This is the essential difference from other various kinds of lubricating oil additives.

2．在线修复：乾承技术彻底改变了设备维修与保养的理念，运用高新科技，以简便实用的方式，对机械设备实现"不解体"、动态中的原位修复，保持和恢复零部件几何尺寸。

In-operation repair：Qiancheng technology thoroughly changes the idea of equipment repair and maintenance and performs in-position repair of in-operation mechanical equipment without disassembling it in a simple and practical manner to keep and recover the geometry dimensions of parts and components.

3．生成陶瓷合金："乾承产品"在金属摩擦表面自动生成的陶瓷合金层，具有超硬、超滑、耐腐蚀、耐高温等特性，因而减少摩擦阻力，提高机械设备的承载能力，降低机械振动和噪音、提高输出功率，还可以使有加工缺陷的金属表面恢复至理想尺寸，可对正在运行当中的机械设备进行品质再造。

Generating ceramal："Qiancheng products" automatically generate a layer of ceramal on a metal friction surface, which is characterized by exceptional hardness, ultra-smoothness, resistance to corrosion and high temperature, etc. For this reason, friction resistance is reduced; the bearing capacity of mechanical equipment improved; mechanical vibration and noise reduced; and output power increased. Besides the dimensions of a metal surface having defects due to machining can be restored to ideal dimensions, and the quality of in-operation mechanical equipment can be recreated.

4．节省：可实现节油或节电10%-20%，延长使用寿命1-3倍，可使各种燃油发动机减少有害尾气排放50%以上。

Economy：10%-20% fuel or electricity can be saved; lifetime extended by one - three times; and harmful exhaust gas emitted by various kinds of fuel engines reduced by more than 50%.

六、项目优势：
Ⅵ. Project Advantage(s):

中国科学院过程工程研究所、清华大学摩擦学国家重点实验室、中国环境科学研究院、中国船级社、瓦轴集团检测试验中心（国家认可实验室）、广西柳工机械有限公司传动研究所、国家石油产品质量监督检验中心、大连市产品质量检测研究院等权威机构验证，是在线修复磨损，其他添加剂只是润滑，2017年的科技查新证明其为世界唯一。摩擦系数优于各种添加剂数百倍，耐高温1600摄氏度，形成陶瓷合金厚度可达50微米。

The company has passed the verification performed by authoritative organizations such as the Institute of Process Engineering, Chinese Academy of Sciences, the State Key Laboratory of Tribology Tsinghua University, Chinese Research Academy of Environmental Sciences, China Classification Society, the Inspection and Testing Center of Wafangdian Bearing Group Corp., Ltd. (a laboratory approved by China), the Transmission Research Institution of LiuGong Machinery Co., Ltd., Chinese National Petroleum Products Quality Supervision and Inspection Center, Dalian Products Quality Inspection Institute, etc. The products repair wear, while other additives are only for lubrication. In 2017, the technology has been proved Number 1 in the world via sci-tech novelty retrieval. Friction coefficient outshines various kinds of additives by hundreds of times. Ceramal can resist high temperature of 1,600℃, and ceramal with a thickness of up to 50μm can be generated.

七、项目需求：
Ⅶ. Project Demand(s):

乾承产品广泛适用于物流、船舶、铁路、航空、出租车；风电、水电、火电；油田、冶金、矿山机械、工程机械、农业机械；军用的教练机、水面舰艇、潜艇、坦克、各种作战车辆等领域。诚与各相关行业合作。

Our products are widely applicable to logistics, vessels, railway, aviation and taxies; wind power, hydropower and thermal power; oil fields, metallurgy, mine machinery, engineering machinery and agricultural machinery; military training airplanes, surface ships, submarines, tanks, various kinds of fighting vehicles, etc. We hope to sincerely cooperate with enterprises in related industries.

移动环保公厕
Mobile Environmental Protection Public Toilet

一、项目公司名称：长沙洁洁环保科技开发有限公司
Ⅰ. Project Company Name: Changsha Jiejie Environmental Protection Technology Development Co., Ltd.

二、项目公司介绍：
Ⅱ. Project Company Introduction:

公司从 2006 年起，十年来专注于生态环保移动公厕车、环保生态移动厕所、全智能环保生态移动厕所、旧厕改造及污水处理、粪便处理、垃圾桶、果皮箱、钩臂式垃圾箱、垃圾收集车、电动清扫车等一系列环卫产品研发、生产、销售。清洁服务；物业清洁、维护；市政道路清扫保洁、维护；公厕保洁服务。

Since 2006, over the decade, the company has been engaged in R&D, production and sales of environmental sanitation products such as ecological environmental protection mobile toilet, environmental ecological mobile toilets, all intelligent environmental ecological mobile toilet, old toilet modification and sewage treatment, fecal treatment, trash can, garbage bin, hook arm type dustbin, refuse collector, electric sweeper etc. Cleaning services: Property cleaning and maintenance; municipal road sweeping and cleaning, maintenance; public toilet cleaning service.

三、负责人介绍：
Ⅲ. Responsible Person Introduction:

王梦洁，公司创始人、现任公司董事长，毕业于湘潭大学法律系。从商以来，始终以"永恒的诚信构筑公司的灵魂"为至理名言来管理公司，因此在业界拥有良好的口碑和广大人脉，使公司稳步发展。

Wang Mengjie, founder of the company, now the Chairman of the company, graduated from the Law Department, Xiangtan University. Since engagement in business, she has inherited the wisdom of "constructing the company's soul with permanent honesty" to manage the company, and has obtained sound reputation and relationship in the industry, making the company develop steadily.

四、项目名称：移动环保公厕
Ⅳ. Project Name: Mobile Environmental Protection Public Toilet

五、项目概况：
Ⅴ. Project Profile:

环保优点：
Environmental protection advantages:

1．可移动性强，因道路的改造或规划的变动可整体移动，避免了土建式厕所必须拆除而造成的资源浪费；
Strong mobility, the product could be moved as a whole because of road modification or changes in planning, avoiding any waste in resource caused by demolition of civil toilets;

2．更加节能环保，比起传统厕所，节约了至少 80% 以上的水资源；
More energy saving, compared with traditional toilets, the product saves more than 80% of water resources;

3．占地面积小，和传统厕所相比，移动厕所大大节约了土地面积；
The product covers a small area, compared with traditional toilets, mobile toilet greatly saves land area;

4．美观大方，在保证实用的基础上，注重了美观的重要性，成为旅游景点、公园小区的一道风景线。
Beautiful and generous, on the basis of ensuring the utility, the product pays attention to the importance of aesthetics, and becomes a tourist attraction or a scenery line in parks and residential quarters.

环保要点：
Environmental protection key points:

1．拒绝污染：采用厌氧微生物来分解粪便液，从而使粪便液降解成水和二氧化碳，实现了粪便的就地处理。
Pollution elimination: It adopts anaerobic microorganisms to decompose fecal fluid, so that the fecal fluid is

degraded into water and carbon dioxide, which achieves in situ treatment of fecal.

2．微生物生长繁殖力强，一次添加，终身使用。

Microorganism has strong growth fecundity, making life-time use of the product by adding once.

3．自动化程度高，PLC 全自动操作：

High degree of automation, and PLC full-automatic operation:

（1）即人入厕：门上方的显示屏自动显示"有人"中英文对照。

Entering the toilet："Occupied" (in both English and Chinese) will display automatically on the screen above the door.

人出厕：门上方的显示屏自动显示"无人"中英文对照。

(Exiting the toilet："Vacant" (in both English and Chinese) will display automatically on the screen above the door.

（2）背景音乐：即人入厕，音乐自动响起，音响设备型号：501，DSPPA，内容可根据采购人要求录制。人出厕自动关闭。

Background music：The music will sound automatically once someone entering the toilet. Sound equipment model：501, DSPPA, the content could be customized according to the requirements of the purchaser. Closes automatically when people exiting the toilet.

（3）人入厕：排气扇、照明灯自动运行。人出厕自动关闭。

Entering the toilet：Exhaust fan and light will run automatically. Closes automatically when people exiting the toilet.

（4）系统操作安全方便。

Safe and convenient system operation.

4．环保公厕施工简捷：只需厕所占地，无须市政管道支持，接通电源即可正常使用。

Convenient construction of environmental protection toilet：Only toilet coverage is required, without needing municipal pipeline support, the product could be used once connected to power supply.

5．无害化：处理过程无二次污染，微生物无毒、无害、无污染。

Harmless：No secondary pollution during treatment, the microbial is non-toxic, harmless and free from contamination.

6．特别是车载式厕所，方便实用，可随便开动。无电、无水、无排污情况下都可使用，并且厕所采用的是生化除臭，使厕所内外无臭味、无异味。

Especially the onboard toilet, which is convenient and practical, and can be started at randomly. The product can be used when there's no electricity, no water or no drainage, and the toilet adopts biological deodorization, making no smell or Oder outside the toilet.

六、项目优势：

VI. Project Advantage(s):

在建造上大大节约了人力、物力和财力，传统厕所的构建通常需要经过选址、购材、施工、完工、投入使用等，而移动厕所是厂家生产好的成品，直接安装就可以使用。

It reduces manpower, material and financial resources in construction. The construction of traditional toilets usually needs to select address, purchase materials, commence construction, complete construction, and put into use etc., while mobile toilets are finished products made by the manufacturer, and could be used right after installation.

七、项目需求：

VII. Project Demand(s):

产品推广：移动环保公厕、车载式环保公厕、垃圾桶、环卫工休息室。

Product promotion：Mobile environmental protection public toilet, car-mounted environmental protection public toilet, trash, and environmental sanitation rest room.

富蓝特酒店
Friends Hotel

一、项目公司名称：张家界富蓝特酒店投资管理有限责任公司
Ⅰ. Project Company Name：Zhangjiajie Friends Hotel Investment Management Co., Ltd.

二、项目公司介绍：
Ⅱ. Project Company Introduction:

公司于2000年成立，是以住宿、餐饮为主的投资管理公司，公司旗下现有两个主打品牌：富蓝特乐酒店，定位为中端时尚品牌；富蓝特和酒店，定位为土家民俗高端品牌，目前在湖南省已开业11家直营连锁分店，计划2018-2020年面向大湘西、贵州、云南等地的拓展，使富蓝特品牌覆盖云、贵、川三省主要城市和旅游景区，将富蓝特发展成为中国西部连锁酒店第一品牌。

Founded in 2000, the company is an investment management company in the accommodation and catering service industry. The company is currently running two brands：Friends Joy Hotel which is a middle-end fashion hotel brand, and Friends Hotel which is a Tujia-themed high-end hotel brand. So far, the company has opened 11 direct chain hotels in Hunan province and is further expecting to extend its business to Xiangxi, Guizhou and Yunnan in 2018-2020. By these efforts, Friends brand will be able to cover all major cities and tourism sites in Yunnan, Guizhou and Sichuan and Friends will develop into the top chain hotel brand in China.

三、负责人介绍：
Ⅲ. Responsible Person Introduction:

向文红女士，大学本科，张家界富蓝特酒店投资管理有限责任公司执行总裁，张家界市工商业联合会副会长，张家界市人大代表。1999年即开始投资酒店，多年来始终秉承"以精立业，以质取胜，以诚相待，以恒持之"的经营理念来管理公司，缔造了富蓝特主题酒店和富蓝特新闻酒店均在同一座城市两年内收回投资成本的商业神话。

Ms. Xiang Wenhong, Bachelor degree, is currently working as Executive President of Zhangjiajie Friends Hotel Investment Management Co., Ltd., Director of Zhangjiajie Federation of Industry and Commerce, and a Zhangjiajie representative to National People's Congress. She began the investments in hotels in 1999 and managed her company by the philosophies of "elaboration, quality, good faith and perseverance". The Friends Theme Hotel and Friends New Hotel, under her management, became a miracle that she had all investment returned in only two years in a single city.

四、项目名称：富蓝特酒店
Ⅳ. Project Name：Friends Hotel

五、项目概况：
Ⅴ. Project Profile：

公司2016年与全国知名的策划公司合作，确立了将土家文化融入公司的经营与管理中，结合西方先进的管理模式，形成具有民族特色的公司形象，并确立以张家界为核心，辐射大湘西，面向全国拓展实现"南战西征，五年百店"的宏伟目标以及公司五年战略规划和方案。2016年8月，公司推出两大主打产品：富蓝特·乐酒店，富蓝特·和酒店，是以土家民族文化为主导，以"将艺术融入服务之中，把服务提升到艺术的高度"为目标，打造具有民族情怀的旅游商务酒店。目前两个品牌共有直营连锁店11家，近2500个床位，提供酒店就业岗位近600个，各分店的经营状况良好，具有较好的获利能力。计划2018-2020年通过向大湘西、贵州、云南等地的拓展，使富蓝特品牌覆盖云、贵、川三省主要城市和旅游景区，发展成拥有包含直营、加盟、托管等多形式的酒店50家；未来十年，富蓝特品牌将成为中国西部连锁酒店第一品牌。

In 2016, the company cooperated with a famous planning company and decided to include Tujia culture in company operation and management and combine it with western advanced management models. With such efforts, the company established a company image with distinct national features and decided to base Zhangjiajie to cover the greater Xiangxi area, and to realize the national expansion goal of "100 hotels in 5 years" and the five-year strategy and plans. In August 2016, the company promoted two major brands：Friends·Joy Hotel and Friends·Peace Hotel. Both brands are rooted in the cultures of Tujia nation and targeted to "include art in services and promote services at the level of arts" to build a travel and business hotel with unique national features. Currently, there have been 11 chain hotels under the two brands, providing 2,500 beds and 600 jobs. All chain stores are now running well with considerable profitability. We are planning to expand the business in 2018-2020 to cover the greater Xiangxi, Guizhou and Yunnan, to cover all major cities and tourism sites in such provinces and regions and to develop 50 chain hotels including direct hotels, franchise hotels and entrusted hotels. In the next 10 years, Friends will become the No.1 brand in West China.

六、项目优势：

Ⅵ. Project Advantage(s):

1．在湖南省内已具有一定的品牌知名度。

Brand popularity in Hunan province.

2．公司有股东从事旅游行业，因此，可以开发股东的旅游资源，满足酒店的经营需要。

Shareholders of the company are practitioners in tourism industry, making it easy to further develop tourism resources of the shareholders and to meet the needs of hotels.

3．营销渠道系统化，富蓝特目前拥有粉丝会员近5万，并建立了包括线上、线下的完整的营销体系，能够做到立体化的全方位营销，达到全国各地客户资源共享的目标。

Systematic sales channels：Friends has currently near 50 thousand member users, and has established an online and offline marketing system. With the 3D marketing model, all chain hotels can share the customer resources at different regions.

4．健全而合理的规范和标准：经过多年的探索与研究，富蓝特公司已经形成了一套成熟的个性化管理运营P&P制度规范和SOP标准作业流程。

Complete and reasonable codes and standards：Through exploration and studies for years, Friends has established a set of customized management and operation P&P systems and SOPs.

5．丰富的人力资源库：通过内部培养和不惜成本从外部发掘人才，现在富蓝特公司已经拥有丰富的酒店职业经理人力资源库。

Rich labor resources：By internal training and attracting external talents, Friends has built up a professional manager library.

6．具有土家民族特色的酒店风格。

Tujia-themed hotel.

七、项目需求：

Ⅶ. Project Demand(s):

目前富蓝特品牌在湖南以外省份的知名还不够高，需要政府予以支持，帮助推广和宣传提高全国知名度，同时希望有实力看好酒店业发展的企业、财团与我公司对接，尽早占有中国西部酒店业市场，共同发展，使得富蓝特酒店品牌发展壮大！

Friends is not yet very popular outside Hunan province and therefore needs governmental supports in promotion and advertising. We also hope that companies or groups that have interest in hotel industry can contact us directly to join us in developing the hotel markets in West China and to further develop the Friends brand!

大气新能源
Atmospheric New Energy

一、项目公司名称：湖南紫伊智能机械设备有限公司
Ⅰ. Project Company Name：Hunan Ziyi Intelligent Machinery Equipment Co., Ltd.

二、项目公司介绍：
Ⅱ. Project Company Introduction：

公司前身为上海紫伊实业有限公司，成立于2010年；起源于高科技智能化系统设备供销；与上海应用技术大学长期战略合作；是联合国采购特殊供应商。各事业部在高科技新能源——大气能节能环保工程；现代农牧业牲畜前期智能化科技饲养，中期屠宰生物卤制与深加工系统，后期"变废为宝"的小肠肝素钠与骨素提取、粪便与牲畜尸体无害化环保利用等系列优势工程领域有相当高的造诣与专业技术水平！

The Company, formerly known as Shanghai Ziyi Industrial Co., Ltd., was established in 2010 and originated in high-tech intelligent system equipment supply and marketing; it has a long-term strategic cooperation with Shanghai Institute of Technology and is the special supplier of United Nations procurements. The various divisions have the very high attainments and professional and technical level in terms of high-tech new energy - the atmosphere save energy and environmental protection projects; early-term intelligent technology breeding of modern agriculture and animal husbandry livestock, medium-term slaughtering bio-halogen marinating and deep processing system, and later-term "turning waste into treasure" – extraction of small intestinal heparin sodium and ostein, feces and animal carcasses harmless environmental protection and other series advantage engineering fields!

三、负责人介绍：
Ⅲ. Responsible Person Introduction：

何正权，上海复旦工商管理硕士。读书期间长期担任学生会干部。工作期间先后担任科密集团、哈德电气、东方集团的总监、副总、执行总裁等职。2010年自主创业、全力推进国际最新高科技新能源环保项目——大气能与太阳能、地热能综合开发环保利用高科技系统项目。

He Zhengquan, Master of Business Administration of Shanghai Fudan, acted as the student union cadres during the study period. During the work, he has served as president, vice president, executive president and so on of Comet Group, HED Electric and Orient Group. In 2010, he founded his own company to promote the latest international high-tech new energy and environmental protection projects. - Atmospheric energy and solar energy, and geothermal energy comprehensive development and environmental protection utilization high-tech system project.

四、项目名称：大气新能源
Ⅳ. Project Name：Atmospheric New Energy

五、项目概况：
Ⅴ. Project Profile：

国际最新高科技新能源环保项目：前期依托空气能热源塔技术在虹桥机场航管楼、上海市政大厦、延安饭店、杭州华北饭店、上海瑞金医院等成功运用；让空调领域减去了锅炉，运用空气中的水蒸气压缩成液体把能量置换出来，实现制冷、供热及生活热水等功能；节能效果约在20%-50%之间，真正开辟了新能源的世界性革命。目前的研发是要开创"把大气能中的氮气、氧气、二氧化碳、氢气等分离出来进行能源重新配置利用"，紫伊智能已经与德国MIT集团达成了技术战略合作、与国内外"大气能"科研方面最有权威的几家科研院所和大学正在进行密切地深度科研开发合作，鉴于最新高科技的保密性在此不便详细阐述，敬请谅解！

The latest international high-tech new energy and environmental protection project：During the earlier stage, relying on the air energy heat source tower technology, the project is applied successfully in Air Traffic Control Building of Hongqiao Airport, Shanghai Municipal Government Building, Yan'an Hotel, Hangzhou North China Hotel, Shanghai Ruijin Hospital and so on; The boiler is eliminated from the air conditioner. The water vapor in the air is compressed into the liquid to replace the energy to achieve cooling, heating and domestic hot water functions; and the energy-saving effect is about 20% -50%, and truly opens up the world revolution of the new energy. The current research and development is to create "the atmospheric energy in the nitrogen, oxygen, carbon dioxide, hydrogen and so on are separated for the energy re-allocation and use," Ziyi Intelligent Co., Ltd. has reached a technical strategic cooperation with German MIT Group and has carried out the close and deep technical strategic cooperation with the domestic and foreign most authoritative research institutes and universities in "atmospheric energy" scientific research aspects. In view of the latest high-tech confidentiality, the elaborated cannot be available here, please understand!

六、项目优势：
VI. Project Advantage(s)：

国际最新高科技新能源环保项目的前期空气能热源塔技术为国内首创、国际领先；目前在"取之不尽用之不竭——大气能"最新高科技的开发下将会"无限量的降低社会成本、并无限量的提高新能源环保水平"，真正开展全世界新能源颠覆式的革命。

The early-stage air heat source tower technology of the latest international high-tech new energy and environmental protection project is the initiative one and the international leader; currently in the latest high-tech development of the "inexhaustible atmosphere energy" will "unlimitedly reduce social costs, and unlimitedly improve the environmental protection level of new energy" to truly create a new era of subversive revolution of the world new energy.

七、项目需求：
VII. Project Demand(s):

市场融资与战略合作、推进国际最新高科技新能源环保项目的开发与应用。

Carry out the market financing and strategic cooperation to promote development and application of the latest international high-tech new energy and environmental protection project.

VR 手机助手 & 易企炫
VR Mobile Phone Assistant & Yiqixuan

一、项目公司名称： 厦门桔子树网络科技有限公司

Ⅰ. Project Company Name： Xiamen Orange Tree Network Technology Co., Ltd

二、项目公司介绍：

Ⅱ. Project Company Introduction：

公司成立于 2014 年，是一家专注于软件开发、软件定制、软件实施的高新技术企业。总部设立于美丽的海滨城市厦门，公司技术和研发实力雄厚，拥有一批经验丰富的软件开发、软件定制的专业人才，全方位满足政府与企业信息化需求，荟萃业界精英，将国外先进的信息技术、管理方法及企业经验与国内企业的具体实际相结合，为企业客户提供全方位的解决方案。

Founded in 2014, the company is a high-tech enterprise specializing in software development, software customization and software implementation, whose headquarters is located in the beautiful coastal city, Xiamen. It has enormous technical and research and development strength and owns a batch of professionals with rich experiences in software development and software customization so as to comprehensively meet the informatization demand of governments and enterprises. Besides, we collect the elites in the field, combine the foreign advanced information technology, management methods and business experience with the reality of domestic enterprises, and provide enterprise customers with all-around solutions.

公司人才结构合理，拥有多名高学历管理骨干，为了不断研发更多符合企业需求的产品，聘请行业知名专家和学者作为咨询顾问，紧密跟踪行业发展特点，不断优化产品，使用户得到最优质的服务。是厦门虚拟与增强现实产业协会常务副会长企业。

With reasonable personnel structure, the company possesses several highly-educated management backbones. In order to continuously develop more products that meet the enterprise needs, invite the well-known experts and scholars in the field as consultants, closely track the industrial development characteristics, constantly optimize the products, and enable users to get the best service. In addition, it is an executive vice president of Xiamen Virtual & Augmented Reality Industry Association.

三、负责人介绍：

Ⅲ. Responsible Person Introduction：

曾俊松 CEO 拥有十年外企管理层经验，熟悉企业管理流程，制定优秀的企业战略方针。并且担任过传统零售业、影视业、avr 行业及互联网行业领导人，能够合理地将传统行业结合于互联网中，从而推动产业的发展。

With 10-year management experience in a foreign company, CEO Zeng Junsong is acquainted with the enterprise management process, and is able to set excellent enterprise strategic policy. Besides, he has served as leader in traditional retail industry, film and television industry, avr industry and Internet industry, so he is capable of reasonably combining the traditional industries with the Internet and thus promoting the industrial development.

四、项目名称： VR 手机助手 & 易企炫

Ⅳ. Project Name： VR Mobile Phone Assistant & Yiqixuan

五、项目概况：

Ⅴ. Project Profile：

VR 手机助手定位于做国内最大的手机 VR 资源整合平台，致力于解决用户获取 VR 资源难、复杂等问题，并立志成为 VR 产业的第一入口整合平台，提供卓越的 VR 资源服务。

Positioned to do the largest mobile phone VR resource integration platform in China, VR Mobile Phone Assistant devotes to solving the problem that are difficult and complex for users to obtain VR resources, aspires to become the first portal integration platform in VR industry, and provides outstanding VR resource service.

VR 手机助手是国内第一家基于手机端 VR 资源整合平台，内容含括 VR 视频、全景、游戏、社区、商城及 VR 素材库等。优质的平台服务体系及内容整合渠道是产品快速成长的核心基础

VR Mobile Phone Assistant is the first VR resources integration platform in China based on the mobile phone side, comprising VR video, panoramic view, games, community, shopping mall and VR material library, etc. The superior platform service system and content integration channel are the core foundation of products to rapidly grow.

易企炫项目将成为个人到企业自营化宣传推广的平台，平台通过结合巧妙的创意点子及抢现金红包形式给用户带来刺激感，打造火爆活动。平台核心优势在于底层运用大数据及人工智能分析，精准定位用户人群及地域等平台的理念在于切中传统广告媒体给广告主带来的痛点：推广费用高、目标不明确等。平台做到不限制广告主投入的广告资金、宣传渠道、地域、人群等，从而达到低广告成本，100普光率及到达率等。是目前国内唯一为内容原创者提供内容分发理念的自营化平台。

Yiqixuan project will become the platform from individuals to enterprise self-support promotion, which brings stimulation for the users by combining the clever ideas and cash red packet grabbing form, and creates popular activities. The core advantage of the platform lies in the use of big data in the bottom and analysis of artificial intelligence, and the concept of precise locating of the user groups and region lies in hitting of the pain points of the traditional advertising media to the advertisers：high promotion cost and unclear goal. The platform should not restrict the advertising fund which is invested by advertisers, publicity channels, geography and population so as to realize the low advertising costs, 100 exposure rate and arrival rate, etc. At present, it is the unique Chinese self-support platform which provides content distribution concept for content creators.

重点战略合作企业：
Key strategic cooperative enterprises：
1．京东集团
Jingdong Group
2．环球小姐中国赛区
Miss Universe China
3．SGG俱乐部
SGG Club
4．东莞市新进巧工艺制作有限公司
Dongguan Xinjinqiao Craft Production Co., Ltd.

六、项目优势：
VI. Project Advantage(s)：

1．大型企业、重大赛事活动、知名娱乐社团及产业化工厂为背书
Endorsed by large enterprise, great competition activity, famous entertainment community and industrial factory
2．被厦门市政府评为VR企业专家组身份
Evaluated as VR enterprise expert group identity by Xiamen Municipal Government
3．最全面的VR资源整合平台
The most comprehensive VR resource integration platform
4．突破传统媒体理念的自营化内容分发平台
Self-support content distribution platform which breaks through traditional media concept
5．运营模式国内首创
Originated operation model in China
6．高尖技术人才为依附
Depend on top technical personnel

七、项目需求
VII. Project Demand(s)

资本需求：寻求更多资本方介入，扩大平台知名度
Capital demand：seek more capital partner to join in, and expand platform publicity
政策需求：项目科技成果专利申请
Policy demand：application for project scientific and technological achievement patent
推广需求：科技众筹，城市推广，发展各区域代理商
Promotion demand：scientific and technological crowdfunding, urban promotion, and development of agents in each region

海陆空运输
Maritime, Land and Air Transport

一、项目公司名称：厦门宜洋物流有限公司
Ⅰ. Project Company Name：Xiamen Yiyang Logistics Co., Ltd.

二、项目公司介绍：
Ⅱ. Project Company Introduction:

公司经中国商务部批准的国家一级国际货运代理企业，同时也由中国交通运输部批准具有无船承运人资质(NVOCC NO:MOC-NV 07016)。公司具有货代、专业报送、集装箱堆场、集卡车队、仓库储存、物流管理等服务功能。公司经营范围：承办海运，空运，多式联运国际货物运输代理，包括揽货、订舱、托运、仓储、包装、集装箱拆箱、分拨中转及相关的短途运输；报送、报检、保险；国际展品、私人物品及过境货物代理；咨询业务及其他国际货运代理业务和综合物流业务。

The company is a national Class-I international freight forwarder certified by the Chinese Ministry of Commerce, and is also a Non-vessel Operating Common Carrier (NVOCC NO:MOC-NV 07016) approved by Chinese Ministry of Transport. The company provides services of freight forwarding, data submission, container yard, container truck fleet, warehousing and logistics management. Business scope：International freight forwarding agent for maritime transport, air transport and multimodal transport, including cargo collection, vessel ordering, consignment, warehousing, packing, container devanning, transit shipment as well as their related short-distance transport; document submission, inspection, insurance; international exhibit, private article and cross-border freight forwarding; consultation service and other international freight forwarding and comprehensive logistics services.

三、负责人介绍：
Ⅲ. Responsible Person Introduction:

谢佳霖，2007年大学毕业后参加工作，入职担任厦门嘉鸿信实股份有限公司业务专员；2009年，担任厦门嘉鸿信实股份有限公司业务部经理；2010年，担任厦门嘉鸿信实股份有限公司副总经理；2014年，担任厦门宜洋物流有限公司担任总经理。

Xie Jialin graduated from university in 2007 and worked in Xiamen Jiahongxinshi Co, Ltd. as a business clerk. In 2009, he worked as a business manager of Xiamen Jiahongxinshi Co., Ltd. In 2010, he worked as vice general manager of Xiamen Jiahongxinshi Co., Ltd. In 2014, he worked as General Manager of Xiamen Yiyang Logistics Co., Ltd.

四、项目名称：海陆空运输
Ⅳ. Project Name：Maritime, land and air transport

五、项目概况：
Ⅴ. Project Profile:

公司将充分发挥整体优势，面向海内外市场，不断开拓经营，通过实施经营规模化、功能多元化和国际化的战略，逐步建成一个规模宏大、实力雄厚、功能齐全、具有市场竞争优势的与国际航运中心相匹配的综合物流公司。公司以准确、迅捷、高效、节省的经营方针，竭诚为各位客户服务，并以科学规范的现代化管理，卓越完备的硬件设施，高水平的优质服务，锐意进取，不断开拓，自我完善，及时掌握市场信息，研究货运趋势，制定合理的运输模式和价廉的收费标准，为广大国内外客户提供完善的服务。

The company will make best use of its overall strengths to explore overseas markets by implementing its scale operation, diverse functions and international strategies. The company is expected to become a large and comprehensive logistics company with strong market competitiveness providing complete services. The company runs with clearly defined targets and quick response with effective and efficient services. Under scientific and standardized modern management as wells as excellent facilities, the company provides customers with high-quality services, while making continuous efforts to improve and expand its business. Besides, supported by real-time feedback of market information, the company studies new developments in freight forwarding and works out reasonable transport models and competitive pricing standards.

六、项目优势：
VI. Project Advantage(s)：

公司在澳大利亚、新西兰、西欧、北欧、地中海、中东、南非、中南美、美国、加拿大、东南亚、印度等世界各地 500 多个港口拥有自己强大的代理服务网络，并与 MAERSK、APL、COSCO、MSC、SITC、CMA、PIL、MCC、EVERGREEN 等多家船公司建立了密切的长期合作关系。可为广大客户提供国际海运拼箱、整箱以及门到门、特殊货物、第三方贸易、仓储、报关、报验以及陆运，空运等国际集装箱运输业务优质、快捷、安全、便利的全方位服务。在爆仓的旺季，能够保证客户的仓位，而不会影响交货时间，制定合理的运输模式和价廉的收费，专业优质的服务，确保每批货物安全，准时到达客户手中。

The company has established its powerful freight-forwarding network at over 500 ports throughout the world, including Australia, New Zealand, Western Europe, Northern Europe, Mediterranean, Turkey, Israel, Middle East, South Africa, Central and South America, the U.S., Canada, Southeast Asia and India. Besides, it has established long-term close cooperation with many shipping companies such as MAERSK, APL, COSCO, MSC, SITC, CMA, PIL, MCC and EVERGREEN. We provide customers with high-quality, express, secure and comprehensive international services, including groupage shipping services, regular container shipping services and door-to-door services, transport of special cargoes, third-party trade, warehousing, customs declaration, inspection as well as land and air transport. During peak seasons, we make all efforts to ensure the availability of shipping space, so as not to affect the timeliness of final delivery. Besides, we have reasonable transportation modes, competitive prices and high-quality services, to ensure the secure and timeliness delivery of cargoes to our customers.

七、项目需求：
VII. Project Demand(s)：

能获得更多的机会将公司的服务产品推广出去，争取用我们最大的专业力度服务于客户，服务于社会。

We expect more opportunities to promote our services and products and serve our customers and the entire society wholeheartedly.

嘉佑－贝吉塔饰材
Jiayou- Vegeta Decorative Material

一、项目公司名称：山东嘉佑木业有限公司
Ⅰ. Project Company Name：Shandong Jiayou Wood Industry Co., Ltd.

二、项目公司介绍：
Ⅱ. Project Company Introduction：

公司成立于2004年，公已从单一贴面板生产企业，发展成为阻燃胶合板、家具板、生态板生产、加工及销售的综合性企业。产品销售覆盖全国各地，并赢得良好的口碑。公司以推进行业绿色进程为己任，积极整合各种优势资源，倡导绿色消费理念，以高品质、高环保产品为载体，致力于打造具有影响力的装饰材料综合服务商，实现由制造业向品牌服务业的转型升级，并努力构建资源优势、创新优势、品牌优势，实现企业跨越式发展。

Established in 2004, the company has developed to a comprehensive enterprise engaged in production, processing and sales of flame- retardant plywood, furniture board and ecological board. Our products are sold to all parts of the country and have won good reputation. We take propelling green process as our own duty, actively integrate various advantageous resources, advocate green consumption concept and devote ourselves to creating the influential comprehensive service provider of decorative materials with high-quality environment-friendly products as carrier to achieve transformation and upgrading from manufacturing industry to the brand service industry and strive to build resources, innovation, brand advantages and achieve leapfrog development.

三、负责人介绍：
Ⅲ. Responsible Person Introduction:

李鹏，董事长，沙漠种植绿色农作物发起人之一、国学爱好者、德润文化发起人、中国中小商业企业会员、北京坐标系商学院教练、捐款改造农村道路改善人们出行领头人。

Li Peng, President of the project company isone of initiators of green crop suitable for planting on deserts, an enthusiast of Sinology, the initiator of Derun Culture, a member of China Association of Small & Medium Commercial Enterprise and a professor of Beijing Coordinate System Business College, once donated for renovation of rural roads and a leader of traffic improvement.

四、项目名称：嘉佑－贝吉塔饰材
Ⅳ. Project Name：Jiayou–Vegeta Decorative Material

五、项目概况：
Ⅴ. Project Profile：

贝吉塔是山东嘉佑木业有限公司旗下重点品牌；公司为此成立专业的销售、设计、生产团队，致力于生产高端、高质、高环保产品，发展无醛、无害产品。

Vegeta is a key brand of Shandong Jiayou Wood Industry Co., Ltd.; we have established a professional sales, design and production team for the project to be devoted to production of high-end, good-quality, environment-friendly products and development of formaldehyde-free and harmless products.

贝吉塔饰材，坐落于中国四大板材基地——朱保工业园，占地面积22000平方米，主要生产浮雕水曲柳、三聚氰胺生态板、家具板、阻燃板等。公司设备精良，技术实力雄厚，检测手段严格。拥有国内先进的浮雕水曲柳生产流水线。充分利用当地的资源优势，采用中国林科院的先进技术，以天然原木和符合国家标准的环保胶为原材料，生产出天然、环保、无污染的常规多层板和家具多层板。公司已形成独特的规模优势、质量优势、价格优势、品质优势。

Vegeta Decorative Material, located at Zhubao Industry Park——one of four sheet material bases in China, covers an area of 22,000 m^2 and mainly manufactures embossed fraxinus mandshurica, melamine ecological board, furniture board and flame-retardant plate, etc. We have excellent equipment, powerful technical strength, strict testing methods and the advanced assembly line of embossed fraxinus mandshurica. With the advanced technology of Chinese Academy of Forestry, making the best of local resources advantage, we manufacture natural, environment-friendly and pollution-free conventional sandwich plate and furniture sandwich plate. Now, we have formed unique advantages of scale, quality, price and quality.

公司始终秉承塑时代精品、建美好家园的发展宗旨，以推进行业绿色进程为己任，积极整合各种优势资源，倡导绿色消费理念，以高品质、高环保产品为载体，致力于打造具有影响力的装饰材料综合服务商，实现由制造业向品牌服务业的转型升级，并努力构建资源优势、创新优势、品牌优势，实现企业跨越式发展。

We always adhere to the development tenet of manufacturing quality products of the era and building beautiful homes. We take propelling green process as our own duty, actively integrate various advantageous resources, advocate green consumption concept and devote ourselves to creating the influential comprehensive service provider of decorative materials with high-quality environment-friendly products as carrier to achieve transformation and upgrading from manufacturing industry to the brand service industry and strive to build resources, innovation, brand advantages and achieve leapfrog development.

六、项目优势：
Ⅵ. Project Advantage(s)：

公司响应"一带一路"号召，提高品质，提升效率，专业的新产品研发和市场调研团队使得产品多样化、齐全化，质量高，适合当代年轻人的消费水平。作为行业的领跑者，贝吉塔开通了24小时服务热线，以完善的售后服务为顾客解决后顾之忧。

We respond to the call of the "Belt and Road Initiative" to improve the quality and efficiency. With professional new products R&D and market survey team, we manufacture diversified and completed high-quality products which are suitable for the consumption level of young people nowadays. As the industrial leader, Vegeta has opened up 24-hour service hotline to provide customers with excellent after-sales services.

七、项目需求：
Ⅶ. Project Demand(s):

推广产品：3-18厘米胶合板及饰面贴面、家具专用胶合板、三胺饰面橱柜板。

Promotional products：3-18 cm plywood and wood veneer, specialized plywood for furniture and triamine veneer cupboard plate.

推广需求：市场拓展对象实木家具厂、实木门厂、大型装饰工程公司、实木工艺品厂。

Promotional demands：Market development objects include solid wood furniture factories, solid door factories, large decoration engineering companies and solid wood art craft factories.

防腐保温工程
Anti-corrosion and Heat-preservation Project

一、项目公司名称： 陕西长建建设工程有限公司

I. Project Company Name: Shannxi Changjian Construction & Engineering Co., Ltd.

二、项目公司介绍：

II. Project Company Introduction:

公司创建于2007年11月，已具有十余年的施工管理经验，其技术精、素质好、设备精良。138名员工中有高级、中级、初级职称的工程师、经济师、项目经理，技术员达40多人,2012年公司通过中国质量认证中心（CQC）对公司质量、安全、环保、健康体系认证。公司是以房屋建筑工程、防腐保温工程、机电设备安装、钢结构工程、市政公用工程施工、化工石油设备管道安装、道路维护工程、场站维护工程等施工为主的综合性服务公司。

Established in November 2007, the company has more than ten years of construction management experience as well as excellent technology, good quality and superior equipment. We have 138 staff, including more than 40 engineers and economists at primary, medium and senior titles, project managers and technicians. In 2012, we passed the quality, safety, environmental, health system certification by China Quality Certification Center (CQC). We are a comprehensive service company engaged in construction of house building project, anti-corrosion and heat-preservation project, mechanical and electrical equipment installation, steel structure work, municipal public engineering, petrochemical equipment pipe installation, road maintenance project and terminal station maintenance project, etc.

三、负责人介绍：

III. Responsible Person Introduction:

吕万有，汉族，甘肃泾川县人，中国共产党党员。2007年创办陕西长建建设工程有限公司现任公司董事长。

Lu Wanyou, the Han nationality, a native of Jingchuan of Gansu province, a member of Communist Party of China. Founded Shannxi Changjian Construction & Engineering Co., Ltd. in 2007 and now serves as its Present.

四、项目名称： 防腐保温工程

IV. Project Name: Anti-corrosion and Heat-preservation Project

五、项目概况：

V. Project Profile:

成熟的技术有玻璃钢防腐，聚脲防腐，锌粉防腐，离子防腐，纳米防腐等技术。玻璃钢防腐是在碳钢、混凝土或其他基材表面制作玻璃钢防止基材在介质或环境作用下破坏或变质，称作"玻璃钢防腐"。这是我们公司最常用的技术。聚脲防腐它有具有高抗张强度、高耐磨性能、良好的抗腐蚀性，与基质材料黏接力强，既牢固又柔韧。是目前所有防腐管道中最耐腐蚀的产品。施工方便，不受潮湿和寒冷环境的影响，对环境无污染。渗锌防腐蚀技术是将锌铝元素渗入钢铁构件表层形成保护层来达到防腐蚀目的的一门技术。采用锌作为保护涂层材料，也是目前应用最广泛的工艺方法。抗氯离子侵蚀防腐剂主要用于防腐蚀混凝土或耐久性要求的混凝土，可将水泥水化硬化中生成大量的不稳定或亚稳状态物质转变成稳定的，有利于均质、密实，对强度、耐久性起贡献作用的水泥石结构物质，延长建筑物的使用寿命。曾参加"长庆气田第四、第五净化厂和苏里格气田的场站建设"，并受到各单位一致好评。

Our mature technologies include GRP anti-corrosion, polyurea anti-corrosion, zinc powder anti-corrosion, ion anti-corrosion and nanometer anti-corrosion, etc. GRP anti-corrosion refers to that glass fiber reinforced plastics (GRP) is made on the surface of carbon steel, concrete or other base materials to prevent base materials from being damaged or deteriorated under the effect of medium or environment, and it is our most common technology. Polyurea anti-corrosion has high tensile strength, excellent wear-resisting property and good corrosion resistance. Polyurea has strong force of bonding with basic material and is firm and flexible. The technology is the most corrosion-resistant in all anti-corrosion pipes, featuring convenient construction, immunity to impact of damp and cold environment and no environmental pollution. Zinc impregnation anti-corrosion technology refers to permeating the zinc-aluminum element into the surface layer of steel components to form a protective layer for the purpose of anti-corrosion. It is the most widely applied technology to use zinc as the protective coating material at present. The preservative resistant to chloride ion erosion is mainly used for anti-corrosion concrete or concrete required to be durable. The preservative can convert a good deal of unstable or metastable substances arising from hydrating and hardening of cement to stable ones, to facilitate homogeneity, compaction, improve cement structure contributing to strengthen and durability and extend the service life of building. We once participated in "Construction of the Fourth, Fifth Purification Plants of Changqing Gas Field and Terminal Station of Sulige Gas Field" and were unanimously praised by all units.

六、项目优势：

VI. Project Advantage(s)：

纳米复合粉末渗锌工艺采用改进的新型渗锌混合物，可获得更为有效的锌/铁(Zn/Fe)合金涂层。这种新工艺的优越性在于，涂层厚度均匀性好；硬度高、耐磨损和抗划伤能力强，耐腐蚀性强等特点。

The improved new type zinc-impregnation mixture is used in the nano-composite powder zinc impregnation technology to acquire more effective Zn/Fe alloy coating. The superiorities of such new technology lie in features of good thickness uniformity of coating; high hardness, strong wear resistance and scratch resistance and excellent corrosion resistance, etc.

七、项目需求：

VII. Project Demand(s):

我公司具有成熟的，最新的防腐保温施工工艺，急需打开市场，把我们的技术推而广之，多方合作，互利共赢。

We have mature and latest anti-corrosion and heat-preservation construction technology. We urgently need to open the market to promote our technologies through multi-cooperation to achieve mutual benefit and win-win result.

阳光照明、光热发电及供热系统
Solar Lighting, Solar Thermal Power Generation and Heat Supply System

一、项目公司名称： 陕西日升源创能科技有限公司
Ⅰ. Project Company Name： Sunring Enersource Corporation

二、项目公司介绍：
Ⅱ. Project Company Introduction：

公司位于西安高新技术产业研发区。多年来公司在技术研发的大力投入，获得了多项国家专利和国家高新技术企业证书，同时获得了陕西省和西安市著名商标证书，公司的太阳能采集传输系统和热能系统在国内外同行业处于领先地位，产品中避免了使用高耗能源材料，真正是高效、节能、无污染的环保、绿色产品，公司产品已入编解放军总装备库目录。

The company is located in Xi'an High-tech Industrial Development Zone. For many years, the company has been greatly invested in technical R&D, obtaining multiple Chinese national patents and a Chinese national high-tech enterprise certificate as well as famous trademark certificates in Shaanxi and Xi'an. The solar energy collection and transfer system and thermal energy system take the lead in the same field at home and abroad. No use of energy-intensive raw materials in the products really realizes efficient, energy-saving, pollution-free, environmentally-friendly, green products. The products have been listed in the catalogue of the General Reserve Warehouse of PLA.

三、负责人介绍：
Ⅲ. Responsible Person Introduction：

王晓荣，陕西神木人，经济管理学本科专业，金融系统工作23年，2009年5月创办陕西日升源创能科技有限公司，2012年公司科研项目获科技部和国家科技奖励办批准设立的中国产学研合作"创新奖"，现继续带领团队深入对太阳能热能技术的研发。

Wang Xiaorong, born in Shengmu, Shaanxi and obtained Bachelor Degree of Economic Management, has been working in the financial system for 23 years, established the company in May 2009 and now is leading the company's team to carry out in-depth R&D of solar thermal energy technology. In 2012, a scientific research project of the company was awarded the Industry-university-research Cooperation "Innovation Award" approved and set up by the Chinese Ministry of Science and Technology and the Chinese National Office for Science and Technology Awards.

四、项目名称： 阳光照明、光热发电及供热系统
Ⅳ. Project Name： Solar Lighting, Solar Thermal Power Generation and Heat Supply System

五、项目概况：
Ⅴ. Project Profile：

公司主要项目为阳光采集自动跟踪传输系统、自动跟踪发电系统、自动聚集热发电系统和自动跟踪供热系统。所有系统皆采用全球热门的尖端技术。前两个系统已研发出成熟产品，后两个系统正在技术革新，将精密生产工艺改进为开模后的部件组装形式及模块化生产。项目产品简化了工艺流程、提高了生产效率、降低了生产成本，是军事、航天、交通、医疗、农业、民用等行业的多用途产品；同时公司的太阳能智慧路灯也是高效节能产品。

The main projects of the company are a sunlight collection, automatic tracking and transfer system, an automatic tracking power generation system, an automatic thermal aggregation power generation system and an automatic tracking heat supply system. All these systems use the most popular sophisticated techniques in the world. The first two systems have completely developed into mature products; and the latter two systems are undergoing technical innovation with the precision production process improved into component assembly and modular production after molding. The foresaid techniques simplify process flow, improve production efficiency and reduce production cost, so they are used in military, aerospace, transportation, medical, agricultural, civil industries, etc.; and the solar smart road lamp is an efficient, energy-saving product.

为了扩大生产规模，提高经济效益，公司于2013年决定在鄠邑区统征土地12亩，新建生产、研发、办公大楼，现已拿到了土地证、规划许可证及项目建设许可证文件，土方工程已完工。该项目建筑面积28500平方米，总投资9380万元，项目建成后将采用公司自有专利技术，投入使用后每年可节约原煤160吨，减少二氧化炭排放，而且地下室完全可以照射纯太阳光，不会有霉变、发臭等异味发生，展览大厅智能电子显示屏即时公示每日的节能量数据。

In order to expand production scale and improve economic benefits, the company decided to rent 12-mu land uniformly in Huyi District, Xi'an in 2013. For the production, R&D and office building newly built, the land certificate, planning license and project construction license documents have been obtained. The earthwork has been completed. The project covers a building area of 28,500 square meters with total investment of RMB 93.8 million. After completion of the project, the adoption of the company's own patent technology will save 160-ton raw coal and reduce-ton CO_2 emission. In addition, the lamps in basements are supplied completely by solar energy, producing no mould, stink and other odors; and a smart electronic display screen in an exhibition hall publishes energy-saving data of each day.

六、项目优势：
VI. Project Advantage(s):

产品的主流市场主要以军队、西部地区的光伏发电和居民的供热为主，为提高大众收入和社会效益、促进地方经济发展而服务。

The products are mainly used for PV generation in military troops and western areas and resident heat supply, and to improve public income and social benefits and provide service for improving local economic development.

公司已和天津大学洽谈校企联盟合作，使技术更新和业务发展有了更好的支持和保障，并和杨凌农林科技大学进行高科技农业蔬菜、大棚的项目研究合作。

The company has started the discussion of university-company alliance cooperation with Tianjin University, which provides better support and guarantee for technical upgrade and business development; besides, it also carries out project research cooperation in high-tech agricultural vegetables and greenhouses with Northwest A&F University in Yangling.

我公司的太阳能自动跟踪系统等四项专利技术，技术尖端适用范围广，前两项功能已研发出成熟产品，后两项技术已经技术革新，正在将精密生产工艺流程改进为模块化组装。项目产品简化了工艺流程，提高了生产效率，降低了生产成本。项目实施将惠及广大用户，推动太阳能的开发利用，引领全球的太阳能热能技术，为拯救全球环境做出应有贡献。

Our patent technology, solar automatic tracking system and technology are sophisticated with a wide range of application. The first two functions have completely developed into mature products; and the latter two technologies, after technical innovation, will improve precision production process flow into modular assembly. These simplify process flow, improve production efficiency, reduce production cost to bring benefits to users, push forward the development and use of solar energy, take the lead of solar thermal technology in the same industry in the world, and make contribution to save the environment of the earth.

七、项目需求：
VII. Project Demand(s):

因公司在技术研发的大力投入，产品还未完全投放市场，加之生产、研发、办公大楼的开工建设投资，公司流动资金出现紧缺，现面向社会及投资机构进行多种模式的融资，计划融资8.5亿（其中有70兆瓦太阳能跟踪电站和2000亩光伏加智能化高科技阳光蔬菜大棚），望有意者洽谈投资。

Our circulating funds become insufficient due to great investment in technical R&D, incomplete marketing of products and the investment in on-going construction of production, R&D and office buildings. Therefore, we launch multiple modes of financing from the society and investment institutions with a financing plan of RMB 850 million (including 70-megawatt solar tracking power plant and 2,000-mu PV smart high-tech sunlight vegetable greenhouse), and we hope that those who have the intent discuss the investment with us.

太阳能灯具及储能产品
Solar Lamps and Energy Storage Products

一、项目公司名称： 深圳市鹏诚新能源科技有限公司

I. Project Company Name： Shenzhen Pengcheng New Energy Technology Co., Ltd

二、项目公司介绍：

II. Project Company Introduction:

公司成立于 2015 年 11 月，运营成熟、规范并已通过 ISO9001、ISO14001 和职业健康安全管理体系 18001 认证。公司主营储能系统、能源转化系统、动力电池系统及管理系统，是国内新能源领域的新兴品牌，发展至今已拥有多项国内领先的储能技术、能源转化技术以及动力电池回收技术。公司产品涉及领域广泛，主要应用于太阳能路灯、家庭储能、智能家电、医疗器械、电动汽车和无人飞机等。

Since its founding in November 2015, the company has achieved mature and normal operation and has passed ISO9001, ISO14001 and 18001 certification of Occupational Health and Safety Management System. It is a new brand in the new energy field in China and focuses on energy source systems, energy conversion systems, power battery systems and management systems. Up to now, the company has developed multiple energy storage, energy conversion and power battery recovery technologies which take the lead in China. Covering a wide range of fields, the products are mainly applied to solar road lamps, domestic energy storage, smart domestic appliances, medical devices, electric automobile, unmanned aircrafts, etc.

三、负责人介绍：

III. Responsible Person Introduction:

谭祖宪，博士，武汉大学电化学毕业，是国内新能源领域的专家，拥有多年的动力电池、储能电池技术开发和工程化工作经验。他曾参与并主持多项国家 863 电动汽车重大专项课题以及太阳能路灯系统等国家标准制定，在电化学技术上有较高的造诣，在动力电池、电池系统以及电池管理等领域有 15 年以上的实际开发工作经验。谭祖宪先生曾任国内外大型新能源科技型企业的总工程师、总经理及执行总裁等重要职务。

Tan Zuxian, a doctor graduated from the electrochemistry of Wuhan University, is an expert in the new energy field in China and has technology development and engineering experiences in power and energy storage batteries for years. He participated in and presided at the formulation of Chinese national standards for multiple National "863" Key Projects of Electric Automobile, solar road lamp systems, etc., and has made important achievements in electrochemistry technology and has more than 15 years of actual development experience in the fields of power batteries, battery systems, battery management, etc. Mr. Tan Zuxian took important positions in new energy technology enterprises at home and abroad, such as chief engineer, general manager, chief executive officer, etc.

四、项目名称： 太阳能灯具及储能产品

IV. Project Name： Solar Lamps and Energy Storage Products

五、项目概况：

V. Project Profile：

随着城市化建设进程的加速以及城市基建设施建设的快速投入，城市对照明产品的市场需求逐渐扩大。近几年，我国乃至其他国家已开始对偏远的农村进行扶持，要求真正实现"亮化"，故照明产品在农村市场的需求也日益剧增。在能源紧张的大背景下，传统照明设备耗能巨大，且存在巨大的能源浪费，进而影响城市生态环境，这显然已不符合我国乃至世界能源利用的发展方向，同时也极大地限制了照明设备的利用效率。公司"太阳能路灯及家庭储能产品"的研发制造，有效弥补了上述不足。太阳能路灯及家庭储能产品是采用太阳能电池供电，免维护阀控式密封蓄电池储存电能，超高亮 LED 灯具作为光源，并由智能化充放电控制器控制，用于代替传统公用电力照明的路灯和家庭照明。

With speedup of urban construction progress and rapid investment in urban infrastructure construction, the demand for lighting products in cities is increasing gradually. In recent years, China and other countries have been providing support for remote rural areas and requiring real realization of "lighting". Therefore, the demand for lighting products in rural markets is increasingly rising sharply. Under the background of energy shortage, huge energy consumption by traditional lighting equipment leads to huge energy waste and affects urban ecological environment. This has obviously failed to comply with the development trend of energy utilization in China and other countries, but also put great limitations on the utilization efficiency of lighting equipment. Our research, development and manufacture of "solar road lamps and domestic energy storage products" have effectively made up the aforesaid disadvantage. Solar road lamps and domestic energy storage products are supplied by a solar battery and store electric power with a maintenance-free valve-regulated sealed battery with super-bright LED lamps as light sources; they are controlled by a smart charge and discharge controller to replace traditional public and domestic lighting lamps.

六、项目优势
VI. Project Advantage(s):

1．太阳能路灯及家庭储能产品在使用过程中无须铺设线缆、无须交流供电；
No need to lay wires or cables or no use of AC supply during the use of such products；

2．不产生电费，采用直流供电、控制；
No electric charge; DC power supply and control；

3．具有稳定性好、寿命长、发光效率高；
High stability, long lifetime and high efficiency；

4．安装维护简便、安全性能高、节能环保、经济实用；
Easy to install and maintain, highly safe, energy-saving and environmentally-friendly, economic, practical, etc.；

5．可广泛应用于城市、农村道路，小区、工厂、旅游景点、停车场等场所以及家庭照明。
Widely used in cities, rural roads, quarters, factories, tourism spots, parking lots, etc. and for domestic lighting.

七、项目需求：
VII. Project Demand(s):

作为太阳能照明灯具及家庭储能产品的一种创新性储能系统，对于推动光伏产业和新能源产业的深度融合有着重大价值。寻求国内外太阳能路灯、家庭离网储能系统工程项目合作。

As a type of innovative energy storage system for solar lighting lamps and domestic energy storage products, solar lamp products contain significant value for promoting in-depth integration between the PV industry and the new energy industry. We are seeking for cooperation on solar road lamps and domestic external energy off-grid system projects.

室内空气污染治理
Indoor Air Pollution Treatment

一、项目公司名称：北京中海国泰环保科技发展有限公司

I. Project Company Name: Beijing Zhonghai Guotai Environmental Protection Technology Development Co., Ltd.

二、项目公司介绍：

II. Project Company Introduction:

公司是专业从事室内环境净化产品及技术进口的高新环保企业。以室内环境净化、室内空气污染检测为方向，专业从事室内净化产品进口、工程治理及销售为一体的综合性环保公司，也是国内最早掌握植物活性酶技术及应用的高科技企业。

The company is a high-tech enterprise engaged in importation of indoor air purification products and technologies. The company is a comprehensive environmental protection company that aims at indoor air purification and pollution detection, importation of purification products, engineering and sales. It is also the earliest company in China that masters active plant enzyme technologies and their application.

自成立以来，以"净化生活空气，缔造洁净空间"为经营理念，以"诚信经营，服务为本，道德至上，客户为尊"的经营宗旨，立足环保产业，锐意进取，努力创新。为每一位客户提供量身定制完善的室内环境治理净化方案，全程监护，郑重向广大客户承诺：一周无味，终生质保；一次净化，永绝污染！

Since its foundation, guided by the philosophy of "Pure air, pure space" and "Good faith, service oriented, moral values and customer first", the company strove to develop in the environmental protection industry and made innovations. We provide customers with a purification solution that is specifically designed and tailored to the conditions. We keep monitoring the indoor conditions and commit to our customers: Smell disappears in one week. Life-cycle warranty; Once for all!

三、负责人介绍：

III. Responsible Person Introduction：

吴永顺，公司法人，全联房地产商会理事；北京广东商会副秘书长/理事；北京建筑设计施工企业协会副会长；中国民主建国会会员；国际狮子会会员；北京山西商会理事；北京黑龙江商会会员；中国管理科学研究院学术委员会特约研究员；北京广西百色企业商会会员；北京住宅房地产企业商会理事。

Wu Yongshun, legal representative of the company, Director of China Real Estate Chamber of Commerce；Vice Secretary General/Director of Guangdong Corporation Chamber of Commerce in Beijing；Vice president of Beijing Association of Building Design and Engineering Enterprises；China Democratic National Construction Association member；International Lion Club member；Director of Shanxi Chamber of Commerce in Beijing；member of Heilongjiang Chamber of Commerce in Beijing；Special researcher of Chinese Academy of Management Science Academy Committee；member of Guangxi Baise Corporation Chamber of Commerce in Beijing；Director of Beijing Chamber of Real Estate Enterprise.

四、项目名称：室内空气污染治理

IV. Project Name: Indoor Air Pollution Treatment

五、项目概况：

V. Project Profile：

新装修房屋和新车内由装饰材料散发出的大量有机物对人类健康产生巨大影响，已经构成人类身心健康的隐形杀手。十八大后政府高度重视人们居住工作小环境的空气污染问题，已在2016年实行车内空气质量强制性标准和室内空气质量强制性标准强化执行。

Newly decorated houses and new cars may give off plenty of organics harmful to human health due to the decoration materials used, which has become an invisible killer threatening people's wellbeing and health. After the 18th National

Congress, governments laid great attentions to air pollution problems in microenvironment and were preparing to issue a series of compulsory standards to control in-car and indoor air quality.

六、项目优势：
VI. Project Advantage(s)：

公司经过十年的潜心研发攻关，成功开发"室内车内空气净化质量项目"，获得国家级全面达到国标的检测报告，获得国家级企业环保施工资质证书，获得国家级工程技术人员施工资质证书。

Through great efforts for decades, the company successfully developed the "Indoor/In-car Air Purification Project" which has been tested and approved according to related national standards. As such, the company was granted a national environmental protection engineering certificate and Certificate for National Engineering Technicians.

1．一次性治理永不反弹。（国标范围内）

Once for all to solve pollution problems. (As per related national standards)

2．治理后无二次污染，无有机物和微生物残留。（国标范围内）

Free of secondary pollution or residual of organics and microorganism after treatment. (As per related national standards)

3．对治理环境和治理对象无腐、锈、损现象。

No corrosion, dust or damage to environment and target object.

4．治理药剂为纯食品级药剂，填补国内空白。

Treatment agent is food and drug level. Make up a short slab in domestic market.

七、项目需求：
VII. Project Demand(s)：

1．在全国30个省市自治区建立省级加盟代理商。向上述加盟代理商推行免费服务加有偿产品的商业模式。

Province sales agents in 30 provinces and cities in China. Promotion of the business model of free service and paid products to agents.

2．在全国各有名的建材商场建立形象店，每家店采用直营+众筹的方式复制式发展。

Brand image stores in well-known building material markets. Stores are to be developed by direct management + crowd funding.

3．与大型房地产公司及装饰公司进行长期合作。

Long-term cooperation with large real estate developers and decoration companies.

4．进驻四大电商，进行室内空气治理产品及环保家居产品销售。

Sales of air treatment and eco-home products on four major E-Commerce platforms.

5．与各小区物业合作捆绑式推广环保家居产品。

Combined promotion of eco-home products through cooperation with local property management companies.

6. 公司将与全国各大汽车厂商及4S店的建立长期合作，在汽车未入市之前进行车内空气污染治理。

Long-term cooperation with major auto manufacturers and SSSS stores, to provide early treatment before cars are sold.

7. 与城市各洗车行合作为已入市的汽车进行车内空气污染治理。

Cooperation with car wash plants to provide in-car air treatment for sold cars.

高新技术产权交易所
High-tech Intellectual Property Exchange

一、项目公司名称：贵州首辰知识产权管理有限公司
Ⅰ. Project Company Name: Guizhou F-Star Intellectual Property Management Co., Ltd.

二、项目公司介绍：
Ⅱ. Project Company Introduction:

公司隶属于首辰集团，集团公司成立于2013年，作为贵州省内领先的企业经营管理配套服务商，为企业提供知识产权、工商财税、项目认证、资质申报、互联网开发、品牌策划等全生命周期服务，致力于成为企业发展过程中"引商、稳商、助商、知商"的企业服务机构，发展四年来，首辰已助力西南地区十万余家中小企业实现了产业转型升级和知识经济竞争力的提升，在企业成长、资产增值领域构建了一套独立完善的孵化体系。

The Company is a subsidiary under F-Star Group which was founded in 2013. As a leading enterprise operation and management support service provider in Guizhou, F-Star provides companies with product life-cycle management services. F-Star strives to become a service provider that helps companies to "identify, grasp, support and understand business opportunities". In the past 4 years, F-Star helped over 100 thousand SMEs in Southwest China to realize industrial upgrading and to improve their intellectual property competitiveness and has established a complete and independent incubation system in company growth and capital value adding fields.

三、负责人介绍：
Ⅲ. Responsible Person Introduction:

龚航，首辰集团总裁，企业服务及知识产权行业新秀，创业三年将首辰集团从六人团队发展到200多人的团队，完成了企业服务从订制化到大数据应用的初步布局。在2017亚洲品牌论坛上，首辰集团荣获"亚洲品牌十大最具创新力企业"和"中国十大创新创业风云企业奖"，首辰集团总裁龚航先生荣获"亚洲品牌十大创新企业家"及"中国知识产权行业最具社会责任企业家"荣誉称号。

Gong Hang, President of F-Star, is an outstanding young man in the company service and intellectual property industry. He successfully developed F-Star from a 6-person team to a 200-person team in only 3 years and completed the preliminary transformation from company service to Big Data application. At the 2017 Asian Brand Forum, F-Star Group was awarded the titles of "Top 10 Asian Innovative Enterprises" and "China Top 10 Influential", and Mr. Gong Hang, F-Star President, was also entitled "Top 10 Asian Innovative Entrepreneur" and "Most Responsible Entrepreneur for Society in Chinese IP Industry".

四、项目名称：高新技术产权交易所
Ⅳ. Project Name: High-tech Intellectual Property Exchange

五、项目概况：
Ⅴ. Project Profile:

为深度落实国务院《"十三五"国家知识产权保护和运用规划》，帮助企业促进高新技术转化，提高自主创新能力，充分发挥知识产权的杠杆融资作用，首辰集团利用四年来在知识产权领域10万+的企业数据积淀，和贵州大数据战略的政策机会，投资建设高新技术产权交易所（简称"高交所"）。目前国内高新技术知识产权转化率不到百分之十，国有高价值知识产权流失海外现象严重，针对此种现状，高交所定位高新技术转化大数据平台，打破传统融资方式的局限性，通过整合大数据、物联网、区块链技术，为企业知识产权转化建立一个赋能平台，帮助技术驱动型企业快速获得社会各方的赋能。赋能包括以下三个方面：

In order to practice the *13th Five-Year* *National Intellectual Property Protection and Application Plan* by the State Council, to help companies to convert their technologies and improve their capacity for independent innovation and to make good use of the financing and loaning effect of intellectual properties, F-Star took advantages of its accumulated data of over 100 thousand enterprises in relation to intellectual properties as well as the big data strategy in Guizhou and built the High-tech Intellectual Property Exchange (HIPE). Currently, the conversion rate of high and new technologies in China is less than 10% and many high-value intellectual properties suffered from unauthorized use in foreign markets. As a solution, HIPE aims to build a big data platform for conversion of high and new technologies to break the traditional way of financing. By integration of big data, IoT and block chain technology, HIPE is expected to establish a platform where technology-driven enterprises can obtain supports quickly from the society. This process includes three aspects：

1．知识赋能。通过平台共享大数据，从趋势、最新解决方案、知识共享等领域，帮助科技型企业更好地理解和应用知识产权标的，推动标的迭代更新，为中国知识产权体系建立全球竞争力提供有利的生态环境。

Knowledge. Through the shared big data on the platform and from views of trends, latest solutions and shared knowledge, HIPE helps enterprises to better understand and apply intellectual properties, to promote their updating and to build an advantageous ecology for Chinese intellectual property systems.

2．科技赋能。科技型企业与高交所提供的增值服务结合，帮助企业改善自身的管理和运营效率，使企业资源能更好地专注于新技术的迭代和推广。

Technology. Technology-driven enterprises may integrate with the value-adding services provided by HIPE to improve the management and operation efficiency of such enterprises, so that they can focus on the upgrading and promotion of new technologies.

3．金融赋能。高交所通过分阶段搭建知识产权交易、知识产权质押金融、知识产权证券化等平台，帮助企业通过多种类型渠道，实现各类技术产品的转化。

Finance. By establishing platforms for IP transaction, IP pledging and financing, IP securitization, HIPE helps enterprises to realize conversion of their technological products through diverse channels.

六、项目优势：
VI. Project Advantage(s)：

首辰集团依托贵阳的大数据中心硬件基础与政策导向，凭借自营企服产业积累的大量数据资源，利用资源互给的方式，扩充高交所的知识产权储备，构建知识产权转化生态，作为区域首发，致力于成为贵阳市的大数据企业名片。

Based on the big data center facilities and policies in Guizhou as well as the data resources accumulated in company services, F-Star expands the reserve of intellectual properties by seeking related resources, and establishes the IP conversion system. As a leader in this domain, HIPE will become a symbol of Guizhou in terms of Big Data.

七、项目需求：
VII. Project Demand(s)：

项目需要引入投资机构、基金公司、银行等相关方共同参与，共同助力企业知识产权转化。

The project needs participation of institutional investors, fund management companies and banks to pool the efforts to facilitate the IP conversion.

黑背景显微镜
Black Background Microscope

一、项目公司名称： 哈尔滨康邦黑背景光学仪器有限公司
Ⅰ. Project Company Name： Harbin KangBang Black-field Optical Instrument Co.Ltd.

二、项目公司介绍：
Ⅱ. Project Company Introduction：

公司成立于 1998 年 10 月，合作伙伴和客户遍及全国各地及美国、澳大利亚、新加坡、马来西亚、印尼、泰国等二十几个国家，AAA 级信用企业。公司目前拥有一项发明专利，三项实用新型专利和两项外观设计专利。哈尔滨康邦公司，可根据客户要求，订制个性化的光纤导光非直射入光黑色背景视频显微镜。同时，哈尔滨康邦公司也是国内唯一一家可提供中文版、英文版和俄文版等多种语种软件的生产企业。

Harbin Kangbang Black-field Optical Instrument Co., Ltd, was established in October 1998, with partners and customers extend all over China and other dozens of countries such as USA, Australia, Singapore, Malaysia, Indonesia, Thailand and so on. It has been affirmed as the AAA level company by China Small and Medium Business Enterprise Association. Up to this days, the company has possessed 1 invention patent, 3 utility model patents and 2 design patents. According to the customer's requirement, Harbin Kangbang Company can provide the many kinds of black-field video Microscope. Meanwhile, it is also the sole manufacturer that can provide software with Chinese version, English version, Russian version and other multiple languages.

三、负责人介绍：
Ⅲ. Responsible Person Introduction：

刘书宝，公司总经理，自 1991 年至今，先后在药品和医疗器械企业从事管理和研发工作二十余年，是一项国家发明专利、三项实用新型专利和两项外观设计专利的发明人和拥有者。

The man in charge of Haerbin Kangbang Black Background Optical Equipment Co., Ltd Mr. Shubao Liu has been pursued the occupation of the management and R&D of medicine and medical equipment for more than 20 years. He is the owner and developer of invention patent, 3 utility model patents and 2 design patents.

四、项目名称： 黑背景显微镜
Ⅳ. Project Name： Black Background Microscope

五、项目概况：
Ⅴ. Project Profile：

公司研发的具有自主知识产权的光纤导光非直射入光黑色背景视频显微镜，可以通过提取标本来为患者进行综合性的全科检查。这种检查方式克服了一般诊查目的单一、复杂烦琐、预见性差的缺陷，从而有效地、最大限度的减少了漏诊。也就是说，可以通过一滴血、一块黏膜或一点分泌物，早期诊断多种可能存在的人体生理、病理变化，全面评估健康状态，特别是对发现临床多发的微循环障碍及肿瘤的早期变化等健康隐患有重要意义。

光纤导光非直射入光黑色背景视频显微镜，可以通过石英光纤导光器把大功率光源光均匀无色差导至显微镜底座内部，使显微镜物镜在大光源下成像效果更佳，使 CCD 在明亮视野下成像更清晰柔和。光纤导光非直射入光黑色背景视频显微镜，通过对定位的设计，使卤素灯光源以最大输出光源，从而减少光损耗，提高发光效率，以使更明亮的光通过石英光纤传导至显微镜底座内聚光镜下。为了更精细更准确中心挡光环形透光，并且更准确确定环形透光的光线射出角度，光纤导光非直射入光黑色背景视频显微镜，通过采用激光＋线切割的方式来实现精确环形透光范围及精确的厚度。从而使聚光镜射出的环形光能够均衡均匀进入物镜，才能保证物镜成像正常。

Fiber optic light; non direct light; black-field; video microscope, with independent intellectual property rights by Harbin Kangbang Black-field Optical Equipment Co., Ltd, Specimens can be extracted for comprehensive general examination of the patient. This kind of inspection method overcomes the defect of the simple, complicated and unpredictability of the general diagnosis, so as to reduce the leakage diagnosis effectively and maximally. That is to say, a drop of blood, a mucous membrane or secretions, early diagnosis of a variety of possible human physiological and pathological changes, the comprehensive assessment of health status, especially in microcirculation and tumor found that clinical multiple health concerns such as early change has important significance.

Fiber optic light; non direct light; black-field; video microscope, light can be achieved by quartz optical fiber light guide to the high-power light source the light uniform no guide to internal microscope base color, make the microscope objective lens in the big light imaging effect is better, to make CCD imaging under bright vision more clear and soft. Fiber optic light not direct into the black background video microscope, through to the positioning of the design, make the halogen light source to maximize the output light, thus reducing the light loss, improve the luminous efficiency, in order to make more bright light, through the quartz optical fiber transmission to under microscope base in the condenser. To finer more accurate center ring of light transmission, and more accurately determine the annular pervious to light the light emitting Angle, fiber optic light not direct into the black background video microscope, by using laser + linear cutting way to achieve precise circular transmission range and accurate thickness. Thus, the circular light emitted by the condenser can be evenly distributed into the objective lens to ensure that the objective image is normal.

六、项目优势：
VI. Project Advantages:

哈尔滨康邦黑背景光学仪器有限公司对光纤导光非直射入光黑色背景视频显微镜进行了独家投入，批量生产。由于此类产品只能由专业厂家生产，行业进入壁垒比较高，替代品和生产厂家较少，在国内没有可以和其竞争的产品。

Harbin Kangbang Black Background Optical Equipment Co., Ltd is the sole investor and massive producer of Fiber optic light; non direct light; black-field; video microscope. Since such products can only be produced by professional manufacturers, the barriers to entry are relatively high, and there are fewer substitutes and manufacturers, and there are no products that can compete with them in China.

七、项目需求：
VII. Project Demand(s):

光纤导光非直射入光黑色背景视频显微镜在医学领域的许多方面显示出其实用性、有效性，被誉为健康的"保护神"和预警器，显微领域的"CT机"。这种显微镜，不但适用于大、中、小型医院和诊所等各医疗单位，同时相关科研院校、体检中心也有大量需求。

In many aspects of the medical field, Fiber optic light; non direct light; black-field; video microscope, has shown its usefulness and effectiveness, being presented as a healthy "protection of god" and an early warning device, a "CT machine" in the microsphere. This kind of microscope is not only applicable to medical units such as large, medium and small hospitals and clinics, but also has a large demand in related research institutes and physical examination centers.

智能安防、智能交通
Smart Security Control, Smart Traffic

一、项目公司名称： 河北腾维科技有限公司
I. Project Company Name： Hebei Tengwei Technology Co., Ltd.

二、项目公司介绍：
II. Project Company Introduction:

公司专注于视频监控系统中的矩阵、监视器拼接墙、网络高清监控设备的生产与销售；为广大用户提供从产品设备到方案设计再到安装调试和售后支持等全方位服务，公司凭着雄厚的技术力量及优质的服务体系，产品及项目案例遍及全国各地，已成功地广泛应用于公检法单位、交通、监狱等安防的监控系统，因其严谨的生产工艺和专业的服务团队，在广大客户中树立了良好的印象，成为安防行业的知名品牌。

The company is specialized in production and sales of monitor matrix, spliced monitor wall, HD network monitoring devices. We provide user with one-stop services from solution designing to installation and debugging, to after-sales services. Supported by technologies and high-quality service systems, we have products and projects throughout China. Our solution has been extensively adopted by public security authorities, traffic control, and jails for monitoring purposes. Thanks to the fine production techniques and professional service teams, we have established very good images among customers and become a famous brand in the security industry.

三、负责人介绍：
III. Responsible Person Introduction:

南国力，公司总经理，生于1985年，河北安防协会会员，主营建筑智能化安装工程施工、信息系统集成服务、安防设备。经过三年的建设发展，公司共服务于62个项目，包括省内与省外的公检法单位、交通、监狱等安防的监控系统、建设工程弱电项目及改造工程。

Nan Guoli, General Manager, born in 1985, is a member of the Hebei Association of Security Control. Our company is mainly engaged in engineering and installation of intelligent building systems; information system integration services; and security control devices. Through efforts of three years, we have completed 62 public projects including the CCTV systems in use by public security authorities, traffic control authorities and jails, as well as LV power distribution and modification projects.

四、项目名称： 智能安防、智能交通
IV. Project Name： Smart Security Control，Smart Traffic

五、项目概况：
V. Project Profile：

随着城市管理措施的日益丰富和完善，交通管理的规则也变得更加充实。而对于道路监控来说，它所承载的责任也变得越来越多，这必然会对交通监控基础设施建设及其设备的性能提出更高的要求。主要集中在道路监控、高速公路收费、3S（GPS、GIS、RS）和系统集成环节。传统的统一化智能交通监控模式已经越来越难以满足不同特点道路的工作需要，因此专业化和定制化将成为未来智能交通管理设备的发展方向，今后智能交通对于设备功能的细化需求，将比以往更加细致、更加严格。比如，对于灵活可变的行驶方向，对于一些行驶规则在时间上的限制以及车辆状态的进一步识别等，都是交通行业对未来设备的新要求。

With the development and improvement of municipal administration measures, traffic control rules are further detailed. For road monitoring systems, they have to process more tasks, which have proposed higher requirements for the traffic control facilities and device performance. Our services mainly focus on road monitoring, express road tolling system, 3S (GPS, GIS, RS) and integration. Traditional integrated traffic monitoring systems can no longer meet the requirements on road with distinct characteristics. As such, professional and customized products and services will become a future trend in traffic control. In the future, smart traffic will bring more elaborate and stricter requirements on traffic control devices and their function. For example, smart traffic devices should be able to identify time restrictions of some traffic rules and vehicle status. All these are new requirements for future equipment.

六、项目优势：
VI. Project Advantage(s):

国内约有 200 多家企业已取得了具有自主知识产权的智能监控智能停车双界面 CPU 卡技术。中高端产品线主要被国外品牌所占领，关键核心技术仍然依赖进口。我国智能化行业仍处于发展阶段，对于国内企业来说，抓住机遇突破核心技术，进一步研究适应中国市场的整体解决方案将是成功的关键，我公司在研究创新设计方面有着非常优秀的团队，欢迎可以合作共赢的企业投入我们的团队中。

Currently in China, about 200 enterprises have acquired their intelligent monitoring and smart parking dual-interface CPU card technologies with independent intelligent property rights. However, middle and high-end product lines are still in the hands of foreign brands and core technologies have to be imported from foreign service providers. Intelligent device industry in China is still at its developing stage. For Chinese enterprises, the key to success lies in taking all opportunities to realize technical breakthrough. Our company has outstanding teams in research and design innovation and is open to cooperation.

七、项目需求：
VII. Project Demand(s):

1．资本需求：发展壮大期间需要银行的融资。
Capital：Bank financing support is required at the developing stage.

2．政策需求：需要政府的支持和对接服务。
Policy：Government supports and broker services.

3．推广需求：全国城市推广，引进更多资源。
Promotion：Nation-wide promotion, more resources.

4．合作需求：希望更多的智能化厂家合作。
Cooperation：Cooperation with more smart device manufacturers.

建筑供应链平台
Building Supply Chain Platform

一、项目公司名称： 广东旗胜建筑装饰工程有限公司
I. Project Company Name: Guangdong Qisheng Building Decoration Engineering Co., Ltd.

二、项目公司介绍：
II. Project Company Introduction:

公司成立于 2010 年，总部位于东莞。公司集工程建设、工业地产投资为一体，专注为客户提供系统的工程建设及融资解决方案，在深圳、重庆、浙江、上海、广州等地设有分支机构，工程项目遍布全国。核心业务包括：装饰工程及装饰设计、工程总承包、市政工程、钢结构、幕墙工程等。管理团队 150 余人，服务世界 500 强企业超过 25 家，与富士康、RB、宝洁等有良好的合作关系。

The company was founded in 2010, with its head office located in Dongguan. The company is mainly engaged in project construction and investments in industrial properties, and provides customers with systematic construction and financing solutions. It has established branch offices in Shenzhen, Chongqing, Zhejiang, Shanghai and Guangzhou and is currently participating in projects all over China. Our core business lines include：decoration engineering and decoration design, project EPC, municipal works, steel structures and curtain wall engineering. The company has a managing staff of over 150 persons, providing services to more than 25 of Fortune Global 500 enterprises and has established good cooperation with Foxconn, RB and P&G.

三、负责人介绍：
III. Responsible Person Introduction:

覃士峰董事长，从事建材、建筑装饰及工程行业 18 年，致力于推进绿色、智能及科技的应用，是模块化装饰、智能建筑管理系统、建筑供应链平台、建筑装饰智能机械等项目的先行者。

Qin Shifeng, Chairman of Qisheng, has 18-year experiences in industry of building materials, building decoration and engineering. He devoted himself to the application of green and intelligent technologies, and is a pioneer of modular decoration, intelligent building management system, building supply chain platform and intelligent building and decoration machinery.

四、项目名称： 建筑供应链平台
IV. Project Name: Building Supply Chain Platform

五、项目概况：
V. Project Profile：

为中小型建筑企业搭建阳光、专业、高效、共赢的供应链服务平台。

This project aims to build an open, professional and efficient supply chain service platform with mutual benefits for SMEs.

六、项目优势：
VI. Project Advantage(s):

利用自身的行业优势，解决市场信息不对称问题，有效连接采购方与供应商资源；利用供应链平台优势，解决中小型建筑企业采购规模小，议价能力低的局面，为中小企业提供强有力的供应链服务；免费提供"采购管理、销售管理、订单及合同管理"等功能的管理平台工具；规范标准，阳光作业，打造产、供、销、管理的共生生态系统。供应链平台的宗旨是集上游优质供应资源为下游中小型企业提供专业、高效的服务，目前已经进入平台的搭建和资源整合的阶段。

The Company makes good use of its advantages in the industry to solve the problem of asymmetric market information by effectively connecting buyers and suppliers. In addition, by its advantages as a supply chain platform, the company helps to solve the awkward situations that SMEs are small in size and weak in price negotiation by providing

SMEs with competitive supply chain services. It also provides free management platform with features of "procurement management, sales management, order and contract management". The company also implements standardized and open operation to build up a biological system with integrated production, supply, sales and management. The goal of a supply chain platform is to aggregate high-quality upstream resources to serve the downstream SMEs professionally and efficiently. So far, the company has come to the stage of platform building and resources integration.

七、项目需求：

Ⅶ. Project Demand(s):

欢迎全国各地各大品牌、有实力的建材厂商加入平台建设，共同推进行业供应链转型；各中小型建筑、装修装饰工程企业有材料采购、项目管理等方面的需求。

We welcome all brands and influential building material manufacturers to join us in the platform construction, to jointly promote the supply chain transformation. Small and medium sized construction and decoration enterprises are confronted with the needs for raw material procurement and project management.

水溶性高分子产品
Water-soluble Polymer Products

一、项目公司名称：上海宇昂水性新材料科技股份有限公司

I. Project Company Name: Shanghai Yuking Water Soluble Material Tech Co., Ltd.

二、项目公司介绍：

II. Project Company Introduction:

公司成立于2005年，以水溶性高分子产品、技术服务以及应用研究为主的高新技术企业。为全国功能高分子行业委员会理事单位，秘书处所在单位，水溶性高分子PVP国标撰写单位。

Founded in 2005, the company is a high-tech enterprise mainly focusing on water-soluble polymer products and technical services and application researches. The company is a managing organization and secretary unit of National Functional Polymer Industrial Committee and an editor of the national standard on water-soluble PVP.

旗下有上海宇昂新材料科技有限公司、上海宇昂生物科技有限公司、上海融澈水性材料有限公司等子公司。

Our subsidiaries include Shanghai Yuking New Material Tech Co., Ltd., Shanghai Yuking Biotechnology Co., Ltd. and Shanghai Rongche Water Soluble Material Co., Ltd.

公司主营业务为水溶性高分子材料技术、环保技术、新能源技术及其相关产品的研究开发、生产和销售，还提供相关技术服务。经营产品包括新型医药缓控释材料、水处理膜材料、新型抗真菌剂和其他水溶性高分子材料，产品涉及的行业领域为医药、化妆品、食品饮料、水处理等新兴或蓬勃发展的产业。

Our main product lines include water-soluble polymer material technologies, environmental protection technologies, new energy technologies and their related product development, production and sales and technical support services. Our products include new medical slow-release materials, water treatment membrane materials, new antifungal agents and other water-soluble polymer products, covering extensive industries including medicine, cosmetics, food and beverage and water treatment.

三、负责人介绍：

III. Responsible Person Introduction:

王宇，宇昂科技公司创始人。上海同济大学有机合成硕士，上海大学材料博士，中欧工商管理学院EMBA，国家"万人计划"入选者，中国CCTV-2016年度创业榜样，全国功能高分子行业委员会秘书长，水溶性高分子行业突出贡献者，PVP国标撰写人，中国水溶性高分子专著主编，国家科技部双创人才。

Wang Yu, founder of Yuking Tech. Master of organic synthetic chemistry from Shanghai Tongji University, Doctor of Material from Shanghai University, EMBA of China Europe International Business School, winner of national "Ten Thousand Talent Program", model entrepreneur by CCTV-2016, Secretary General of National Functional Polymer Industrial Committee, outstanding contributor to water-soluble polymer industry, editor of PVP national standard, Chief Editor of Water-Soluble Polymer in China; Innovative and Entrepreneurial Talent by Chinese Ministry of Science and Technology.

四、项目名称：水溶性高分子产品

IV. Project Name: Water-soluble Polymer Products

五、项目概况：

V. Project Profile:

1. 水性聚维酮碘消毒产品，为公司自主研发的，荣获"国家重点新产品"称号，拥有国内外专利。水性聚维酮碘系列消毒产品最大的特点是：无痛、无刺激；不黄染、无污染、更环保；成膜缓释；更低的致敏性；更高的稳定性；PVP医药辅料产品，产品符合USP\EP标准。

Water-soluble povidone-iodine disinfection products developed independently by our company was selected as "a national key new product", to which we own full patents both in China and international markets. Main features of water-soluble povidone-iodine series disinfection products: Free of pain and irritation; environment-friendly and free of yellow staining or pollution; film protected slow release; less sensitization; better stability; PVP medical accessories meet USP\EP standards.

2. 水溶性高分子日化品，是以水溶性高分子为基础的日化产品。旗下所有品牌产品均经过十数年研究，结合多项独家专利技术，综合了自然界植物提取物（草本精华）、生物基因科技及水溶性高分子三者的优点，形成的系列产品包括面膜系列护肤品等。最大的特色是绿色、环保、自然及健康。

Our water-soluble daily chemical products are produced on basis of water-soluble polymer materials. All our brand products are developed through researched for more than ten years, combining the advantages of natural plant extracts (herbal essences), biological gene technologies and water-soluble polymer materials. Our product series include facial masks and other skin care products. Our products are very popular because they are green, environment-friendly natural and healthy.

3. 水净化产品：以水溶性高分子材料为基础原料，通过本公司的研发技术，使得水质达到绿色环保、健康安全的净化剂以及净水器系列产品。

Water purification products: With our water-soluble polymer materials and proprietary technologies, we provide purification agents and water purifier products that can produce safe and healthy water after treatment.

六、项目优势：
VI. Project Advantage(s):

1. 品牌优势：创立的 yuking 品牌已经在国内外形成了广泛的影响力，产品行销欧洲、北美、南美、澳洲、非洲、亚太、中东等数十个国家和地区。

Brand: Our yuking brand has established extensive influence in Chinese and international markets and our products are sold in dozens of countries and regions in Europe, North America, South America, Australia, Africa, Asia Pacific and Middle East.

2. 技术优势：拥有核心专利技术及自主知识产权，公司拥有二十余项国家专利，一项美国专利，七项 PCT 国际专利及数十项拟申请的国家发明专利，部分专利技术经中科院评定处于国内领先、国际先进的水平。

Technology: We have core-patented technologies and independent intellectual properties, including more than 20 Chinese patents, 1 US patent, 7 PCT international patents and dozens of patents reading for filing. Some of our technologies have been reviewed by the Chinese Academy of Sciences as leading technology both in China and in international markets.

3. 产品优势：产品质量稳定优良，深获广大客户的信赖。

Products: Our products provide stable quality and won trusts from extensive users.

七、项目需求：
VII. Project Demand(s):

1. 推广产品

Product promotion

2. 希望借助"一带一路"进行成果转化，在"一带一路"沿线国家和地区共同投资建厂

Product conversion with help of the "Belt and Road Initiative" to establish new plants in countries along the "Belt and Road"

3. 市场拓展

Market exploration

种群耘平台
Zhongqunyun Platform

一、项目公司名称：广州南国农业有限公司
Ⅰ. Project Company Name：Guangzhou Nanguo Agriculture Co, Ltd.

二、项目公司介绍：
Ⅱ. Project Company Introduction:

公司以创始人的系列发明专利技术为核心，通过研发引领、平台带动，打造以专利技术为纽带，种群产品为载体，融合产业链（育繁用）各方，以长板对接长板，建立共享生态圈的新型种植业模式，为消费者提供从种子到餐桌的健康安全食品。同时通过种群品种内部多样性，实现"回归种子多样性，惠泽农业与生态"的历史使命。种群耘平台将以种子到餐桌的全程溯源模式，链接育种家、种子生产者、种植大户与健康食品消费者，走可持续农业发展道路。公司具有授权发明专利11项，授权商标11项，新产品10多项，主持承担省部级以上项目6项，公司本部及控股子公司，具有全国领先的种群技术研发团队15个，遍布全国11省区，8大作物，正在以新的模式共享和吸纳产业链各方加盟。

The company is founded on basis of a series of inventions by its founder. Driven by research and development and platform, the company aims to build an innovative and shared crop farming model that takes technology as the link and seed products as its carrier, integrates the advantages of all parties on the industrial chain (breeding, farming and application), to safeguard the food security of consumers from seeds to final products. Besides, the company aims to realize its mission of "back to seed diversity and benefit agriculture and ecology" by improving the species diversity. Zhongqunyun Platform keeps track of the whole process from seeds to food on tables, and connects seed breeding experts, producers, large farmers, and consumers of healthy food, to realize sustainable agricultural development. The company owns 11 invention patents, 11 trademarks, over 10 product species and undertakes 6 provincial/department level projects. The headquarters and wholly-owned subsidiaries of the company has established 15 advanced seed R&D teams covering 11 provinces and 8 crop species. It is open to all practitioners on the industrial chain to share the innovative model.

三、负责人介绍：
Ⅲ. Responsible Person Introduction:

创始人李晓方，中国第一个农业女博士，专注作物育种技术创新数十年，取得中国、美国、日本等国内外授权种群育种技术及种群耘互联网平台商业模式等系列发明专利11项，曾主导创立了某科研单位种子企业，名列全国同行前茅，享受国务院特殊津贴的专家，第九届、十届全国人大代表，主持国家级和省部级多个技术创新项目，国家行业专项首席专家。

Ms. Li Xiaofang, founder of the company, was the first female Doctor of Agricultural Science. She was devoted to crop breeding technologies for decades and was granted 11 invention patents in China, U.S. and Japan for licensed breeding technologies and the breeding Internet platform model. She once led and created a seed breeding company under a research institute. Due to her outstanding contribution, she was accepted as a State Council expert for special allowance, and was elected a representative to the 9th and 10th National People's Congress. She once directed many a technological innovation project under national and provincial programs and was thus recognized as a top national industrial expert.

四、项目名称：种群耘平台
Ⅳ. Project Name：Zhongqunyun Platform

五、项目概况：
Ⅴ. Project Profile:

本项目通过自有的授权发明专利和商标、专有技术培训、种群耘平台开放加盟等方式，整合当地资源，充分利用品种内多样性，以可持续发展为核心，避免化工性农业技术对生态系统的破坏，以"一带一路"沿线国

家当地消费习惯和作物特色为主线，打造新产品、新品牌和新服务，为沿线国家农业资源利用、产品升级、扩大市场和升级消费做出贡献。

This project integrates local resources by its proprietary patents and trademarks, expertise training, seed-breeding platform, so that it can make the best use of diversity in the crop species to build up a sustainable development model and to avoid the damages to local ecological systems by chemical agriculture. It focuses on the consuming habit and featured crops in countries along the "Belt and Road" and develop new product lines, brands and services. By these efforts, the project can contribute to the utilization of agricultural resources, product upgrading, market expansion and consumption upgrading in such countries.

六、项目优势：

Ⅵ. Project Advantage(s):

本项目的技术属于本平台首创，在国内外获11项发明专利授权，已获得国家成果登记（3392016Y0076）：认为种群技术具有鲜明的特色和优势、创新性强，技术水平国际领先，创造了一种新型环保和可持续农业发展的新路子。

The technology under this project is specific to this platform and 11 patents have been granted and registered as a national research achievement (3392016Y0076)：the artificial seed population technology has its distinct features and advantages and is a highly innovative and internationally leading technology, and has created a new environment-friendly and sustainable model for agriculture development.

七、项目需求：

Ⅶ. Project Demand(s)：

推广由种群种子生产的活性胚萌芽产品等，加盟方式培育新的种群品种和推广种群产品，推展沿线国家市场，招商融资。

Promotion of active embryo germination products；breeding of new seed population species and promotion of seed population products in forms of franchise；promotion in countries along the Belt and Road；Financing.

凤凰中药材花卉种植基地
Phoenix TCM and Flower Plantation Base

一、项目公司名称： 重庆禾蓓农业科技有限公司

Ⅰ. Project Company Name: Chongqing Hebei Agricultural Technology Co., Ltd.

二、项目公司介绍：

Ⅱ. Project Company Introduction:

公司成立于2014年，主要承担"重庆凤凰中药材花卉种植基地"的规划建设。主要经营范围：生态农业开发，研发中药材培育、种植技术服务，技术咨询，技术转让；中药材的种植、销售；花卉的种植、销售。公司与四川农业大学、中国农业科学院合作，采用中国农业科学院多功能生物肥，培育种植以川黄精、白芨、铁皮石斛、黄栀子和油用牡丹、佛手等药食两用、具有观赏价值的名贵中药材品种，以中药材种植、加工，互联网＋中药材交易，健康生态游，中药材文化科普知识普及，中药材健康养生、养老等内容打造绿色生态健康的中药材产业基地。

Founded in 2014, Hebei Agricultural Technology was devoted to the planning and construction of "Chongqing Phoenix TCM and Flower Plantation Base". Business scope: ecological agriculture development, traditional Chinese medicine materials breeding, growing technology service, technological consultation, technology transfer; TCM plantation and sales; flower plantation and sales. The company established cooperation with Sichuan Agricultural University and Chinese Academy of Agricultural Sciences, and adopted the multi-purpose biological fertilizer developed by Chinese Academy of Agricultural Sciences in breeding of edible and ornamental rare medical herbs, such as Rheum palmatum essentials, bletilla striata, dendrobium officinale, gardenia jasminoides and Paeonia suffruticosa Andr, and fingered citron. The company is also engaged in plantation and processing of medical herbs, Internet + TCM transaction, health travel, TCM culture popularization, TCM and health, etc. It strives to build a green and healthy TCM industrial base.

三、负责人介绍：

Ⅲ. Responsible Person Introduction:

咸旭胜，男，山东临沂人。于2007年在渝创办重庆可益荧新材料有限公司，并担任董事长一职。2014年3月，企业主动承担起了农村带头人的作用，新成立了重庆禾蓓农业科技有限公司，并担任总经理。

Xian Xusheng, male, born in Linyi, Shandong. Xian Xusheng founded Chongqing Keyiying New Material Co., Ltd. in 2007 and acted as its Chairman of BoD. In March 2014, the company worked active in leading the rural development by establishing a new agricultural company known as Chongqing Hebei Agricultural Technology Co., Ltd. Mr. Xian Xusheng worked as the General Manager of such new company.

四、项目名称： 凤凰中药材花卉种植基地

Ⅳ. Project Name: Phoenix TCM and Flower Plantation Base

五、项目概况：

Ⅴ. Project Profile:

凤凰中药材花卉种植基地，位于重庆市沙坪坝区凤凰镇八字桥村，重点发展建成中药材特色产业村，以中药材种植、加工、互联网＋中药材交易，健康生态游，中药材文化科普知识普及教育，中药材健康养生、养老等内容。一、二、三产业融合发展模式，采取公司＋股民成立新的村级合作社，走股份制合作之路，全民集体共同发展，共同致富的路子，以发展"川黄精、川佛手……"等地道药材为重点，多种药材种植科普教育为辅的中药材文化健康村，做到上有蓝天白云，下有健康生态。实现绿水青山，就是金山银山的梦想。

Phoenix TCM and Flower Plantation Base is situated in Baziqiao Village, Fenghuang Town, Shapingba District of Chongqing. The company made great efforts to develop an industrial village covering medicine herb plantation and processing, Internet + TCM transaction, health travel, TCM culture popularization, and TCM health care. The company adopted a business model of company + rural cooperative, under which the company cooperated with local villagers by shares, in order to pool the efforts of the entire village to achieve common prosperity. The company focused its business on local herbs such as "Rheum palmatum, fingered citron ...", and promotes TCM education in the village. With these efforts, the company expects to build an ecological industry while protecting the local natural environment. The company aims to develop local economy and protect the local environment at a same time.

项目于2014年3月流转土地开建，经发改委备案，由重庆禾蓓农业科技有限公司负责实施，计划分三期实施，初期流转土地1500亩，规划建设玻璃温室大棚设施、中药材加工中心、中药材冷冻仓储冷藏冻库、中药材交易中心、中药材养生养老中心、中药材文化休闲广场、群众大舞台，及中药材生长环境监控追溯系统。研发适合市场需求的新产品（如佛手保健酒、佛手养生茶、佛手饮料等）。

In March 2014, the company acquired necessary land use rights and reported to the local National Development and Reform Commission for registration. The project was undertaken by Chongqing Hebei Agricultural Technology Co., Ltd. and was expected at three phases. According to the first phase project, 1,500 mu land piece had been granted for construction of glass greenhouse, herb processing center, a cold warehousing facility and transaction center, a TCM health care center, a TCM-theme leisure square, a mass stage and a TCM growing environment monitoring and tracing system. The project also makes efforts to develop new products that cater to market needs (such as fingered citron wine, tea and beverage products).

六、项目优势：
VI. Project Advantage(s):

1．交通便利：基地位于重庆沙坪坝区，距离渝新欧铁路、中亚铁路起点站约4公里，外环高速路边，高速路口约2公里，距离重庆大学城约15公里，距离成渝高铁约20公里，交通条件十分便利。

Traffic facilities：The base site is located in Shapingba District of Chongqing, and is 4km from the starting point of Chongqing-Sinkiang-Europe International Railway and Middle Asia Railway, 2km from the outer ring express road of Chongqing, 15km from Chongqing College Town and 20km from Chengdu-Chongqing railway. Therefore, it enjoys great advantages of physical location.

2．稳健的销售渠道：公司与国内多家药业公司合作，建立了长期稳定的业务关系。

Robust sales channels：the company has established business cooperation with many pharmaceutical companies in China.

3．技术力量雄厚：依托中国农业科学院、四川农业大学、多家药业合作公司成熟技术及公司专业人才团队。

Technology：Supports mature technologies from Chinese Academy of Agricultural Sciences, Sichuan Agricultural University, and many pharmaceutical companies and professional teams of the company.

4．环境优势：项目位于缙云山脚下，山清水秀、空气清新，是生产绿色产品的天然场地。

Environment：The project is situated at the foot of Jinyun Mountain where there is well-protected mountains and rivers and fresh air, which make it an ideal production site for green products.

5．产品优势：产品种植过程均采用生物有机肥（抗虫增肥），农药零使用。

Products：All our products are grown with organic fertilizer (with deinsectization effect) which is pesticide-free.

七、项目需求：
VII. Project Demand(s):

为加快项目建设进度，早日推向市场，希望得到政府更多财政支持，同时希望投融资机构介入共同打造凤凰中药材花卉种植基地项目。

In order to facilitate the project construction and market promotion, we are looking forward to more financial supports from governments and expect the cooperation with investing organizations in developing the phoenix TCM and flower plantation base project.

安全社区智能管理平台
Secure Community Intelligent Management Platform

一、项目公司名称：广州织网通讯科技有限公司
Ⅰ. Project Company Name：Guangzhou Weaving Communication Technology Co., Ltd.

二、项目公司介绍：
Ⅱ. Project Company Introduction:

公司是富力地产、实地地产全国项目的通信网络（光纤到户）及智能化系统集成建设、智能家居软硬件配套及智慧社区（楼宇）运营的战略合作商，与时代地产、中海地产、越秀地产为深度合作伙伴，是广东智慧城市产业技术创新联盟理事单位之一；公司提供完整智慧城市/园区/住区弱电智能化、酒店公寓智能化、家居智能化、建筑能源管理系统等综合解决方案。

The company is a strategic partner of R&F Properties and Seedland responsible for communication network (FTTH) and intelligent systematic integration, smart home software and hardware support and smart community (building) operation. It has established in-depth cooperation with Times Property, China Overseas Property and Yuexiu Property and has become a council member of Guangdong Alliance of Smart City Industrial Technology Innovation. The Company provides complete solutions for smart city/park/community LV power distribution, smart hotels and apartments, smart home and building energy management systems.

三、负责人介绍：
Ⅲ. Responsible Person Introduction:

钟广宏，总裁，在中国电信股份有限公司广州分公司工作24年，经历了电信的固网、移动业务分拆，在综合和市场线条换了多个部门和岗位；2015年7月，从国企下海到织网公司任职，将公司从传统的只与一家战略地产开发商合作的单一通信业务工程商转型为智慧城市服务商，实施"走出去"的战略，先后与多家地产开发公司开展业务合作。

Zhong Guanghong, President, once worked in China Telecom Corporation Limited Guangzhou Branch Company for 24 years, during which period he experienced the separation of mobile and fixed network businesses and worked at several positions from general department, market department to many other departments and divisions. In July 2015, he quit the job and joined Weaving Communication, where he successfully changed Weaving Communication from a traditional single communication engineering service provider with only one strategic real developer cooperator to a comprehensive smart city service provider. By practicing the "going abroad" strategy, he successfully established business cooperation with many other real property developers.

四、项目名称：安全社区智能管理平台
Ⅳ. Project Name：Secure Community Intelligent Management Platform

五、项目概况：
Ⅴ. Project Profile:

为文冲社区制定了全市首创的，以"物联网+"打造的八大功能整合创新方案，将智慧APP、智能门禁、视像监控、安全锁控、联网烟感、公共信息屏、延迟电插座、语音广播生态整合。每一个功能都是经过充分的调研和论证，结合城中村消防和治安隐患防范的实际需要，通过"智慧门禁+安防"、"智慧门禁+社区平台"、"智慧门禁+物业"、"智慧社区+托管"和"智慧社区+体验"五种模式。

The company successfully built the first "Internet +" based overall solution for Wenchong Community that integrates eight major functions including smart APPs, smart access control, CCTV system, secure lock control, network smoke detectors, public information panel, delay socket and voice broadcasting systems. Each function is developed on full investigations and demonstration in combination with the practical needs in urban villages for fire and security control. It integrates five modes："smart access control + security control", "smart access control + community platform", "smart access control + property management", "smart community + entrusted management" and "smart community + experience".

六、项目优势：
VI. Project Advantage(s):

织网公司旗下的"旧城区系列智能门禁系统"是公司目前着力打造的明星项目和产品，该方案以其安全性、易用性、创新性和实用性受到广大用户的喜爱，在同类项目方案和产品市场中获得良好的口碑。

The "Old Urban Area Smart Access Control System" solution is a popular project and product developed by Weaving Communication. The solution is very popular among users for its security, easy operation, innovative and practical features and won very good reputation and recognition in comparison with similar solutions and products.

全市首创的以"物联网+"打造的八大功能整合创新方案，已经得到了黄埔区各级政府部门的认可，各大媒体争先报道，包括广州电视台、广州电视花城频道、《新快报》、《信息时报》、大洋网、《广州黄埔》、广州政法网等。

The innovative "Internet +" based solution integrating eight features has been extensively recognized by governmental authorities at all levels in Huangpu District, and was reported by many mainstream media, including without limitation to Guangzhou TV, Guangzhou TV Huacheng Channel, *New Express*, *Information Times*, dayoo.com, *Guangzhou Huangpu*, and gzszfw.gov.cn.

七、项目需求：
VII. Project Demand(s):

以智慧社区为核心，通过智能门禁系统的建设，实现社区人口管理、出租屋管理、人员管理和管控，满足城市治安综合管理、城市化管理等要求，提供社区治安防控水平、为居民提供安全、高效、便捷、舒适的智慧化生活环境。

The project realizes community population management, rent apartment management, personnel management and control, and satisfies the needs for urban security control and municipal administration on basis of the Smart Community solution and by the smart access control systems. It also helps to improve the local security level and provide local residents with secure, efficient, easy and comfortable smart lives.

"手机控"养生产品
Health Products for "Phone Freaks"

一、项目公司名称：北京华富隆科贸有限公司

I. Project Company Name: Beijing Huafulong Technology Trade Co., Ltd.

二、项目公司介绍：

II. Project Company Introduction:

公司成立于2004年,是一个以绿能环保科技、天然健康养生、文化艺术创意等为导向的具有高科技含量的国际化综合性科技贸易公司。公司运营规范,操作标准,涉及行业广泛。主要经营多款膳食食品和绿能奈米健康用品等,弘扬中华民族传统健康养生观念,以食疗、理疗代替医疗,旨在根本解决广大民众的健康问题。

Founded in 2004, the Company is an international comprehensive technology trade company with green and environment-friendly technology, natural health maintenance and cultural and artistic creativity as the guidance and of the high-tech content. With the normative management and standard operation, the Company involves extensive industries. Mainly engaged in multiple dietary food and green energy Nano health products, it carries forward the traditional health maintenance ideas of the Chinese nation and replaces the medical treatment with Chinese food therapy and physical therapy to fundamentally solve the people's health problems.

三、负责人介绍：

III. Responsible Person Introduction:

公司董事长张建军先生1982年毕业于青岛科技大学,化工高级工程师,在中央企业工作20多年,并担任过重要领导职务,有丰富的技术管理、市场营销和企业管理经验。曾多次参加国内外商务活动,并与海内外企业和科研机构建立了很好的业务关系。

Graduating from Qingdao University of Science and Technology in 1982, a senior engineer of chemical industry, President of the Company Mr. Zhang Jianjun, he has worked in the central enterprises for more than 20 years and served as important leader ever; thus, he has rich experience in technology management, marketing and enterprise management. He participated in the domestic and foreign business activities for many times and has built the good business relations with the domestic and overseas enterprises and scientific research institutes.

四、项目名称："手机控"养生产品

IV. Project Name: Health Products for "Phone Freaks"

五、项目概况：

V. Project Profile:

针对当前手机控、电脑迷、长坐办公室、工作强度大、较少运动及不良饮食习惯等导致身体气血循环不畅、末梢血液微循环不良,由此产生的各类骨关节疼痛、腰椎颈椎病、心脑血管疾病等,可使用绿能奈米科技有限公司与台湾工业研究院奈米中心共同设计、研发、生产的绿能奈米健康用品。绿能奈米α波(超能量)产品通过了专业机构的测试评估以及GMP、FDA、CE、台湾卫生福利部等认证,取得了12项海内外专利。主要品类有非动力式治疗床/椅垫、奈米枕(巾)、多功能治疗垫及披肩(围巾)、护颈/肘/腰、眼罩、穴道按摩袜、享瘦带、软针灸医疗用贴布等。

Green energy Nano health products jointly designed, researched and developed as well as produced by Green Energy Nano Technology Co., Ltd. and Nano Center of Taiwan Industrial Institute can be used for all kinds of bone and joint aches, lumbar vertebrae spondylosis and cervical spondylosis as well as cardiovascular and cerebrovascular diseases generated due to poor blood circulation and bad peripheral blood microcirculation caused by the phone freaks, computer fans, sitting in the office for long, high-intensity work, bad diet habits, less movement, etc.. Green energy α-wave (super-energy) products have passed the test and evaluation conducted by the professional institution and the certifications of GMP, FDA, CE and Taiwan Ministry of Health and Welfare and have obtained 12 domestic and overseas patents. Its main categories include the non-powered treatment bed / cushion, Nano pillow (towel), multi-function treatment cushion and shawl (scarf), neck / elbow / waist guards, eye patches, acupoint massage sock, slim down belt and soft acupuncture medical-use patch and so on.

针对不同人群身体退化性关节炎、骨刺、骨质疏松、肩周炎，以及因关节液缺失造成的骨关节磨损等常见骨骼疾病，食用台湾康和生技有限公司与台湾国防医学院联合研发生产、具有自主知识产权、通过国际生产认证和 SGS 检验合格的"康乐健"骨关节炎最佳膳食品，可有效增进钙吸收，补充关节液，间接保护（补充）骨营养素，改善骨质疏松，加速软骨细胞（弹性组织）的再生与修复，刺激软骨间质生成（预防软骨失去弹性），润滑骨关节，减少骨间摩擦受损，减轻关节、软骨、骨头和邻近结构的损害等。

For the common bone diseases of different groups of people, such as degenerative arthritis, bone spur, osteoporosis, scapulohumeral periarthritis as well as the bone and joint wear caused due to the loss of joint fluid, eating "Kang Le Jian" Best Food for Osteoarthritis with the proprietary intellectual property right and passing the international production certification and SGS inspection, which is jointly researched and developed and produced by Taiwan Kanghe Biological Technology Co, Ltd. and National Defense Medical Center can effectively promote calcium absorption, supplement the joint fluid, indirectly protect (supplement) the bone nutrients and improve the bone rarefaction, accelerate the regeneration and repair of the chondrocyte (elastic tissue) and stimulate generation of cartilage stroma (prevent the cartilage from the loss of elasticity), lubricate the bones and joints and reduce the friction damage between the bones, and reduce the damages of the joints, cartilages, bones and the adjacent structure and so on.

根据公司"绿色、天然、健康、快乐、长寿"的经营理念和战略发展需要，为进一步完善相关产品在国内外市场的布局，迅速提高产品的市场占有率，我们将继续投入技术研发，增强产品品质的多样化，彰显"无药物保健养生"，以适应市场需求。

According to the Company operation idea of "Green, Natural, Healthy, Happy, Long-life" and the demands of strategic development, to further improve the layout of the relevant products in the domestic and overseas market and rapidly improve the market share of the products, we will continue to invest in the technical research and development, enhance the diversified product quality and highlight "Medicine-free Health Maintenance" to adapt to the market demands.

六、项目优势：
Ⅵ. Prject Advantage(s)：

绿能奈米 α 波（超能量）用品以奈米贵金属复合式粉体配方植入多孔中空棉取代传统的微米颗粒附着，突破了远红外线产品单纯的蓄热保暖功能，促进血液量与血流速度，强化血液微循环，实现无药理疗、标本兼治。

green energy Nano α -wave (super-energy) products replace the traditional micrometer particle attachment with the Nano precious metal compound power recipe implanting porous hollow cotton to break through the pure heat storage and warmth preservation function of the far infrared products, promote the blood volume and blood flow rate, strengthen the blood microcirculation and realize medicine-free physical therapy and treatment from the roots and symptoms.

七、项目需求：
Ⅶ. Project Demand(s)：

品牌推广，加盟合作。

brand promotion, joining and cooperation.

妈妈安－小儿推拿连锁加盟
Mamaan – Infant Massotherapy Chain Store

一、项目公司名称： 香港乐甲生物科技有限公司
I. Project Company Name: Hong Kong Lejia Biotechnology Co., Ltd.

二、项目公司介绍：
II. Project Company Introduction:

公司以"传承中华五千年中医之经典，强健华夏儿女子孙之体魄"为宗旨，目前拥有"乐甲""妈妈安"两大系列产品及相对应的加盟连锁店数百家。2016 年公司下属的"妈妈安妇婴保健中心"汇聚国内众多著名中医小儿推拿专家，用独创的推拿手法，配以公司独家研制的保健敷贴，成立了"妈妈安小儿推拿连锁服务中心"，并开设了公益中医保健培训班，拥有数百家加盟连锁店，形成了覆盖全国的营销网络，随时为国内外客户提供优质快捷的产品服务和技术咨询。将全力打造全国规模最大的小儿保健行业的综合体。

Guided by the mission of "Passing on traditional Chinese medicine of five thousand years, body building for Chinese people", the company is currently running two product series: "Lejia" and "Mamaan" and several hundred chain stores. In 2016, the "Mamaan Motherhood and Infant Health Care Center" gathers many famous infant massotherapy experts and with their peculiar massage skills and our plasters, the "Mamaan Infant Massotherapy Chain Service Center" was established. The company also sets up a public healthcare training program and opened hundreds of chain stores, covering entire sales network in China. We are always ready to provide quick and quality services, products and advices to customers at home and abroad. The company will make all efforts to build up the largest a complex organization in the industry of infant healthcare.

三、负责人介绍：
III. Responsible Person Introduction:

于枫，2009 年成功启动"乐甲手足修护"连锁项目，目前拥有数百家连锁店，2016 年带领研发团队开发出"妈妈安"小儿保健系列产品，并成立了公益保健培训大课堂，反对小儿小病大治，提倡有病推拿，无病防病的小儿健康保健口号，必将带动全国的"小儿推拿连锁项目"走上新的里程碑。

Yu Feng, successfully launched the "Lejia Finger and Foot Care" chain operation project in 2009. Currently, and has so far developed hundreds of chain stores. In 2016, under his leadership, the R&D team successfully developed "Mamaan" series infant healthcare products and set up a public healthcare training program. By these efforts, he appeals for actions against overtreatment and advocated massotherapy and daily health care. This will surely lead the "infant massotherapy project" to a new stage.

四、项目名称： 妈妈安 - 小儿推拿连锁加盟
IV. Project Name: Mamaan - Infant Massotherapy Chain Store

五、项目概况：
V. Project Profile:

公司独创的小儿推拿术与"妈妈安"系列产品完美结合后，能显著提高调理范围、见效快且无副作用。目前公司已开展了五期培训班，培训出百名优秀小儿调理师。培训课程包括：小儿系统调理技术、门店运营技巧、新媒体应用、团队建设等。希望让每位学员都能学有所成，学有所用；让小儿推拿精髓永续传承 让绿色疗法走进每个家庭。

The unique infant massotherapy works perfectly with our "Mamaan" Series products. They can significantly improve the massage and are totally free of side effects. Currently, we have completed 5 sessions and trained a hundred outstanding infant nursing expects. Our training sessions include systematic infant nursing skill, store operation expertise, new media application, team building, etc. Every trainee will become a real nursing expert. We hope that the infant massotherapy can pass on and safeguard each family.

六、项目优势：

VI. Project Advantage(s)：

产品质量优势：产品制造工艺成熟，疗效稳定可靠。

Product quality：Mature production process, stable and reliable effect.

丰富经验优势：公司拥有多年的加盟连锁经验。

Experiences：The company has experiences for years in running chain stores.

免费师资优势：公司拥有多名资深小儿推拿专业导师，免费传授相关小儿保健推拿知识。

Free training：The company has a large number of experience infant massotherapy experts who provide free training on the massotherapy skills.

产业时机优势：

Industry maturity:

1．抗生素的管制，输液的风险，都给传统中医外治疗法带来机遇；

Controls of antibiotics and risks in transfusion bring opportunities for traditional Chinese therapy；

2．中医已成为国家战略项目，把握政策趋势，成就事业；

Traditional Chinese Medicine (TCM) has become a national program and the policies are best chances for entrepreneurs；

3．基层诊所小、散、乱，没有特色，对输液的管制让诊所雪上加霜。特色才能生存，小儿绿色疗法深受基层诊所欢迎，合作前景巨大；

Local clinics are small in size and poor organized and are lack of differentiated service. Strict controls over transfusion put local clinics in even poorer conditions, and they have to differentiate themselves from others to survive the competition. The infant green therapy is very popular among residents and there is endless possibilities for the future；

4．二胎政策的放开，市场将出现爆发性增长；

Withdrawal of the childbirth control policy will lead to explosive growth of market size；

5．小儿市场基本没有医保的压力，家长对小儿的投资不考虑价格，安全疗效和服务是关键。"小儿推拿"产业的巨大财富，势必会又培养出一批创业成功者。

Infant therapy market is free of pressure from medical insurance. Parents are not price-sensitive in therapy to their children, but values safety and effects most. "Infant massotherapy" is an industry with great fortune and will surely create a large number of winners.

七、项目需求：

VII. Project Demand(s)：

公司项目前景及其看好，为加速成功的脚步，现寻求相关单位与优秀人士的加入合作，公司给予技术支持提供垄断产品，并给予股份或高分成的优惠政策。

The company project has very promising future and in order to facilitate our process, we faithfully expect cooperation with interested organizations and individuals, for which we provide technical supports and exclusive products together with stock shares or profit shares of our company.

流量计
Flow Meter

一、项目公司名称： 安徽天维仪表有限公司
I. Project Company Name： Anhui Tianwei Instrument Co., Ltd.

二、项目公司介绍：
II. Project Company Introduction：

公司是集科研、生产、销售和服务于一体的专业流量仪表生产厂家，位于安徽省合肥市庐阳工业区，占地1万平方米，现有职工86名。以"天道酬勤、维经有度"的企业精神，经过多年发展，公司拥有精良的加工设备和先进的技术，不断完善内部运行机制，引进科学管理制度，先后通过了国际质量管理体系、职业健康管理体系认证和环境体系认证。2013年获得国家高新技术企业和安徽省著名商标荣誉。

the company is a professional manufacturer of specialized flow meters which integrates scientific research, manufacture, sales and service, and is located in the Luyang Industrial Zone, Hefei, Anhui, covering an area of more than 10,000 sq.m. and having 86 employees at present. With the enterprise spirit of "God help those who help themselves" and "normal management", the company, after development for years, has possessed excellent processing equipment and advanced technologies, make constant improvement of its internal operation mechanism, introduce of scientific management system, and has successively passed the certification of the International Quality Management System, the Occupational Health Management System and the Environmental System. In 2013, it obtained Chinese national high-tech enterprises and Anhui famous brand honors.

三、负责人介绍：
III. Responsible Person Introduction:

孔庆胜，职务：总经理，北京大学EMBA工商管理学位。2007年组建安徽天维仪表有限公司，并担任总经理兼技术总监，全权负责公司运作与产品开发，近三年获得2项发明专利、13项实用新型专利。

Kong Qingsheng, General Manager, EMBA of Peking University In 2007, he established Anhui Tianwei Instrument Co., Ltd., acted as the General Manager and Technical Director, taking full responsibility for the operation and product development, and has obtained two invention patents and 13 utility model patents in the last three years.

四、项目名称： 流量计
IV. Project Name： Flow Meter

五、项目概况：
V. Project Profile:

容积式流量计是我公司主导产品，分别包括螺旋转子流量计、椭圆齿轮流量计、腰轮流量计、三转子流量计。具有结构简单、使用可靠、准确度高，对进出口管道内的流场无特殊要求，被测介质的黏度范围和流量范围都很宽广等特点。被广泛用于石油、化工、船舶、医药、交通、食品等工业及商业贸易计量的工程管理控制。

Volumetric flowmeters are our leading products, including helical rotor flowmeter, elliptic gear flowmeter, roots flowmeter and three-rotor flowmeter. These flowmeters are characterized by simplicity, reliability, high accuracy, no special requirements for flow fields in inlet and outlet pipelines, wide range of viscosity and flow of measured mediums, etc. Therefore, they are widely used in the process management and control of petrochemical, chemical, vessel, medicine, transportation, food industries, etc. and commercial trade measurement.

速度式流量计是我公司研制的新型流量计，分别包括电磁流量计、涡街流量计、旋进旋涡流量计、涡轮流量计。速度式流量计是以测量管道内流量的平均速度来测量流量的仪表，该系列产品设计新颖、外形美观，具有重量轻、流量范围大、精度高、使用寿命长等特点。被广泛用于石油、化工、医药、环保等行业。

The velocity-type flowmeter developed by our company is a new type of flowmeter, including electromagnetic flowmeter, vortex flowmeter, vortex precession flowmeter and turbine flowmeter. The velocity-type flowmeter is a meter to measure flow by measuring the average velocity of flow in a pipeline. This series of products is characterized by novel design, attractive appearance, lightness, wide flow range, high precision, long lifetime, etc. Therefore, they are widely used for petrochemical, chemical, medicine, environmental protection industries, etc.

六、项目优势：
Ⅵ. Project Advantage(s):

公司拥有一支高素质、高效率研发团队，近三年获得2项发明专利、13项实用新型专利。是安徽省第一家拥有300口径容积式流量计检测设备。目前长期与中石化、中石油等大型国有企业保持合作关系。

The company has a high-quality and efficient R&D team and has obtained two invention patents and 13 utility model patents in the last three years. It is the first company in Anhui which owns the volumetric flowmeter with an internal diameter of 300. At present, it keeps a long-term cooperation relationship with large state-owned enterprises such as Sinopec, CNPC (China National Petroleum Corporation), etc.

七、项目需求：
Ⅶ. Project Demand(s):

1. 寻找国内外合作伙伴，共同开发流量仪表行业市场。

Seek for partners at home and abroad to jointly develop the industrial market of flowmeters.

2. 将公司系列产品，容积式流量计与速度式流量计在"一带一路"沿线各个国家的石油、天然气、水处理、化工原料等计量领域打开销路。

Find a market for the series of the company's products such as volumetric flowmeter, velocity-type flowmeter, etc. in the metering fields of oil, natural gas, water treatment, chemical raw materials, etc. in every country alongside the "Belt and Road".

中药材种植与深加工
Cultivation and Deep Processing of Chinese Medicinal Herbs

一、项目公司名称： 广西一带一路健康产业投资有限公司

Ⅰ. Project Company Name： Guangxi Belt and Road Health Industry Investment Co. Ltd.

二、项目公司介绍：

Ⅱ. Project Company Introduction：

公司成立于美丽的绿城南宁市，总资产3.6亿元，是一家集制药业、医疗业、养老养生产业、健康产业投资、研发、技术咨询服务转让、技术管理、健康食品加工生产、中药材种植、苗木培育、农副产品、健康养生生态旅游观光种植开发等为一体的大型民营企业。公司现有人员86人，其中技术人员有36位，管理人员28位。公司已租用土地面积达10万多亩，现已种有5万多亩仿野生中药材，公司旗下有省级研发中心及中草药营养食品生产加工车间1万多平方米。与国内外多家知名代理销售企业建立了良好战略合作伙伴关系。

The company locates in the beautiful green City—Nanning. As one of the large-scale private enterprises, it enjoys a total asset of RMB 360 million and professionally engaged in its main business scope as followings：pharmaceutical, healthcare, old-age and health preservation industry, health industry investment, research and development, technical consulting service transfer, technology management, health food processing and producing, traditional Chinese medicinal herbs cultivation, seedling cultivation, agricultural and sideline products, planting and development for health-preservation ecological tourism and sightseeing, and etc. The company now has 86 personnel, including 36 technicians and 28 managers. It has leased a land area of more than 100 thousand mu (6.7 thousand hectares), and has planted more than 50 thousand mu (3.3 thousand hectares) of imitation wild Chinese medicinal herbs. It has more than 10,000 square meters of R & D center at provincial-level and processing workshop for nutritious foods which belong to Chinese herbal medicine. It has established a good strategic cooperative partnership with a number of well-known brand manufacturers and distributors at home and abroad.

三、负责人介绍：

Ⅳ. Responsible Person Introduction：

周厚霖，董事长，研究员，中药师，从事多年的医疗保健工作，获得国家多项专利配方，2013年第十届全国中医肝胆学术获奖者，2014年获得中华人民共和国国史两弹一星历史研究会"红色青年"，国家机关老干部健康顾问团成员，广西东盟城中医药研究院院长，国内外多家单位个人健康顾问，受智利总统，阿根廷大使馆等国家邀请参加"一带一路"国际合作高峰论坛，2017年参加"一带一路"国际商业领袖人才高级研修班学习。

The Chairman, Researcher and Traditional Chinese Pharmacists, Zhou Houlin has engaged in health care for many years and accessed to national patents. He was also the winner of the Tenth National Traditional Chinese Hepatobiliary Academic Award in 2013；meanwhile, in 2014, he was awarded as the honor of "Red Youth" titled by the PRC Chinese History Two Bombs and One Satellite History Institute, awarded as the state organs senior cadres health advisory member, awarded as the Dean of Guangxi ASEAN City Institute of Traditional Chinese Medicine Research, and awarded as personal health consultant for many units and individuals at home and abroad in 2014. He has attended the "Belt and Road" International Cooperation Forum, invited by the president of Chile and by the embassy of Argentina and other countries. In 2017, he took a part in advanced training seminar of "Belt and Road" international business leaders.

四、项目名称： 中药材种植与深加工

Ⅳ. Project Name： Cultivation and Deep Processing of Chinese Medicinal Herbs

五、项目概况：

Ⅴ. Project Profile：

项目由2012年开始建设的200亩，发展至今已达5万多亩，计划未来三到五年达到20万亩，公司按照中药材GAP标准，建立20万亩的仿野生种植中药材基地；新建10000多平方米中草药保健品营养食品生产加工

厂，打造中国高寒山区仿野生中草药种植最大的"定制药园"。

The construction of this project started in 2012, and occupied 200 mu (13.3 hectares). In 2017, now it occupied more than 50,000 mu (3.3 thousand hectares), and it will be planned to occupy 200,000 mu (13.3 thousand hectares) in the next 3 to 5 years. In accordance with the GAP standard of Chinese herbal medicines, the company established 200,000 mu (13.3 thousand hectares) imitation wild medicinal herb plant base; built more than 10,000 square meters' health care nutrition food producing and processing workshop to create the biggest imitation wild herbs planting "customized herbal garden" of cold highland area in China.

六、项目优势：

VI. Project Advantage (s)：

公司地道药材种植，高寒山区中草药仿野生种植耐旱耐虫高产技术是国内首创，填补了国内高寒山区石漠化地区仿野生中药材种植技术。适合石漠化地区的农民脱贫致富的项目。

The drought resistance, insect resistance and high-yield technology of geo-authentic crude drug planting and cold highland area' imitation wild planting, is initiated by the company in our country, which have filling a domestic gap in the field of imitation wild herbs planting techniques in stony desertification of cold highland area. The project is suitable for farmers to get rid of poverty in rocky desertification areas.

七、项目需求：

VII. Project Demand (s):

市场融资与战略合作，推进国际中药材种植技术与加工、医药文化交流，原材料销售。

We hope to obtain market financing and strategic cooperation to promote the cultivation and processing of international herbal medicine, medical cultural exchanges and raw materials sales.

雲山椿山茶油
Yunshanchun Camellia Oil

一、项目公司名称： 福建云山椿生物科技有限公司
I. Project Company Name: Fujian Yunshanchun Biotechnology Co., Ltd.

二、项目公司介绍：
II. Project Company Introduction:

公司位于福建厦门，注册资本为 1000 万，云山椿是一家集山茶油科研、生产、营销和服务为一体的公司，在福建龙岩的汀江河畔拥有天然油茶种植基地，并签约泼墨画大师钟京先生为公司品牌代言人。云山椿山茶油自面世以来，深受广大客户喜爱。

Located in Xiamen of Fujian with registered capital of RMB 10 million, Yunshanchun is a company integrated the researches and development, production, marketing and services for camellia oil, and possesses plantation base for natural Camellia oil at riverside of Ting Rive in Longyan of Fujian. The Company has signed the contract for Company brand spokesman with splash-ink painting master, Mr. Zhong Jing. Yunshanchun Camellia oil is loved by the majority of customers since marketing.

三、负责人介绍： 胡虹
III. Responsible Person Introduction: Hu Hong

2000 年	海龙贸易公司	财务
Year 2000	Hailong Trading Company	Financial staff
2005 年	庆威针织公司	担任报关员
Year 2005	Qingwei Knitting Company	Customs declarer
2000 年	海龙贸易公司	担任财务
Year 2000	Hailong Trading Company	Financial staff
2010 年	中裕达商贸公司	担任副总经理
Year 2010	Zhongyuda Commercial Trading Company	Vice General Manager
2015 年	福建云山椿生物科技有限公司	担任总经理
Year 2015	Fujian Yunshanchun Biotechnology Co., Ltd.	General Manager

四、项目名称： 云山椿山茶油
IV. Project Name: Yunshanchun Camellia Oil

五、项目概况：
V. Project Profile:

山茶油是从山茶科油茶树种子中获得的，是我国最古老的木本食用植物油之一。中国是世界上山茶科植物分布最广的国家，是世界上最大的茶油生产基地，除此之外只有东南亚、日本等国有极少量的分布。中国是油茶的原产地，油茶是我国特有的油料树种，其栽培历史有 2300 年以上，它的中心产地则分布在我国的大别山区域、西南及湘、赣南部。油茶树生长在没有污染的亚热带南岭湿润气候区，整个生长过程中不施农药、化肥等。山茶油营养成分高，不含芥酸、胆固醇、黄曲霉素等对人体有害物质；色泽金黄或浅黄，品质纯净，澄清透明，气味清香，味道纯正；为中国政府提倡推广的纯天然木本食用植物油，以及国际粮农组织首推的卫生保健植物食用油。当前国家粮油安全形势不容乐观，外资油脂企业已基本垄断了中国食用油市场，股权、定价权均被外方控制着。只有自力更生，大力生产自己的油，方能确保我们国家粮油安全。茶油，是我们中国人所独有的食用油！

Camellia oil is obtained for seeds of Camellia oleiferaAbel of Camellia and is one of the oldest woody edible vegetable oil in our country. China is the most widely distributed with Camellia plants in the World, is the world's largest

Camellia oil production base, in addition, there is only few distribution in Southeast Asia, Japan and other countries. The core planting area of Camellia is in Dabie Mountain region, Southwest as well as south parts of Hunan and Jiangxi, the planting history is over 2,300 years, is a China special oil tree and China is the place of origin for Camellia. Camellia trees grow in subtropical south humid climate zone free from pollution, nether pesticide nor fertilizer is needed during the whole growth. The geographic locations, soil and climates are suitable with high nutritional ingredients. The Camellia oil excludes substances harmful to human body such as erucic acid, cholesterol and aflatoxin. It is golden or pale yellow in color, pure quality, clear transparent, fragrant smell and pure flavor. It is the natural woody edible vegetable oil advocated and promoted by Chinese government, and is the first health care plant oil recommended by International Food and Agriculture Organization. The security situation of China's grain and oil is not optimistic, as foreign oil companies almost monopolized the China's edible oil market, and the equities, pricing rights are controlled by foreign companies. In changeable international market, however, only self-reliance and producing our own oil products can ensure grain security of our country. Camellia oil is the unique edible oil for Chinese.

六、项目优势：

Ⅵ. Project Advantage(s):

1．产地：源自闽西红土地，气候适宜，酸性土壤，日照、降水充足。

Place of origin：originate from red earth in west Fujian with adequate climates, acid soil, sufficient sunshine and rainfall.

2．工艺：采用纯物理压榨工艺，更好地保留茶油中的营养。

Processes：adopt pure physical squeeze techniques, for better keeping the nutrition in Camellia oil.

3．区位：营销中心位于福建厦门，五大经济特区之一、计划单列市。地处东南沿海，便于对外交流。

Location：The marketing center is located in Xiamen of Fujian which is one of five special economic zones and special planned city. The Company is located in China's South-East coastal areas, convenient for foreign exchanges.

七、项目需求：

Ⅶ. Project Demand(s)：

礼品团购，商超合作，渠道经销，高档酒店，月子中心。

Group buying gifts, cooperation with shops and supermarkets, channel marketing, luxury hotel and confinement center.

光伏太阳能景区道路指示牌
Photovoltaic Solar Road Sign in Scenic Areas

一、项目公司名称： 湖南至易工程技术有限公司

I. Project Company Name: Hunan Zhiyi Engineering Technology Co., Ltd.

二、项目公司介绍：

II. Project Company Introduction:

公司集研发、生产、销售、工程服务于一体。主营光伏太阳能道路指示牌、太阳能电池板、太阳能光伏发电热水器、太阳能电池板升降微调装置、空气源热泵、光伏幕墙等系列产品。以上产品自主研发生产，并拥有多项技术专利。运营成熟、规范管理。获得了 IBC 知识产权认证、商业企业品牌评价三星认证、中国商业联合会知识产权会员、湖南省绿色建筑委员会会员单位，是国内新能源领域的新兴品牌。

Hunan Zhiyi, oriented at an integration of R&D(research & development), production, sales distribution and construction service, mainly provides PV (photovoltaic) solar road sign, solar panel, PV solar water heater, micromatic setting device for lifting solar panels, air-source heat pump and PV curtain wall. The company is solely independent in developing and manufacturing those products and has been granted with multiple technology patents. Rising as a new star in domestic development of new energy, the company, with its mature operation system and well-regulated management system, has been acknowledged by various societies, winning honors and awards like IBC (Intellectual Business Connection) Intellectual Property Right Certification, 3-Star Business Coporate Brand, China General Chamber of Commerce IP (Intellectual Property) Member and Hunan Green Building Council Member.

三、负责人介绍：

III. Responsible Person Introduction

李先成，总经理，拥有多年的新能源领域技术开发和工程工作经验。他曾参与并主持省多项新能源领域等标准制定。

Mr. Li Xiancheng, serving as general manager of the project, has been seasoned by over 14 years in the field of new energy technology development and construction service. He has been involved in and led several programs of preparing provincial standards to guide new energy development.

四、项目名称： 光伏太阳能景区道路指示牌

IV. Project Name: Photovoltaic Solar Road Sign in Scenic Areas

五、项目概况：

V. Project Profile

太阳能作为一种取之不尽、用之不竭的安全、节能、环保能源越来越受到世人的关注，它的应用已经涉及日常生活的各个方面。光伏太阳能景区道路指示牌在道路广告中广泛应用，我公司研发这款光伏太阳能景区道路指示牌产品采用太阳能光伏发电装置、储能装置、指示牌、广告位、其他装置（垃圾桶、手机充电桩等）独立系统组成，适应性很强，用于代替传统道路广告牌。太阳能光伏发电是当前世界性的能源革命，绿色环保可再生，是高科技的形象代言，可以提高道路广告牌的外在形象，成为夜晚的一道亮丽风景，从而提升广告主的品牌效应。

The project is considered as an application of photovoltaic solar road sign in the road advertising industry. There appears a growing interest in solar energy which has been widely used in various life aspects due to its advantages of being inexhaustible, safe, energy-saving and environmental friendly. The solar road sign, an independent power system developed by our company, consists of photovoltaic generation part, power storage devices, sign board, advertising screen and other attachment like trash bin and phone charge point. With its great adaptivity, the product aims to replace the traditional road signs. PV solar power generation has upended the energy industry. Being green and renewable, it becomes a representative of high technology. Application of solar road signs not only presents better-looking road advertising boards, also creates a shining beautiful view at night, making the advertiser's brand more impressive.

道路广告牌多安装在道路两旁，分布比较广，不具备安装普通电源的条件，夜晚无光源照射，无法达到预期的宣传效果。通过安装太阳能光伏供电系统，充分解决夜晚无光源照射问题。

The advertising boards are usually mounted at road sides, distributed across a large area. It's tricky to lay out a traditional electrical system to power the road boards. Dark boards at night due to lack of illumination source weaken the advertising effect. The problem can be solved by installing the photovoltaic solar power system.

安装在道路两旁的道路广告牌在夜间灯光的照射下，打破了路上环境单调的气氛，具有非常强烈的视觉冲击力，让驾车、乘车、步行、骑行者易于接受。太阳能电池板寿命达25年以上。可广泛应用于城市、农村道路，小区、工厂、旅游景点、停车场等场所。

The roadside advertising boards, glaring among the night lighting, break through the cloud of gloom hovering along the road and present very strong visual impact, cosy and sensible to drivers, passengers, walkers and riders. With a service life as long as over 25 years, the solar panels can be widely used in urban areas, rural roads, communities, plants, scenic spots and parking areas.

六、项目优势：

Ⅵ. Project Advantages:

1．可以提高广告主的品牌效应；

Create better brand effect at day and night for the advertiser；

2．充分解决夜晚无光源照射问题增强宣传效果；

Provide night illumination for stronger advertising effect；

3．它打破了路上环境单调的气氛；

Break through gloomy atmosphere along the roads；

4．太阳能电池板使用寿命可达25年以上；

Guarantee a service life of the solar panels as long as over 25 years；

5．免去电力部门手续，易维护、全自动控制。

Eliminate the formality and procedure of the electrical power department；easy maintenance and fully automatic control.

七、项目需求：

Ⅶ. Project Demand

根据目前新能源产业的发展，新能源领域的开发或利用已经逐渐成为一种必然趋势，我们希望在新能源的利用上得到协会及社会各界的大力支持，利用太阳能这种环保、节能、安全的能源寻求国内外建设具有代表性的示范工程。

The current developing trend in new energy industry inevitably leads to further utilization or exploitation of the new energy. We are sincerely seeking support from relative societies and other industries to put the solar power into full utilization by undertaking international and domestic sample projects which bears the feautres of safe, economical and green.

译境语言服务平台
Project E-ging Language Service Platform

一、项目公司名称：布凡网络技术（北京）有限公司
Ⅰ. Project Company Name：Bufan Network Technology (Beijing) Co., Ltd.

二、项目公司介绍：
Ⅱ. Project Company Introduction：

布凡网络技术（北京）有限公司（母公司为天津乐译通翻译服务有限公司），专业从事优质多语种翻译服务、本地化服务、国际会议会展、国际出版、国际舆情、多语培训及国际化人才派遣等跨语言、跨文化服务，并通过科技互联网优化产能和提升服务效率，消除企业语言和文化障碍。至今，已与新华社、国务院、国家发改委、中科院、中石油、中石化、葛洲坝集团、中国国际商会、天津大学、南开大学、同济大学、宝马汽车以及捷克、以色列等国大使馆建立深度合作关系，服务领域涵盖国际工程、汽车、机械、电子、石油化工、法律、医学、专利、财经、水利水电等行业。

Bufan Network Technology (Beijing) Co., Ltd. (BNTC, the Subsidiary of Tianjin HP Trans Service Co., Ltd.) is a company specialized in multi-language translation, local service, international conference and exhibition service, international publication, international public sentiment and cross-linguistic and transcultural service with multi-language training and international talent dispatch. And also, it intends to optimize productivity, lift efficiency and to eliminate the obstacle of enterprise languages and culture. By now, it has established broad partnership with the Xinhua News Agency, the State Council, NDRC, Chinese Academy of Sciences, CNPC, Sinopec, CGGC, CCOIC, TJU, NKU, Tongji University, BMW and embassies of Czech, Israel and other countries and its service covers the range of international engineering, automobile, machinery, electronics, petrochemical industry, law, medical science, patents, finance, water conservancy, hydroelectricity and other industries.

三、负责人介绍：
Ⅲ. Responsible Person Introduction：

邵福生，男，1983出生，毕业于天津外国语大学金融本科，毕业后，凭借在校期间从事电子产品推广、网站运营、家教、翻译等工作积累的人脉、社会资源以及创业的原始资本，陆续创立天津乐译通翻译服务有限公司以及北京布凡网络技术（北京）有限公司，致力于消除企业国际合作中语言和文化障碍！

Mr. Shao Fusheng, male, born in 1983, was graduated from the Department of Finance, Tianjin Foreign Studies University. After his graduation, he engaged himself in eliminating the obstacles of languages and cultures and established in succession HP Trans, and Bufan Network Technology Co., Ltd. relying on the connections, social resources and initial capital collected and accumulated in his spare-time work of promoting electronic parts, running the websites, home-teaching and translation.

四、项目名称：译境语言服务平台
Ⅳ. Project Name：Project E-ging Language Service Platform

五、项目概况：
Ⅴ. Project Profile：

译境语言服务平台，简单称译境网，该项目立足于中国，从有效解决各类翻译需求的角度，整合全球翻译人才、机构、资讯、技术、教育等行业资源。随时随地，您的语言需求将能在此平台上得到一站式解决，使翻译服务（包括中译外、外译中、外译外）的各环节全部在平台上实现，打造全链条式的语言服务。

E-ging Language Service Platform (E-ging Net) is a China-based project which, from the perspective of effective solutions for the social needs of translation, aims to globally integrate the resource of translation talents, institutes, information, technology, education and other facilities so that any language requirement, anywhere and at any time, can be met with one-stop solution on the platform and the all the links of translation service (including Chinese into foreign languages, foreign a language into Chinese and a foreign language into another one) can be realized therefore with a full chain language service.

译境网提供的是无实物形态的语言服务,"翻译"这两个字本身即已消除了深度国际合作中的语言和文化壁垒。在译境网上,深度国际化合作渠道可以瞬间打通,译境网在汉语版本的基础上,将通过数据分析,快速准确地进行英语、法语、俄语、西班牙语、阿拉伯语等不同语种的版本的研发,涵盖联合国通用语种,并在全球设立分公司,在目前与中国建交国家的主要城市上线译境网,服务于全球用户。

E-ging Net provides language service which is non-physical and the word "translation" itself gives the meaning of going through the linguistic and cultural threshold. In E-ging Net, deep international cooperation channels can be immediately unobstructed in need as Chinese based net, can soon be accurately developed into the versions of English, French, Russian, Spanish, Arabic and other languages to cover those generally used in UN with the help of data analysis. The net will globally set up its subsidiaries and push online in the main cities in those countries of diplomatic relationships with China to serve users all over the world.

六、项目优势：

Ⅵ. Project Advantage(s)：

作为中国第一家将自身翻译项目管理实践纳入国家高等教育专业课的翻译公司。多年来,积极探索让翻译行业插上互联网的翅膀,并已构建互联网产品体系和深刻理解语言服务行业及具备丰富经验的产品设计和运营团队。

As the first company in China bringing its own practical translation project management into the national academic education system as a major, BNTC has made the industry of translation assisted with the wings of internet after years of active exploration and has constructed the system of internet product, the design and operation teams well understanding and being rich experienced in language service.

七、项目需求：

Ⅶ. Project Demand(s):

引导市场对语言服务业有更客观、深刻的认知,意识到专业语言服务的价值和意义,获得人才、资金、技术、社会渠道资源方面的支持。

Guiding a more objective and profound cognition on language in the market so that the value and significance of specialized language service can be aware of and obtaining the supports of talents, funds, technology and social resources.

乐居公社
Leju Community

一、项目公司名称： 大连乐居社电子商务有限公司
Ⅰ. Project Company Name: Dalian Lejushe Electronic Business Co., Ltd.

二、项目公司介绍：
Ⅱ. Project Company Introduction

乐居社——社区品质生活倡导者。公司本着来源于社会、奉献于社会、服务于社会、回报于社会的宗旨，把幸福、快乐、优越直接传达给每一个客户，乐居社用走出去宣传、请进来服务的方式，通过刊物、联谊、公益活动和团购等开放性模式，综合满足客户的消费和情感需求，用你提要求我来办的方式把家庭、个人和消费整合于快乐中，从而打造中国最专业的社区综合服务平台，建立最权威的社区家庭信息与消费信息数据化服务平台。

Lejushe is an initiator for high quality community life. Our goal is originating from, making contribution to, serving and giving back to society, which directly provides happiness, joy and superiority to every customer. Our service mode is external propagation and internal service. Customer's demands on consumption and emotion are generally met through opened forms such as publication, friendship tie & socially useful activity and group purchase. Family, individual and consumption are integrated with happiness by handling customer's request, so that the most professional and comprehensive service platform for community in China can be created. The most authoritative datamation & service platform for information on community, family and consumption are founded.

三、负责人介绍：
Ⅲ. Responsible Person Introduction

马玉国，董事长，在社区领域有着十余年的从业经验，深谙客户消费需求与变化特点，在产品整合和服务营销方面经验极其丰富。同时，他因在社区服务领域的突出贡献，在2015年度，成功入选"健康中国名人殿堂"。

Ma Yuguo, chairman, has working experience for more than 10 years in community field. He is very familiar with demand and change characteristic for customer. He has rich experience in product integration, service & marketing. Meanwhile, Mr. Ma was awarded "China Health Hall of Fame" in 2015 due to his remarkable contribution in community service field.

四、项目名称： 乐居公社
Ⅳ. Project Name: Leju Community

五、项目概况：
Ⅴ. Project Profile

乐居社以实体店面（乐居公社）为依托，以社区为中心，用优质的服务搭建社区家庭客户与乐居公社之间的信任平台。在服务同时针对社区家庭客户健康、生活、消费、娱乐等方面信息，进行信息数据整合归类，有针对性的提供客户所需，完成客户所想，打破传统营销思维，把客户需求和商品信息化完美融合于终端服务中，让商品数据化战略真实落地。

Lejushe depends on physical store (Leju Community) with focusing on community, which creates a trust platform between community & family customers and Leju Community through high quality service. Information and data are integrated and classified for information on health, life, consumption and entertainment for community & family customers during service. It is specific and customized to customer's demand. Traditional marketing theory is changed. Customer's demand and commodity informationization are perfectly integrated with end service, which makes commodity datamation strategy come true.

公司通过刊物、联谊、公益活动和团购等开放性模式，综合满足客户的消费和情感需求，从而打造中国最专业的社区综合服务平台，建立最权威的社区家庭信息与消费信息数据化服务平台。

Customer's demands on consumption and emotion are generally met through opened forms such as publication, friendship tie & charity activity and group purchase, so that the most professional and comprehensive service platform for community in China can be created, and the most authoritative datamation service platform for information on community, family and consumption can be founded.

六、项目优势：
VI. Project Advantage(s)

乐居社真实落地的数据化平台，公司着力于实体门店覆盖社区，在真正实体服务的基础上构建网络平台，销售与服务同步发展，双线启动，齐头并进，是真正的信息与服务完美结合的公司。2017年4月，大连乐居社成功在深圳前海股权交易中心挂牌，6月，首届中国连锁节上又荣获"中国连锁最具投资价值奖"，以及"中国连锁商业模式创新奖"。

Lejushe is a real and actual datamation platform. We focus on physical store covering community. Network platform is established based on the real physical service. Sales and services are developed synchronously with two-line start and advance side by side. We are a company to perfectly combine information with service. Dalian Lejushe Electronic Business Co., Ltd. was listed on the Shenzhen Qianhai Equity Trading Center in April 2017. In addition, Dalian Lejushe gained prizes "Most Valuable for Chinese Chains" and "Innovative Business Mode for Chinese Chains" in June 2017.

七、项目需求：
VII. Project Demand(s)

公司目前正处于扩展阶段，欢迎在源头生产领域的农副产品、特产类产品、深加工类产品的供应商洽谈合作，共同开拓国内、国际市场。同时，为更快、更好地推进项目，目前公司正处于A轮融资阶段，对社区服务领域比较感兴趣的投资机构或个人可与我们洽谈。

At present, we are in expanding stage. Welcome the suppliers of source manufacturing fields for negotiations and corporations, including agricultural & sideline products, native product and deep processing product. We can explore domestic and international markets together. In addition, in order to better and faster promote products, we are financing in Round A. Investment organization or investor who is interested in community service field can contact us.

企业 SP 集合服务商
Enterprise SP Integrated Service Provider

一、项目公司名称：霍尔果斯成功必询九牛远德创业咨询有限公司
Ⅰ. Project Company Name： Horgos Nine Cattle & Yonder Success and Startup Consulting Co., LTD.

二、项目公司介绍：
Ⅱ. Project Company Introduction：

公司由九牛人力、投资人李鑫和远德集团共同发起设立，致力于为企业提供一站式定制化专业服务，让专业的企业服务触手可及。公司拥有六大实操顾问团队，可为企业人、财、税、法、资本、资金、资产提供系统解决方案和实施服务。

The company was founded by Nine Cattle Human Resource Company, investor Lixin and Yonder Corporation. It is committed to provide one-stop customized professional service for enterprises, and make professional enterprise services within reach. It has six practical operation consultant teams, which can offer systematic solutions and implementation services for enterprises in terms of personnel, finance, tax, law, fund, capital and asset.

三、负责人介绍：
Ⅲ. Responsible Person Introduction:

李鑫，董事长，毕业于北京建筑大学，曾在大型上市金融集团、跨国集团，太平洋保险及利宝保险等知名金融机构任职高管，拥有八年金融机构战略运营经验，在机构拓展和管理，风险控制等方面具备丰富的经验。2013 年 11 月创建大同航（北京）网络科技有限公司，次年销售额过亿，在企业决策上也有着独到的见解。

Lixin, board chairman, graduated from Beijing University of Civil Engineering and Architecture, worked as senior executive for large listed financial corps, transnational corporations, China Pacific Insurance, Liberty Mutual Insurance and other famous financial institutions. He has 8-year strategic operation experience in financial institutions, and rich experience in institutional expansion, management and risk control. In November, 2013, he established Da Tong Hang Network Technology Ltd. Its sales volume in 2014 was over 100 million, and it has very unique views on business decision making.

四、项目名称：企业 SP 集合服务商
Ⅳ. Project Name： Enterprise SP Integrated Service Provider

五、项目概况：
Ⅴ. Project Profile：

企业 SP 集合服务商集合了拥有丰富企业管理实战经验的顾问团队和国内优质的专业企业服务商。专心助力中国企业，支持企业管理的升级和改造，为企业客户提供量身定制的创业咨询服务及落地实施解决方案；专注于精准解决企业战略发展、融资规划、人才梯队建设、内部运营管理、财务管理、法务风控、税务筹划等创业和企业发展过程中的常规管理问题；专业为企业资本金短缺、分支机构设立撤销、劳务纠纷、法务纠纷等突发问题提供有效解决方案。我们以优质系统的服务，一站式解决企业运营管理过程中的现实问题。

This project integrates consultant teams with rich practical management experience and domestic professional business service providers with high quality. It focuses on helping Chinese enterprises, supporting the upgrade and transformation of enterprise management, providing customized startup consulting services, implementation and solution; it concentrates on accurately solving management problems related to enterprise strategic development, financing planning, talent construction, internal operation, financial management, legal risk control, tax planning and other conventional problems occurring in enterprise development; it specializes in offering effective solutions for capital shortage, establishment and repeal of branches, labor disputes and other emergencies. With high-quality systematic service, we can solve those practical problems of enterprise operation and management in just one stop.

六、项目优势：
VI. Project Advantage(s)：

成功必询九牛远德的企业 SP 集合服务商项目是从企业运营的人、财、税、法、资金、资本、资产七大方面为企业客户提供系统的解决方案，集合国内优质专业企业服务商实施落地，一站式解决企业运营管理过程中的现实问题。

The enterprise SP integrated service provider project of Horgos Nine Cattle & Yonder Success and Startup Consulting Company, LTD. is to provide systematic solutions for enterprises in the following 7 aspects：personnel, finance, tax, law, fund, capital, and asset. It integrates domestic excellent and professional service providers to solve operation and management problems within one stop.

七、项目需求：
VII. Project Demand(s)：

希望与相关企业合作，为更多企业完善制度提供支持。希望与各地商协会及服务机构合作，共同为企业提供多元化服务。

We hope to cooperate with related enterprises to provide more support for system improvement. We would also like to cooperate with local business associations and service agencies to provide diversified services for enterprises.

沙发、汽车座套革
Sofa and Car Seat Cover Leather

一、项目公司名称： 成都鑫瑞发商贸有限公司

Ⅰ. Project company name： Chengdu Xinruifa Trading Co., Ltd.

二、项目公司介绍：

Ⅱ. Project Company Introduction：

公司2000年成立，一直致力于中国家具、箱包、制鞋、汽车座套等行业用皮的研发和推广。2001年与中国合成革制造基地-烟台万华合成革股份有限公司合作，共同研发出当时国内外皮革行业影响深远的超细纤维合成沙发革。并延伸到服务国防装备用皮、汽车座套、制鞋领域，使之成为目前为止无论耐化学性能、物理性能、抗老化、防霉变等性能都超越了天然真皮，超纤皮环保、无污染是替代天然真皮最理想的皮革制品材料！

Since established in 2000, the company has been committed to the research and development and popularization of leather in Chinese furniture, bags, shoemaking, and car seat cover industry. We cooperated with China synthetic leather manufacture base-Yantai Wanhua Synthetic Leather Co., Ltd in 2001 to jointly develop the superfine fibre synthetic sofa leather with far-reaching effect on the leather industry at home and abroad, and extend to serve defense equipment leather, car seat cover and shoemaking fields, so that it surpasses the natural leather in chemical resistance and physical properties, anti-aging, prevent mildew and other properties. The environmental and non-polluting superfine fibre leather is the most ideal leather material to substitute the natural leather.

三、项目负责人：

Ⅲ. Responsible Person Introduction：

钟立新，从事皮革行业的研发和销售25年，经历并见证了中国合成革的变革与发展，从1993年就在合资公司从事皮革销售工作，从服装皮革、鞋用皮革、汽车座套再到家具用革，期间经历了多个行业，对用革理念的需求和变化。积累了丰富的行业知识和经验，同时与国内外皮革行业的专家和生产厂商也建立了良好信誉和友谊！

Zhong Lixin, engaged in the research and development and sales of 25 years in the leather industry, has experienced and witnessed the changes and development of China synthetic leather. He has worked in leather sales in the joint venture company since 1993, and gone through a lot of industries from garment leather, shoe leather and car seat cover to furniture leather, so he has accumulated rich industry knowledge and experience on leather concept demands and changes, and meanwhile he has also established good reputation and friendship with the domestic and foreign experts and manufacturers in the leather industry!

四、项目名称： 沙发、汽车座套革

Ⅳ. Project Name： Sofa and Car Seat Cover Leather

五、项目概况：

Ⅴ. Project Profile：

鑫瑞发皮革主要经营高端超纤皮仿真系列的家具用革，满足消费市场环保、健康要求，该产品具有无污染、抗老化、耐候、耐磨、防霉变等特性。是世界环保组织推荐，更是软体家具、汽车座套替代真皮的首选皮料！

Xinruifa Leather is mainly engaged in furniture leather of high-end microfiber leather series so as meet the environmental protection and health requirements of consumption market. With the non-polluting, anti-aging, weather-proof, wear-resisting and anti-mildew features, the product is the preferred leather material which is recommended by the world environmental organization and replaces the leather with upholstered furniture and car seat cover!

六、项目优势：

Ⅵ. Project Advantage(s)：

超纤仿真皮系列产品，花色品种丰富，手感丰满、柔软，色彩艳丽、华贵、逼真！

品质优良，性能卓越，应用广泛，性价比超高！最适合皮革制品企业对皮革的生产加工！

superfine fibre simulated leather series of products is rich in assortment, plump and soft in hand feeling, and beautiful, gorgeous, elegant and vivid in color! Good in quality, outstanding in performance, wide in application, and high in cost performance! It best fits manufacture and processing of leather product enterprises on leather!

七、项目需求：

Ⅶ. Project Demand(s)：

希望能与国内大型软体家具制造、汽车座套生产企业的合作，共同打造中国品质、品牌制造的典范。

we hope to cooperate with large domestic soft furniture manufacturing and car seat cover production enterprises to jointly build the model of China's quality and brand manufacture.

豪运盈发汽车
Haoyun Yingfa Auto

一、项目公司名称：四川豪运盈发汽车销售服务有限公司
Ⅰ. Project Company Name：Sichuan Haoyun Yingfa Auto Sales and Service Co., Ltd.

二、项目公司介绍：
Ⅱ. Project Company Introduction：

汽车销售；汽车租赁；销售（含网上销售）：汽车用品、汽车零配件、五金交电、照明设备、电子产品、机电设备、通信设备及相关产品、汽车装饰品、皮革制品；从事汽车专业领域内技术开发、技术咨询；机动车保险代理；承办汽车展览展示服务。

Our scope of business covers the following：automobile sales；automobile rental；sales of the following items (including online sales)：automotive supplies, automobile parts, hardware and electrical and lightening equipment, electronic, mechanic and electrical products；telecommunications products, automobile accessories and leather products；Professional technical research and development and technical consulting of the automobile industry；Automobile insurance agency；Organizing car exhibitions.

三、负责人介绍：
Ⅲ. Responsible Person Introduction：

杨鸿宇，从事金融行业12年，自从2017年放弃自己十几年的老本行银行这个职业就决心做一个可以持续发展、可以称得上事业的事儿。同时也坚信一点：一个可以持续发展的事业必定要承载一份社会责任。

Yang Hongyyu had been in the finance industry for 12 years before he decided, in 2017, to quit his career as a banker and to get into a business which he can count as a continuous career with the strong belief that a sustainable career is one that comes with certain social responsibility.

四、项目名称：豪运盈发汽车
Ⅳ. Project Name：Haoyun Yingfa Auto

五、项目概况：
Ⅴ. Project profile：

公司以创新性的经营模式和所有有志之士一起为共同实现伟大的中国梦而努力。面对新形势我们需要新的购车理念和方式，彻底改变传统的消费观念和习惯，盈发汽车，让您轻松拥有代步工具；让您快速享受宝马良驹；减轻您的购车负担；购车手续简单方便，选择灵活多样，是一种全新的购车方式。

Our highly innovative operating mode has gathered a group of people with great aspirations to strive for the Chinese dream. The current situation requires us to renew our concepts and ways of car purchase, and change our views and habits of consumption. Yingfa is here to give you the perfect solution to having the car of your dream ASAP, by offering you loads of options and simplified procedures while releasing you from the overwhelming burden. It is indeed a brand-new mode of car-purchase.

近年来，一种新型的购车模式悄然而生，很多人对于"新型的购车模式"并不了解，其背后又存在有多大的市场，其发展的趋势如何？其消费人群是谁？盈发汽车，带你了解"新型购车模式"发展趋势。公司旨在建立一个颠覆传统的购车模式，让买车换车像买包包一样简单。让消费者轻松拥有代步工具、快速享受宝马良驹、减轻购车负担。

In recent years, a new mode of car purchase has come into being without the general public realizing. A lot of people don't know much about it, how much potential the market has, in which direction it is going or who the target consumers would be. Yingfa will take you to get to know the future trend of this "new automobile-purchasing mode". Yingfa is dedicated to building an unconventional automobile-purchasing mode which makes getting a new car just as easy as buying a handbag, so that the consumers could get a nice car in the easiest, quickest and least stressful way.

六、项目优势：

Ⅵ. Project Advantage(s)：

公司将用两年时间在全国建立 200 家以上的四川豪运盈发汽车销售服务有限公司仓储卖场管理销售一体化的分公司和子公司，1 万个品牌服务馆，将通过铸造连锁品牌价值成功成为国内上市公司中的一员。

Within the next two years, Yingfa Auto will be setting up more than 200 warehouse store branches and subsidiaries in the country integrating management and sales, 10000 Brand service centers, and finally become one of the listed companies in the country through building up the value of the chain brand.

七、项目需求： 寻加盟合作，实现零元购车，共享赚月供！

Ⅶ. Project Demand(s)： We are looking for partners to join us, to make the dream of costless car purchases come true, and to get the monthly mortgage payment back together!

纯滚动轴承
Pure Rolling Bearing

一、项目公司名称：上海天创纯滚动轴承有限公司

I. Project Company Name：Shanghai Tianchuang Pure Rolling Bearing Co., Ltd.

二、项目公司介绍：

II. Project Company Introduction：

公司已拥有国际首创的"纯滚动轴承"专利技术及其成熟的生产技术、测试技术和生产工艺，并建成了一条P4级全自动数控生产线（正式通过外单位轴承界专家验收）。是世界上唯一实施该专利技术的研发、生产和销售的高新技术的企业。并获得国家权威机构的认证以及中国官方权威认可。该项目与不同的投资人先后经历了三轮股权投资合作，相应地纯滚动轴承完成了从实验室、中试到产业化批量生产三个阶段的成功飞跃。公司通过国际权威机构美国AQA的国际汽车行业最高标准TS16949的全面质量管理体系认证。并获得"中国科技创新型中小企业100强"荣誉证书。

the company has possessed the patent technology of "pure rolling bearing" invented in the world for the first time and has built a P4-level full-automatic NC production line (which has passed the acceptance of the bearing experts of other companies) by using its mature production technology, test techniques and production process. The company is the only high-tech enterprise which implements the research, development, production and sales of such patent technology, and has obtained the certification by Chinese authoritative organizations and the acceptance by China's official authorities. The project has experienced three cycles of equity investment cooperation successively with different investors, and successful leap of pure rolling bearing from laboratory and pilot scale test to batch production has been completed accordingly. The company has passed the comprehensive quality management system certification of TS16949, which is the highest standard for the international automobile industry, carried out by the international standard institution American AQA, and has awarded an honor certificate of "Top 100 of China's Technological Innovation Small- and Medium-sized Enterprises".

三、负责人介绍：

III. Responsible Person Introduction：

上海市科技创业领军人物俞大邦教授曾先后八次获得重大科技和发明奖、持有十多项发明专利。特别是其中两项对世界科技进步和发展做出了重大贡献：一项是"叶栅跨声速流场分区计算激波拟合"（获中国科学院科技进步一等奖），在重大国际学术会议上俞大邦博士因此被大会组委会推选为分会执行主席；另一项发明为国际首创的"纯滚动轴承"专利项目，解决了在轴承领域中长期存在的世界难题。

Professor Yu Dabang, one of the leaders of Shanghai in technology entrepreneurship has successively obtained eight major technological and invention prizes and holds more than ten invention patents. Especially, two of such patents have made significant contribution to the technological improvement of development of the world：one is "cascade transonic flow field calculation shock fitting" (awarded the first prize of national scientific and technological progress by Chinese Academy of Science), and for this, Dr. Yu Dabang was made executive chairman by a meeting organization committee in a major international academic meeting; the other is the patent of "pure rolling bearing", which has solved a long-lasting world difficulty in the bearing field.

四、项目名称：纯滚动轴承

IV. Project Name：Pure Rolling Bearing

五、项目概况：

V. Project Profile：

纯滚动轴承高新技术产业的诞生，对提高国际竞争力，建设先进制造业、先进装备制造业高地具有十分现实的意义。

The birth of the pure rolling bearing high-tech industry has practical significance to improve international competition and obtain advanced manufacturing industry and advanced equipment manufacture advantages.

纯滚动轴承重点突出节能减排和环保的绿色理念。其核心是俞大邦博士在世界上首次提出的"纯滚动"理论及其应用。用滚动约束代替滑动约束，用滚动摩擦代替滑动摩擦。从根本上消除了传统轴承中的滑动摩擦阻力，显著降低了能耗和噪音，极大地提高轴承的使用寿命。与世界最著名品牌轴承相比，使用寿命至少达到三倍以上；承载能力大幅提高，而且可以承受双向载荷。可以用普通碳钢代替轴承钢或者用较小的轴承替代较大的轴承，节省了安装空间和能源。

The pure rolling bearing mainly focuses on the ideal of energy saving, emission reduction and environment protection. The core is the "pure rolling" theory raised by Dr. Yu Dabang for the first time in the world and its application. Rolling constraint is used to replace slipping constraint, and rolling friction to replace sliding friction. These features radically remove the sliding friction resistance force in traditional bearings, significantly reducing energy consumption and noise and greatly expanding the lifetime of bearings. Compared with the bearings of the most famous brands in the world, the foresaid pure rolling bearings surpass them by at least three times; the loading capacity is improved greatly and the bearings can bear bidirectional loads. Common carbon steel can be used to replace bearing steel or small bearings to replace large bearings, which saves installation space and energy.

纯滚动轴承各项优越的性能指标得到了国家轴承质量监督检验中心和上海机械工业（部）轴承产品质量检测中心的认定；通过了上海市经委、科委组织的批量新产品鉴定并一致通过最高等级："国际首创"的鉴定结论；获得了上海市高新技术成果项目认定。已在全球94个国家申请了发明专利。无形资产价值被香港权威评估机构评估为28亿港币。

All of the excellent performance indexes of the pure rolling bearing have passed the appraisal by Chinese National Bearing Quality Supervision and Inspection Center and the Bearing Quality Inspection Center of Shanghai Ministry of Machinery Industry; passed the appraisal of new products in batches organized by Shanghai Economy Committee and Shanghai Committee of Science and Technology and the highest level - the appraisal conclusion of "the first international creation"; and obtained the appraisal of hi-tech technological achievements in Shanghai. The invention patent has been applied in 94 countries. The value of intangible assets of the company is evaluated by a Hong Kong authoritative assessment agency to be $HK 28 billion.

六、项目优势：
VI. Project Advantage(s):

用该生产线生产的"纯滚动轴承"，经过分别送至机械工业轴承产品质量检测中心和中国轴承最高权威检测机构——国家轴承质量监督检测中心的检测，使用寿命达到额定寿命的十倍，轴承精度和噪音等级不仅达到P4级，几乎达到全球轴承最高等级的P2级，完全达到低噪声水平，从理论到实践达到了遥遥领先的国际水平。

The "pure rolling bearing" produced by this production line has been sent to China's Mechanical Industrial Bearing Product Quality Testing Center and the Chinese National Bearing Quality Supervision and Inspection Center (the highest authoritative bearing organization in China) for testing and use. According to the test result, the lifetime is up to 10 times of rated lifetime; the precision and noise level of the bearing are not only up to P4 level, but also nearly reaches P2 level, the highest level of bearings in the world; completely low noise level is achieved and far ahead of the international level from theory to practice.

七、项目需求：
VII. Project Demand(s):

通过"一带一路"拓展产品市场，促进产品的推广和出口，为扩大产品生产规模和型号的多样化招商融资。

Expand the product market through the "Belt and Road", push forward the promotion and export of products, and attract investment and financing to expand production scale and multiple models.

液晶书画板
LCD Sketchpad

一、项目公司名称：深圳市我好数码科技有限公司
Ⅰ. Project Company Name：Shenzhen WOOHOO Digital Technology Co., Ltd

二、项目公司介绍：
Ⅱ. Project Company Introduction：

公司是一家以生产幼儿智慧教育终端产品为主的高科技企业。我好数码坐落在深圳市光明新区，拥有国内首创的零功耗柔性液晶生产技术，是目前国内唯一一家，集液晶电子书画板研发制造销售为一体的幼教科技企业。

WOOHOO is a high-tech company manufacturing intelligent education terminal products for children. It's located at Guangming New District in Shenzhen. With ground-breaking manufacturing techniques of zero power flexible liquid crystal display, WOOHOO is the only early-childhood education technology company in China integrating the R&D, manufacture and sales of LCD sketchpads.

三、项目负责人介绍：
Ⅲ. Responsible Person Introduction:

叶文新，深圳市我好数码科技有限公司（以下简称"我好数码"）创始人、董事长。他陪伴了我好数码公司的起落与发展，先后领导推出了液晶书画板、触控一体机等产品，深刻改变了现代书写方式，便捷了教学、开会，将环保与科技融入人们的生活，促进社会的进步。

Ye Wenxin— founder and chairman of the board of WOOHOO Digital Technology Co., Ltd (referred to as WOOHOO). He has been with the company since the start and went with it through bumps on the road, and led the launching of LCD sketchpad, Touch-control all-in-one products among other products, changing ways of writing in the modern world and making teaching and conferences easier; it has brought to people's daily life the concepts of environment protection and science and technology, thus pushing the forward social developments.

四、项目名称：液晶书画板
Ⅳ. Project Name：LCD Sketchpad

五、项目概况：
Ⅴ. Project Profile:

液晶书画板是一种可以替代传统书写方式的书画工具，它采用高科技零功耗柔性液晶技术，可反复书写十万次，不用笔、不用纸、不用电，采用环保材质，轻按擦除键，即可清除画面，看画板就和看普通黑板一样。

LCD Sketchpad is a writing and drawing tool that can replace traditional writing methods. It uses hi-tech zero power flexible LCD technology, enabling the owner to write repeatedly for a hundred thousand times without using a pen, paper or electricity. All materials are environmentally friendly. With a simple tap on the erasing button, what have been written could easily be erased, while giving customers the same visual experience as using a traditional blackboard.

六、项目优势：
Ⅵ. Project Advantage(s):

液晶书画板——采用高科技零功耗柔性液晶技术，可反复书写十万次，不用笔、不用纸、不用电，采用健康塑胶、环保材质。轻按擦除键，即可清除画面，依靠自然光线就能呈现极佳的书写画面，看画板就和看普通黑板一样，零辐射、不伤眼。

LCD sketchpad uses hi-tech zero power flexible LCD technology, enabling the owner to write repeatedly for a hundred thousand times without using a pen, paper or electricity. The product uses plastic harmless to the body, and all materials are environmentally friendly. With a simple tap on the erasing button, the screen could easily be cleaned. It gives you excellent visual experience with natural light, which is same as a traditional blackboard of zero radiation and no harm done to the eyes.

七、项目需求：
Ⅶ. Project Demand(s):

希望通过"一带一路"的平台将产品销售到其他国家，为地球的环保事业做出贡献，希望争取到沿线国家更多的产品展示与合作对接机会。

On the platform of the "Belt and Road", WOOHOO hopes to present its products on the international market, thus making a contribution to the environment of the whole world. It would be great for WOOHOO to get more opportunities for exhibition of products in, and cooperation and docking with neighboring countries.

阳光赛赛公司绩效价值管理系统
Sunshine Saisai Performance &Value Management System for Company

一、项目公司名称： 深圳前海赛赛网络科技有限公司

Ⅰ. Project Company Name: Shenzhen Qianhai Succestech Co., Ltd.

二、项目公司介绍：

Ⅱ. Project Company Introduction:

阳光赛赛公司绩效价值管理系统，由深圳利坤管理咨询机构旗下深圳前海赛赛网络科技有限公司研发。利坤咨询自2011年成立先后为TCL、美的、中国联塑、华宝国际、洲明电子、百果园等大型公司做管理体系咨询服务。特别在绩效管理领域帮助客户规范绩效管理，提升组织效率方面得到客户高度认可。阳光赛赛在众多客户的建议和支持下由利坤咨询自建研发团队，先后投入近500万元于2016年底正式上线发布，立刻得到客户的认可，并先后获得天使投资近300万元。

Sunshine Saisai Performance &Value Management System for Company is researched and developed by Shenzhen Qianhai Succestech Co., Ltd., subsidiary of Shenzhen Likun Business Management Consulting Co., Ltd.. Since establishment in 2011, Likun has provided consulting services for lots of large companies, such as TCL Group, Midea Group, China Lesso Group Holdings Limited, Huabao International Holdings Limited, Unilumin Group Co., Ltd and Shenzhen Pagoda Industrial Development Co., Ltd. Organization efficiency is improved with customer's acceptance, especially in helping customer with regulating performance management field. With suggestions and supports from lots of customers, the system was on-line and published by own research & developing team of Likun in the end of 2016 after about 5 million RMB yuan was invested. The system gains customer's satisfactory with nearly 3 million RMB yuan financed by Angel Investment.

三、项负责人介绍：

Ⅲ. Responsible Person Introduction

祁生胜，原华为大学筹建人之一、华为高级人力资源管理专家、教育部特聘公司教育专家、中国管理科学研究院创新研究所副所长。

Qi Shengsheng, one of founders for Huawei University, senior expert for human resource management for Huawei, company education expert employed by Ministry of Education of PRC, and vice director of Innovation Research Division, China Institute of Management Science.

四、项目名称： 阳光赛赛公司绩效价值管理系统

Ⅳ. Project Name: Sunshine Saisai Performance &Value Management System for Company

五、项目概况：

Ⅴ. Project Profile：

公司之间的竞争本质上不是资金、人脉、技术、设备、人才，而是人才管理的竞争！不能将高科技人才凝聚在一起，做到上下同欲，步调一致。再好的战略、商业模式都是没有办法落地和执行。阳光赛赛是一款公司绩效与价值管理的大数据系统，通过OKR系统、KPI系统、项目管理系统、任务跟进系统、积分打赏系统等多个方面来彻底解决公司内部人的问题，解决人才管理的问题，解决人才价值创造、价值评价、价值分配的问题。帮助公司高层与基础之间建立统一的目标，明确各部门与岗位需要输出的价值贡献，通过大数据和分析科学公正的评价员工的价值，用最后的结果和荣誉来激发员工工作积极主动性，使公司干部员工真正实现"自驱动"。

Competitions for companies are not essentially about funds, contacts, technology, equipment or talents, but talent management! We shouldn't gather hi-tech talents together who have the same intention, desire and thought. No matter how the strategy or business form is good, it cannot be executed or achieved. Sunshine Saisai is a big data system for performance &value management of company. Issues on company's internal human, talent management, and creation, evaluation & distribution of talent value are resolved completely through OKR, KPI, Project Management, Task Follow-up and Point Tip Systems. Company's high level and base are helped to establish unified goal. Required output value contribution for departments and positions are clarified. Values of employees are evaluated fairly and scientifically through big data and analysis. Positivity and activeness of employee are inspired by final achievement and honor to realize "self drive" for leader and employee.

六、项目优势：
VI. Project Advantage(s)

大数据＋智能算法实现量化员工绩效价值贡献和执行力、敬业精神、手机版应用实时观测公司经营状况、员工工作状态、六个维度供公司自由选择考核的内容、积分制打赏实现游戏化管理，让员工工作更积极主动。

Big data + intelligent algorithm quantifying contributions of performance & value, executive force and professional dedication spirit for employee, cell phone application real-time monitoring company operation condition, employee working status, six dimensions supplied to company for freely selecting qualified contents, and point-typed tip realizing game-mode management to get employee to work more actively and positively.

七、项目需求：
VII. Project Demand(s)

得到更广泛的推广和应用，帮助更多中小公司提高员工执行力，提高价值贡献、提升内部绩效管理，彻底实现公司人才管理的规划化，使公司市场竞争力更上一个台阶。

We hope to gain more broad propagation and application, to help more middle & small-sized companies to improve employee's executive force, value contribution and internal performance management, completely realizing arrangement of company talent management, and making company's competitiveness in the market rise.

高精度标准齿轮
High-precision Standard Gears

一、项目公司名称：江阴市宏冠机械有限公司

Ⅰ. Project Company Name：Jiangyin Hongguan Machinery Co., Ltd.

二、项目公司介绍：

Ⅱ. Project Company Introduction：

公司成立于2004年，主营"高精度标准齿轮"项目的投资与建设。2014年经由相关部门审批购置合法土地，入驻江阴市临港街道工业园区，实现空间上生产的规范化与自主化。2012年被评为"支残模范单位"，2015年顺利通过ISO9001认证，连续三年以高标准、严要求通过复查审核。

The company, established in 2004, mainly deals in the investment and construction of "high-precision standard gear" projects. In 2014, the company purchased legal land after examination and approval by related departments, entered Lingang Street Industrial Park, Jiangyin and realized the standardization and independence of production in space. In 2012, the company was evaluated to be a "Disabled Support Model Unit"; in 2015, it passed ISO9001 successfully and recheck with high standard and strict requirements for consecutive three years.

公司目前主要生产普通圆柱直齿、普通圆柱斜齿、胶木齿轮、行星齿轮、轴齿轮，历经13年的专业发展之路，诚信的服务理念与可靠的品质保障，使得我们的客户群体遍布全国。其间，江阴市宏冠机械有限公司提供过加工与生产的企业有近千家，本土企业100家，外来企业300家，外资企业13家，为江阴本土机械单位提供加工与生产近八成。江阴市宏冠机械有限公司有幸历经整个机械行业的轮回四季，而今寒潮退却，暖春初现，我们有惊有喜，同时也更坚信，唯有当下坚定、踏实的每一步才能更好地走向未知的远方，我们一直在努力，也一直在成长，敬请期待我们的新蜕变！

At present, the company mainly produces common spur gear, common helical gear, textolite gear, planetary gear and shaft gear. After 13 years of development, sincere service idea and reliable quality help us win many customers across China. During those years, the company supplied machining and production for nearly 1,000 enterprises. Among them, 100 are domestic enterprises; 300, foreign ones; and 13, foreign-funded ones; and 80% of machining and production is provided for local mechanical units in Jiangyin. The company has the honor to undergo the cycle of the whole machinery industry. Now economy recoveries, and we get surprised and have more confidence to go into an unknown future firmly and surefootedly. We have been always making efforts and growing, and look forward to our new changes!

三、负责人介绍：

Ⅲ. Responsible Person Introduction：

陈建华，董事长，生于1965年。2004年怀揣着一股对机械行业的热血情怀，从一个非专业人士跨行转投进入高精密齿轮的加工与制造。

Chen Jianhua, born in 1965, now is chairman of board of directors of the company. In 2004, he switched as a non-professional person to the machining and manufacture of high-precision gears with a zeal of the machinery industry.

四、项目名称：高精度标准齿轮

Ⅳ. Project Name：High-precision Standard Gears

五、项目概况：

Ⅴ. Project Profile：

公司从建立之初，就定位于高精度标准齿轮的生产，主要生产类别有：普通圆柱直齿、普通圆柱斜齿、胶木齿轮、行星齿轮、轴齿轮。高精度标准齿轮产品选用优质的轴承钢（20CrMnTi、40Cr）制造，并经过严格的热处理和稳定化处理，每件齿轮都经过检测中心的严格检验，能够保证产品的精度，齿面光整，硬度高，耐磨损，使用寿命长。

Since its founding, the company has been focusing on manufacture of high-precision standard gears, mainly including common super gear, common helical gear, textolite gear, planetary gear and shaft gear. High-precision standard gears are made from high-quality bearing steel (20CrMnTi, 40Cr) and undergo strict thermal and stabilizing treatments, which ensures the precision and precision durability as well as smooth complete tooth surface, high rigidity and wear resistance.

六、项目优势：
VI. Project Advantage(s):

公司有合法的土地，有与整个产品生产工艺相配套的设施设备，其中数控车床 8 台；磨床 8 台；钻铣床 5 台；线切割 5 台；滚齿机 13 台；高速滚齿机 2 台；秦川成型磨机床 5 台，项目可实现快速投产及量产。同时我们还建有高精密的检测中心，为高品质的量产提供有力保障，把好产品质量关。

The company has legal land and the facilities and equipment matching with the whole production process, including 8 NC lathes, 8 grinders, 5 driller and millers, 5 wire cutting machines, 13 gear hobbers, 2 high-speed gear hobbers and 5 Qinchuan form grinding machines. Therefore, it can realize fast production and batch production for the project. Besides, we have a high-precision inspection center to ensure high quality of batched products.

七、项目需求：
VII. Project Demand(s):

1．项目需求：新常态下宏观经济形式走势及行业发展趋势，国内外市场需求分析等；

Project Demand(s): macro-economy situation and industrial development trends under the new normal of the economy, analysis of demands on the markets at home and abroad;

2．技术需求：调整产品结构和产业升级的技术支持，抗疲劳长寿命制造技术、齿轮先进成型技术、新材料、轻量化技术、齿轮传动技术最新动态、先进加工装备、工具和刃具、先进实验设备和先进检测手段等；

Technology Demand(s): to adjust product results and the technical support for industrial upgrading, anti-fatigue long service life manufacturing technology, advanced gear forming technology, new materials, light-weight technology, the latest dynamic states of gear transmission technology, advanced machining equipment, tools and cutting tools, advanced test equipment, advanced detection methods and the like;

3．资本需求：多种方式的筹融资渠道，企业兼并、重组方式，海外并购信息及并购风险控制等；

Capital Demand(s): financing channels of multiple methods, enterprise merger and reconstruction methods, foreign merger information, merger risk control, etc.

4．国际化经营需求：与国外企业和相关行业组织对接交流，积极开拓国外市场。

International operation demand(s): organize and carry out communication with foreign enterprises and the organizations in the related industry, and actively expand foreign markets.

阀门
Valves

一、项目公司名称：上海科科阀门集团有限公司
Ⅰ. Project Company Name: Shanghai Koko Valve Group CO., LTD

二、项目公司介绍：
Ⅱ. Project Company Introduction:

上海科科阀门集团有限公司成立于1987年，在上海和浙江有两大生产基地，总部设立于交通信息便利的上海嘉定区，距离虹桥机场20分钟车程。公司拥有数控车床、加工中心等高新加工设备和各类检测装置600多套。我公司从2000年开始相继获得TS、PED、API6D、API607、API F6A、ISO、CE、APIQ1、API600、API609、SIL等国内国际专业认证。上海科科阀门集团，以专业化、科技化、国际化为行动方针，公司生产的金属硬密封球阀、高低温阀、高压临氢阀、全焊接球阀已成功应用于各种石油石化、电站、长输管线、煤化工等国内外大型项目。科科阀门是中石油、中石化、中海油、伊朗石油、伊朗天然气、马来西亚石油公司、日本JGC等国内外知名业主和EPC公司的合格供应商。我们致力于为各种苛刻工况提供一体式解决方案。"好阀门，科科造"一直是科科人的一致追求。

Established in 1987, Shanghai Koko Valve Group CO., LTD has two main production basements in Shanghai and Zhejiang. Our headquarters is located in transportation & information facilitated district, Jiading, Shanghai City, 20 minutes' drive from Hongqiao Airport. We have more than 600 advanced equipment including CNC lathes, machining center, high-tech processing equipment and various testing devices. From 2000, Koko was authorized TS, PED, API6D, API607, API F6A, ISO, CE, APIQ1, API600, API609, SIL etc.

Shanghai KOKO Valve Group take the specialization, technology, international as the action policy, the metal seated ball valve, high and low temperature valve, high pressure hydrogen valve and fully welded ball valve have been successfully applied to a variety of petroleum and petrochemical, power station, long Pipeline, coal chemical and other large projects in domestic and oversea .KOKO valve is a major supplier of CNPC, SINOPEC, CNOOC, NIOEC NIGC, PETRONAS, JGC and other well-known domestic and foreign owners and EPC company. We are committed to providing a integral solution for variety of service conditions. "Good Valves Made By Koko" is our Mission!

三、负责人介绍：
Ⅲ. Responsible Person Introduction:

张佩佩，专业负责外贸十余年，对各种阀门及相关的产品都有业务经验。在出口业务、风险把控、成本核算等方面有相关工作经验。负责公司的出口业务。

Zhang Peipei has been working on foreign trade for over ten years and is especially experienced in business in relation to valves and related products. She is also veteran in export business, risk control, and cost accounting and is now in charge of export business of the company.

四、项目名称：阀门
Ⅳ. Product Name：Valves

五、项目概况：
Ⅴ. Project Profile:

我们的产品涵盖了球阀、蝶阀、平板闸阀、闸阀、截止阀、止回阀、过滤器、电站阀、旋塞阀等系列产品，并具有领先同行业的加工制造设计生产能力，公司采用API、ANSI、BS、DIN、NF、JIS、JPI、GB等国际先进标准，生产通径1/4"-128"（DN6-3200mm），压力级别150LB-2500LB（0.1MPa-42Mpa），工作温度—196℃－680℃，材料主要有碳钢、合金钢、不锈钢、蒙乃尔、青铜、20号合金等，并可根据用户要求制造各种特殊阀门。

Our products cover ball valve, butterfly valve, through conduit gate valve, gate valve, globe valve, check valve, strainer, power station valve, plug valve and special valves as per API, BS, DIN, NF, JIS, JPI, GB and other advanced international standard of size range 1/4"-128" (DN6-3200mm), pressure range 150LB-2500LB (0.1MPa-42Mpa), and working temperature range-196℃-680℃. Main materials include carbon steel, alloy steel, stainless steel, Monel, bronze, 20# alloy steel and other special materials to users' request.

六、项目优势：
VI. Project Advantage(s):

公司全焊接单焊缝，双焊缝球阀被广泛应用到各种国内外供热和长输管线。目前公司研发的48inch-900LB单焊缝球阀已经通过了TUV的严格测试，科科全焊接球阀会成为未来几年国内外长输管线的主力军。公司在政府部门的"国产化"号召下，研发生产了很多国际领先水平的产品并改变了一直以来依靠进口的局面，为国家和社会节约了很多经济和社会资源。公司生产的锁渣阀在煤化工领域经过十几年的实验和实用取得了骄人的成绩，成为取代国际先进同类产品首选产品。

Company Advantage：Our single-welded and double-welded ball valve are widely used in a variety of domestic and foreign heating and long-distance pipeline. At present, our original 48inch-900LB single-welded ball valve has passed the TUV rigorous testing. KOKO fully welded ball valve will become the main force of domestic and foreign long-distance pipeline in the next few years .In response to government call of Indigenous Innovation, we develop many high-level products , which change the situation that we rely on import for many years and save a lot of economic and social resources for our country and society.Our slag valves obtain enormous achievement in the field of coal chemical industry during more than 10 years of practice and application, which became the best choice among the similar products in the world.

七、项目需要：
VII. Project Demand(s):

寻求各种需要工业阀门的客户包括各行业业主、承建商、代理商、贸易商等长期合作的伙伴客户。并可以以项目代理、区域代理的方式开发当地市场。

To seek all kinds of clients in need of industrial valves, including owners、contractors、agents、traders and other long-term cooperation partners. And you can be regarded as our project manager or regional agent to develop your local market.

篆刻艺术·皇家珍藏品
Art of Seal Cutting · Imperial Collection

一、项目公司名称：北京金莲花文化艺术中心

Ⅰ. Project Company Name: Beijing Golden Lotus Culture & Art Center

二、项目公司介绍：

Ⅱ. Project Company Introduction:

中心成立于2000年，主要业务是组织文化艺术交流，收藏、鉴赏、挖掘、整理、继承和发扬我国优秀传统文化艺术。2003年在北京中国革命军事博物馆组织"共和国开国老将军书画大展"，2010年在内蒙古展览馆组织"第二届中国扇子书画艺术大展"、在韩国首尔"中韩皇宫美术品交流展"、在北京组织开展了"中华瑰宝扇面书画"邀请展。公司成立以来，组织开展了"玉器"、"书画"、"瓷器杂项"多场交流学习和拍卖会。2017年1月25日，中共中央办公厅、国务院办公厅印发《关于实施中华优秀传统文化传承发展工程的意见》，按意见指示精神，保护传承具有中国特色、中国风格、中国气派的文化产品和文化遗产，推动中外文化交流互鉴，加强"一带一路"沿线国家文化交流合作，让更多体现中华文化特色、具有竞争力的文化产品走向国际市场。

Beijing Golden Lotus Culture & Art Center was established in 2000 mainly dealing with the activities of cultural and artistic communications, collecting, appreciating, excavating, settling, inheriting and promoting the excellent traditional culture and art of our country. The center held the Art Galllery of the Paintings of the Founding Fathers at Chinese Revolutionary Millitary Museum in 2003, the 2nd Term of Fan Painting Art Exhibition in Inner Mengolia, Sino-Korean Palace Arts Exchanging Show in Seoul and the Inviting Exhibition of Chinese Treasures---Fan Paintings in Beijing in 2010. The center has hosted many communication conferences and auctions of jade wares, paintings and caligraphies and porcelain since it was established. On January 25, 2017, General Office of the CPC Central Committee and General Office of the State Council issued the Comment on *the Implementation of the Traditional Chinese Cultural Heritage Development Projects* which instructed to protect, inherit and conduct sino-foreign exchanges on those cultural products of Chinese characteristics, style and manner in carrying forward the excellent Chinese traditional culture by strengthening the cultural communication and cooperation with the countries along "the Belt and Road" and marketing more of typical and competitive Chinese cultural products to the whole world.

三、负责人介绍：

Ⅲ. Responsible Person Introduction:

水恩海，收藏家、企业家，中国管理科学研究院行业发展特邀高级研究员、中国收藏家协会会员、中国文物学会理事、中国书法艺术研究院理事、中国扇子艺术学会副会长、中嘉国际拍卖有限公司高级顾问、中国乡土艺术协会佛教艺术专业委员会主任、内蒙古国拍公益救助金高级顾问、内蒙古北京商会会长、中国文物学会名誉理事中国第一历史档案馆名誉馆员梁华京先生授权（皇家珍藏品）在全球进行有偿转让的唯一全权代理者。

Shui Enhai is a collector, entrepreneur, the guest advanced researcher on industrial development in China Institute of Management Science, the member of China Association of Collectors, the director of China Cultural Relics Academy, the director of China Art and Calligraphy Research Institute, the vice-chairman of Chinese Society of Fan Art, the senior consultant of Beijing Zhongjia International Auctioneering Co.,Ltd., the director of Specialized Committee of Buddhist Art of the Association of Chinese Localart, the senior consultant of Inner Mengolia Guo Pai Charity Funds, the chairman of Beijing Chamber of Commerce in Inner Mengolia, the only authorized agent of global paid transfers of imperial collections approved by Mr. Liang Huajing, the honored librarian of the First Historical Archives of China and the honored director of China Cultural Relics Academy.

四、项目名称：篆刻艺术·皇家珍藏品

Ⅳ. Project Name: Art of Seal Cutting · Imperial Collection

五、项目概况：
V. Project Profile:

中国书法篆刻印章是中国独有的世界上独一无二的艺术表现形式，是中华民族悠久灿烂辉煌的5000多年文明史中不可缺少的一部分；2008年北京奥运会中国印代表着中华民族独特的精神标识和大国工匠精神，过去历朝历代皇权更是将其发展到登峰造极的集政治权威一统天下的顶峰，北京故宫博物院交泰殿就是大清王朝存放（乾隆帝钦定25宝玺）皇家玉玺的宫殿，中国第一历史档案馆（新中国成立伊始明清档案整理部门）随着改革开放和香港、澳门回归祖国，响应祖国文化大繁荣大发展号召，使过去皇家艺术品走入寻常百姓，和有关单位合作"手工钤印"并由皇族后裔爱新觉罗·毓瞻、爱新觉罗·兆瑞、中国文物专家清史专家朱家溍、故宫博物院中央文史馆员文物专家文物鉴赏家王世襄、史学家文物鉴定收藏家史树青以及中国著名书法家、名流亲自书写题跋限量孤品《清宫交泰殿皇帝宝谱》（真品真迹并配收藏证书），高仿或高级珂罗版（限量编号）清·嘉庆《澳门图说》、清·雍正郎世宁《瑞谷图》等一批（皇家珍藏品）。2008年在韩国首尔举办了"中韩皇宫艺术品交流展"，《清宫交泰殿皇帝宝谱》已被国内外100多位国家元首政要、500多位社会知名人士和收藏机构、收藏家收藏。

Chinese caligraphy and seal cutting are unique artistic expression in the world and are an inalienable part of the splendid history of civilization of more than 5,000 years. "China Seal" for 2008 Beijing Olympic Games represented the unique Chinese Nations' spirit and the craftsmanship of a large country. For dynasties, the emperors had made it to its extreme with their power under the heaven and the Hall of Union in the Palace Museum was the place storing royal seals in the Qing Dynasty (25pcs were made by Emperor Qianlong's order). With the opening policy and the return of HK and Macau, First Historical Archives of China (the department of the new country managing the archives of Ming and Qing) responding to the summon of the country to let the people learn more about the imperial arts, with the cooperation of other departments, published in limited quantity the Pattens of *the Seals from the Hall of Union in the Palace of Qing* (real stamps with certificats), high stimulation and high grade collotype *the Description of Macau, Blessed Farming* by Giuseppe Castiglione in the years of Yongzhen in Qing and other imperial collectons by hand-stamping and with preface and postscrip by Aisin Gioro Yuzhan, Aisin Gioro Luo Zhaorui, who were the imperial descendants, togeter with those by Zhu Jiajin, an expert on Chinese Relics and the history of Qing, Wang Shixiang, a relic expert, appreciater and the librarian of Central Relic and History Section of the Palace Museum, Shi Shuqing, a historic relics collector and appreciater and other famous caligraphers and celebrities. In the Exchange Exhibition of Sino-Korean Imperial Art held in Seul in 2008, *the Pattens of the Seals from the Hall of Union in the Palace of Qing* was collected by more than 100 chiefs of states and more than 500 noted public figures, institutes and collectors.

六、项目优势：
VI. Project Advantage(s)

1．全球中国独有艺术表现形式；
The unique Chinese Artistic Expressions in the world；

2．《清宫交泰殿皇帝宝谱》真迹孤品限量；
The Pattens of the Seals from the Hall of Union in the Palace of Qing in limited quantity

3．权威、独有、唯一，配发相关资料、收藏证书。
Authorized, exclusive and only related material and certificate of collection.

七、项目需求：
VII. Project Demand(s)

向"一带一路"沿线国家宣传中华优秀传统文化，使具有中国特色、中国风格、中国气派的文化产品走向国际市场。

Advertising the excellent Chinese traditional culture to the countries along "the Belt and Road" and marketing more of typical and competitive Chinese cultural products to the whole world.

中药生态旅游观光庄园
Traditional Chinese Medicine Ecological Tourism Manor

一、项目公司名称：辽宁旭美乾园现代农业发展有限公司

I. Project Company Name：Liaoning Xumei Qianyuan Modern Agricultural Development Co., Ltd

二、项目公司介绍：

II. Project Company Introduction:

公司成立于2017年，是一家从事生态旅游观光、现代农业、食品、苗木、园林景观工程设计施工、农产品销售、网络技术于一体的生态公共服务综合平台型企业。本公司下设调兵山市乾景园林工程有限公司、调兵山市逸实乾园生态食府、抚顺市绿都园林工程有限公司、辽宁源洋光电科技有限公司。

Founded in 2017, we are an ecological public service integral platform type enterprise, specializing in the ecological tourism, modern agriculture, food, nursery stock, landscape engineering design and construction, sales of agricultural products and network technology. It sets up under Diaobingshan Qianjing Landscape Engineering Co., Ltd, Diaobingshan Yishi Qianyuan Ecological Restaurant, Fushun Lvdu Landscape Engineering Co., Ltd, and Liaoning Yuanyang Photoelectric Technology Co., Ltd.

三、负责人介绍：

III. Responsible Person Introduction:

刘明，出生于1975年，毕业于辽宁省林业职业技术学院。擅长专研用古法制作的生态养生食品和生活用品，生态庄园的管理及运营，生态食品的种植及养殖，掌握养殖饲料秘方及土壤改良方法，并拥有近20年的生态园林绿化工程、生态修复及河道生态治理工程施工的经验，在所管理公司旗下还拥有辽宁源洋光电科技公司，主营照明系统设计与施工，及EMC能源改造工程的项目。

Liu Ming, born in 1975, graduated from Liaoning Forestry Vocation-Technical College. He is good at special research on ecological health food and living articles by using traditional methods, management and operation of ecological manor, planting and breeding of ecological food, and understanding the aquaculture feed recipe and soil improvement method, with nearly 20-year construction experience in ecological garden landscape engineering, ecological restoration and river ecological treatment project. It also possesses Liaoning Yuanyang Photoelectric Technology Co., Ltd, which is engaged in illuminating system design and construction, and EMC energy modified works.

四、项目名称：中药生态旅游观光庄园

IV. Project Name：Traditional Chinese Medicine Ecological Tourism Manor

五、项目概况：

V. Project Profile：

乾园生态观光，为东北三省唯一一家江南景观的中药养生特色旅游庄园，本庄园坐落在调兵山市区东1.5公里处，园区占地30多万平方米。其中建筑面积270000多平方米。乾园将居所融入水岸园林中，并将南方建筑风格与北方的自然风光交融。

Qianyuan Ecological Sightseeing is the unique traditional Chinese medicine health-caring characteristic tourism manor with Jiangnan landscape in the three northeast province, which is located 1.5km to the east of Diaobingshan, covering the park area of more than 300,000 m^2 and the construction area of 270,000 m^2. Qianyuan integrates the house into water front garden, and blends the architectural style in the south with natural scenery in the north.

乾园以接待旅游团队和社会团体活动为主，更为社会各阶层人士创造了商务洽谈和休闲度假的理想场所。身在园中，不仅可以将调兵山地区历史文化典故一览无余，还可以品尝到中医养生食谱为发展主线的特色养生美食套餐，另外还有为补充现代人五行不足而制作纯木火铁锅炖。在创造了智慧庄园、乐活农业、乾园盒子等新的经营模式的同时，正逐步建立起文化旅游、生态观光、生态修复、少年儿童研学基地等一整套新体系下绿色产业经营模式。

Qianyuan mainly receives tourist groups and social group activities, and even creates an ideal place for all levels of society for business negotiation and vocation. In Qianyuan, you can not only get a sweeping view of the historical and cultural allusions of Diaobingshan, but also taste the featured health-caring food set which takes traditional Chinese medicine health-caring recipes as the major development route. Besides, there is pure wood fire iron pot stew to supplement insufficient five elements of modern people. When creating wisdom manor, happy farming and Qianyuan box, it also gradually establishes the green industry business model under a set of system such as cultural tourism, ecological sightseeing, ecological restoration and children research and study base.

乾园的休闲项目现主要包括：农耕体验、文化定制及自然摄影、植物科普、果实采摘、动物观赏、山野菜种植、景观造型欣赏等。

Leisure projects of Qianyuan mainly contain farming experience, culture customization, nature photography, plant science popularization, fruit picking, animal enjoyment, wild vegetable planting, landscape modeling appreciation, etc.

计划 2017 年再完善一期园林生态项目，同时启动婚宴广场项目、民宿项目、儿童乐园项目等部分二期项目，并申请国家 AAA 级景区，在周边城市增加 3-4 个"乾园盒子"门店。在主要城市增设一家生活馆或体验馆。2018 将启动沙浴等养生康体项目，并将"乾园盒子"门店增设至 10-15 个，同时继续增加生活馆或体验馆数量。

It is planned to improve phase 1 landscape ecological project in 2017, and simultaneously starts the wedding plaza project, home stay facility project and children's park project, and apply for the national level AAA scenic spot. In the surrounding city, increase 3-4 "Qianyuan box" stores. In major cities, establish one life house or discovery hall. In 2018, launch the health-caring and fitness project such as sand bath, add "Qianyuan box" stores to 10-15, and meanwhile continue to increase the quantity of life houses or discovery malls.

六、项目优势：
VI. Project Aduantage(s)：

乾园为东北三省鲜有的一家江南景观的中药养生特色旅游庄园，并与地方书法、美术、诗歌协会等机构建立联系积极发展特色旅游，是对集生态休闲、旅游观光、文化交流于一体的绿色产业经营新模式的有益"探索"和"实践"。

As a rare health-caring characteristic tourism manor of Jiangnan landscape in the three northeast provinces, Qianyuan makes contact with local calligraphy association, art association and poetry association to actively develop characteristic tourism, which is beneficial "exploration" and "practice" on green industry business model which integrates ecological leisure, sightseeing and cultural exchange.

七、项目需求：
VII. Project Demand(s)：

由于区位、宣传、规模等方面的不足，该项目需要进一步加强推广工作及合理化建议，同时也需要和各个旅行社取得有效的联系。争取资金上或技术上的支持和合作。

due to insufficiency of location, promotion and scale, we shall further enhance promotion and put forward reasonable proposal. Simultaneously, we need to get effective contact with various travel agencies for the sake of support and cooperation in funds or technology.

天伦网·一站式服务
Tianlunwang · One-stop Service

一、项目公司名称： 沈阳天伦网企业管理有限公司

I. Project Company Name： Shenyang Tianlunwang Enterprise Management Co., Ltd

二、项目公司介绍：

II. Project Company Introduction：

公司成立于 2015 年，总部位于沈阳市沈河区沈阳北站，金融商贸开发区华府天地商场四层。隶属于沈阳紫慧华韵文化传播有限公司。由紫慧华韵文化传播有限公司 90% 总控股与自然人股东周永斌、苑凯各 5% 股权共同发起。天伦网健康生活家，是紫慧华韵产业集团打造的中国东北首家健康行业（产品）集采中心服务商城。

Founded in 2015, the headquarters is located in Floor 4, Huafu Tiandi Mall, Financial Business Development Area, Shenyang North Station, Shenhe District, Shenyang. Subordinated to Shenyang Zihui Huayun Cultural Transmission Co., Ltd, the company is jointly launched by 90% shares of Shenyang Zihui Huayun Cultural Transmission Co., Ltd and 5% stock equity respectively by natural person shareholders Zhou Yongbin and Yuan Kai. Tianlunwang healthy life home is the first health industry (product) collection center service mall which is built by Zihui Huayun Industrial Group in northeast China.

三、负责人介绍：

III. Responsible Person Introduction：

紫慧华韵文化产业集团董事长张昊宇先生，是道教龙虎山正一派传人，道号张三墨，深谙国学传统文化和道家文化，从中提炼出健康科学的养生方式，推动健康产业的发展。是东北健康产业的领头人。紫慧华韵四大产业创始人。

President of Zihui Huayun Cultural Industry Group, Zhang Haoyu, is successor of Zhengyi sect of Longhu Mountain of Taoism, with the Taoist monastic name, Zhang Sanmo. Familiar with Chinese traditional culture and the Taoist culture, he extracts the healthy and scientific way to preserve health and promote the development of health industry. He is a leader in the northeast health industry, and founder of four industries of Zihui Huayun.

四、项目名称： 天伦网·一站式服务

IV. Project Name： Tianlunwang · One-stop Service

五、项目概况：

V. Project Profile：

天伦网·健康生活家实体商城位于沈阳市沈河区沈阳北站金融商贸开发区华府天地商场四楼，占地 5400 平方米，内含高品质天然氧吧洽谈区、健康产品体验区、理疗区、休闲娱乐茶室、太极室等。同时配备了大、中、小型健康产品专柜精品区、健康生活日用品区、礼品区、生活服务区等。天伦网·健康生活家是健康产品连锁商城＋互联网企业，健康产业（产品）一站式连锁服务招商零售商城。天伦网·健康生活家实体商城是以人类健康为出发点，服务于社会，全面提供全民健康导向的平台商城；提供日常所需的健康生活用品、养生保健、文化休闲，以及养老、旅游等一站式便民服务；以健康产业核心需求为出发点，集研发、传播、推广、生产、销售、服务、渠道、网络、连锁、投资、整合为一体的平台；面向所有追寻健康人群，建设及开发健康产品和方式的机构，联合缔造健康产业的同行业者提供综合性服务的平台商城。

The entity shop of Tianlunwang · healthy life home is located in Floor 4, Huafu Tiandi Mall, Financial Business Development Area, Shenyang North Station, Shenhe District, Shenyang, covering an area of 5,400 square meters; it contains high-quality natural oxygen bar discussion area, health product experience area, physical therapy area, recreation teahouse, Tai chi room, etc and is also equipped with large, medium and small health product counter boutique area, healthy life commodity area, gift area, life service area, etc. Tianlunwang · healthy life home is a healthy product chain store + Internet company, and health industry (product) one-stop chain service investment retail mall. Tianlunwang · healthy life home—the entity shop, based on human health as a starting point, serves the society, and provides a people health-oriented platform mall. It will provide health supplies for daily life, health care and culture leisure, as well as pensions and tourism one-stop convenient services. It is a platform which takes the core demand of health industry as a starting point, and integrates research and development, transmission, promotion, production, sales, services, channels, networks, chain and investment. It is also a platform mall which offers the comprehensive service for personnel who build the health industry, institutions which construct and develop health products and ways, and experts who build the health industry.

六、项目优势：
VI. Project Advantage(s):

天伦网·健康生活家是健康产品连锁商城＋互联网企业。提供日常所需的健康生活用品，养生保健、文化休闲，以及养老、旅游等一站式便民服务，联合缔造健康产业的同行业者提供综合性服务的平台商城。

Tianlunwang · healthy life home is a healthy product chain store and Internet company, which will provide the health supplies for daily life, health care and culture leisure, as well as pensions and tourism one-stop convenient services. It is a platform mall which offers the comprehensive service for experts who build the health industry.

七、项目需求：
VII. Project Demand(s)：

面向所有追寻健康人群推广我们的健康产业，整合建设及开发健康产品和方式的机构，希望得到政策支持及项目融资。

To promote our health industry to people who pursue health, integrate the institutions which construct and develop health products and ways, and hope to get the policy support and project financing.

自然之诺自然活酒
Promise of Nature Natural Live Wine

一、项目公司名称：贵港市东方传奇食品科技有限公司

Ⅰ. Project Company Name：Guigang Legendary East Food Technology Co. Ltd.

二、项目公司介绍：

Ⅱ. Project Company Introduction：

2014年成立，产品连续获得了两届中国-东盟商务与投资峰会宴用酒，2015年欧亚经济论坛宴用饮品，东亚商务理事会宴用酒。第一、第二届中国创新创业百强企业，微生物樊氏法列入国家《2016年度重点推荐技/2016年度重点推荐项目》白皮书等，获得十六项国家荣誉。拥有由十一位院士专家组成的自然之诺院士专家委员会，目前已经有23个城市代理。

Guigang Legendary East Food Technology Company was established in 2014. It has been awarded 16 national honors consecutively since its establishment: Banquet Wine for China-ASEAN Business and Investment Summit (2014/2015); Banquet Drink for Euro-Asia Economic Forum (2015); Banquet Wine for East-Asia Business Council (2015); Top 100 Enterprises in 1st and 2nd China Innovation and Entrepreneurship Competition; Microbial Fan's Methods, included into National White Paper *2016 Annual Key Recommended Technology/2016 Annual Key Recommended Project*. Moreover, it has possessed "Promise of Nature" Expert Committee which consists of 11 academicians. Till now, it has authorized sales agents in 23 cities.

2017年6月20日公司与华堂国际广告公司签订协议，正式成为华堂国际广告公司的战略合作伙伴。自然之诺华堂宴用酒生产基地项目坐落在贵港江南工业园，项目年产能可达1亿瓶自然活酒。预计2017年10月份投入生产．

On June 20, 2017, it has signed agreement with Hua Tang International Advertising Company, and become strategic partner of Hua Tang International Advertising Company formally. "Promise of Nature" Huang Tang Banquet Wine production base is located in Guigang Jiangnan Industrial Park; the annual capacity of this project will be up to 100 million bottles of natural live wine. It is expected that the production base will be put into operation in Oct., 2017.

三、负责人介绍：

Ⅲ. Responsible Person Introduction:

樊海麟，男，现年45岁，广西贵港市壮族人，"微生物樊氏法"创始人，世界第六大酒类——自然活酒创始人，自然之诺自然活酒品牌创始人，带领公司三年开拓二十多个城市销售代理，创造了十六项国家级荣誉。

Fan Hailin (Male), 45 years old, is of Zhuang nationality in Guigang city, Guangxi Province. He is the founder of Microbial Fan's Methods, Natural Live Wine (The world's six largest type of alcohol), and brand of Natural Live Wine (Promise of Nature). He has led the company to develop sales agents in over 20 cities since the company established for 3 years, and create 16 national honors.

四、项目名称：自然之诺自然活酒

Ⅳ. Project Name：Promise of Nature Natural Live Wine

五、项目概况：

Ⅴ. Project Profile:

樊海麟在二十三年的微生物发酵研究的过程中，创造了微生物生态法、微生物营养阻断法、微生物破壁抑制法、微生物破壁活性提取法，被学界命名为"微生物樊氏法"。开启了微生物科研新领域。

Project Profile：During 23 years' research on microbial fermentation, Fan Hailin has created microbial ecological method, microbial nutrient blocking method, microbial wall-broken suppression method, and microbial wall-broken activity extraction method. All these methods are named as "Microbial Fan's Methods" by the academic community, which have opened a new field of microbial research.

"微生物樊氏法"为有机肥和有机饲料生产、粮食果蔬深加工、微生物医药制造、微生物医疗等方面提供系统解决方法。这些方法的应用对上述领域的生产将是革命性的，其所产生的社会价值和经济价值将是不可估量的，将成为经济社会取得新发展的新生力量。

Via "Microbial Fan's Methods", proper solutions can be provided for such aspects as production of organic manure and organic feed, deep processing of food,fruits and vegetables, manufacturing of microbial medicine, and development of microbial health care. The application of these methods will be revolutionary for the fields mentioned above; the social and economic values due to the application of these methods will be immeasurable. They will become new forces for the social and economic development.

应用"微生物樊氏法"生产的酒类开创了世界第六大酒类——自然活酒。自然活酒具有以下优点：

Natural Live Wine produced via "Microbial Fan's Methods" has created the world's sixth largest types of alcohol. It has the following advantages:

1．"零酒精度酒，喝出酒感觉"，解了酒瘾，又不醉酒。

Zero alcohol：It is a kind of wine with zero alcohol, which can make people enjoy the flavor of wine. In other words, it is a type of wine that can feed people's alcohol addiction, but does not make people drunken；

2．活酒：富含生态链活性益生菌，富含人体必需的近百种小分子活性营养元素。

Live wine：It is rich in active probiotics of ecological chain; moreover, it is also rich in nearly 100 types of active nutritional facts, which are required by human body；

3．口感淳美：研发二十多年来，近十万消费者的体验，好评率达95%。

Beautiful taste：Since it has been developed and launched to the market for more than 20 years, the experience on nearly 100 thousands of consumers has accumulated, and the praise rate has reached 95%；

4．广泛的受众度——小朋友能喝爱喝，不爱喝酒精酒的女士可开怀畅饮，男士喝了有酒的感觉，办事不糊涂，中老年人首选调理养生酒品。解决了无酒不成席的传统饮酒文化问题。

Extensive audience：The little kids can not only drink it, but also love drinking it; the women who do not love alcohol can drink it freely with great joy; the men can enjoy the flavor of the wine after drinking it, and can handle affairs normally; moreover, it is the best choice if the health care alcohol needs to be chosen for the middle-aged and elderly people. In one word, it has helped to solve the traditional drinking culture problem that no wine no seats and no wine a feast.

六、项目优势：

Ⅵ. Project Advantage(s):

拥有科技核心竞争力，国际领先的技术应用广泛，产品受众广泛。

The company has core competitiveness in science and technology, adopts widely-used international leading technologies, and possesses extensive product audiences.

七、项目需求：

Ⅶ. Project Demand(s)：

需要融资三千万元。

We hope to attract financing of RMB 30 million yuan.

宜速家
Yisujia

一、项目公司名称：宜速家网络科技有限责任公司
Ⅰ. Project Company Name ： Yisujia Network Technology Co., Ltd.

二、项目公司介绍：
Ⅱ. Project Company Introduction ：

公司（便宜、快速、到家，简称宜速家）2015年成立于辽宁沈阳，注册于国家工商总局，注册资本10 000万元，总部办公面积4000余平，在职员工一百余人。

The company (cheap, fast, and excellent, called Yisujia for short) was established in Shenyang of Liaoning Province in 2015, and registered in State Administration for Industry and Commerce of the People's Republic of China, with the registered capital of 100 million Yuan. It covers the headquarters office area of 4,000 m^2, and owns over 100 employees.

公司集商业软件开发、网上商城推广应用、现代化物流仓储投资建设、大数据云计算中心、快递物流配送于一体，以超快速、超低价、优质正品的商品速送为基础业务，致力于提高居民的生活消费质量，降低社会生存成本，打造线上线下仓储物流为一体的全新零售模式。

The company integrates business software development, online mall popularization application, modern logistics warehousing investment construction, big data cloud computing center and express logistics delivery, takes the super-fast and super-low-price and high-quality goods delivery as the basic business, devote o improving the quality of people's life consumption, reduces the cost of social existence, and create the new retail model by combing online and offline storage logistics.

三、负责人介绍：
Ⅲ. Responsible Person Introduction ：

王勇，生于1960年，1993年取得中国政法大学政治经济学硕士学位，1991年任辽宁省工合集团总经理；1994年创建了辽宁第一家连锁企业，同期拥有200多家直营店，并获得辽宁知名品牌，多年经营食品批发零售、百货、服务、软件开发等多种行业，在管理连锁企业方面有着特殊的极深造诣。

Wang Yong, born in 1960, got the master's degree in Political Economy of China University of Political Science and Law in 1993, and assumed as general manager of Liaoning Gonghe Group in 1991；In 1994, he created the first chain enterprise in Liaoning, owned more than 200 directly-managed stores in the same period, and got famous brand in Liaoning. He has been engaged in food wholesale and retail, department stores, services, software development and other industries for many years, so he has special and deep attainments on management of chain enterprise.

四、项目名称：宜速家
Ⅳ. Project Name：Yisujia

五、项目概况：
Ⅴ. Project Profile ：

项目以线上智能购物、线下动态平衡物流、千户服务站及大数据收集三大体系构成。

The project consists of online smart shopping, offline dynamic balance logistics, thousand-household service station and big data collection.

线上智能购物体系为企业自主研发的一款智能机器人语音购物系统，可完全脱离打字等烦琐功能进行简单操作，可实现无论是5岁孩子还是70岁老人均无障碍操作APP，率先突破了只有年轻人能使用APP的瓶颈。

Online smart shopping system is a smart robot voice shopping system which is independently researched and developed by the enterprise, can be simply operated by completely separating from typing, realize free operation of APP no matter you are 5 years old or 70 years old, and firstly breaks through the bottleneck that only young people can use APP.

线下动态平衡的物流体系为企业自主研发的一套自动化动态补货系统,该系统配合高效的军事化管理,使物流成本降到了冰点,进而大幅度降低了商品的销售成本。

Offline dynamic balance system is a set of automatic dynamic replenishment system which is independently researched and developed by the enterprise, and is executed by matching with high-efficiency militarization management, so as to drop the logistics cost to the freezing point and then reduce the sales cost of goods.

千户服务站及大数据收集体系中,千户服务站扎根于园区中央位置,低成本的运营确保低于便利店20%-50%的低价体系及十分钟送货上门服务,除了大数据采集外,同时提供免费共享便民工具、医疗、娱乐等福利设施及便民服务、收发快递、广告精准投放、义务辅助办理、义务探视等细节工作。

In the thousand-household service station and data collection system, the thousand-household service station is located in the park central position; low-cost operation ensures the low-price system lower by 20% -50% than convenience store and 10-minute door-to-door delivery services. Besides big data collection, it also offers free sharing convenient tool, medical facilities and entertainment welfare facilities as well as convenient service, sending and receiving express, accurately targeted advertising, obligatory details auxiliary handling, and obligatory visit.

六、项目优势:
Ⅵ. Project Advantage(s):

1. 社区中心位置选址=十分钟极速送达;

Site selection of community center position=10 min fast delivery;

2. 动态平衡的低成本物流体系=价格低于传统便利店20%;

Low-cost logistics system of dynamic balance=price is lower by 20% than traditional convenience store;

3. 高效的军事化管理=高标准的服务质量;

High-efficiency militarization management=high-standard service quality;

4. 非开放式的供应链体系=高质保真的产品;

Non-open supply chain system=high-quality and high-fidelity product;

5. 地毯式的覆盖=80%的终端消费者与50%的民生市场;

Carpet coverage=80% terminal consumers and 50% people's livelihood market;

6. 线上线下同步数据采集=大数据。

Online and offline synchronous data collection=big data.

七、项目需求:
Ⅶ. Project Demand(s):

项目拓展至各区域时,希望得到政策支持和资源对接,包括政企联合业务办理,大型仓库选址,正面推广宣传,低息创业贷款等。

When the project is extended to all regions, we hope to get the policy support and resource docking, including government enterprise alliance business handling, large warehouse site selection, positive promotion, low-interest start-up loans, etc.

大健康公共服务平台
Great Health Public Service Platform

一、项目公司名称：辽宁省宁厚堂科技有限公司
Ⅰ. Project Company Name： Liaoning Province Ninghoutang Technology Co., Ltd.

二、项目公司介绍：
Ⅱ. Project Company Introduction：

公司是一家集研发、推广于一体的高科技有限公司。致力于心血管内科、神经科、肿瘤科、儿科等医药领域的药品及医疗器械专业化推广。2017年在辽宁股权交易中心成功挂牌，股权代码：宁厚堂S50125。公司自主设计开发的"大健康公共服务平台"得到全国各级医院的支持。公司前期软件开发投入500万。市场推广投入200万。以期构建解决老百姓看病难，买药贵等问题的大健康公共服务平台。

The company is a high-tech limited company integrating R & D and promotion. Its business covers the professional promotion of medicine and medical devices in cardiovascular medicine, neurology, oncology, pediatrics and other medical fields. It was successfully listed in the Liaoning Equity Trading Center in 2017. Equity Code： Ninghoutang S50125. "Great Health Public Service Platform" designed and developed independently by the company has been supported by hospitals all over the country. The company has invested 5 million in pre-software development. And 2 million was invested in market promotion. The purpose is to build the "Great Health Public Service Platform" to solve the problem of difficult medical treatment, expensive drug purchase, etc. among the common people.

三、负责人介绍：
Ⅲ. Responsible Person Introduction：

阎剑崙先生具有多年从事医疗行业服务销售经验，熟悉医疗行业。并对医疗行业有独到的认知和见解。在过去几年的工作中与各医院建立了良好的合作关系，并且与国际诸多大的医疗器械厂商和机构有着良好的合作关系。

Mr. Yan Jianlun has many years of service sales experience in the medical industry and is familiar with the medical industry. And has the unique cognition and insight into the medical industry. He has established a good cooperative relations with various hospitals in the past few years of working experience. And it has a good cooperative relationship with many large international medical device manufacturers and institutions.

四、项目名称：大健康公共服务平台
Ⅳ. Project name：Great Health Public Service Platform

五、项目概况：
Ⅴ. Project Profile:

该项目致力于解决"看病难、看病贵、看病烦"的焦点问题。目前医疗信息资源缺乏整合。医院与就医者存在医疗信息不对称，医疗信息分散，难以互通，求医群众和医护人员均无法通过网络实时了解多家医院的医疗信息动态和实现医疗信息的共享。因此公司自主设计开发的"大健康公共服务平台"得到全国各级医院的支持。公司前期软件开发投入500万。市场推广投入200万。通过建设区域医疗信息共享平台，实现医疗信息资源的整合，可满足就医、治疗、科研、管理、提高五位一体的医疗服务的目标，病人是信息资源整合的最终受益者。实现"整合"后，病人可以享受到更透明、便利、高效、便宜的医疗服务。通过网络共享平台，病人可以了解各医院包括医生、床位、单病种治疗价格等医疗资源分布情况；病人可以享受预约、咨询等互动式服务；病人可更全面地掌握自己的诊疗记录，形成"一站式"服务模式。医学研究和教学人员也是医疗信息资源整合后的受益者。注重中西医结合，注重老百姓的科学普及以及大夫的日常咨询。我公司还将在该项目的操作之下，进行康复治疗的普及项目。与基层社区医院合作，针对脑卒中，脑梗死，残疾，神经外科，心脏外科等术后以及病后病人进行指导性康复治疗。

The project aims to solve the core problems of "Difficult Medical Treatment, Expensive Medical Treatment and

Complicated Medical Care". Lack integrated medical information resources. The asymmetrical medical information, scattered medical information has existed between hospitals and patients, which is difficult to communicate. The patients and medical staff are unable to understand the medical information development of several hospitals and the realization of the sharing of medical information in real time through the network. "Great Health Public Service Platform" designed and developed independently by the company has been supported by hospitals all over the country. The company has invested 5 million in pre-software development. And 2 million was invested in market promotion. The integration of medical information resources has been realized through the construction of regional medical information sharing platform, which can meet the medical care, treatment, scientific research and management, and improve the "Five In One" medical service goals, and the patient is the ultimate beneficiaries of the integration of information resources. The patient can enjoy more transparent, convenient, efficient and cheap medical services after the "Integration". The patient can understand the distribution of medical resources, including doctors, beds, single diseases, treatment prices and so on through the network sharing platform; The patient can enjoy the interactive services such as the appointment and consultation; The patient can master their own medical records more comprehensively, forming the "One-Stop" service model. Simultaneously, the medical research and teaching staff shall also be the beneficiaries of the integration of medical information resources. Focus on the combination of Chinese and western medicine as well as the scientific popularization of common people and the daily consultation of doctors. Our company will also undertake the popularization program of the rehabilitation treatment under the operation of the project. The rehabilitation treatment shall be conducted for the stroke, cerebral infarction, disability, neurosurgery, cardiac surgery and postoperative patients in collaboration with the community hospitals.

六、项目优势：
VI. Project Advantage(s)

公司自主设计开发的"大健康公共服务平台"得到全国各级医院的支持。在政府相关部门的支持下，公司在东北已拥有 1500 个社区资源及庞大的老百姓求医数据库。

"Great Health Public Service Platform" designed and developed independently by the company has been supported by hospitals all over the country. There are 1,500 community resources and a vast population of medical treatment database in the northeast with the support of the relevant government departments.

七、项目需求：
VII. Project Demand(s)：

公司准备在软件开发上加大投入力度，期待各种形式合作。

The company has been prepared to increase the investment efforts in software development to look forward to various forms of cooperation.

新尼燕窝饮
Xinni Bird's Nest Drink

一、项目公司名称：沈阳新尼商业连锁企业管理有限公司
Ⅰ. Project Company Name：Shenyang Xinni Commercial Chain Enterprise Management Co., Ltd.

二、项目公司介绍：
Ⅱ. Project Company Introduction:

公司成立于2007年，主要经营燕窝、燕窝饮等系列养生品，以五星级酒店餐饮平台为依托，致力于打造中国养生心仪品牌，填补中国燕窝饮品市场空白。2012年成功加入了中国燕窝委员会，被国燕委授予常务理事单位，并成为中国东北唯一一家与印度尼西亚、马来西亚燕窝供应基地合作的燕窝专营企业。2016年又成功研制出独具特色的便捷罐装饮品——新尼燕窝饮，开启了燕窝消费平民化、即食化、便捷化新时代，并获得各界人士的好评与青睐。

The Company was founded in 2007, mainly engaged in bird's nest, bird's nest drinks and other series of health-maintenance products, relying on the five-star hotel restaurant platform, and committed to creating China's favorite brand for health maintenance and filling the market blank for bird's nest drinks in China. In 2012, it successfully joined the China Bird's Nest Committee by which it was awarded the standing director unit, and became the only one bird's nest franchise business in northeast China to cooperate with the bird's nest supply base in Indonesia and Malaysia. In 2016, it also successfully developed the unique and convenient canned drinks, called Xinni bird's nest drink, which has opened a new era for the common, instant and convenient bird's nest consumption, and won the praise and favor of people from all walks of life.

三、负责人介绍：
Ⅲ. Responsible Person Introduction:

刘金梁总裁自2007年与燕窝结缘，便多次携团队到印尼燕窝基地实地考察和选材，成功选取属于新尼公司自己的燕窝供应基地，还带领研发团队研制生产多款新尼燕窝系列爆款产品，并受到广大消费者的热捧和信赖。

Since attached to bird's nest in 2007, President Liu Jinliang has personally taken the team to the bird's nest base in Indonesia to carry out the on-the-spot investigation and material selection several times and has successfully selected the bird's nest supply base belonging to Xinni Company itself. He has also personally led the research and development team to research and develop a variety of hot Xinni bird's nest products which are liked and trusted by the vast number of consumers.

四、项目名称：新尼燕窝饮
Ⅳ. Project Name：Xinni Bird's Nest Drink

五、项目概况：
Ⅴ. Project Profile:

新尼燕窝饮拥有成熟的研发团队，与美国生物科技研究院先进的国际科研机构合作。并在印尼有自己合建的六大燕屋及采购基地，历经八年考察研究，足迹遍布马来西亚、印度尼西亚，对燕窝的培育、采集、初加工、精加工、燕窝饮的配方和选料都有严格要求与生产标准，建立国内第一个燕窝饮行业标准。"即食胶原蛋白燕窝饮品"新尼燕窝饮，天然选材、真空杀菌、慢火熬炖、原汁原味、性价比高、品质优选上乘。原料采用小分子团活性水、燕窝、冰糖、胶原蛋白、琼脂，男女老少孕妇皆宜。新尼燕窝饮四大功效：抗霾洗肺、润肤养颜、健脑防衰、降解三高。

Xinni Bird's Nest has a mature research and development team, and cooperates with the advanced international scientific research institutions of American Institute of Biological Sciences. It has its own 6 major bird houses and purchasing bases jointly built in Indonesia. After eight years of investigation and research, its footprints have been all over Malaysia and Indonesia. There are strict requirements and production standards for the cultivation, collection, preliminary processing, finishing, and recipe and material selection of bird's nest drinks. It has also established the first standards for bird's nest industry. The Xinni bird's nest drinks, namely "instant collagen bird's nest drinks", are made of the natural materials, sterilized in vacuum and stewed on slow fire, which are of original taste and flavor, with high performance cost ratio and selected superior quality. The raw materials are small molecular active water, bird's nest, crystal sugar, collagen and agar, which are suitable for people of all ages and both sexes as well as the pregnant women. Xinni bird's nest drinks have four effects: anti-haze & lung lavage, moisturizing & beauty, brain-strengthening & anti-aging, degradation of three highs.

六、项目优势：

VI. Project Advantages:

1．巨大市场的空白：据数据统计，每年中国饮品市场的年消费量是730亿升，燕窝饮市场却一片空白，如果新尼燕窝饮仅仅占这个市场份额的0.5%，就是3.65亿升，这样算下来销售额就是270亿元，燕窝饮上市后不到六个月时间仅在沈阳一个城市就销售30万罐，销售额达到540万元。

Blank huge market space: according to the statistics, the annual consumption of the Chinese drink market is 73 billion liters, while the bird's nest drink market is blank. If the Xinni bird's nest drinks only accounted for 0.5% of this market share, that is, 365 million liters, it would be 27 billion by calculating this way, therefore, 300 thousand cans of bird's nest drinks would be sold just in Shenyang in less than 6 months after they are on the market and the sales volume would be as much as RMB 5.4 million.

2．成熟的研发团队：（1）先进的国际科研合作机构——美国生物科技研究院；（2）深厚的燕窝研究经验；（3）成熟的研发队伍。

Mature research and development team: (1) advanced international scientific research institutions——American Institute of Biological Sciences; (2) deep bird's nest research experience; (3) mature research and development team.

3．庞大的生产基地：在印尼有自己合建的六大燕屋及采购基地。

Huge production base: it has its own major bird houses and purchasing bases jointly built.

4．深厚的行业经验：历经八年考察研究，足迹遍布马来西亚、印度尼西亚，对燕窝的培育、采集、初加工、精加工、燕窝饮的配方和选料都有严格要求与生产标准，建立国内第一个燕窝饮行业标准。

Deep industry experience: after eight years of investigation and research, its footprints have been all over Malaysia and Indonesia. There are strict requirements and production standards for the cultivation, collection, preliminary processing, finishing, and recipe and material selection of bird's nest drinks. It has also established the first standards for bird's nest industry.

5．独特的产品配方：独自研发，独特配方，独特配料——天然纯正燕窝、小分子团活性水、上等胶原蛋白、天然植物琼脂、无添加剂等。

Unique product recipe: independent research and development, unique recipe and unique ingredients - natural pure bird's nest, small molecule active water, superior collagen, natural plant agar and no additives, etc.

七、项目需求：产品宣传、市场拓展。

VII. Project Demand: Product publicity and market expansion.

聚氨酯及热缩材料
Polyurethane and Pyrocondensation Materials

一、项目公司名称：陕西蓝源科技有限公司
Ⅰ. Project Company Name: Shanxi Lanyuan Technology Co., Ltd.

二、项目公司介绍
Ⅱ. Project Company Introduction:

陕西蓝源科技有限公司成立于 2013 年，其前身是 2007 年成立的西安蓝源工贸有限责任公司，为发展需要于 2013 年通过增资成立陕西蓝源科技有限公司。现公司具备了更加成熟的聚氨酯技术，集人力，科技、工贸于一体，致力于西北地区聚氨酯行业的发展，在城市集中供热、石油管线运输等一系列国家大节能项目做出突出贡献。

Shannxi Lanyuan Technology Co., Ltd. was founded in 2013 by capital increase for the development needs, whose predecessor is Xi'an Lanyuan Industry and Trade Co., Ltd. founded in 2007. Now the company has a more mature polyurethane technology, integrating manpower, technology, industry and trade in one and committed to the development of the polyurethane industry in the northwest, and makes significant contributions to a series of important national energy conservation projects such as central heating in cities and oil pipeline transportation, etc.

三、负责人介绍
Ⅲ. Responsible Person Introduction:

李建军，男，西安交大本科生。在技术开发、工业实施等方面具有丰富的经验，能够在生产过程以及工作现场运用中提供专业方法，以分析及解决问题。

Li Jianjun, male, undergraduate of Xi'an Jiaotong University, with rich experience in technology development and industrial implementation and able to provide professional methods during production and applications in job site, so as to analyze and solve the problems.

四、项目名称：聚氨酯及热缩材料
Ⅳ. Project Name：Polyurethane and Pyrocondensation Materials

五、项目概况
Ⅴ. Project Profile:

硬质聚氨酯发泡原液是偶聚醚多元醇、泡沫稳定剂、复合催化剂、发泡剂等混合组成，然后便可与 MDI 或 PAPI 按一定比例混合，既成聚氨酯硬泡。聚氨酯厂生产的组合聚醚有普通型、浇注型、石油管道专用型、耐高温型、喷涂型、低氟、无氟发泡料、高密度仿木型等。

The stock solution of the rigid polyurethane foam is a mixture of polyether polyol, foam stabilizer, composite catalyst and foaming agent, etc., which then can be mixed with MDI or PAPI according to a certain ratio, to become the rigid polyurethane foam. The combined polyether produced in Polyurethane plant factory has the common type, pouring type, special oil pipeline type, heat-resistance, spray, low-fluorine, fluorine-free foam material, and high-density imitation wood.

热收缩带是为钢管防腐而设计的带有独立固定片的包裹套，该产品具有操作时焊接处不滑脱，有较高的机械强度、耐老化、耐化学腐蚀、黏力强，易操作等特点。适用于各种型号防腐管道品，保湿管道保护层，及伤外补口。

The heat shrinkable belt is designed for the protection of the steel pipe from radiation, which is equipped with a separate package for the fixed piece. The product has the advantages of no slippage at the welding place, high mechanical strength, aging-resistance, chemical-resistance, strong adhesive force and easy operation, etc. during the operation, which is suitable for various types of anti-corrosion pipeline products, for moisturizing pipeline's protection layer, and for coating the external opening damaged.

六、项目优势
VI. Project Advantages

1．本公司生产的一步法聚氨酯组合聚醚以发泡稳定、空洞少、抗压强度高等优良品质得到广大用户的好评；

The combined polyether of the one-step polyurethane produced by the Company is widely praised by the users for its stable foaming, few holes, high-compressive strength and other excellent qualities；

2．热收缩其内层涂敷在钢管表面的环氧底漆，中层为特种热熔胶，外层为改性的辐射交联聚乙烯基材。

The inner layer of heat shrinkage is coated on epoxy primer on the surface of the steel pipe, the middle layer is a special hot melt adhesive, and the outer layer is a modified radiant crosslinked polyethylene substrate.

七、项目需求
VII. Project Demands

1．推广产品

Promotion of products；

2．希望借助"一带一路"进行成果转化

Intending to carry out achievement transformation with the virtue of the "Belt and Road"

3．市场拓展

Market development

凤英·智慧外交 APP 平台
Fengying · Smart Diplomatic App Platform

一、项目公司名称：东莞市凤英跨界文化咨询有限公司
Ⅰ. Project Company Name：Dongguan Fengying Cross Boundary Culture Consulting Co., Ltd.

二、项目公司介绍：
Ⅱ. Project Company Introduction：

公司主营"一带一路"国际接轨外语外贸实战职业经理人高端就业培训，打造对外（社交）交流、（对外贸易）交易，让中外农民能用简易智能化全球 APP 端招商引资资源对接平台。

The company is mainly engaged in high-end employment training for practical professional manager of The "Belt and Road" international convergence foreign language and foreign trade to create foreign (social) exchanges and transactions (foreign trade), so that Chinese and foreign farmers can make the resource docking platform of "Business Invitation and Investment Attraction" of intelligent global app terminal easier.

三、负责人介绍：
Ⅲ. Responsible Person Introduction：

陈苏董事长，商务英语，清华大学 EMBA 硕士，潮州人居深圳，20 年大型制造业与外贸公司全球总经理全盘运营实战经验，曾任火凤凰空中英语联盟组委会创始人会长，在东莞成功举办过十期纯公益英语沙龙，服务于广东狮子会，现任深圳市华睿源教育公益事业发展中心副主任（总部深圳妇联指导）、中亚硅谷教育产业基地副院长（与北京大学联合办学）、国际新闻联盟主编，第 13 届中国超级模特大赛深圳赛区副秘书长，世界华商同学会副会长。拥有全球 500 多位商协会会长资源。

Chen Su, the chairman of the board, Tsinghua University EMBA master, born in Chaozhou, living in Shenzhen, has 20 years of the practical experience of the overall operating of the large-scale manufacturing and foreign trade company global general manager, served as the founder chairman of the Organizing Committee of the "Phoenix Air English Union", has successfully held 10 pure public welfare "English salon" in Dongguan and serves the Guangdong Lions Club. Chen Su is currently the deputy director of Shenzhen Huaruiyuan Education Public Welfare Development (headquarters in Shenzhen federation guidance), and is the vice president of education industry base in Central Asia (jointly run with Peking University), and is the chief editor of the International News Union, and is the deputy secretary general of the 13th China Super Model Contest Shenzhen Division, and is vice president of World Chinese Entrepreneurs Association. Chen Su has more than 500 global business association president resources.

四、项目名称：凤英·智慧外交 APP 平台
Ⅳ. Project name：Fengying · Smart Diplomatic App Platform

五、项目概况：
Ⅴ. Project Profile：

凤英·智慧外交 APP 平台即外语外贸职业经理人高端就业培训+智慧外交网。以创新智能互联网+蓝海科技教育，培养跨国高端紧缺外语外贸实战职业经理人，链接环球经贸资源从而建立国际接轨和谐友好关系，助力推动中外进出口贸易与文化旅游的招商引资资源，整合让中外农民简易互联与自动翻译智慧做外贸四网合一的 APP 全球平台，该项目也得到团队股东国家级 IT 网络行业巨头深圳市信息化和工业化研究院院长兼深圳市社会组织总会副会长魏劲合的大力支持与赞助。项目将实现"多语交流""在线预约""供需共享""物联清货""在线成交支付"等功能。

The platform is the high-end employment training of the professional manager of foreign language and foreign trade + mart Diplomatic networks. To cultivate transnational high-end shortage foreign language and foreign trade practical professional manager to link the global economic and trade resources to establish the harmonious and friendly relationship with international standards, help promote the import and export trade between China and foreign countries and "Business Invitation and Investment Attraction" resources of cultural tourism, integrate Chinese and foreign farmers simple inter language automatic translation wisdom to the App global platform of foreign trade four net one in accordance with Innovative Smart Internet + Blue Ocean Science and Technology Education, the project has also been supported and sponsored by Wei Jinhe who is the team shareholder, national IT network giant, president of Shenzhen Information and Industrialization Research Institute and vice president of Shenzhen society organization association. The project will realize "Multi-lingual Communication", "Online Booking", "Supply and Demand Sharing", "Goods clearance", "Online transaction payment" and other functions.

课程（外语外贸实战职业经理人高端就业培训班）：

Courses:（foreign language and foreign trade practical professional manager high-end employment training course）

1．英文导游班

English Tourist Guide Course

2．英文主持人演讲家班

English Host Speech Course

3．英文金融班

English Finance Course

4．英文身心灵觉醒班

Physical and Mind Awakening Speech Course

5．英文外企外贸高管班

English Foreign Enterprises and Foreign Trade Executive Course

6．老外国学班

协助解决五对象：①工作：猎头对象；②学习：出国游学移民对象；③家庭：婚恋对象；④事业：销售客户老外对象；⑤人脉资源全球平台：商会政要明星对象。

Foreign Sinology Course Assist in solving the follow 5 objects：① Work：Headhunting object；② Learning：Travel and study abroad immigration object；③ Family：Marriage object；④ Career：Sell customer foreign object；⑤ Interpersonal network resources global platform：Commerce dignitaries and stars object.

六、项目优势：

Ⅵ. Project Advantage(s)

1．政府"一带一路"人才补贴优势：为"一带一路"国际接轨培养高端稀缺紧缺人才而助力环球经贸。

Government The "Belt and Road Initiative" talent subsidy advantage：Promote global economic trade for The "Belt and Road" international convergence to cultivate high-end scarce talent.

2．智能智慧网络科技创新优势：智能O2O互联网＋蓝海教育市场，自动同步翻译互联语，外交外贸商家在线预约，资源共享，在线成交支付，物联网清库存。

Intelligent smart network technology innovation advantages：Intelligent O2O Internet + Blue Ocean Education Market, automatic simultaneous translation inter language, online booking of foreign trade and foreign merchants, resource sharing, online transaction payment, Goods clearance.

3．颠覆传统外贸障碍变成智慧互联语外语外贸高薪就业创业外交交易优势：非语言工具培训的外语外贸实战经验传授，中外农民简易智能智慧做社交外贸。

To overturn the traditional foreign trade barriers and make it become smart inter language foreign language and foreign trade high salary employment and entrepreneurship diplomatic transaction advantage：The foreign language and foreign trade practical experience teaching of the non - language tools training, Chinese and foreign farmers simple smart wisdom to do social and foreign trade.

七、项目需求：

Ⅶ. Project Demand(s)：

众筹融资、科技成果专利申请、软件技术开发人才APP研发团队的引入、全球推广。

Public financing, patent application of scientific and technological achievement, introduction and global promotion of software technology development personnel App R & D team.

传统艺术推广平台
Traditional Art Promotion Platform

一、项目公司名称：北京识雅博文化传播有限公司
Ⅰ. Project Company Name：Beijing Shiyabo Culture Communication Co., Ltd.

二、项目公司简介：
Ⅱ. Project Company Profile:

公司是中国校园健康行动领导小组办公室中国关心下一代爱心行组委会副主任单位，集艺术领域评审推介、出版画册、网站运营、工艺名家作品宣传、推广（拥有1200余家网站、报纸、央视、政协画界·工艺美术杂志等传媒资源）、销售于一体的专业文化传播运营公司。旗下中国工艺美术联盟网（简称：中工联）主要服务于工艺美术从业者、工艺美术企业及文化传承机构，为展示宣传工艺美术（大）师、工艺品、艺术品兼销售于一体的综合性网站。

The Company is the deputy directing unit of Let Love Travel for China Cares for the Next Generation Working Committee of Leading Group Office of China School Health Action, and an operation company for professional culture communication integrating review and marketing in art field, publishing album of painting, website operation, advertising, promoting and marketing artworks of masters with media resources of over 1,200 websites, newspapers, television stations of China Central Television, Arts and Crafts of CPPCC Art Fields and alike. The subordinate China Arts and Crafts Alliance Web (hereafter to be referred as China Crafts Web) is mainly serve for the practitioners of arts and crafts, companies for arts and crafts and cultural inheritance organizations, which is a comprehensive website for presenting craft artists, masters, artwares, artworks as well as sales.

三、负责人介绍：
Ⅲ. Responsible Person Introduction:

孙百珍，1996年12月服役于中央警卫局，2008年部队转业，历任中国紫檀博物馆办公室主任、北京识雅博文化传播有限公司总经理、中国工艺美术联盟秘书长、中国校园健康行动关心下一代爱心行组委会副主任、中国关心下一代爱心行组织委员会党支部书记。

Mr Sun Baizhen, served in Central Security Bureau from December of 1996, transferred to civilian work in 2008, was the Office Director of China Red Sandalwood Museum, General Manager of Beijing Shiyabo Culture Communication Co., Ltd., Secretary-General of China Arts and Crafts Alliance, Deputy Director of China Cares for the Next Generation Working Committee of Leading Group Office of China School Health Action and the Secretary of CPC Branch of Let Love Travel for China Cares for the Next Generation Working Committee.

四、项目名称：传统艺术推广平台
Ⅳ. Project Name：Traditional Art Promotion Platform

五、项目概况：
Ⅴ. Project Overview:

中国工艺美术和手工艺历史悠久、源远流长，是中华文化发展和世界文化发展的重要组成部分。我们社会主义文艺要繁荣发展起来，必须认真学习借鉴世界各国人民创造的优秀文艺。只有坚持洋为中用、开拓创新，做到中西合璧、融会贯通，我国文艺才能更好发展繁荣起来！

The long history and long standing of China's arts and crafts as well as handicrafts is the important part of China's culture development and the World's culture development. To boom and develop socialist arts and literatures, we must carefully study and learn from the outstanding people's arts and literatures from the whole world. The arts and literatures of China can only develop and boom when insists in adapting foreign things for Chinese use, exploration and innovation as well as combining Chinese and Western elements and achieving mastery through a comprehensive study of the subject.

平台自2009年在全国运作以来，主要以挖掘中国传统的民间艺术家和手工艺传承艺术家为己任，为全国从

事手工艺传承的民间艺术家提供一个艺术交流的平台，对艺术家为人师表、责任担当、技艺选拔、艺术传承等方面建立健全资料库，弘扬大国工匠精神，以艺术博览、艺术论坛、艺术展销交流和游学等形式多样的渠道，实现在平台上的宣传推广、在线销售、网上培训、线下交流、非遗体验等功能版块，运用互联网技术实现一体化。通过"一带一路"的倡导，平台的功能定位以展示、宣传、推广、交易、融资等为基础，以商务、公益和文化三大服务平台为依托，用"构建平台、整合资源、优享商机、互利发展"的运作模式，结合线下展览、展销、手工体验、民俗文化、节庆文化等活动形式由国内向国际延伸发展。

Since the operation throughout China in 2009, the platform mainly devotes in unearthing China's traditional folk artists and handicraft inheriting artists, provides an art communion platform for folk artists involving in handicraft inheriting all over China, establish and perfect the data base in terms of artists of exemplary virtue, accountabilities, artistry selection, artistic inheritance and alike, develop and expand the craftsman spirits of great country. Through various channels such as art expos, art forums, exchange of art exhibitions and learning tours, realize advertisement and promotion on platform, on line sales, on line training, off line communications, experiences for non-material cultural heritage and such functions, and achieve the integration by applying Internet technologies. Through The "Belt and Road Initiative", function orientation of the platform would be based on display, publicity, promotion, trade and finance, relied on three major service platforms for business, public welfare and culture, utilize the ration mode of building platform, integrating resources and superiorly enjoying business opportunities, win-win development, to extend development from domestic to international by combining off line exhibitions, sales exhibitions, manual experience, folk cultures, festival cultures, and other forms of activities.

六、项目优势：
VI. Project Advantage(s):

以商务、公益和文化三大服务平台为主要内容结合宣传推广、在线销售、网上培训、线下交流、非遗体验等功能版块，运用互联网技术全面实现线下展览、展销、手工体验、民俗文化、节庆文化等活动的开展。

Take three service platforms for business, public welfare and cultural as the main content, combine the promotion, on line sales, on line training, off line communication, experiences for non-material cultural heritage and such function sections, utilize Internet technologies to achieve off line exhibitions, sales exhibitions, manual experiences, folk cultures, festivals and cultural activities.

七、项目需求：
VII. Project Demand(s):

希望有政府、企事业单位、文化机构和天使投资人，以及从事文化艺术机构的负责人和生产创作在一线的艺术家、团体组织等加入平台，强强联合，创新发展，抱团取暖，共同为中华文化的发展和繁荣做出应有的贡献。

Hope governments, enterprises and institutions, cultural institutions and angel investors, and responsible persons from organizations engaging in cultural and art as well as artists and organizations involving in first line production and creation to join the platform, to achieve alliance between gaints, innovation and development, collaboration, and contribute together for the development and rise of the Chinese culture.

元古页岩画艺术
The Art of Proterozoic Shale Painting

一、公司名称： 天津蓟县瑛辉页岩书画院

Ⅰ. Project Company Name: Tianjin Jixian Yinghui Shale Painting and Calligraphy Academy

二、公司简介：

Ⅱ. Project Company Introduction:

本书画院是以院长张瑛辉名字冠名的，成立于2008年，被当地政府定名为"元古页岩画研发基地"。

The academy was founded in 2008 being named after the founder Zhang Yinghui and it was entitled as "Research and Development Base of Proterozoic Shale Painting" by the local government.

元古页岩画是一种新型的具有厚重历史底蕴的书画艺术。它采用蓟县中、上元古界标准地层剖面出产的天然页岩矿石，经过选料、研磨、描绘、配色、填涂、晾晒等十几道工序绘制而成。

Proterozoic shale painting is an innovative art of painting and calligraphy with the profound connotation of age, that is to paint or write on shale pieces form in Epiproterozoic or Mesoproterozoic era and mined in Jixian after the process of selection, grinding, painting, coloring, coating and sun-curing.

书法系列、敦煌系列、山水系列、佛教系列、姓氏文化和民族风情等作品展现出古朴、厚重、典雅、唯美。而且每件作品都是不可复制独一无二的艺术珍品。被国内外各界艺术家称赞为"令人叹为观止的艺术"。页岩画这一艺术承载着厚重的历史沉淀，融入独特的艺术表现形式，远古与现代的巧妙结合，让艺术呈现了巨大的震撼力和永恒的生命力。

The series of works of calligraphy, paintings of Dunhuang, landscape, Buddhism, family name culture and folk custom fully display the sense of primitive simplicity, dignifying, elegance and aestheticism. Every work is a non-copyable piece of art and can be stunning in the eyes of the artists all over the world. The artistic form of shale painting carries the deposits of history and is infused with unique artistic expressions. The ingenious combination of modern and antiquity gives the art with gigantic deterrent force and eternal vitality

页岩画曾多次在各地展会展出，得到社会各界的青睐和好评，并有多家媒体进行报道。

Shale paintings have been exhibited in different places and have been highly praised by all sectors of society. And this form of art has been reported by many media.

三、负责人介绍：

Ⅲ. Responsible Person Introduction:

张瑛辉：瑛辉页岩书画院院长、元古页岩画创始人。国际工艺美术大师。早年参军，从事医务工作。回乡后，曾从事根雕、石雕工艺品开发。20世纪80年代初开始元古页岩画探索与研究。2013年获得国家发明专利。

Mr. Zhang Yinhui, an international master of arts and crafts, is the director of Yinghui Shale Painting and Calligraphy Academy and the founder of Proterozoic shale painting. He had served in the army and worked at medical works in his early years. After returning back, he engaged himself in developing root and stone carving. He started his exploration and research of Proterozoic shale painting in the 80s and gained national invention patent license in 2013.

四、项目名称： 元古页岩画艺术

Ⅳ. Project Name： The Art of Proterozoic Shale Painting

五、项目概况：

Ⅴ. Project Profile：

本项目是一个以世界闻名的"中上元古界"境内，世界上最稀有、最古老而独特的距今8.5亿年至18.5亿年的页岩而创作的"元古页岩画"。具有极高的观赏价值及收藏价值。可根据不同国家不同民族信仰创作出不同的高端艺术品。目前已在加拿大、美国、捷克、巴勒斯坦等国和北京、上海等城市设有销售平台。

The project is called the art of Proterozoic shale painting that is to create paintings on the rarest, the most ancient and unique shale pieces which were formed in the world famous area of Proterozoic shale 850 million to 1.85 billion years ago. The artistic works, therefore, are of high value of ornamentation and collection and can be high-end compositions according to the religious faiths in different countries and for different nations. Now, the marketing platforms have been set in Canada, US, Czech, Palestine overseas and in Beijing, Shanghai at home.

项目响应国家"一带一路"的倡议,学习国外优良的管理理念。在页岩画的装饰装裱上引进国内外优质材料和技术,开拓页岩画市场,创作出更多更好的艺术作品。通过与国际接轨,让这一艺术瑰宝走向世界,从而让更多的国际友人了解中华文化艺术!

The project is in conformity with the nation's the "Belt and Road" Initiative and will learn the advanced management concepts from outside. In decorative framing of the paintings, high quality material and advanced technology at home and abroad have been found and adapted to make better works and to extend the market of shale paintings. With internationalization of the works, the artistic treasure is marching forward into the world and getting recognized as a Chinese cultural art by more and more international friends.

六、项目优势
VI. Project Advantage(s):

核心竞争力:
Core Competence:

1．元古页岩画全国只有本画院一家绘制。
The academy is the only one in the country engaged in Proterozoic shale painting

2．持有国家发明专利证书、受国家法律保护。
Shale painting is patent licensed and protected by the national law

3．原材料唯有本地才有,故极其珍贵,且不可再生。
The raw material only exists locally, extremely rare and non-renewable

4．目前在国内外市场没有可比性、不存在同样表现手法的竞争对手,所以没有竞争之忧。
There is no comparable cultural product in the world. Nor there is a competitor in the world market.

七、项目需求:
VII. Project Demand(s):

欢迎国内外有识之士投资合作!更快更好的使页岩画走向世界!
We welcome those with breadth vision to invest and cooperate to push shale painting better into the world.

泉龙佛像雕塑工艺
Quanlong Buddha Statue Sculpture Craft

一、项目公司名称：诸暨市泉龙雕塑工艺品厂

I. Project Company Name: Zhuji Quanlong Sculpture Handicraft Factory

二、项目公司介绍：

II. Project Company Introduction:

本公司为村办企业，成立于1980年，投资300万元，被当地政府定为佛像造像传承基地。公司产品2001年2月12日获得诸暨街亭长塘各种佛像菩萨塑像荣誉奖状；2003年9月10日诸暨五峰寺四大天王塑像（6.50米）7米获特别荣誉奖；《中国梦》作品集登刊并获金奖杯；2016年荣获国际收藏文化节暨手工艺大师邀请展"工合杯"银奖。

the Company is a village-run enterprise, founded in 1980, with an investment of RMB 3 million, which is set as a heritage base for Buddha statue by the local government. The Company's products won various honor certificates for Buddha statue and Bodhisatva on February 12, 2001 in Changtang, Jieting, Zhuji; the four heavenly kings (6.50m) as high as 7m in Wufeng Temple, Zhuji, won the special honorary award on September 10, 2003; the works, called Chinese Dream, won the honor certificate for publication of works collection and gold trophy; the silver award of "Industrial Cooperative Cup" in International Collection Art 2016 & Handicraft Master Invitational Exhibition was won.

三、项目负责人介绍：

III. Project's Responsible Person Introduction:

郭东平，总经理，国际工艺美术传承师。1999年9月28日在诸暨市化泉乡人民政府举办的绘画作品比赛中荣获一等奖。2015年6月25日荣获民间人才高级证书。获第五届中国传统工艺美术精品展暨行巧夺天工金马奖金奖。2017年国际职业规划鉴定中心授予国际工艺美术传承师荣誉称号。

Guo Dongping, the General Manager and International Craft Artist heritage master, won the first-prize honor certificate for the people's government paintings in Huaquan Village Zhuji on September 28, 1999; the senior certificate for folk talents on June 25, 2015; the gold award of Golden Horse Prize in the fifth Chinese Traditional Arts and Crafts Exhibition & Wonderful Workmanship Excelling Nature; awarded the honorary title of the International Crafts Art heritage master by the International Occupation Planning Identification Center in 2017.

四、项目名称：泉龙佛像雕塑工艺

IV. Project Name: Quanlong Buddha Statue Sculpture Craft

五、项目概况：

V. Project Profile:

可提供寺庙泥塑、木雕及堆灰垒塑，真漆、瓦灰、麻布、玻璃钢佛像工艺装真金，绘画神仙菩萨，各种佛像雕塑、高级油漆工艺等。中央宗教信仰自由的政策落地，老百姓宗教信仰自由的到来，将为村庙佛像需求开创新局面，中国民族文化的崛起必将影响"一带一路"延边村镇的发展，对佛像造像需求市场潜力巨大。

It can provide clay sculpture, wood carving, ash stacking, and building and carving technology for temples all over the world, provide lacquer, tile ashes, flax and technological genuine gold for fiberglass Buddha statue, draw the immortals and Buddha, sculpture various Buddha statues and provide the advanced paint technology, etc. The policy for freedom of religious belief from the central government has been implemented, therefore, the arrival of freedom of ordinary people's religious belief in the village temple will create a new situation for the Buddha statues in the village temple, and the rise of Chinese national culture will influence the development in villages and towns in the countries along the "Belt and Road", where the market potential for the demand of Buddha statues is huge.

六、项目优势：
VI. Project Advantages:

1．泥塑流程：因地制宜，就地取材，以砖块打佛座，用木料钉架子，用草绳固定架子，再用泥土浇筑，塑坯成型，再用棉花拌泥、浇塑等塑像干燥再刮泥和泥子，然后，油漆再做五彩亮光成型。

Process of clay sculpture：it adjusts measures to local conditions and uses the local materials, in which the base of the Buddha is built with bricks and the frame is build with woods and fixed with the straw rope, which, then, is casted with mud. When the blank is molded, then the cotton shall be used to be mixed with the mud and the statue shall be put on fire. When the statue is dry, the mud shall be scraped and applied with putty, and then paint, to make it colorful and shiny for molding.

2．木雕流程：先镶缝、批灰，用真漆瓦灰麻布包好佛像，继续批灰，要批三遍，然后打磨光后油漆、打底，然后油漆三遍，打磨光滑，除净灰尘，开始贴真金，然后处理金碎片，干净抛面油。

Process for wood carving：first insert the joints and plaster, wrap the Buddha statue with the lacquer, tile ashes and flax, continue to plaster 3 times, then apply the paint 3 times and render after the statue is polished to be smooth, clean the dust, start to paste the genuine gold, then clean the gold fragments and apply the clean surface oil.

3．古代的堆灰工艺流程：用于古老祠堂、寺庙、墙壁堆灰，石门堂修复等，传统用石头粉和石灰，平整墙面，用现代水泥、石头粉加石灰，沙子加用粳米拌成材料，再加细麻丝和棉花，用铁钉固定位置，用拌料堆墙面做成图形，画墙古代传统用烟煤，用瓦片一张，放在煤油灶上烧成烟煤，用桐油和青油拌变成黑色燃料，画色采用藏族颜料，画壁不会变色，流传百世。

Ancient ash stacking process：it is applicable to ash stacking for the ancient ancestral temple, temple, wall and repair of stone hall. The wall is traditionally leveled with the stone powder and lime, in which the materials are made from modern cement, stone powder with lime and sand mixed with japonica rice along with fine hemp thread and cotton. The iron nails are used to fix and the pattern is made by building the wall with the mixed materials. The wall was traditionally painted with the soft coal in the ancient times, that is, the title was burnt into the soft coal on the kerosene stove, which was mixed into a black fuel with tung oil and tallowtree seed oil. The paint is painted by the Tibetan pigments and the color of the wall painted will not change, but will circulate forever.

七、项目需求：
VII. Project Demands:

融资扩厂，前期厂房工程建设（工作区和展区等）500万元，原材料开发、储备及相关设备300万元，人才引进、运输等200万元，共需资金1000万元。可根据不同国家不同民族信仰和村庙特点创作出不同的高端艺术品，销往世界各地。

The factory is expanded by financing, with RMB 5 million for the engineering construction of factory in the early stage, RMB 3 million for the development and reserve of raw materials and relevant equipment, RMB 2 million for talent introduction and transportation, etc., with a total of RMB 10 million. Different high-end artworks can be created in accordance with the characteristics in different countries with different national belief and village temples and sold around the world.

蒙古族根雕及旅游商品
Mongolian Root Carving and Tourism Commodity

一、项目公司名称：正蓝旗乌尼民俗文化有限公司

I. Project Company Name: Zhenglan Banner Unni Folk Culture Co., Ltd.

二、项目公司介绍：

II. Project Company Introduction:

公司成立于2014年4月，经营范围是民俗文化推广，工艺品制作，蒙元文化开发研究，蒙古族根雕艺术宣传推广，旅游商品研发制作。公司下设乌尼根雕艺术馆、乌尼木雕加工厂。2013年蒙古族根雕艺术被列入自治区级非物质文化遗产名录；2014年乌尼根雕艺术馆被列入自治区级民间博物馆。

Founded in Apr. 2014, the company is mainly engaged in promotion of folk culture, production of crafts, development & research of Mongolian culture in Yuan Dynasty, propaganda and promotion of Mongolian root carving art, as well as R&D and production of tourism commodity. The Unni Root Carving Art Museum and Unni Wood Carving Processing Plant are subordinate to the company. In 2013, the Mongolian root carving art was listed in the Intangible Cultural Heritage List of Autonomous Region Level; In 2014, the Unni Root Carving Art Museum was included into the Folk Museum of Autonomous Region Level.

三、负责人介绍：

III. Responsible Person Introduction:

公司总经理苏乙拉图，男，蒙古族，1972年出生于内蒙古正蓝旗。2001年开始从事察干伊德申报非物质文化遗产工作；2001年在正蓝旗注册乌尼民俗文化有限公司；2012年创办乌尼木雕加工厂；2013年成立乌尼根雕艺术馆。

As the General Manager of company, SuYiLaTu, male, Mongol nationality and born in 1972, lives on Zhenglan Banner of Inner Mongolia. In 2001, he started up in declaration of ChaGanYiDe as the intangible cultural heritage; In 2001, he registered Zhenglan Banner Unni Folk Culture Co., Ltd. in Zhenglan Banner; In 2012, he launched Unni Wood Carving Processing Plant; In 2013, he established Unni Root Carving Art Museum.

四、项目名称：蒙古族根雕及旅游商品

IV. Project Name: Mongolian Root Carving and Tourism Commodity

五、项目概况：

V. Project Profile:

项目以蒙古族根雕为切入点，围绕蒙元文化进行学术研讨、产品研发，打造蒙元文化旅游商品系列，包括开发复原元代建筑、发掘元代民俗文化（散曲、戏剧、诗词、书法、绘画、手工艺），通过编撰出版研究书籍，对上述蒙元文化旅游商品进行推广。

Taking the Mongolian root carving as the breakthrough point, the project conducts academic discussion and product R&D based on Mongolian culture in Yuan Dynasty, to build a series of tourism commodity characterized by Mongolian culture in Yuan Dynasty, including development of building rehabilitation in Yuan Dynasty and folk culture in Yuan Dynasty (Sanqu, drama, poem, calligraphy, painting and handicraft), and promote these tourism commodities by means of compiling and publishing the research books.

六、项目优势：

VI. Project Advantage(s):

内蒙古自治区唯一一处世界文化遗产元上都遗址坐落于正蓝旗境内，而且正蓝旗人民至今保留着正宗的传统蒙古族习俗，对研究收集蒙元文化具有得天独厚的优势。正蓝旗处于中国四大沙地之一的浑善达克沙地腹地，盛产野生沙地榆树——蓝旗榆，此物种由于生长环境恶劣，树干和树根特别密实，是制作根雕的上好材料。

The sole Site of Xanadu as a world cultural heritage in Inner Mongolia Autonomous Region is located in Zhenglan

Banner, in which local people have still been preserving the authentic and traditional Mongolian customs and have distinctive advantage on research and collection of Mongolian culture in Yuan Dynasty. The Zhenglan Banner is located in central Hunshadake Sandy Land, one of four sands in China where rich in wild elm in the sand – Zhenglan Banner Elm. Due to tough growth environment, its trunk and root are very dense, which can be used for producing the root carving as a kind of superior material.

七、项目需求：

Ⅶ. Project Demand(s)：

需要寻求合作企业，通过招商融资，进一步扩大生产规模，进一步拓展蒙古族根雕艺术和蒙元文化旅游商品市场。

By seeking cooperative enterprises and attracting investment and financing, to further expand the scale of production and market of Mongolian root carving art and tourism commodity with the featured Mongolian culture in Yuan Dynasty.

营养型奶酒
Nutrition-type Milk Wine

一、项目公司名称：内蒙古多尔太乳酒有限公司
Ⅰ. Project Company Name : Inner Mongolia Duoertai Milk Wine Co., Ltd.

二、项目公司介绍：
Ⅱ. Project Company Introduction:

公司成立于 1998 年 1 月 12 日，具有独立法人资格，是中国首家营养型蒸馏奶酒生产销售企业。目前，年生产能力为 90 万瓶 450 吨。公司的核心竞争力技术形成了本公司的自主知识产权，生产的营养型蒸馏奶酒，填补了世界酒品市场的空白，是世界级稀缺产品，迎合了二十一世纪健康革命的高端需求。公司立志紧跟国家大趋势，打造高端制造业，制造高端稀缺文化产品，进入世界高端酒品市场，占领世界酒文化高地。

The company was founded on January 12, 1998 as an independent legal person, and is the first nutrition-type distilled milk wine producer in China. Currently, the company has a yearly production capacity of 900 thousand bottles or 450 tons. The core competitiveness of our company helps to build our independent intellectual properties. Our nutrition-type distilled milk wine opened up a new product line in international wine markets and therefore is a world-class rare cultural product that caters to high-end demands for healthy products in the 21st century. The company follows Chines national strategies in building a high-end production industry and producing high-end cultural products. Besides, it successfully took some shares in world high-end wine market.

三、负责人介绍：
Ⅲ. Responsible Person Introduction:

王希尧，男，现年 78 岁，内蒙古包头人，祖籍山东济宁。中国营养奶酒创始人、中国营养奶酒老年工匠。已在内蒙古工作生活了六十余年。长年热爱学习与传承中国奶酒文化。现任内蒙古多尔太乳酒有限公司法定代表人、董事长。

Mr. Wang Xiyao, 78 years old, born in Baotou, Inner Mongolia, with the native place being Jining, Shandong. Creator of nutrition-type milk wine and a senior wine maker in China. He has lived in Inner Mongolia for over 60 years. Wang has keen interest in Chinese cultures in relation to milk wine. He is now acting as legal representative and Chairman of Inner Mongolia Duoertai Milk Wine Co., Ltd.

四、项目名称：营养型奶酒
Ⅳ. Project Name : Nutrition-type Milk Wine

五、项目概况：
Ⅴ. Project Profile:

1．项目是农副产品的深加工，是牛奶的高效能转化。目前国内外市场空白。

The project realizes deep processing of farm products in rural areas. Highly efficient conversion of milk products. It is currently a new product line in China.

2．项目所需要的原料为牛奶、马奶、羊奶、驼奶均可。产品是营养型蒸馏奶酒，是世界首创，也是世界稀缺文化产品。

Milk used by the project as raw materials may be obtained from cows, horses, sheep and camels. The product is nutrition-type distilled milk wine, which is a remarkable creation and rare cultural product in Chinese and international markets.

3．本公司目前营养型奶酒的生产规模是：日产 3000 瓶，月产 9 万瓶，年产 90 万瓶计 450 吨，年产值 2.7 亿元，年利税 9000 万元。

The company production capacity is 3 thousand bottles per day or 90 thousand bottles per month or 900 thousand bottles per year, equivalent to 450 tons. The annual output value is CNY 270 million including CNY 90 million profits.

4．需要扩大生产规模：本公司需要引进资金扩大生产规模。建设规模可大可小，投资 3 亿元 、30 亿元 、300 亿元均可。以投资 3 亿元为例，建设周期一年，投产后一年收回全额投资，属高回报项目。

Further expansion of production capacity：The company needs to introduce external capital to expand the production volume. The investments may vary according to the needs, which may be CNY 300 million, 3 billion or 30 billion. If investment is CNY 300 million, the construction will be completed in one year period, and all investment will be returned in one-year period, therefore this is a highly rewarding project.

5．项目落地后，由参与方根据项目所在地的原料价格土地价格、劳动力价格、水电价格等，共同做出项目可行性报告。

After the project plan is approved, a feasibility report will be worked out by all participants on basis of the local material prices, land prices, labor prices and utility prices.

6．营养型奶酒项目建设运营后，将带动以牛奶为原料的化妆品项目和以牛奶为原料的制药项目。当三个项目同步运营时，就是中国千亿元规模的高端制造业。

After the nutrition-type milk wine project is completed and put in operation, it will facilitate cosmetics projects and pharmaceutical projects that take milk as raw materials. When all three projects are in operation, they make a high-end ten million level manufacturing industry.

六、项目优势：
VI. Project Advantage(s)：

1．项目拥有核心竞争力的技术和自主知识产权，具备了技术合作与技术转让的条件。

The project is supported by core competitive technologies and independent intellectual property rights and is ready for technical cooperation and transfer.

2．项目拥有已投放市场的稀缺文化产品，具备了产品推广和品牌宣传的条件。

The project is supported by cultural products that have been available in market, and is ready for product promotion and brand advertising.

3．项目的高额回报和发展远景，具备了招商引资联合建厂的条件。

With high return and good development prospect, the project has the condition of establishing factories jointly through investment invitation.

七、项目需求：
VII. Project Demand(s)：

1．国家给予政策支持，支持企业迅速发展。

National policy support for fast company growth.

2．支持企业拓展国内外市场。

Supports for exploration of domestic and foreign markets.

3．帮助企业做产品推广和品牌宣传。

Supports for product promotion and brand advertising.

4．支持企业技术推广，技术合作，技术转让。

Supports for technical promotion, cooperation and transfer.

5．支持企业跨地区发展，包括技术合作联合建厂。

Supports for cross-region development, including technical cooperation.

6．为企业招商引资帮企业迅速发展。

Supports for attracting external investments to facilitate fast company growth.

首铝铝材
Shoulv Aluminum

一、项目公司名称： 首铝铝业（廊坊）有限公司

I. Project Company Name: Langfang Shoulv Aluminum Co., Ltd.

二、项目公司介绍：

II. Project Company Introduction:

公司始建于1988年，位于第三大经济区环渤海经济圈内，合作伙伴和客户遍及全国各地，如：北京、天津、上海、广东、河北、内蒙古、新疆、西藏、山东、陕西、山西、甘肃等省市，是纳税信用等级评价A级企业。公司目前拥有一项实用新型专利。被军工部三五二二厂列为指定供应单位，公司的断桥铝型材阔步走进了酒泉卫星发射基地，被列为指定供货商。

Founded in 1988, the Company is located in the Bohai Economic Circle, the third major economic circle, with its partners and customers spreading all over the country, in provinces and cities such as Beijing, Tianjin, Shanghai, Guangdong, Hebei, Inner Mongolia, Xinjiang, Tibet, Shandong, Shaanxi, Shanxi and Gansu, etc. As an enterprise with tax credit rating at Level A, the Company currently owns a utility model patent, and has been identified as the designated supplier by the Military Industry Department 3522. The Company's aluminum broken bridges aluminum profile has entered Jiuquan Satellite Launch Center with the Company becoming the designated supplier.

三、负责人介绍：

III. Responsible Person Introduction:

首铝铝业（廊坊）有限公司企业负责人闫万凯先生，自2013年至今，先后在企业从事采购、生产、销售管理工作四年，经常勉励自己"工作多干、困难多上、荣誉多让"，事事、处处、时时严格要求自己，讲实话、办实事、求实效，不断超越自己，挑战极限，在公司的生产经营管理中做出了突出的业绩。

Mr. Yan Wankai, head of Langfang Shoulv Aluminum Co., Ltd., has been successively engaged in purchasing, production and sales management works for 4 years with the enterprise since 2013, and he often encourages himself to "work more, overcome difficulties and keep humility when winning honors", to have strict demands on himself about everything at anywhere and anytime, tell the truth, do practical works, seek actual results, constantly go beyond himself, challenge the limits, and thus he has made outstanding achievements in the company's production and operation management.

四、项目名称： 首铝铝材

IV. Project Name： Shoulv Aluminum

五、项目概况：

V. Project Profile:

首铝铝业有限公司致力于铝型材的研发、生产、销售。主要生产各种建筑型材以及各种工业型材。公司现拥有全自动挤压生产线十条，其中七条广东金沥机械生产线，三条日本三菱全自动生产线。全自动着色电泳生产线一条，可生产银白、香槟、黄金等多种颜色电泳料。喷涂设备引进世界先进的瑞士进口金马全自动喷涂生产线两条。粉末均选用国际优质品牌阿克苏产品，原材料选择山东茌平的国标铝棒，隔热系列选用广东万格士全自动生产线两条，使产品在满足先进工艺的同时，达到国际质量要求。

Committed to research & development, production and sales of aluminum profile, Shoulv Aluminum Co., Ltd. mainly produces all kinds of building profiles and various industrial profiles. Now, the Company has 10 automatic extrusion production lines, of which seven are Guangdong Jinli mechanical production lines and three are Japanese Mitsubishi automatic production lines. One automatic coloring electrophoresis production line can produce electrophoretic materials in silver, champagne, gold and other colors. The spraying equipment consists of two world's advanced Gema automatic spraying production lines imported from Switzerland. We have powders selected from the international good-quality brand Aksu's products, Shandong Chiping's international standard aluminum rods selected as raw materials, two Guangdong Wangeshi fully automatic production lines selected as insulation series, so that our products meet the advanced technology and meet international quality requirements as well.

首铝人坚信质量是企业的生命保障，诚信是企业的寿命保障。从原材料检验到出厂都实行严格的检验检测，126 道工序层层把关，每一环节都进行自检和互检，绝不允许有一根、一片有质量问题的产品出厂。同时，公司采用内部市场经济方式进行经营与管理，各岗位都有严格的操作规则和训练科目标准，每位员工都配有一本员工手册和一本岗位操作及训练科目手册，管理者每人都配有一本首铝文化手册和一本管理者手册，量化的首铝文化及操作规则达 200 多万字。产品通过 ISO9000 国际质量体系认证，"首铝"商标也被省工商局评为著名商标。

Shoulv employees firmly believe that the quality guarantees the survival of an enterprise and integrity guarantees the length of an enterprise. From the raw material inspection to the delivery from factory, we implement strict inspection with 126 processes subject to quality control at every level. Every part requires self-test and mutual inspection, and we never allow a single product with quality problem to leave the factory. In addition, the Company adopts the internal market economy mode for operation and management. All posts have strict rules of operation manual and training subject standards. Each employee is provided with an employee manual and a post operation and training subject manual. Each manager is provided with a Shoulv culture manual and a manager's manual. The quantified Shoulv's culture and rules of operation documents contain more than 2 million characters. Products have passed ISO9000 international quality system certification, and "Shoulv" trademark has also been rated as a famous trademark by the Provincial Administration for Industry and Commerce.

六、项目优势：
VI. Project Advantage(s):

首铝铝业（廊坊）有限公司是专业生产隔热断桥门窗铝材的厂家，从原材料检验到出厂都实行严格的检验检测，126 道工序层层把关，量化的生产操作流程说明 200 多万字，每一环节都进行自检和互检，绝不允许有质量问题的产品出厂。

Langfang Shoulv Aluminum Co., Ltd. is a manufacturer specialized in producing insulation broken bridge aluminum doors and windows. From raw material inspection to the delivery from factory, we implement strict inspection with 126 processes subject to quality control at every level. The quantified production operation process description contains more than 2 million characters. With each part subject to self-test and mutual inspection, we never allow products with quality problem to leave the factory.

七、项目需求：
VII. Project Demand(s):

随着国内建材环保节能标准的进一步提高，断桥隔热门窗型材的需求量呈现持续增长的趋势；此外，室内装饰用建筑铝材的需求量的扩大，也带动了公司铝材产能的增加。公司坚持"立足京津冀，面向全中国"的发展方针，在保持原有优势地位的基础上，将在全国各地开设新的销售网点。正是由于国内市场需求的增长及公司在新产品研发和市场开拓方面的努力，使得经销商队伍进一步壮大。

With the further improvement of domestic environmental protection and energy conservation standards for building materials, the demand for insulation broken bridge window and door profiles has shown a continuous growth trend. In addition, the expansion of the demand for interior aluminum for interior decoration has also driven an increase in the Company's aluminum production capacity. Adhering to the development principle of "being based in Beijing-Tianjin-Hebei and covering China", we will open new sales outlets throughout the country while maintaining our original dominant position. It is precisely because of the growth of domestic market demand and the Company's efforts in new product research & development and market development, our network of dealers is further expanding.

风机
Blowers/Fans

一、项目公司名称：沈阳盛纳机械制造有限公司

Ⅰ. Project Company Name：Shenyang Shengna Machinery Manufacturing Co., Ltd.

二、项目公司介绍：

Ⅱ. Project Company Introduction:

公司成立于 2008 年，是一家股份制企业。合作伙伴和客户遍及全国各地及朝鲜、印度、埃塞俄比亚、莫桑比克等十几个国家。被沈阳市国家税务局和沈阳市地方税务局评为 2014-2016 年度纳税信用等级 A 级纳税人"称号，并在 2016 年 12 月获得国家级高新技术企业称号，2017 年 6 月 20 日获得沈阳市科技创新"双百工程"项目证书。2017 年列入《沈阳市"双培育计划"入选企业名单（2017 年）》。2017 年 7 月被评为"小巨人"企业。

The company, established in 2008, is a joint-stock enterprise. Its partners and customers are across China and more than ten countries including North Korea, India, Africa, Ethiopian, Pemba(Mozambique), etc. The company was awarded 2014-2016 "Tax-paying Credit Class A Taxpayer" tile by Shenyang Municipal Office, SAT and Shenyang Local Taxation Bureau; won the state-level high-tech enterprise title in December 2016; obtained Shenyang Technological Innovation "Double-hundred Engineering" Project Certificate in June 20, 2017. In 2017, it was listed in the enterprise list for *Shenyang "Double Cultivation Plan" (2017)*. In July 2017, it was evaluated to a "Small Giant" enterprise.

三、负责人介绍：

Ⅲ. Responsible Person Introduction：

徐成先生，2012 年 11 月再次当选为"辽中县人大代表"，2016 年 5 月获得"沈阳市劳动模范"称号，2016 年 2 月获得"杰出企业家"称号，当选辽宁省第十二届人大代表。

Mr. Xucheng continued as "Liaozhong County NPC member" in November 2012；obtained the "Shenyang Labor Model" title；was awarded the "Outstanding Enterprise" title in February 2016；and was selected as "Liaoning NPC member".

四、项目名称：风机

Ⅳ. Project Name：Blowers/Fans

五、项目概况：

Ⅴ. Project Profile:

公司的主要产品有：工业离心风机系列、罗茨风机系列、电厂风机、中石化风机系列、锅炉鼓引风机系列、煤粉离心通风机系列、轴流、斜流、消防风机系列、箱式风机系列、建筑、民用、厨房排烟风机系列、耐高温、耐磨离心通风机系列等多用途风机、中大型焊接结构件加工高精度零部件等。

The main products of the company includes multi-purpose blowers such as industrial centrifugal blower series, Roots blower series, blowers for power plants, series of blowers for Sinopec, Boiler forced and induced draft fan series, pulverized coal centrifugal ventilation fan series, axial, diagonal and fire control fan series, box-type blower series, building, civil and kitchen smoke exhaust fan series, high temperature resistant and wear-resistant centrifugal fan and the like, as well as large and middle welded structure parts, the machining of high-precision parts and components, etc.

六、项目优势：

Ⅵ. Project Advantage(s)：

长期为沈阳忠旺集团有限公司、沈阳忠旺机械设备制造有限公司、沈阳机床股份有限公司、中铁沈阳铁道装备有限公司、中国北车集团、三一重型装备有限公司、泰豪沈阳电机有限公司、沈阳远大集团等提供精密备件及产品。

the company has been long supplying precise spare parts and products for Shenyang Zhongwang Group Co., Ltd., Shenyang Zhongwang Mechanical Equipment Manufacturing Co., Ltd., Shenyang Machine Tools Co., Ltd., China

Railway Shenyang Railway Equipment Co., Ltd., China CNR Corporation Limited, SANY Group, Taihao Shenyang Motor Co., Ltd., Shenyang Yuanda Enterprise Group, etc.

七、项目需求：

Ⅶ. Project Demand(s)：

风机主要应用于冶金、石化、电力、轨道交通、纺织和船舶等国民经济各领域以及各种场所的通风换气。除传统应用领域外并在煤矸石综合利用、新型干法熟料技改、冶金工业的节能及资源综合利用的市场领域将有较大量需求，欢迎合作。

The blowers/fans are mainly used for all fields of national economy (including metallurgy, petrochemical, electric power, rail transit, textiles, vessels and the like) and air ventilation in various kinds places. Apart from the use in traditional fields of application, they are also widely used in the market fields of comprehensive coal gangue utilization, new dry-process clinker technological transformation, energy conservation in the metallurgy industry and comprehensive energy utilization. Welcome your cooperation.